KANT
SARTRE
BIKO
PHILOSOPHY IDENTITY AND LIBERATION
FANON
HEGEL

MABOGO PERCY MORE

HSRC PRESS

NATIONAL INSTITUTE
FOR THE HUMANITIES
AND SOCIAL SCIENCES

Published by HSRC Press
Private Bag X9182, Cape Town 8000, South Africa
www.hsrcpress.ac.za

First published 2017

ISBN (soft cover) 978-0-7969-2571-8
ISBN (pdf) 978-0-7969-2538-1

© 2017 Human Sciences Research Council

This book has undergone a double-blind independent peer-review process overseen by the HSRC Press
Editorial Board.

This publication was made possible through a grant received from the National Institute for the
Humanities and Social Sciences.

The views expressed in this publication are those of the authors. They do not necessarily reflect the views
or policies of the Human Sciences Research Council (the Council) or indicate that the Council endorses
the views of the authors. In quoting from this publication, readers are advised to attribute the source of the
information to the individual author concerned and not to the Council.

The publishers have no responsibility for the continued existence or accuracy of URLs for
external or third-party internet websites referred to in this book and do not guarantee that any
content on such websites is, or will remain, accurate or appropriate.

Thank you to the University of Limpopo who contributed to the funding of this publication.
Copy-edited by Debbie Rodrigues
Typeset by Hothouse South Africa
Cover design by Nic Jooste

Printed and bound by Novus Print Solutions, a Novus Holdings company

Distributed in Africa by Blue Weaver
Tel: +27 (0) 21 701 4477; Fax Local: +27 (0) 21 701 7302; Fax International: 0927865242139
www.blueweaver.co.za

Distributed in Europe and the United Kingdom by Eurospan Distribution Services (EDS)
Tel: +44 (0) 17 6760 4972; Fax: +44 (0) 17 6760 1640
www.eurospanbookstore.com

Distributed in North America by River North Editions, from IPG
Call toll-free: (800) 888 4741; Fax: +1 (312) 337 5985
www.ipgbook.com

This book is dedicated to the late

Moeketsi More (2002–2017)

With fond memories

Contents

Acknowledgements

WHY WRITE A BOOK about Steve Biko today – especially when his most famous work, *I Write What I Like*, is so clearly an expression of the specific historical moment? Are there 'philosophical' lessons to be learned or principles to be gleaned from Biko's work? This book is an attempt to deal with these questions. It is indeed a book about a philosopher whom other conventional establishment professional philosophers would categorically refuse to regard as a philosopher of any kind. A philosopher whose book establishment academic philosophy would not consider as belonging to the ordinary canons of philosophical literature or include in their curricula – 'an intellectual gadfly', to use George Yancy's words, who operates outside the confines of the academy; a philosopher who belongs to 'that breed of philosophers who takes it as his or her responsibility to extratextually intervene in the process of our unfinished history' (2002: x). This attitude is, however, not surprising given that even the big philosopher Jean-Paul Sartre had his philosophical credentials questioned by Anglo-Saxon analytic philosophy in general, except for Iris Murdoch and Arthur Danto.

Biko, like many others (such as Sartre, Frantz Fanon, Kwame Nkrumah and Julius Nyerere) did not worry much about being recognised as a philosopher, and did not expect philosophy to be the absolute answer to problems. However, in his struggle to offer innovative ways of perceiving, new ways of acting, new ways of thinking, indeed new ways of being-black, new ways of black 'Somebodiness' and new ways of escaping black 'Nobodiness', Biko evolved a philosophy that went beyond philosophy itself. For example, his criticism of liberalism as a philosophy implicated in the oppression of black people is, by that very fact, a philosophy that refuses to extricate itself from philosophy. It is important to note here that Biko's conception of blackness is inclusive of the black/African, coloured and Indian people of South Africa. In seeking the death of liberalism as an oppressive philosophy, Biko joins Karl Marx, Friedrich Nietzsche, Martin Heidegger and others who in their proclamation of the death of philosophy invariably gave philosophy an extension of life. Each of them, in their own manner, continued philosophising in the very attempt to bring an end to philosophy, an endeavour which Lewis Gordon calls a 'teleological suspension' of philosophy.

This is the kind of philosopher Steve Biko was – a philosopher, as it were, who was involved in politico-philosophical activism. He refused to separate theory from practice, a feat which most academic philosophers are incapable of achieving. But what has become even clearer today is that Biko (like Fanon and Sartre) speaks to a multitude of young minds, especially to young black philosophers; political, social, and cultural activists; and civil society organisations in a manner unequalled – except for Fanon – by any other thinker in this country and abroad.

The answer to the question 'Why write a book on Biko today?' is staring us in the face. His ideas speak to the present human condition, especially the black condition, not only in South Africa but also in the USA and other antiblack societies where blatant racism continues to manifest in various forms. Almost forty years after his untimely and brutal death in detention at the hands of the apartheid security police, his life's work continues to be debated and discussed around the world. Biko, like Fanon, has been celebrated and idolised by student radicals, with his face on their T-shirts and his ideas used to interpret and understand their existential condition. There are certainly many young people who are reading Biko today and are learning about his thought through serious engagement with it. Part of the reason for this resurgence of Biko is that his major philosophical preoccupation – white racism – has not disappeared. This very fact, captured in the many incidents of invidious racism against black people reported almost daily in the media, constantly turns his physical absence into a haunting philosophical presence, a concrete invisibility into a visibility that simultaneously produces a lucid consciousness of the post-apartheid South African condition. This also explains why both Biko and Fanon have been invoked as authorities for the #MustFall student movements of whatever form and civil society organisations that have been engaged in struggles for transformation, decolonisation and antiracism.

This text has long been in the making; therefore, a full account of its evolution and the assistance of the many people who contributed to its development and completion would be too lengthy for a mere preface. Suffice to say that the idea of ultimately writing about Black Consciousness as a philosophy emerged during my student days when the first elective conference of the South African Student Organisation (SASO) was held at Turfloop (University of the North), where I was a student. Given South African academic philosophy's attitude towards Africana philosophy, the chances of writing my doctoral thesis on Black Consciousness were absolutely non-existent. My spirits were, however, re-ignited in the late-1980s when Prof. Mala Singh of the then University of Durban-Westville came to me after she presented a paper on Black Consciousness and said: 'I thought you'd challenge some of the claims in my paper'. This conversation was to be followed by my first published paper on Biko, 'The Philosophical Bases of Biko's Thought' (1998), in which I argued that Biko was a philosopher. When this paper appeared, many dismissed my claim as utterly absurd. My second piece of writing on Biko the philosopher (published in 2004 in the journal *Alternation*) was reprinted in the book *Biko Lives!* (edited by Andile Mngxitama, Amanda Alexander and Nigel Gibson) in 2008 and again later in Derek Hook's *Voices of Liberation* in 2014. Since then a number of progressive philosophers (including Lewis Gordon, Nigel Gibson, Mogobe Ramose, Richard Pithouse and Tendayi Sithole) have, amid intense resistance, given recognition to Biko's philosophical voice. Put differently: I lived with this project for a long time, unable to bring myself to give it a definite shape or form, nor a definite path and unity. I dreamed about it; visualised it; thought deeply about it; wrote parts of it; deserted it; forgot about it without giving up; and was reminded of it by the persistence of invidious racism, student protests such as #RhodesMustFall and #FeesMustFall, demands for a decolonised curriculum, and the continual presence of neo-colonialism, neo-liberalism and a detotalised black identity. There it was, in front of me, shapeless yet demanding to be shaped, summoning me toward itself, appealing and beseeching to be recognised and completed.

This book is both a study *on* and an engagement *with* Biko's philosophical ideas and tenets. Indeed, I regard Biko as a *locus* of many pressing questions in contemporary black philosophy, particularly issues relating to the Africana philosophy of existence. Issues crucial to Biko such as antiblack racism, alienation, identity, whiteness, liberalism and Marxism, and liberation from oppression are examined through an existentialist lens. Although studies on Biko are becoming a fast-growing field, this book breaks new and uncharted ground in approaching these issues through the lenses of philosophy. My concerns with the philosophical dimensions of Biko's thought place it in a different genre and category from the ones published so far.

As mentioned, this book has been in the making for over a decade. Some reworked parts of it have appeared in journals over a period of 20 years. Because of this, the book benefitted from a lot of people, some of whom I might unintentionally forget to mention – people who have, through their advice, discussions, editing, encouragement, prodding, questioning and so on played a major role in making its publication possible.

First and foremost, I owe a huge debt of gratitude to Lewis Gordon for his friendship, brotherly love, generous and unselfish help, and encouragement throughout the years. He is just one of those people who are truly out of the ordinary, an amazing philosopher who is – most importantly – a wonderful human being. As he would say: 'Life's journey offers an opportunity to meet few souls and pass many more. I'm glad that we both stopped for a moment and reached out to each other, in solidarity and friendship.' Not to be outdone though is the amazing Jane Anna Gordon, who has been a source of intellectual inspiration. I am heavily indebted to all the past and present members of the Caribbean Philosophical Association (CPA) for their contribution to my intellectual growth. Special thanks, however, go to Paget Henry, not only for being my roommate during conferences but mainly and simply for being who he is – a great philosopher, sociologist and special person. Charles Mills deserves special thanks for being such a wonderful friend and person in the CPA. My special gratitude also goes to the founder and organiser of 'Philosophy Born of Struggle' conferences, a pioneer in African-American philosophy, Leonard Harris, and his ever-enthusiastic collaborator, my good friend J Everet Green.

Three people here at home deserve special recognition for their unbelievable confidence and belief in my work and ability: Richard Pithouse, Tendayi Sithole and Mogobe Ramose. My sincerest gratitude goes to all my students at the former University of Durban-Westville and the University of KwaZulu-Natal, particularly those who took my classes on Fanon, Biko, political philosophy, social philosophy and so on. I have in mind Ernest Moikangwe, Isaac Khambule, Khondlo Q Mtshali, Lukhona Mnguni, Luntu Hlatshwayo, Siyasanga Zibaya, Jethro Abel, Rachel Marrow, Micaela de Freitas, Seham Areff, Khanya Vilakazi, Cyprian Ndlela, Andrew Joseph, Prava Pillay, Emmanuel Sairosi, Nkosinathi Mzelemu, Nokubonga Mazibuko, Kiki Senatla, Sanele Gamede, Siyabomga Ntombela and many others whom I have not mentioned.

Thanks also to my recent students at the University of Limpopo: Bongisizwe Mpangane, Marta Tsebe, Mpilo Mkhonto and particularly Buyiswa Zulu. Not to be forgotten at this university is the administrative assistant of the TV White Space Centre, Ms Franscina Lemekoana, for her infinite patience with my clumsiness and incompetence that resulted in my constant demands for help in administrative and technological matters. Without her skills, patience and readiness to help, my project would have been delayed by many months. Dr Jeffrey Mabelebele has been phenomenal. I fondly remember the serious discussions we had in the evenings and the problems we experienced together at the house we shared. Finally, I owe a huge debt of gratitude to the University of Limpopo for affording me the opportunity to fulfil my last wish of ending my career where it all started. I have also benefitted from research funding by the university, for which I am tremendously appreciative.

Outside the academy, my special thanks go to Nelson Mwale for his generosity and being there when and wherever I needed to talk to someone. My gratitude also goes to Steve Nale, whose love and concern for my well-being are unquestionable. Mdu Nene, my brother from another mother, thank you for the brotherly love you always give. I thank Nkateko Peter Mageza for our constant email conversations about serious global issues. Finally, a word of appreciation goes to Mtshali Phore for our often frustrating realisation that sometimes, for a black person in an antiblack world, ignorance is bliss and knowledge generates anguish and often existential despair.

My very special thanks to those closest to me, whose mere presence in the world provides justification for my continued existence: my children Takatso Semenya and Ndondo Matsimane and my nephews Kgomotso More and Moeketsi Ndumo (More). Moeketsi's courageous and indomitable management of enormous adversity is an example to all. He has courageously taught us how to be strong in the face of immense emotional and physically painful circumstances. Thank you to my sister, Limakatso Sebati, for taking care of Moeketsi. Your love is unequalled. Finally, I thank Buli who has hung in there with uncompromising and often stubborn me, for her endurance, patience and understanding of the situation in which I have put her.

I wish to thank Peter Vale, Lawrence Hamilton and Estelle Prinsloo for granting me permission to use part of the chapter I contributed to their book *Intellectual Traditions in South Africa: Ideas, Individuals and Institutions* (2014). Permission was also granted for the use of revised versions of the following articles: 'Black Consciousness Movement's Ontology: The Politics of Being' (2012), 'Gordon and Biko: Africana Existential Conversation' (2010/2011) and 'Biko: Africana Existentialist Philosopher' (2004a).

Introduction: Biko's Multiple Identities

Emancipate yourselves from mental slavery,
None but ourselves can free our minds
– Bob Marley: 'Redemption Song'

THERE IS AN ONGOING tendency in certain quarters, Lewis Gordon (2000) says, of locking African thinkers and their productions in the biographical moment and political activism. Biko was to some extent a victim of this practice. Bemoaning this reductionist tendency, Gail Smith notes how commemorative discourse on the 25th anniversary of Biko's death elided confrontation with the contents of his writings and his critical philosophy, focusing rather on Biko the 'gap-toothed activist who had charisma, commitment and liked to party' (2002: 6). According to Smith, the commemorative publications that boasted struggle icons such as Nelson Mandela and Archbishop Desmond Tutu were inexcusable and unique precisely because of 'the absence of Steve Biko's voice – it carried not a single one of his articles or speeches' (2002: 6). Worse still, Mandela reduced Biko's radical analysis to a shallow philosophy of aesthetics in his assertion that '[Biko's] message to the youth and students was simple and clear: Black is Beautiful! Be proud of your Blackness' (in Smith 2002: 6). Resonating with Smith's observations, Amiri Baraka (aka LeRoi Jones) a wrote: 'Once opponents of the bourgeoisie are dead, the rulers transform these class enemies into ciphers or agreeable sycophants of Imperialism...who are now "rehabilitated" all the way into being represented as the very opposite ideologically of what they actually were in life' (1992: 18).

Yet the truth is that Biko defied simple reduction to a politician or activist by assuming other equally important identities. He combined the cultural, the political and the philosophical in the same person. He and his comrades espoused what is normally described as a philosophy. Hence Biko himself, together with commentators, spoke of 'the philosophy of Black Consciousness' or the 'Black Consciousness philosophy'. Paradoxically, very few people referred to Biko, popularly known as the 'father' of the Black Consciousness Movement in South Africa, as a philosopher. Exceptions such as Themba Sono describe Biko as 'a formidable and articulate philosopher' (1993: 90), a philosopher not in the usual academic sense of a university professor but more precisely a man of theory and action, an 'organising philosopher' (Sono 1993: 102), perhaps a sort of social and political lay philosopher. But to describe someone as a philosopher, as Sono does, is merely to state a generality without specificity. Therefore, this book, following on Lewis Gordon's extensive phenomenological work on Frantz Fanon, seeks to locate Bantu Stephen Biko within the philosophical terrain – more pointedly, the Africana existentialist tradition. The aim, in short, is to constitute Biko as part of what Benita Parry describes as the attempt 'to disclose the dead victim's...[philosophical] claims' (1996: 12).

Although Biko's entire philosophical legacy has been ignored and dismissed by academic institutions, academics, liberals, Marxists and political opponents, his popularity has never dwindled among a cadre of young black radicals, activists, journalists and independent intellectuals who – for over 35 years – have debated seriously the significance of his intellectual contributions to South African politics and society. It is these debates that have created huge waves of tension over the interpretation of the meaning of Biko in this age and time.

In the face of 'post-apartheid apartheid' (that is, the continued post-1994 racism in the country, which many people believed or hoped had been outlawed), Biko's renewed popularity – both his ideology and image despite being suppressed by the ruling party – has taken on a new dimension of importance. The signs of his rise – posters, T-shirts, the commercialisation of his name, the revisiting of the movie *Biko*, the ever-increasing number of articles in academic journals, the increasing recognition in the academy, the number of biographies being published and so on – are all primarily a function of a need: the current need for a confrontational attitude or mindset against continuing South African racism.

Hence it is that Biko's name no longer belongs to him and no longer refers to his 'facticity'(the word Sartre adopts to refer to a whole range of given facts which apply to a person in the world) – that is, Biko's name no longer names this particular person born in a particular place to particular parents at a particular point in space and time. The name has transcended the owner and has become more than the owner. Like Nelson Mandela, Biko is progressively becoming more than himself, not a saint like the post-1994 Mandela but evidently something more than himself. For some, Biko was a racist; for others, he was an antiracist of the first kind. For some, he was a hedonist, a party lover; for others, he was a serious and committed revolutionary. For some, he was a womaniser; for others, he was a devoted husband. Still some view him as merely an activist; while others, such as myself, regard him as a serious thinker – a philosopher. Biko himself anticipated some of these perceptions, for he stated: 'Some will charge that we are racists.' And it is this charge that would later make Mandela a saint much more than Biko because Mandela's style and the content and aims of his leadership were largely inoffensive and visibly attractive to white South Africa, especially liberal white people. Biko's leadership style, because of its confrontational character against white supremacy, appealed to most black people and invited scorn, ridicule and contempt from white South Africans (both progressive and conservative).

Bongani Madondo has reported that at the time when he wrote the newspaper article 'Fawning over St Nelson is no way to do justice to Mandela',¹ 'a whopping 41 books on the man alone' had been published, besides the fact that Mandela's *Long Walk to Freedom* had been reprinted several times. Add to this *Mandela: The Authorised Portrait*; Nelson Mandela gift books, children's reference books and cartoon books; and a host of other texts that followed during his illness and after his death. Assuming that Mandela's global attention derives from his political involvement and given that he did not single-handedly bring about the political transformation in South Africa, a pertinent question to ask, Madondo insists, is: 'What about other past and present political activists, strategists and indeed community leaders?' What about Jeff Masemola, the man who was incarcerated longer than Mandela? What about Robert Mangaliso Sobukwe, the Pan-Africanist visionary leader whose role in the 1960 Sharpeville pass march (a political 'march that set the tone for all political engagements with the apartheid government thereafter') and subsequent massacre were stellar? Indeed, 'What about Bantu Steve Biko?' Madondo continues to ask. In his view, the focus on Mandela alone – almost to the exclusion of other significant political leaders such as Zeph Mothopeng, Govan Mbeki, Oliver Tambo (whose 'memory has been salvaged by the naming of an airport after him'), Harry Gwala, Oscar Mpheta or Bram Fischer – limits the very big canvas on which 'to paint the story of the nation'. To expand this political canvas, we need to tell the stories of these other leaders as well. Mandela did not build the new South Africa alone.

The other corners of the political canvas are, however, beginning to be slowly painted on as well. Thabo Mbeki has been and still is the focus of the political painters and narrators of the South African story. For all the wrong reasons, Jacob Zuma is also receiving attention. What about Biko? There is a significant resurgence of interest in Biko and the Black Consciousness Movement. Texts written on them include Pityana et al.'s (Eds) *Bounds of Possibilty: The Legacy of Steve Biko and Black Consciousness* (1991); Linda Price's *Steve Biko* (2005); Donald Woods' *Biko* (1987); Lindy Wilson's *Steve Biko* (2011); Millard Arnold's (Ed.) *Steve Biko: No Fears Expressed* (1987); Chris van Wyk's (Ed.) *We Write What We Like* (2007); Saleem Badat's *Black Man, You Are On Your Own* (2009); the Steve Biko Foundation's *The Steve Biko Memorial Lectures: 2000–2008* (2009); Xolela Mangcu's *Biko: A Biography* (2012); Daniel Magaziner's *The Law and the Prophets: Black Consciousness in South Africa, 1968–1977* (2010); Robert Fatton's *Black Consciousness in South Africa* (1986); Andile Mngxitama et al.'s (Eds) *Biko Lives! Contesting the Legacy of Steve Biko* (2008); Derek

Hook's (Ed.) *Steve Biko: Voices of Liberation* (2014); and, recently, Tendayi Sithole's *Steve Biko: Decolonial Meditations of Black Consciousness* (2016). Except for a few texts, almost all deal with Biko's biography, placing much emphasis on his political life and the autobiographical narrative of his influence on the author. The text of Mngxitama et al. is an attempt (as is that of Magaziner) to correct this shortcoming; Mngxitama et al. do this in the first section, entitled 'Philosophical Dialogues', and the chapter entitled 'The Age of the Philosophers'. My contribution to the Mngxitama et al. text is a shortened attempt at establishing Biko's credentials as philosopher. This book, developing the philosophical themes contained in my contribution to Mngxitama et al.'s text, posits Biko as a philosopher and excavates his philosophical ideas, which are located within what I describe as Africana existential philosophy.

There is another tendency to one-dimensionally iconise Biko by reifying his legacy to simply the political. This iconisation, unfortunately, has the capacity to close out possibilities of exploring other dimensions of his legacy that are not politically heroic. One of the most important ways in which this book differs from the existing literature on Biko is the willingness to confront many of those commentaries which attempt to reduce him to a mere political activist. I therefore attempt to limit my focus to the philosophical *leitmotif* or recurrent theme of Biko's political life. This approach is taken with the hope that this heretofore somewhat neglected aspect of his thinking may in fact yield a kind of privileged insight into some of the tensions and contradictions embedded in his philosophical enterprise. My aim here is to disclose the immanent philosophical foundations of Biko's political thought as such. Although Sono does make claims about Biko being a philosopher, what is lacking in his otherwise insightful observation is the moment of 'philosophical specificity' which in some way determines the conditions of possibility or grounds for Biko's empirical political convictions.

Biko nowhere provides a sustained and systematic articulation of a philosophical treatise. He gave us no coherent philosophical theory, but did leave a site for Africana philosophical discourse. His essays contain numerous critical and expository passages from which it is possible to draw together an account of his philosophical orientation. This conception is to be found in his collected essays *I Write What I Like* (1996), speeches and interviews. From these materials, it is easy to notice that from Biko's point of view, philosophy is not a disembodied system of ideas or a mechanical reflection of the world; rather, it is a way of existing and acting. It is because of this philosophical orientation that I locate his philosophy within what has come to be known generally as Africana philosophy, but more pointedly as Africana existential philosophy. To be a philosopher, especially an Africana existential philosopher, is not just to hold certain views; it is also a way of being and a way of perceiving in the world, what Biko himself described as 'a way of life'. As Maurice Merleau-Ponty (1962) confirms, philosophy is not an activity centred in itself but one which questions the world around the philosopher; it is, in short, an existential phenomenological activity. It is not just permissible but necessary that the philosopher should start from her own experience of the world and not from abstract problems. In this context, therefore, it was from his own personal experience, for example with the liberals during his membership of the National Union of South African Students (NUSAS), which taught him how hypocritical liberals are prone to be when it comes to issues of race. His encounter with students of different political persuasions at the medical school helped him to refashion and rethink his political, ideological and philosophical outlook.

But why is Biko's philosophy relevant now? The magnitude of the contradictions and the complexity of the problems of present-day post-apartheid apartheid reality suggest that Biko's adamant insistence that black people learn to think for themselves is particularly relevant today. For example, there is an emerging post-1994 consensus in South Africa – a consensus seriously called into question by the recent youth and student movements and political organisations such as the Black First Land First movement led by Mngxitama – that race is a myth which (as Anthony Appiah would say) has no semantic nor scientific respectability, biological basis or philosophical legitimacy. What has acquired constitutional respectability, however, is the liberal attitude that race is irrelevant and that South Africa is a democratic state founded on the principle of non-racialism. Flowing from this is the belief that since racism is predicated on race, and since the myth of race has disappeared, racism also must have disappeared (that is, since the death of apartheid, racism has also died). If this is the case, then Black Consciousness should – in the context of this newly acquired non-racial democratic dispensation in South Africa – be unnecessary and disappear precisely because what necessitated its existence (racism) no longer exists. Is the project of non-racialism, as envisaged by Biko and the Black Consciousness Movement, realised? Is South Africa a truly non-racial country such that the existence of Black Consciousness as articulated by Biko is superfluous? Can we say that with the death of legal institutional apartheid, antiblack racism is also dead? In the face of Penny Sparrow's animalisation of black (African) people – followed by Matthew Theunissen, Judge Mabel Jansen and Pretoria University philosophy lecturer Louise Mabille – the constant attacks on black people and students by white men and white students, and a host of other racist incidents that have occurred since 1994 after a black government came into power, can we truly afford to ignore Steve Biko?

These are the questions that this book deals with. In Chapter 1, I attempt to understand Biko the man, his character and what made him what he became – a fabulously courageous man willing to put his life on the line for freedom, not only his freedom but the freedom of his people and, by a dialectical inversion, their oppressors as well. To be courageous in an oppressive totalitarian society, to question authority and society's value system, is in a fundamental way to be a rebel – a rebel against the inhumanity of a system that went to the extent of questioning the humanity of other human beings. Thus, Chapter 1 is a phenomenological exploration of being-a-rebel. Rebels come in different shapes and forms of being. We get political, religious, social, existentialist, ontological, metaphysical, oedipal and even scientific rebels. In many ways, Biko's rebellion was an expression of all these versions, often combined or sometimes individually.

Note

1   Madondo B, Fawning over St Nelson is no way to do justice to Mandela, *Sunday Times*, 25 February 2007.

Biko the rebel

*The only way to deal with an unfree world is to become so absolutely free
that your very existence is an act of rebellion.*

(Camus 1974)

*No doubt...part of the approach envisaged in bringing about 'black consciousness'
has to be directed to the past, to seek to rewrite the history of the black man and to
produce in it the heroes who form the core of the African background...
But only scant reference is made to African heroes. A people without
a positive history is like a vehicle without an engine.*

(Biko 1996: 29)

*Truth, because of its compelling nature, makes him defiant and unyielding
and it is this quality, amongst others, that makes the rebel such a
difficult thorn in the flesh of established authority.*

(Manganyi 1981: 172)

STEVE BIKO HAS BECOME a contested figure around the world. The contestations range from him being perceived and portrayed as a hero or villain, psychologist or politician, nationalist or liberal, socialist or Africanist, racist or humanist, martyr or recklessly courageous man, activist or philosopher, and so on. His name has even found a home in academic institutions where it is used in psychology, politics, history, cultural studies, Africana studies, theology, literature (including poetry), sociology, poetry, music and philosophy. Like those of Malcolm X and Ernesto Che Guevara, his image appears on struggle organisations' T-shirts and fashion clothing brands such as Stoned Cherrie. Having been iconised like Malcolm X, Che Guevara and Nelson Mandela, Biko has become commodified, bought and sold in the marketplace. Consequently, he has become a fashion statement, deradicalised, depoliticised and – if I may say so – dephilosophised. Which Biko is the real one? Is this, in earnest, a fair question to ask about any human being?

To a lot of people in South Africa and the rest of the world, Steve Biko was a hero. What is a hero? A hero is someone who, among other things but primarily, is willing to risk or sacrifice her own life for another person for justice. What constitutes justice differs from one group of people to the next. Consequently, someone might be considered a hero by one group of people and not be a hero to another group of people. This is acknowledged by Biko one of this chapter's epigraphs. Indeed, those he considered African heroes were villains to other groups of people. Similarly, for example, not everyone will agree with Sono, who in his book *Reflections on the Origins of Black Consciousness in South Africa* declares: 'I propose to begin with the premise that Biko was a hero...[His] heroic qualities revolved around the power and symbol of contrast' (1993: 91–92). And among those who disagree with Sono, I suspect, might be Biko himself. He probably would not have considered himself a hero, not out of modesty but out of conviction. Be that as it may, if Nelson Mandela is globally regarded as a hero because he declared during the Rivonia Trial that freedom is an ideal for which he was prepared to die and later sacrificed 27 years of his life in prison to free his country from oppression, Biko should – in fact, even more than Mandela – be considered a hero because he paid the ultimate price (death) to free his people from oppression. Could he have done otherwise? Yes. He could have easily pursued his medical studies and ended up a rich middle-class medical doctor like so many of his fellow students. Being unable to do so, Biko chose a life of freedom rather than slavery – a choice that ended in his tragic death. In other words, his heroism is part of his rebelliousness against unfreedom and thus he constructed himself into the quintessential rebel. Undoubtedly, Biko was (as the epigraph indicates and as I will attempt to show in this and subsequent chapters) so free that his very existence, his very being, was an act of rebellion against the brutally unfree and violent world of apartheid. It is precisely this mindset that made Biko a rebel, and in the words of Manganyi, 'such a difficult thorn in the flesh of established authority' (1981: 172).

This being said, I certainly do not want to fall into the hero-construction trap. However, since a human being is nothing but the sum of her actions, it is possible, given Biko's actions, to describe him as a rebel whose mere existence (as Camus declared in the first epigraph above) was 'an act of rebellion'. The 'power and symbol of contrast' which Sono identifies, are the qualities not only of a hero, I would say, but – most importantly – those of a true rebel. Not all heroes are rebels and not all rebels are heroes. Some heroes may be perceived as rebels and some rebels may be regarded as heroes. This means that what Sono and I are claiming may or may not be the same. Thus, instead of declaring 'Biko was a hero' as Sono does, I want to begin with the premise that Biko was a *rebel*. After all, a dead person is defenceless before the judgements of the living. In death, only our past defines us: 'The terrible thing about Death is that it transforms life into destiny' (Sartre 1956: 112).

The rebel

Camus (1974) asks: 'What is a rebel?' 'A man who says NO', he answers. But such a person is not all negativity. A rebel is also a person who says 'YES as soon as he begins to think for himself'. A rebel says NO to oppression, suffering, dehumanisation, exploitation, degradation and unfreedom. To say NO, as James Cone (1969) correctly indicates, means that the oppressor, the exploiter or the master has crossed and overstepped the limits and boundaries beyond which he should not go. To say NO is to refuse to allow anyone to touch what one is; to fight for the integrity of one part of one's being, to 'persistently refuse to be humiliated…accept pain provided that [one's] integrity is respected' (Camus 1974: 24). To be a rebel is to adamantly refuse to accept the oppressive situation in which one finds oneself. In short, a rebel is one who is constantly in search of authenticity through the pursuit of freedom. This is not metaphysical rebellion but ontologico-existential rebellion. When, for example, the slave says NO to the master, she has decided that there are boundaries that the master cannot cross, limits beyond which the master may not go. The NO delineates boundaries and sets up parameters of human action. What the rebel demonstrates with her refusal is that the slave cannot allow her humanity to be questioned, annihilated or degraded; that if this nihilation of possibilities continues, the slave has to declare 'Give me liberty or death'.

In an autobiographical moment that sounds more like the experiences of a slave, Biko wrote: 'Born shortly before 1948, I have lived all my conscious life in the framework of institutional separate development. My friendships, my love, my education, my thinking and every other facet of my life have been carved and shaped within the context of separate development. In stages during my life, I have managed to outgrow some of the things the system taught me' (1996: 27). The growing out of the system required an act of rebellion which other black people living within the system and unfortunately submerged in its deadly morass could not and did not outgrow. It required saying NO – in anger – to having his friends, love, education and even his thoughts determined from without by a vicious system bent on keeping him in perpetual servitude. As an act of rebellion, Biko introduced the concept of 'consciousness' into his lived-experience of oppression: 'I have lived all my conscious life' in apartheid oppression, he declared, and subsequently became 'conscious of the urgent need' for a new consciousness. His family, comrades, environment, education (including his medical school, political circumstances and informal experiences) gave him the substance with which to combine consciousness with actual life experience as a function of philosophical revelation. In fact, it is this consciousness that became the catalyst for the emergence of a philosophical theory and practice later to be known as the Black Consciousness philosophy.

In a biography of Malcolm X, Bruce Perry describes his subject's rebellious attitude by stating that Malcolm's 'war against the white power structure evolved from the same inner needs that had spawned earlier rebellions against his teachers, the law, established religion, and other symbols of authority' (in Dyson 1993: 123). In a similar way, because of the rebel he was, Biko very early in his political and social formative years refused to take the back seat and be reticent on matters concerning his existence. As a consequence, his rebelliousness – fashioned by a new consciousness – cost him a year out of high school. He was expelled from Lovedale High School for political activity. This experience and the constant harassment by prison warders, security police and white people in general led him to develop 'an attitude which was much more directed really at authority than anything else. I hated authority like hell. I used to have lots of arguments on a personal basis with the prison warders and so on' (interview with Gerhart 1972: 17). These confrontations were not confined to the warders; Biko also had personal wars with the presumably liberal missionaries at St Francis College in Marianhill: 'I personally had many wars with those guys [liberal Catholic teachers]. Most of them non-political wars in a sense, but again this kind of authority problem' (interview with Gerhart 1972: 18). This early attitude developed into a form of rage or anger. In fact, it was the consequence rather than the cause of his anger; anger over the way black people were oppressed, dehumanised and brutalised; anger at white arrogance and hypocrisy; indeed, anger at white racism and supremacy.

Undeniably, the title of his book *I Write What I Like* is a rebellious assertion of selfhood in a context bent on coercively suppressing that very self, a context bent on limiting the boundaries of possibility. In fact, the 'I' in Biko's 'I Write' is not a disembodied and abstract Cartesian *cogito* (the principle establishing the existence of someone from the fact of her thinking or awareness), but a situated, concrete, embodied and racialised 'I' or self. It is an 'I' that signifies what Herbert Marcuse described as 'The Great Refusal', meaning 'the protest against unnecessary repression, the struggle for the ultimate form of freedom' (1955: 149). It is an 'I' that refuses to be intimidated by a powerful state ideology backed by an equally powerful and repressive state apparatus and machinery. This title is a NO to intimidation, to oppression and, above all, to *fear*. The text graphically articulates in existentialist and phenomenological terms that 'if you can overcome the personal fear of death, which is a highly irrational thing, you know that you're on the way' (1996: 152) to freedom. Biko's rebellion was a revolt which, in the words of William (WEB) du Bois, said: 'No to the scorn of man. No to the degradation of man. No to the exploitation of man. No to the butchery of what is most human in man: freedom' (in Gordon 1997a: 210).

The writings were a refusal to be silenced since, as he himself declared, '[t]here is no freedom in silence (1972: 10)'. He refused to be silenced despite the banning orders placed on him which forbade him to speak to a crowd, write anything or travel. He refused to take the insults and restrictions in silence. Such a NO was the NO of a man whose rebellious spirit against inhumanity ironically, through his death at the hands of the security police torturers, disclosed and revealed the utmost inhumanity against which his very rebellion was directed. Furthermore, where in the 'Republic of Silence' others were forced to hold their tongues, where the right to speak truth to power and to write were denied, Biko chose to speak, and when he did, 'every word became precious as a declaration of principle' (Sartre 2013: 83). He became 'Frank Talk' (his writing pseudonym) and spoke truth to power. As black people, we speak because we dare to look in the mirror and see what we are not; we speak because blackness has come to represent negativity, nothingness; we speak because we seek to name ourselves, define ourselves, re-invent ourselves – and we speak because we want to free ourselves. For him, speaking represented and constituted a *Weltanschauung* (world view) and a mode of being-black-in-the-world, what he called 'a way of life'. He used words, both spoken and written, to express himself. As Sartre would say, the writer is simultaneously a speaker. Biko's writings, in the face of banning orders, censorship and detentions, were an act of rebellion in the sense that they were intended as an awakening of consciousness, and thus they became not only committed literature but also revolutionary writings.

The title of his book is also a defiant response to white (liberal) paternalistic attitudes towards black people, an attitude which for Biko found its earliest expression in the missionaries: 'Blacks cannot or are incapable of saying or writing anything about themselves. We can do it for them.' This is a longstanding missionary and colonial attitude graphically articulated by, among others, Father Placide Tempels in his *Bantu Philosophy*. In this text, Tempels claims that although the Bantus (Africans) had a philosophy (ontology), they were incapable of systematising it; only Europeans possessed the capacity to formulate and enunciate it for them and on their behalf. He paternalistically writes:

> We do not claim that the Bantus are incapable of presenting us with a philosophical treatise complete with an adequate vocabulary. It is our intellectual training that enables us to effect its systematic development. *It is up to us to provide them with an accurate account of their conception of entities, in such a way that they will recognize themselves in our words* and will agree. (Tempels 1959: 24 – italics added)

At the close of the twentieth century, a white South African philosopher following on the 'civilising mission' of missionaries such as Placide Tempels wrote a book entitled *Philosophy for Africa*. In it he attempts to outline 'a philosophical conception of humanity that incorporates and *systematizes* the African insights'

(Shutte 1993) through the mediation and use of certain European philosophical traditions, because traditional African thought, in his view, has not by and large undergone rigorous philosophical scrutiny and assessment. This philosopher had evidently not read anything by Mazizi Kunene, Ezekiel (Es'kia) Mphahlele or Manganyi in South Africa, let alone the many philosophical treatises by African philosophers on the continent – hence his patently absurd belief that African thought has not undergone philosophical scrutiny. It is this kind of paternalistic attitude and white arrogance that Biko rejected. He refused to be told what his thinking and his writing should or ought to be, and could not allow it to be dictated to him by others. In many ways, therefore, the discovery of blackness and the acceptance of its factual aspect constitute one way of describing Black Consciousness as a major influence on the rebellious nature of Biko's *I Write What I Like*. It is one of the more militantly defiant assertions of Black Consciousness that provided Biko with the title of his book. In a similar rebellious fashion, Fanon's *Black Skin, White Masks* opens with a rebellious declaration: 'Why write this book? No one has asked me for it.' Fanon continues: 'I think it would be good if certain things were said' (1967a: 7).

While Biko was a rebel *par excellence*, a man who said NO, in a sense, NO is dialectically related to YES. Negation is dialectically the opposite of affirmation. There is a sense in which saying NO implicitly becomes saying YES to something. Saying NO to something or a condition implies that a correlative YES determines that NO. So when Biko said NO to oppression, he simultaneously said YES to freedom – a YES which in the apartheid context constituted an act of rebellion. While he rebelled against being silenced, he also said YES to silence when talking was demanded of him by the security police. In other words, he said NO when the all-powerful apartheid regime force silenced him through restrictions and YES when he refused to talk when interrogated by the security police. He kept silent even in the heat of torture: 'I only understand one form of dealing with police, and that's to be as unhelpful as possible. So I button up' (Biko 1996: 152). Yet, in his own words, '[a]ny issue that you win because of your "no" implies that you are being listened to by those in power' (1996: 135–136). As a consequence, he said NO to racism, oppression, exploitation, dehumanisation, degradation and unfreedom that characterised the situation of black people in an antiblack apartheid world; he simultaneously said YES to freedom, equality, non-racialism and human dignity.

Biko was in many ways a rebel and a martyr like Fanon, Malcolm X and Patrice Lumumba. Consider Lumumba's words, which may apply with equal force to all these rebels:

> Everything possible was done to break my spirit, but I knew that in every
> country in the world freedom is the ideal for which all men in all times have

fought and died. Having made a choice...I was jeered at, vilified, dragged in the mud – simply because I insisted on Freedom...I have never been against whites...but what I have always rebelled against was injustice. (in Heinz & Donnay 1969: vi)

Their rebellion was a manifestation of their willingness to insert themselves into the world, their willingness to risk their lives, their determination, as Friedrich Nietzsche would say, 'to live dangerously'. Such existence typifies Heideggerian authenticity, the courage and ability to face and confront one's death as one's 'ownmost possibility [which is] non-relational, certain and as such...not to be outstripped' (1962: 303). Knowing how the apartheid regime reacted to rebellious individuals, Biko predicted that he would be murdered in his early adulthood.[1] To say NO means that death is preferable to life, if the latter is devoid of freedom. As Camus indicated, it is '[b]etter to die on one's feet than to live on one's knees' (1974: 15), which Biko himself understood so very well: 'You are either alive and proud or you are dead' (1996: 152). This relationship between the rebel and death is predicated on the relationship between the rebel and freedom, for she who learns how to die unlearns slavery and servitude and thus becomes free. Rebels for the liberation of black people against white racism, in Cone's words, are people 'who stand *unafraid* of the structures of white racism. They are men [sic] who risk their lives for the inner freedom of others' (1969: 41 – italics added).

In his poem 'Elegie', Goethe says that where other people become silent in their trouble, God gave him the power to express his suffering. With some slight modification, it may be said of Biko that where other black people became speechless in their pain, it was given him to express their suffering. As a man who was conscious of himself, Biko took the whole of human suffering upon himself and in turn, through his death at the hands of his oppressors, suffered for all – even for the white person. But suffering, as Sartre brilliantly declares, contains within itself the refusal to suffer. Hence, in his and black people's suffering, Biko fought to eliminate that very suffering. In fact, black suffering should not be confused with Christian suffering characterised by masochistic humility and 'give-the-other-cheek' resignation of 'dolorism'. Black suffering is that kind of suffering which 'carries within itself its own refusal; it is by nature *a refusal to suffer*, it is the dark side of negativity, it opens onto revolt and liberty' (Sartre 1988: 323 – italics added).

Authenticity

Through this rebellion, Biko constituted himself as a personification of what Sartre describes as authenticity. Authentic existence, in Sartre's words, consists 'in assuming a lucid and true consciousness of the situation, in accepting responsibility and risks incurred in that situation, and in maintaining it in the moment of pride or of humiliation and sometimes in the moment of abhorrence and hatred' (1956: 75–76). To exist authentically is to exist in full consciousness of one's freedom and to choose one's self within the conditions of this freedom and one's situation. From Martin Heidegger's point of view, authenticity, besides having the ability to choose one's possibilities and assuming responsibility for Being oneself, also importantly consists of the resolute decision to face that which is our 'ownmost potentiality-for-Being' (1962: 299) – that is, our death. If an individual, as Biko did, is able to stand before death, understand and accept it as that possibility which is her 'ownmost potentiality-for-being', then she exists authentically. If anyone can realise and resolutely face the reality that death is her non-relational (individualised and undelegatable), not-to-be-outstripped (inescapable), certain (undeniable) and indefinite possibility, accept it without fear and 'indifferent tranquillity' (Heidegger 1962: 309), then she exists authentically. In anticipating his death as his ownmost possibility, Biko liberated himself from the clutches of fear and – most importantly – the fear of death. Heidegger explains that anticipation of death 'turns out to be the possibility of understanding one's *ownmost* and uttermost potentiality-for-Being – that is to say, the possibility of *authentic existence*' (1962: 307 – italics added). Biko's anticipation of his death was the self-disclosure of his freedom. Hence, to say NO implies that death is much more preferable than a life without freedom.

The existence of an authentic being-towards-death immediately suggests its opposite, namely inauthentic being-towards-death. It is precisely this mode of existence gripped by 'Fear', especially the fear of death, which Biko (as I will show in a later chapter) denounced among black people during apartheid repression as a form of bad faith or false consciousness. In inauthenticity, an individual is in constant flight not only from who she is or from her freedom, but also from the reality of her impending death. She refuses to recognise and acknowledge that death is her ownmost potentiality-for-being, that it is non-relational, certain, indefinite and cannot be outmanoeuvred. This inauthenticity becomes manifest in what Heidegger calls 'fallenness' of existence, where an individual participates in the idle talk of everydayness. Everyday idle talk avoids the reality of the immanent presence of personal death. In this kind of talk, death is constantly conceived as occurring somewhere, to someone else. Everyday talk depersonalises death by reducing it to an abstract and universal category. Instead of saying 'I shall die', everyday talk says 'one dies'. It refuses to recognise that death is a concrete phenomenon which all human beings, whether they like it or not, must of necessity suffer. The character of death as my ownmost possibility, mine and mine alone, is reduced to the death of someone far removed from myself. In other words, everyday talk anaesthetises, deodorises, tranquilises and desensitises the reality of one's death. To the individual of average everydayness, the consciousness of death generates not only fear but also *angst* or existential anguish. Philosophers (particularly existentialists) have given different names to this mode of inauthentic existence, although they all refer to the same phenomenon with slight individual variations. For Georg Hegel, inauthenticity can be understood as 'unhappy consciousness'; for Karl Marx, it is 'false consciousness'; for Søren Kierkegaard, it is the 'aesthetic mode of existence'; for Sartre, it is 'bad faith'; and for Camus, it is 'absurdity'.

Through resolute choice to pursue 'truth' and 'the good' by means of the philosophy of Black Consciousness, Biko emancipated himself from false consciousness, inauthenticity and bad faith produced by apartheid oppression. He realised that his condition as an oppressed person was not as natural, immovable and unchangeable as it was made out to appear, and that no choice of how to live his situation appeared impossible. Mystification and ignorance of the oppressed render their condition natural and constitute it as a given. For example, the distribution of wealth during the height of apartheid was made to appear so natural, so God-given, that it was unquestioned by most black people. Simone de Beauvoir describes this sense of false consciousness thus: '... one of the ruses of oppression is to camouflage itself behind a natural situation since, after all, one cannot revolt against nature' (1994: 83). This means that the situation of the oppressed black person has been made such that she is unable even to recognise that she is oppressed. Such an oppressed person is in the grip of false consciousness. Free from false consciousness, Biko saw his situation more clearly and thus took responsibility for his being in that situation with a decisiveness and resoluteness derived from an act of pure reflective rebellion. It becomes clear, therefore, that authenticity demands not only resoluteness but great courage (the courage-to-be). In other words, Biko admitted to himself that the apartheid situation did not need to be as it *was* but that it could be transformed into what-it-*ought-to-be*.

Biko's life was thus a search and a quest for authenticity. Authenticity, as Sartre noted, is also the self-recovery and the self-affirmation of being which was previously corrupted – that is, an alienated self. Authentic being-black-in-the-world necessitated liberation from the terror of fear and death. As a rebel, Biko (like Fanon) recognised one right only – a right that led to his untimely death: 'That of demanding human behavior from the Other' (Fanon 1967a: 219).

The rebel as philosopher

Some rebels are not simply people who pursue disorder or lawlessness for its own sake; they are also fundamentally revolutionaries. In a society where racism and oppression are endemic, a society characterised by the ever-present possibility of death, indeed a world of the living dead – in such a world, as Fanon remarks, anyone who rebels against the status quo becomes a revolutionary. Some revolutionaries are also philosophers in their quest to bring about change. They are, as it were, philosophers of change. Thus a rebel can assume the mantle of a revolutionary philosopher by the truth and the good that she pursues and embraces. Besides, rebels too can be and are often philosophers. Consider Nietzsche's shocking declaration 'God is dead!' and Sartre turning down the Nobel Prize in Literature, saying: 'I don't align myself with anybody else's description of me. People can think of me a genius, a pornographer, a communist, a bourgeois, however they like. Myself, I think of other things.'[2] Part of what it is to be a philosopher, as I will attempt to demonstrate later, is the pursuit of the 'True' and the 'Good'. The pursuit of truth (what-is) and the good (what-ought-to-be) constitutes a philosophical theory of transcendence, of liberation, of freedom. Biko's awareness of the urgent need for a new consciousness became a catalyst for a philosophy that would eventually be a midwife for *what-ought-to-be*. A revolutionary looks to the future, to a change from 'being' (*what-is*) to 'becoming' (*what-ought-to-be*).

The rebellion of the kind that Biko exemplified is in itself a philosophy of transcendence, a going beyond *what-is* and a becoming of *what-ought-to-be*. The 'ought' in this case is not simply an ethical imperative but, more importantly, an existential notion of change. It is in short, a philosophy of change whose main *raison d'être* or reason for being is to annihilate *what is* and usher in *what-ought-to-be*. As a revolutionary philosopher, the rebel claims to be a contingent being, unjustified but free, wholly plunged into society through her effort to change it. But in living her contingency, the revolutionary philosopher accepts the *de facto* existence of her oppressor and the absolute value of the ideologies they have produced. She becomes a rebel only through a movement of transcendence which challenges these ideologies. Such a rebel as revolutionary philosopher adheres to a philosophy whose principles are: (i) that a human being is unjustifiable, since human existence is contingent in that neither she nor any providence has produced it; (ii) that, as a consequence of this contingency, any collective order established by human beings can be transcended towards other orders and any systemic limits placed on the individual can be crossed; (iii) that the system of values current in society reflects the structure of that society and tends to preserve it; (iv) that it can thus always be transcended towards other systems which are not yet clearly perceived since the society of which they are the expression does not yet exist.

Unlike the revolutionary philosopher, oppressors and antiblack racists always believe that their existence in the world is pre-given or pre-ordained and therefore that they exist by (divine) right or natural right, that theirs is a necessary and justified existence, the kind of existence which Sartre describes as 'existent-that-exists-because-it-has-the-right-to-exist' (1984: 111). This attitude in effect means that the racist or oppressor grasps herself as existing by necessity, or possessing a certain justification or reason for being. To the revolutionary philosopher (rebel), however, human beings of divine right (who exist by right) do not exist. The rebel is conscious of the fact that as human beings, they also lead an existence that is equally unjustifiable. The declaration that 'we too are human beings' is at bottom a declaration that the racist and oppressor whose main *telos* or ultimate aim is to deny the humanity of others are human beings too, not gods. Because the consciousness of her contingent condition inclines her to recognise herself as an unjustifiable fact, she regards those who claim divine right to exist as simple facts like herself. Thus, the revolutionary philosopher is not a person who demands rights, but rather a person who destroys the very idea of rights which she regards as products of force and custom. This means, for example, that unlike the ANC leaders who wished to raise themselves to the level of the ruling white people and be identified with them by the fact that they also existed by right, Biko the rebel wished to deny the validity of white right-to-exist, to bring them down to the level of the contingent and unjustified.

Conclusion

My focus in this chapter has been on existential rebellion rather than metaphysical rebellion. While metaphysical rebellion speaks to the revolt of the individual against existence itself and creation itself, ontological rebellion makes the rebel proclaim and profess her individual existential authenticity in the Heideggerian sense. I have indicated that Biko personified Camus' rebel, that he was an embodiment of what it is to say NO and YES. Thus, precisely because when he first become conscious of his situation as a black man in an extremely antiblack society and felt rudely and penetratingly the total contradiction between *what-is* and *what-ought-to-be*, he acquired what Lewis Gordon calls 'potentiated double consciousness' (Gordon 2008: 177). This means that when he saw and identified the contradictions embedded in apartheid antiblack racism and white supremacy, his immediate reaction was rebellion. His rebelliousness made him one of the first black people in South Africa who looked the brutality of white racism right in the eye and, within the short period of his life, was able to tell South Africans about this blatant atrocity in a courageous and defiant manner.

   In the final analysis, what constituted Biko a rebel and – I may say – a heretic (not in the usual religious sense) was best described by a New York cab driver speaking about Malcolm X: 'Malcolm ain't afraid to tell Mr Charlie [the white man], the FBI or the cops or nobody where to get off. You don't see him pussyfootin' 'round the whites like he's scared of them' (in Silberman 1964: 57). This sentiment was echoed by a former president of the USA's National Association for the Advancement of Colored People (NAACP) who confessed:

> 'Malcolm says things you or I would not say. When he says those things, when he talks about the white man, even those of us who are repelled by his philosophy secretly cheer a little outside ourselves, because Malcolm X really does tell 'em, and we know he frightens the white man. We clap' (in Silberman 1964: 57).

Indeed, both Malcolm X and Biko were conscious of and did not flee the possibility of their death. Both died knowing full well that they might be killed. They faced their death authentically.

While certain philosophers might assert the Cartesian 'I think, therefore I am', Biko – together with a lot of black philosophers – asserted: 'I rebel, therefore I am.' What all that has been said here about Biko comes to is 'freedom'. It was his ability to say NO that constituted the measure and meaning of his freedom in the world.

Notes

1   For a lengthy discussion on Biko and death, see my article 'Biko and Douglass: Existentialist Conception of Death and Freedom' (2016).
2   Sartre J-P, quoted in Existentialism, *Life*, 6 November 1964.

Black Consciousness: The movement and its historicity

IN THE PREVIOUS CHAPTER, I suggested that Biko was not only a rebel but also a philosopher. However, it seems impossible to discuss Biko without taking into account the historical origins and development of his ideas. Furthermore, his ideas cannot be understood in isolation, without taking into consideration the context and the social and political milieu in which they originated. In other words, one cannot do justice to Biko's ideas without locating them within the organisational framework from which they emerged. There is simply no way one can talk of Biko without talking about the Black Consciousness Movement, and one cannot talk of the Black Consciousness Movement without talking about Biko. He is the foundation of Black Consciousness in South Africa. Thus, we need to understand the movement and the philosophical context in which his thinking developed: Black Consciousness. Black Consciousness is both a movement and a philosophy. Much has already been written about the historical development and political aspects of the movement;[1] therefore, in this chapter, I briefly consider the origins and formation of the movement before plunging into its philosophical orientation – although a strict delineation of the two is a somewhat complex task.

Some people argue that the Black Consciousness Movement was a product of the political vacuum created by the banning of the ANC, the Pan Africanist Congress (PAC) and other political organisations; the arrests of the African nationalist leadership; and many activists going into exile. True as this perception is, it ignores the fact as argued by Ibbo Mandaza that 'there are no vacuums in history, least of all in that of the struggle'.[2] The more correct approach is to view Black Consciousness as part of a long line of black activism and radical philosophical tradition traceable, as Lewis Gordon (2002) indicates, to the thinking of Martin Delaney three centuries ago and to what is now known as the 'black radical tradition'. Delaney, for example, developed the view that black people's coming to consciousness of their blackness is a necessary condition for their eventual liberation. In fact, the archaeology may be traced back to the Haitian

Revolution led by Toussaint L'Ouverture and includes Marcus Garvey, Aimé Césaire and Fanon on the Caribbean islands; Du Bois, Alain Locke and Richard Wright during the Harlem Renaissance in North America; the African intellectual tradition of the eighteenth to twentieth centuries, from Pan-Africanism to African socialism; and, finally, from Negritude to the Black Power Movement. In order to correct certain misconceptions, let me begin with the influence of the Black Power Movement in the USA on the formation and ideological orientation of the Black Consciousness Movement in South Africa.

The Black Power Movement

There is general consensus among the critics of Black Consciousness in Azania that the movement owes a great debt to the theories and political practices of the Black Power Movement in the USA.[3] In an attempt not only to deny Black Consciousness in this country any originality but also to maliciously implicate it in violent intentions and practices similar to the Black Panthers' self-defence strategy, some critics – and what Pityana calls 'minions of this racist oppressive giant in South Africa'[4] – simply painted it as 'nothing but an importation of Black power ideas from America', an imitative ideology (Pityana 1979: 3). According to this view, Black Consciousness basically re-articulated and reproduced certain already existing ideologies such as that of the Black Power Movement. Correct as this interpretation seems, and 'as if that was wrong in itself' (Pityana 1979: 3), it is however a half-truth. Indeed, it is incorrect to claim (as Sono, a former expelled SASO president does) that 'Black Consciousness as it is known and articulated in South Africa...is lock, stock and barrel Black American invention, exported to the South African black radicals almost *verbatim*', that Black Consciousness in Azania is 'a Black American proposition' and that the Azanian version of Black Consciousness 'as an *ideological* weapon, as a political *doctrine*, is a thinly veiled Afro-American weapon with all its faults – warts and all' (1993: 34, 55, 40 – italics in original). As support for this extreme claim, Sono cites the dubious, biased and unresearched views of apartheid's white Minister of the Interior Theo Gerdener and member of the white parliament Marais Steyn, who characterised Black Consciousness as constituting 'a dangerous situation...created for us by the transfer to South Africa of dangerous Black Power doctrines from the United States of America' (Steyn, in Sono 1993: 55). Needless to say, with reference to the two cited Afrikaners, the '*swart gevaar*' (black threat) doctrine of the apartheid regime was similar to the 'communist inspired' doctrine of the McCarthy era in the USA, a doctrine which saw Black Consciousness as a threat to white survival.

In a recent publication, Magaziner (2010) makes almost the same bizarre claims as Sono. He even accuses some Black Consciousness exponents of plagiarism.

Referring to Sono and other critics' charges, Magaziner writes: '*They had a point.* As with Biko's use of Kaunda, SASO activists did not exactly respect copyright' (2010: 48 – italics added). For me, this is plain agreement with Sono despite Magaziner's later hedging: 'Activists *copied,* but they also translated, they read words from one context and wrote them into their own' (italics added). Magaziner then proceeds to give what he calls an example of the 'copying' applied in a different context. He refers to Bennie Khoapa's 1972 speech, which he claims was 'almost entirely lifted from an article by Lerone Bennett'. Further on, he writes: 'Just as I will show how Black Consciousness's faith-infused politics rejected narrow structures of "rational" political practice, so too might we argue that *activists' use of text appropriately violated modernist, legalistic notions of intellectual property and propriety*' (2015SSO: 49 – italics added).

Biko and other Black Consciousness adherents unquestionably read and were influenced by Stokely Carmichael (aka Kwame Ture) and Charles Hamilton's *Black Power and the Politics of Liberation in America* (1967); Eldridge Cleaver's *Soul On Ice* (1968); George Jackson's *Soledad Brother* (1970) and *Blood in My Eye* (1971); Malcolm X's *The Autobiography of Malcolm X* (1965); Angela Davis's *If They Come in the Morning: Voices of Resistance* (1971); James Cone's *Black Theology and Black Power* (1969) and so on. Most members of SASO and of the Black Consciousness Movement acknowledged their debt to the Black Power Movement in the USA. However, it is incorrect to exaggerate the African-American contribution in the manner that Sono does. These were not the only influence, as Sono, Magaziner and others would have us believe. Even though we acknowledge the impact of Black Power on Black Consciousness, Biko insisted that those Black Power ideas were not simply absorbed and appropriated with disregard for the different existential, social and political peculiarities and contexts of South Africa. In a SASO publication on formation school discussions, Biko reported that the study of the African-American approach to the race problem 'offered interesting comparisons' between apartheid and American Jim Crow practices. One study group, for example, was assigned the task of studying the significance of Carmichael and Charles Hamilton's statement that 'before entering the open society, we must first close ranks'. The group concluded that 'an open society in this country can only be created by blacks and that for as long as whites are in power, they shall seek to make it closed in one way or the other. We then defined what we meant by an open society' (*SASO Newsletter* 1970: 6). The report goes on to demonstrate the difference between black conditions in the USA and in South Africa. Because of historical, political and social differences, the statement was changed from 'entering' to 'creating' the open society. To imply, therefore, that SASO is 'lock, stock and barrel Black American invention' (as Sono does) or that SASO plagiarised Carmichael and Charles Hamilton (as Magaziner claims) is at best mistaken and at worst disingenuous. Indeed, Sono himself wrote a piece entitled 'Some Concepts of Negritude and Black Identity' in a *SASO Newsletter,* stating among other things: 'It was a West Indian poet, Aimé Césaire, who coined the word Negritude. *But we sharpened the concept into an armament of our existential confrontation with the world'* (1971: 18 – italics added).

In an apparent rebuttal of the Sono thesis of absolute American influence, Biko responded:

> The growth of awareness among South African blacks has often been ascribed to influence from the American 'Negro' movement [Black Power Movement]. Yet it seems to me that this is a sequel to the attainment of independence by so many African states within so short a time. In fact, I remember that at the time I was at high school, Dr Hastings Kamuzu Banda [the first president of Malawi] was still a militant and used to be a hero of a friend of mine. His often quoted statement was, 'This is a black man's country; any white man who does not like it must pack up and go.' Clearly at this stage the myth of invincibility of the white man had been exposed. When fellow Africans were talking like that, how could we still be harbouring ideas of continued servitude? We knew he had no right to be there; we wanted to remove him from our table, strip the table of all trappings put on it by him, decorate it in true African style, settle down and then ask him to join us on our own terms if he liked. This is what Banda was saying. The fact that American terminology has often been used to express our thoughts is merely because all new ideas seem to get extensive publicity in the United States. (1996: 69)

And Fatton notes:

> What the American Black Power ideology provided was a theoretical source for the renewal of Black South African thinking. It accelerated the development of the Movement, helping to transform existential feelings into ethico-political conceptions of the world. The black South African intelligentsia discovered in Black Power ideology the basis for generating a new theoretical paradigm, but one which had to be adapted and reconciled with its own peculiar social condition. (1986: 75)

George Fredrickson supports this view when he states that at first glance, the Black Consciousness Movement of South Africa appears to have imitated the American Black Power Movement. However a close examination of the circumstances of its development and the contents of its ideology reveals that the local conditions and indigenous current thought in South Africa had much more influence on Black

Consciousness than the American influence. The reading of Black Power literature was, according to George Frederickson, 'clearly a stimulus, but the adoption of African-American concepts and slogans was selective rather than wholesale, and the ideas that were appropriated were often reinterpreted to fit South African conditions' (1997: 298). Having also emphasised the influence of the Black Power Movement in the USA on Black Consciousness in South Africa, Neville Alexander (a fierce critic of Black Consciousness) admits that he had overstated the point. According to him, in tracing the influences on Black Consciousness, one should emphasise much more the indigenous – especially the African – influences on the evolution of the ideology and politics of the movement. He acknowledges that he later 'discovered that some of the more famous ideas and passages in the writings of some of the BC publicists were drawn directly or indirectly from PAC, ANC, and NEUM sources. Only very few of the more fashionable ideas ("Black is Beautiful") can be traced back to their US origins' (in Pityana et al. 1991: 239).

Commentators such as Sono want us to believe that the influence was a one-way phenomenon (is, that Africans were influenced by black Americans, and that the opposite was not the case). The rise of independent African states encouraged African-Americans to reconstruct their history and restore their cultural ties with Africa, which were systematically destroyed by slavery. Not only did Du Bois and Garvey resuscitate African-Americans' interest in Africa, but the Black Power Movement itself was heavily influenced by African leaders such as Lumumba, Jomo Kenyatta and Kwame Nkrumah. These African leaders became idols and heroes to the young black militants of the 1960s. African art, history, poetry, music, food, dress and so on – the whole culture of Africa – had a tremendous impact on young African-Americans. Ordinary African-American men and women stopped attempting to be white and adopted African hairstyles, dress and so on.

It is surprising that Sono downplays the African connection and contribution to Black Consciousness. The notion of African Consciousness, for example, precedes the notion of Black Consciousness as articulated by black Americans. Despite the fact that Sono speaks only of the Black Consciousness Movement, influential individuals in the movement itself – who steered the course of the movement – were also profoundly influenced by what Robinson (1983) calls the black radical tradition, African liberation traditions and African political thinkers and activists. Biko was a great admirer of African intellectual and political elites such as Sobukwe, Banda, Oginga Odinga, Nkrumah, Kenneth Kaunda and of course Julius Nyerere. Asked whether his ideas were derived purely from the Black Power literature, Biko consented with a proviso which many commentators either dispute or ignore, namely: the African influence. In his words: 'The influence from Africa...was *very* important at that time...We were receptive to other influences, strange enough, influences much more from Africa, guys who could speak for themselves' (interview with Gerhart 1972: 11). Note that Biko does not talk of 'I' but of 'we' – an indication, *pace* Sono, that the Black Consciousness adherents had other major influences other than the Black Power radicals in the USA. Each volume of the *SASO Newsletter* had a regular 'Africa Series' (written by Charles Sibisi) which updated the readers about developments in other African countries; it also engaged and often criticised leaders such as Houphouët-Boigny of the Ivory Coast and articulated the philosophical views of progressive leaders such as Nyerere, Nkrumah, Kenyatta, Kaunda and others. Mosibudi Mangena confirms the 'we' when he states: 'There was a hunt for relevant reading material, especially works by the Nkrumahs, Fanons, du Boises and so forth' (1989: 11).

Since Biko grew up among PAC members, the influence of Sobukwe cannot be a far-fetched assumption. Sobukwe's challenge of the unquestioned domination of white liberals in shaping the struggle of black people within the liberation movements of Azania (an issue which dominated Biko's attitude towards liberal white people) is an example of his influence on Biko. Sobukwe's position against white liberals shifted and located the responsibility of struggling against oppression and racism squarely on the shoulders of black people themselves. Black people, Sobukwe insisted, could no longer stand as powerless victims and watch from the touchline a game they should be playing. He insisted that black people should be at the forefront of the liberation struggle, on their own terms, and that if 'we want to build a new Africa, only we can build it' – a statement that perfectly resonates with the Black Consciousness's mantra 'Black man, you are on your own'. The presence of PAC members and sympathisers in SASO had a tremendous impact on the direction of the organisation, and Biko followed. For example, Nchaupe Aubrey Mokoape, one of the leading members of SASO at the medical school and a close confidant of Biko, was also a PAC member. He was arrested for his political activities at the tender age of 17 years and was later imprisoned on Robben Island in the famous SASO Nine Trial. Mokoape was a dominant figure in the formation of the Black Consciousness Movement.

Another rarely acknowledged figure who influenced Biko and the Black Consciousness Movement was the Brazilian Paulo Freire. It was from his *Pedagogy of the Oppressed* (1985) that the ever-revolutionary notion of 'education for liberation' and the transformative concept of 'conscientisation' were derived. Freire came up with a revolutionary method of teaching and training that empowered both the teacher and the learner. This training method, appropriated by members of the Black Community Programme, 'influenced Biko considerably and dovetailed with his style of leadership' (Wilson, in Pityana et al. 1991: 35). In her recent book *Liberation and Development: Black Consciousness Community Programs in South*

Africa (2016), Leslie Hadfield articulates the influence of Freire's work on Black Consciousness activists in teaching literacy to the communities where they worked. For Freire, *conscientização* meant 'learning to perceive social, political, and economic contradictions, and to take action against the oppressive elements of reality' (1985: 19). Put differently, conscientisation refers to the awakening of critical consciousness. In Fanon's view, a new consciousness among the oppressed is forged through the process of conscientisation or what he calls 'educating the masses' (1968: 197).

Negritude

It was the Negritude Movement (initiated mainly by Césaire, Léon-Gontran Damas and Léopold Sédar Senghor) that later exercised an immense influence on the Black Consciousness Movement in South Africa. Ironically, it was Sono himself during his tenure as president of SASO who constantly appealed to Negritude. Later, Sono contradicts his claim that Black Consciousness was completely American, as the previous section's quotation of his words in SASO's newsletter showed – '...*we sharpened the concept into an armament*...' (1971: 18 – italics added). The very Sono who accuses Black Consciousness of having framed itself 'lock, stock and barrel' in terms of Black Power, then argues that in the capacity of 'transvaluation of values', Negritude is the *modus operandi* of SASO in its refined form. He writes: 'The black man is Negritude because he cannot hate himself, he cannot hate his being without ceasing to be. Being cannot be non-being. Black cannot be Non-White...So Negritude, i.e. Black identity, is never self-negation...It is...confirmation of one's being' (1971: 18).

As an indication of the importance of Negritude to the Black Consciousness Movement, regular debates and discussions on the topic took place. Biko and Gees Abrahams, both medical students at the time, shared a platform at a symposium on 'Positivity in Negritude' held at the University of Natal's (Black Section) medical school in 1971. SASO leaders occasionally organised cultural events appropriately entitled 'Into the Heart of Negritude'. These events included theatre performances and productions, and readings of and discussions on the poetry and works of Negritude authors such as Césaire, Senghor, David Diop and Cheikh Anta Diop as well as South Africans such as Oswald Mtshali, Sipho Sepamla, Mafika Gwala, Lefifi Tladi, Essop Patel and others. A jazz, poetry and drama session was a regular feature presented by a SASO-affiliated group called TECON. The group examined the concept of negritude and, through their music and poetry, affirmed the path of black assertion (*SASO Newsletter* 1971). Mamphela Ramphela, a leading member of SASO, confirms that Black Consciousness Movement activists read not only American Black literature: 'Fanon, Césaire, the Black Panthers, Martin Luther

King Jr and Malcolm X were the popular authors, orators and heroes of the time' (in Pityana et al. 1991: 218). When asked by Gail Gerhart about specific people who had an influence on him and the Black Consciousness Movement, Biko responded: 'Much more people like Fanon, people like Senghor, and a few other poets, Diop and company. They spoke to us' (interview with Gerhart 1972). In *I Write What I Like*, for example, Biko invokes the name of Césaire more than three times as an explanatory model for understanding Black Consciousness.

The circumstances under which the Negritude Movement came into being and the reasons for adopting a seemingly negative, pejorative and offensive term as an identity tag significantly parallel those of the Black Consciousness Movement – and these movements indeed were, to a large extent, fundamentally the same. In the early 1930s, black students in Paris from various parts of the 'black world' (especially the Caribbean islands and Africa) formed a cultural and political group around the concept of negritude. Negritude as an intellectual, ideological, philosophical and cultural upheaval was constituted as a response to the alienating situation of being-black-in-a-white-world.

For Césaire (one of the leading founders of the Movement and accredited with being the first to use the word 'negritude'), the Negritude Movement also embodied resistance to the French politics of assimilation – the attempt to turn a black person into a French person with a black skin. Speaking about their struggle against *racism*, alienation and dehumanisation when they were students in France, Césaire articulated a philosophy whose origins and content read as if it were a narrative about the origins of SASO and Black Consciousness in Azania three to four decades later:

> We adopted the word '*négre*' as a term of defiance. It was a defiant name. To some extent it was a reaction of enraged youth. Since there was shame about the word *négre,* we chose the word *négre*...There was in us a defiant will, and we found a violent affirmation in the words *négre* and *négritude*. (Césaire 1972: 74)

Damas, a Guyanese-born poet and one of the leading founders of Negritude, described the reasons behind the adoption and coinage of the term 'negritude' by a group of black students in Paris in the 1930s:

> The word 'negritude'...had a very precise meaning in the years 1934–35, namely the fact that the black man was seeking to know himself, that he wanted to become a historical actor and a cultural actor, and not just an object of domination or a consumer of culture...The word 'negritude' was

coined in the most racist moment of history, we accepted the word *négre* as a
challenge. (in Macey 2000: 181)

The re-appropriation of the term 'black' (negro) from its negative connotation to
a positive one is articulated in Césaire's famous epic poem 'Return to my Native
Land'. Fanon later acknowledged: 'For the first time a *lycée* teacher – a man
therefore, who was apparently worthy of respect – was seen to announce quite
simply to West Indian society "that it is fine to and good to be a Negro". To be sure,
this created a scandal. It was said at the time that he was a little mad...' (Fanon
1967a: 21)

In like manner, Black Consciousness originated as a student reaction to
apartheid racism. Just as the black students studying in Paris in the 1930s came
together to form the Negritude Movement as a result of their common experiences
of alienated consciousness, living in an antiblack white world without really
belonging, so the black students in South Africa came together to form SASO – the
cradle of the Black Consciousness Movement – because of their alienated existence
not only within the broader arena of their social and political experiences governed
by apartheid oppression but also as black students within the white-dominated
NUSAS. While the Negritude Movement re-appropriated the negative term 'negro'
and gave it a positive signification, in like manner the Black Consciousness
Movement in a conscious turnaround gesture transformed the negative term
'black' and attached a positive meaning to it. Through the very act of reclaiming the
identity and definition the white world had taught them to loathe, and affirming
it as an identity to celebrate and valorise, both the Negritude Movement and the
Black Consciousness Movement eradicated from their consciousness the 'double
consciousness' that Du Bois saw afflicting black existence.

In Paris, the black students' journal *L'Etudiant Noir* (The Black Student) was
launched as a medium to articulate their views on the African condition in Europe.
In fact, this journal served as a response to the French assimilationist policy
regarding its colonial subjects. This policy was aimed at transforming Africans
into black French people, if not into imitations of the French. The description
of the origins of Negritude as initially a student movement and its founding of
student journals such as *Légitime Défense* (Legitimate Defence) and *L'Etudiant
Noir* undeniably bear a striking resemblance to the origins and philosophical and
ideological orientation of the Black Consciousness Movement in South Africa as
SASO and its various journals such as the *SASO Newsletter* and *Black Viewpoint*.

Responding to René Depestre, Césaire articulated a philosophy of Negritude in
the 1930s which sounds like a narrative about the origins of Black Consciousness
in South Africa three decades later: '[If] someone asks me what my conception of
Negritude is, I answer that above all it is a concrete rather than an abstract coming

to consciousness...We lived in an atmosphere of rejection and we developed an inferiority complex' (1972: 76). In his famous and controversial essay 'Black Orpheus', written as a preface to Senghor's *Anthologie de la Nouvelle Poésie Nègre et Malgache de Langue Française* (a collection of poems by black people espousing a black outlook known as 'Negritude'), Sartre confirms the significance of 'blackness' as negro identity:

> The Negro cannot deny that he is Negro, nor can he claim that he is part of some abstract colorless humanity: he is black. Thus he has his back up against the wall of authenticity: having been insulted and formerly enslaved, he picks up the word 'nigger' which was thrown at him like a stone, he draws himself erect and proudly proclaims himself a black man, face to face with white men. (1988: 296)

Negritude, in other words, was a preoccupation with questions of identity and liberation through self-consciousness and self-definition. Similar sentiments and concerns were echoed by the editorial staff of the South African black student publication *SASO Newsletter*. Referring to the reasons for the adoption of the concept of blackness, they argued:

> The term [blacks] must be seen in the right context. No new category is being created but re-Christening is taking place. We are merely refusing to be regarded as non-persons and claim the right to be called positively... Adopting a collectively positive outlook leads to the creation of a broader base which may be useful in time. It helps us to recognise that we have a common enemy. (in Buthelezi 1987: 28)

In Césaire's understanding, Negritude was not only negatively an intellectual reaction to an alienated black consciousness, a struggle against white racism and its degrading effects, but was also above all positively an affirmation of the being of the black person. Negritude, in his definition, was 'a concrete rather than an abstract coming to consciousness' of black people who lived in an atmosphere of rejection and not only developed an inferiority complex but were also ashamed of their blackness. This coming into concrete consciousness in an antiblack world generated one of the most persistent questions among black people: Who or what am I? In other words, the question of identity becomes a pressing one in an antiblack social context. Césaire declares on the issue of identity:

> 'I have always thought that the black man was searching for his identity. And it has seemed to me that if what we want is to establish this identity, then we

must have a concrete consciousness of what we are – that is, of the fact of our lives; that we are black, that we were black and have a history' (1972: 76).

This description of the origins of Negritude contains four themes that are similar to those contained in Black Consciousness, namely: (i) the meaning of the word 'black', (ii) the question of identity, (iii) the effects of racism and reaction to it, and (iv) historicity. Combining the first and second themes involved the adoption of the word 'black' as a form of personal identity; affirming one's black consciousness. To do this required taking into account the history of black people which throughout modernity was characterised by an encounter with white racism. This encounter with racism in turn obviously demanded a kind of response to its effects on those who suffer because of it (that is, black people). Again, just like the Negritude Movement, the Black Consciousness Movement consisted of two currents: (i) the political Césairean current which was racially inclusive (African, Indian and coloured people) and (ii) the cultural current which took on a Senghorian position of exalting the African culture through poetry and art. The latter current turned against the cultural self-alienation of African people and instilled in them an awareness of their own historical and cultural tradition, which in turn embraced a consciousness of all the deformation and dehumanisation suffered at the hands of apartheid racism.[5]

While Senghor's Negritude was much more oriented towards cultural consciousness and a metaphysical element that concentrated on the ontology of the being of the African, Césaire's Negritude was much more existentialist and thus focused on the consciousness of black people in the context of colonial and racist situations. For him, Negritude was more of a mode of being-black-in-the-world, a consciousness of colour, race and history. In other words, Césaire posed the question of black existence through the lens of Negritude. Even though Fanon's ideas exerted a tremendous influence on the direction and philosophical underpinning of Biko and the Black Consciousness Movement, they gave philosophical substance and content to what Césaire and the Negritudists had already imparted. Indeed the major lessons Biko and the Black Consciousness Movement acquired from Césaire and Negritude was that a Negritudist had to perform certain functions: first, he had to educate his fellow black people (conscientise); second, he had to serve as the spokesperson of black people, be their voice and never allow white liberals and white leftists to speak on their behalf; finally, he had to free black people psychologically, culturally and politically. Césaire's significance to the thinking of Biko and the Black Consciousness Movement, therefore, was not only the appropriation of a negative term and its transformation into a positive signification, but also the role he played as a teacher and inspiration to Fanon and Biko.

Fanon

I pointed out that most Black Consciousness exponents acknowledged their immense intellectual debt to Fanon, the Martinican revolutionary psychiatrist and philosopher who authored two of the most widely read books by black people all over the world: *Black Skin, White Masks* and *The Wretched of the Earth*. Fanon's insertion into Azania came through these famous texts, which became the bibles and the guiding lights of the student movement of the late-1960s and 1970s. In both these texts, and indeed even in *Toward the African Revolution*, Fanon repeatedly makes direct and indirect reference to South Africa (Azania). In Fanon's eyes, as Sekyi-Otu attests, South Africa (Azania) was 'an emblematic instance... of the colonial condition' (1996: 2) and, in Fanon's own words, an embodiment of the colonial system's 'geographical layout' (Fanon 1968: 37) with its system of compartments and the 'dividing line' (1968: 38) that constructs human existence into racial collectives within a 'motionless Manicheistic world' (1968: 51).

While it is evident in his work that Fanon's fundamental concerns were with the colonial condition in general and Algeria in particular, he was as much concerned about apartheid – which, for him, was the quintessence of the colonial order. He states: 'If we have taken the example of Algeria to illustrate our subject, it is not at all with the intention of glorifying our own people...but simply...that other peoples have come to the same conclusion in different ways' (1968: 193). Let me substantiate this claim with a few germane citations from Fanon's work announcing him as the first to name South Africa's apartheid an archetype of the division of human experience. In *Black Skin, White Masks*, he states: 'What is South Africa? A boiler into which thirteen million blacks are clubbed and penned in by two million whites. If the poor whites hate the Negroes...it is because the structure of South Africa is a racist structure' (1967a: 87). Mounting a critique of Tempels' *Bantu Philosophy* (1959), Fanon cites a long passage from IR Skine's *Apartheid en Afrique du Sud* which describes the oppressive condition of black people in apartheid South Africa. In anger, Fanon asks: 'What use are reflections on Bantu ontology when...Bantu existence subsists on the level of nonbeing, of the imponderable?' (1967a: 184–185). For Fanon, there was nothing ontological about apartheid.

If *Black Skin, White Masks* is, as Fanon declares, a wish to liberate the black person from the 'zone of non-being' that is imposed upon him by a antiblack racist society, and if as he proposes 'nothing short of the liberation of the man of color from himself' because '[t]here is a fact: white men consider themselves superior to black men' such that '[f]or the black man there is only one destiny. And it is white', then this book is undoubtedly about the invidious racism of apartheid South Africa and its dehumanising effects on the existential reality of black people living there.

This explains why there are more than nine references to South Africa in the chapter 'The So-Called Dependency Complex of Colonized Peoples'.

Later in *The Wretched of the Earth* when Fanon speaks of the colonial world as 'a world divided into compartments', a world in which there exists 'native quarters and European quarters, of schools for natives and schools for Europeans' (1968: 37), there is no necessity to recall apartheid in South Africa. Describing South Africa's apartheid as archetypical of the division of human experience, he states:

> The colonial world is a world divided into compartments. It is probably unnecessary to recall the existence of native quarters and European quarters, of schools for natives and schools for Europeans; in the same way, we need not recall apartheid in South Africa...
>
> This world divided into compartments, this world cut in two is inhabited by two different species. The originality of the colonial context is that economic reality, inequality and *the immense difference of ways of life* never come to mask the human realities. (Fanon 1968: 39–40 – italics added)

Fanon explains that this apartheid colonial world:

> ...is a narrow world strewn with prohibitions...a world cut into two...The zone where the natives live is not complementary to the zone inhabited by the settlers. The two zones are opposed, but not in the service of a higher unity. Obedient to the rules of pure Aristotelian logic, they both follow the principle of reciprocal exclusivity. (1968: 38–39)

In short, the apartheid world is a Manichean world, 'a motionless Manicheaistic world' of the good white person and the evil black person, in which 'the native is hemmed in' (1968: 51, 52). Apartheid then, for Fanon, is to be understood as 'simply one form of the division into compartments of the colonial world' (1968: 52), a paradigmatic case of the logic of colonial antagonism, an existential prohibition fixed in space, coercive segregation and a relation of social closure.

Finally, in *Toward the African Revolution*, Fanon describes South Africa in crisp words as 'that very deep South Africa before which the rest of the world veils its face' (1967b: 192). In other words, it is a world Fanon likens to the American Deep South of black slavery which together with Algeria 'are the citadels of colonialism and probably the territories in which the European settlers are defending themselves with the greatest frenzy and ferocity' (1967b: 156). Just as the countries against which Nazism manifested itself had to show solidarity to break the backbone of Nazism, so African peoples had to do because they 'had to remember that they have had to face a form of Nazism, a form of exploitation of man, of physical and spiritual liquidation clearly imposed, that the French, English, and South African manifestation of that evil need to engage their attention' (1967a: 171). For Fanon, then, the enforcers of apartheid as a form of Nazism committed acts of genocide, and African peoples did not have to be neutral to the genocide carried out in South Africa.

In this 'deep' South Africa, race and class converged so that '[w]hat parcels out the world is to begin with the fact of belonging to or not belonging to a given race, a given species...the economic substructure is also a superstructure. The cause is the consequence; you are rich because you are white, you are white because you are rich (Fanon 1968: 37, 39–40 – italics added).

Indeed, what really parcelled out the apartheid universe was 'to begin with the fact of belonging to or not belonging to a given race'. Race, though some Marxists such as Robert Young will object, was the determining factor in what one got, how one lived and how long one would live.[6] In the above citation, Fanon – contrary to Marxist interpretations – moves beyond the deterministic model of base and superstructure as cause and effect, and dialectically juxtaposes them so that the base can be viewed as the superstructure and the superstructure as the base. Hence he insists that in the colonial situation, white people exist as the 'rich classes' and the 'rich class' exists as white people. Fanon then counsels that when it comes to the colonial situation, Marxism must be 'slightly stretched'.

In a reassuring tone, Fanon asserts that the colonised people of South Africa should know that they are not alone: 'In spite of all that colonialism can do, its frontiers remain open to new ideas and echoes from the world outside' (1968: 70). Indeed, these 'new ideas and echoes from the outside world' did reach the young black radical students of the late-1960s, despite the presumably closed frontiers of the apartheid Manichean world expressed through the Censorship and Publications Board's restrictive laws (the Publications and Entertainments Act) prohibiting influential literature of Fanon, Marx and a host of other revolutionaries from being distributed and landing in the hands not only of anti-apartheid activists but also of the South African people in general.

Those readers minimally acquainted with South African apartheid realities and confronted with the above extracts from Fanon's work will undeniably understand why these texts had such irresistible attraction and influence on the radical young black students of the 1960s and 1970s. His work spoke directly to the existential situation of black people by articulating their misery, despair, anxiety, anguish and desires under apartheid while at the same time keeping the light of hope alive. As Lou Turner and John Alan say in their book *Frantz Fanon, Soweto and American Black Thought*, the title of which clearly indicates the unbreakable bond between Fanon and the Azanian struggle:

It is not accidental that Fanon's thoughts are relevant to the liberation struggles in South Africa, as manifested in the Black Consciousness Movement...Fanon's philosophy of revolution has assumed the quality of actuality in the brutal life-and-death struggle between the Black masses of South Africa and the arrogant white ruling class that would, if they could, reduce Black humanity to a thing – an object among objects. (1986: 38)

It is no accident therefore that Fanon became, ironically in the manner of Tempels, the 'Vital Force', the catalyst behind the thinking of South African black existentialists (especially that of Biko and Manganyi). For it is through this Fanonian philosophy and its emphasis on black identity and liberation that the Black Consciousness philosophy became embedded in the collective consciousness of the black masses that ultimately brought the apartheid regime to its knees. The attraction of Fanon is that he wrote as a black man at the pre-reflective level about antiblack racism. As a result, there exists concrete knowledge of the black situation and an accompanying depth of passion in Fanon, which could not have escaped the probing eyes and attentive ears of Biko, Manganyi, Mafika Gwala, Pityana, Mokoape and the other activists of the Black Consciousness Movement of Azania. This influence is expressed by Pityana, one of the original architects of the Black Consciousness Movement and a very close comrade of Biko, who approvingly cites Fanon at length:

'I am not a potentiality of something' writes Fanon. 'I am wholly what I am. I do not have to look for the universal. No probability has any place inside me. My Negro consciousness does not hold itself out as a lack. It IS. It is its own follower.' This is all that we blacks are after, TO BE...This, therefore, necessitates a self-examination and rediscovery of ourselves. Blacks can no longer afford to be led by and dominated by non-Blacks. (Pityana 1972: 180)

Hence, as Turner and Alan observe, it was no accident that Fanon's philosophy proved to be relevant to the liberation struggle of the Black Consciousness Movement, for '[i]t was Fanon who had...deepened the Hegelian concept of self-consciousness and in his sharp *critique* of "reciprocity", denied that there is any reciprocity when the relationship of Master and Slave has the additive of color' (Turner & Alan 1986: 38 – italics in original). I consider Fanon's specific influence on Biko in subsequent chapters.

Those who have not been victims of colonialism or racism, or who have not personally experienced apartheid or colonial conditions as victims, will most likely miss the import of Fanon's reference to apartheid as colonialism. Having had no direct experience with the colonial or apartheid situation, 'that narrow world full of prohibitions', they would most likely miss the symbiotic connection between Fanon's phenomenological description of colonialism and its intimation to apartheid. To those participants like us who have lived to witness the brutality of apartheid and experienced it as victims, Fanon's text, in the words of Sartre, 'mediates, names, and shows' us the life we led under apartheid conditions 'from day to day in its immediacy', the life we 'suffered without finding words to formulate [our] suffering' (1988: 79). In his writings, Fanon related to black South Africans' subjectivities, in other words the same experiences of racism and colonialism, the same difficulties, the same complexes, such that a mere hint from him was enough to produce some form of understanding that enabled us to relate to his sufferings. A reading of the writings of Biko, Manganyi, Mphahlele, Bloke Modisane, Sepamla and a host of other black South African authors will show how Fanon actually articulated the conditions and experiences of black life under apartheid. Indeed, some of them even applied Fanon's ideas to understand the existential conditions of South Africa. Thus, in trying to become clear about his own personal situation, Fanon made our situation clear to ourselves. To put it in Sartre's appropriate words again, the black world 'finds *itself* and speaks to *itself* through his voice' (1968: 10). Put simply, Fanon was the conscience of black South Africans. What is more, in the preface to *The Wretched of the Earth*, Sartre warns European readers that Fanon did not write the book for them. The book, Sartre cautions, 'speaks of you often, never to you... it speaks to the colonized only'. If Fanon exposes the crimes of colonialism, Sartre argues that exposition is for his colonised brothers: 'his aim is to teach them to beat us [Europeans] at our own game' (1968: 10).

It is therefore all these individuals, movements, ideologies and philosophies put together – not the Black Power Movement alone – that had tremendous influence and shaped the direction and philosophical foundations of the Black Consciousness Movement in South Africa.

Black Consciousness: Philosophical orientation

The back page of the SASO newsletters describes one of the aims of the student movement in this manner: 'To examine relevant philosophical approaches to South African problems.' The most 'relevant philosophical approach' examined and appropriated by the movement, in my view, is existential phenomenology. Since, at the fundamental level, Black Consciousness is primordially and for the most part a philosophy of consciousness, it falls within the existential-phenomenological approach to the problem of black existence in an antiblack world. As such, it clearly considerably predates the emergence of the label 'Black Consciousness'. A philosophy may exist regardless of whether or not it is labelled or named.

What is certain, however, is that it was inspired by the emergence of three most problematic phenomena that have plagued black people's existence historically and globally, namely: slavery, colonialism and racism. The experiences of systems that put black humanity into question forced black people (especially African people and people of African descent in the diaspora) to start giving serious thought to the reality of their identity. They consequently began to ask questions such as 'Who am I?' and 'What am I?' Since slavery, colonialism and racism are fundamentally forms of oppression, their emergence invariably generated certain responses aimed at liberating victims of these cruel and oppressive systems from their vicious hold. This means that Black Consciousness became a philosophy of identity and liberation. Furthermore, in an attempt to respond to the existential question 'Who am I?' or the ontological question 'What am I?', Black Consciousness assumed the mantle of Africana philosophy in general and black existential philosophy in particular – which concern the examination of the emergence of that question when posed by those whose humanity is being questioned.

This questioning of the humanity of black people generated a central question in philosophical anthropology, namely: What does it mean to be a human being? It is this area of research with which Africana philosophy is concerned. 'The consequences of lost personhood, of denied humanness, are severe in that they lead to groups or kinds of people being treated as property (slavery), as waste to be eliminated (genocides, holocausts), as subhuman or animals (racism)' (Gordon 2008: 13). Since Black Consciousness takes modern concerns such as race, racism and colonialism seriously, it explores – in like manner as Africana philosophy – problems which Lewis Gordon identifies as: consciousness, the self, the body, identity, intersubjectivity, the social world, social transformation, communicability, ethics, politics, bondage and most importantly freedom.[7] Within this context, therefore, black consciousness is indeed a philosophy, a form of Africana existential philosophy which has as its starting point human consciousness.

The marriage of the two terms 'black' and 'consciousness', as Manganyi and many others have pointed out, just as the marriage between 'black' and 'power', generated not only reactions of hostility and fear but also confusion about their philosophical or political meanings.[8] It is appropriate, therefore, to begin this section with a philosophical analysis and understanding of the concepts of black and consciousness, and locate them within the context of the philosophy of Black Consciousness.

Blackness

Before a philosophical discussion of Black Consciousness can be comprehensible, certain preliminary observations about the term 'black' and the negative connotations attached to it are necessary. From traditional colour theory, white and black are colours just like all the other colours such as red, yellow or green. However, colours have both an indicatory (denotative) and a suggestive (connotative) meaning. At the indicatory level, colour is neutral; white is simply white and red is red – that is, colour is a physical and optic phenomenon. At the suggestive level, colours are the centre and focus of passionate sentiments and values – and thus often elicit particular types of feelings and emotions, depending on the colour at hand. This means that colour can be either a sign or a symbol. As a sign, we have for example the colours green and red as traffic signs. Red indicates 'stop' and green indicates 'go'. However, as a symbol, the colour black is viewed in the West and some other parts of the world as connoting negativity, and the colour white is viewed as connoting positivity. As a result, the two colours came to be conceptualised as oppositions. But this imposed opposition, to the exclusion of other colours, is not a visual one; it is strictly psychical, symbolic and even moral. This imposition originates from the Bible and has persisted throughout the Enlightenment and ultimately to modernity, and throughout the associated systems of slavery, colonialism and modern racism.[9] In an interesting article entitled 'An Illuminating Blackness', Mills (the African-American and Caribbean philosopher) shows the conventional distinction between the words 'black' and 'white' in his conception of 'Black Philosophy' and says: 'Moreover – in terms of actual electromagnetic radiation – any physicist will be happy to inform us that white light already includes all the colors of the visible spectrum, while blackness turns out to be not really a color at all, but the absence of all light and color' (2013: 32).

Language symbolism is an important source of prejudice against those who are black. The Enlightenment lexicography's depiction of 'black' as darkness, ugly and devilish and of 'white' as light, innocence and good is a perfect example of the opposition imposed on the two colours. This was passed on to the twentieth century, as expressed in *Webster's New Twentieth Century Dictionary* (1952) in which the word 'black' is defined as:

> (1) figuratively, dismal, gloomy, sullen, forbidding, or the like; destitute of moral light or goodness; mournful; evil; wicked…thus Shakespeare speaks of black deeds, thoughts, envy, tidings, despair, etc. (2) soiled; dirty. (3) disgraceful. (4) without hope, as a black future. (5) inveterate, confirmed, deep-dyed, as a black villain. (6) humorous or satirical in a morbid, cynical or savage way, as black comedy.

The same dictionary gives the word 'white' the exact opposite meaning to 'black':

(1) having the color of pure snow and milk...opposite of black. (2) morally and spiritually pure; spotless; innocent. (3) free from evil intent; harmless; as white magic; white lie. (4) happy; fortunate; auspicious. (5) (a) having light colored skin; Caucasian; (b) of or controlled by white race; as *white* supremacy; (c) honest; honorable; fair; dependable etc.

A look at other dictionaries such as the *Shorter Oxford English Dictionary* reveals the same negative meaning of the word 'black'. Even the first American edition of the *Encyclopaedia Britannica* (1798) describes the negro (black/African) as being idle, dishonest, cruel, treacherous, nasty, a liar, impudent, revengeful, a thief and so on.

Another instance is the practice of depicting black in negative terms in regard to the natural world. According to this conception, consider all things in nature that are good, pleasant, beautiful and desirable. These are always symbolically associated with whiteness, light or brightness. Conversely, whatever is evil, repulsive, ugly and undesirable is always already symbolically associated with blackness and darkness. In nature, there are permanent pairs of binary oppositions: day and night, growth and decay, life and death, cleansing and dirtying, and so on. Vegetation flourishes in the sunlight; in the absence of sunlight, and consequently in the presence of darkness, vegetation dies. In blackness or darkness, there cannot be life. Blackness is fundamentally opposed to life, while whiteness or light promotes life. Similarly, night and its accompanying darkness bring about all that is dreaded, hence the popular expression 'fear of the dark'. Cleanliness brings about health and life, while dirt is the repository of sickness and death. Each pair of the binaries from nature, therefore, has the dual characteristic of being good or evil. That which is evil is associated with blackness and that which is good with whiteness. A Manichean world emerges from which the cosmos is conceived in terms of a struggle between Good and Evil.

From this conception emerges the association of human bodily being and the colour of the skin with the value attached to whiteness and blackness, the two connected terms that cover the great cosmic division of day and night. Since blackness connotes evil, ignorance, sin, death and so on, those who have a 'black' or dark skin colour are alleged to participate in the reality symbolised by the colour. Conversely, since white symbolises goodness, salvation, knowledge, beauty and other positive aesthetic and moral attributes, those who are regarded as 'white' participate in these positive values. The human body thus becomes a raced body. However, it should be noted that there are neither 'white' people in the sense of the whiteness of snow or the colour of white paper, nor 'black' people in the sense of the black colour of objects such as a black car or even a black cat. The 'whiteness' and 'blackness' of people are constructed or imagined whiteness and blackness.

At most, phenomenologically speaking, there are light and dark human beings and not 'white' and 'black' ones. People with 'white' skin colour became evaluated or evaluated themselves positively in line with the positive or good characteristics associated with whiteness, light, brightness in nature; whereas 'black'-skinned people became negatively evaluated and associated with all the bad or evil things of darkness. Consequently, for a racist consciousness, that which is good is white and that which is bad is black.

In a short play on 'black' and 'white' words, Robert Moore demonstrates the bigoted nature of the English language:

> Some may *blackly* (angrily) accuse me of trying to *blacken* (defame) the English language, to give it a *black eye* (a mark of shame) by writing such *black* words (hostile). They may denigrate (to cast aspersions, *to darken*) me by accusing me of being *blackhearted* (malevolent), of having a *black outlook* (pessimistic, dismal) on life, of being a *blackguard* (scoundrel) – which would certainly be a *black mark* (detrimental fact) against me. Some may *black-brow* (scowl at) me and hope that a *black* cat [ill luck] crosses in front of me because of this *black deed* [evil act]. I may become a *black* sheep (one who causes shame or embarrassment because of deviation from the accepted standards), who will be *black-balled* (ostracized) by being placed on a *blacklist* (list of undesirables) in an attempt to *blackmail* (to force or coerce into a particular action) me to retract my words. But attempts to *blackjack* (to compel by threat) me will have a Chinaman's chance of success, for I am not a yellow-bellied Indian-giver of words, who will *white wash* (cover up or gloss over vices or crimes) a *black lie* (harmful, inexcusable). I challenge the *purity of and innocence* (white) of the English language. I don't see things in *black and white* (entirely bad or entirely good) terms, for I am a *white man* (marked by upright firmness) if there ever was one. However, it would be a *black* [sad] day when I would not 'call a spade a spade', even though some will suggest a white man calling the English language racist is like the pot calling the kettle black. While many may be *niggardly* (grudging, scanty) in their support, others will be honest and decent – and to them I say, that's very *white* of you (honest, decent). (in Andersen & Collins 1992: 318 – italics added)

This regrettably long citation is of course not a true statement but was merely intended by its author to illustrate some examples of negative connotations and positive connotations attached to the words 'black' and 'white'. What this suggests is that language is not only a medium of communication but also reflects a society's attitudes, values and practices. It does not only express ideas and concepts but actually shapes thought. Involved in the white/black oppositional logic are positive/

negative, superior/inferior, beautiful/ugly, right/wrong, pure/impure, moral/immoral and so on valuations. In fact, it goes beyond mere symbolism; it assumes a Manichean conception of the world in terms of which goodness and evil are at war. This attitude, Sartre argues, is inscribed in the very languages of Europe, in which 'white' and 'black' are connected in a hierarchical system so that when a teacher gives the negro the term 'black', he also conveys a hundred language habits which consecrate the white person's rights over those of the black person.

> The Negro will learn to say 'white like snow' to indicate innocence, to speak of the blackness of a look, of a soul, of a deed. As soon as he opens his mouth, he accuses himself...can you imagine the strange savor that an expression like 'the blackness of innocence' or 'the darkness of virtue' would have for us? (Sartre 1988: 304)

Not only do we have these dictionary meanings of 'black' and 'white' and the accompanying various connotative meanings of the words 'black' and 'white', Western philosophy also provided the words with sophisticated epistemological, aesthetic and moral justification. Western philosophers such as David Hume, Immanuel Kant, Hegel, Montesquieu (Charles-Louis de Secondat), Voltaire (François-Marie Arouet), John Locke and even Marx articulated antiblackness views that had an immense impact on modern antiblack thinking.[10] Even the Bible, in which most black people believe, is heavily laden with negative images, symbolism and narratives of blackness. It identifies blackness with evil, disaster, famine, plagues, doom and ugliness. In the biblical narrative of Ham, as the epitome of antiblackness, blackness is the colour of those who have been condemned to perpetual servitude of being 'the hewers of wood and drawers of water'.

In an antiblack racist world, to be black is to be not only sin and devil but also criminal. The black historian Benjamin Quarles once remarked: 'When we pick up a social science book we look in the index under "Negro"; it will read, "see Slavery", "see Crime", "see Juvenile Delinquency"...perhaps see anything except Negro. So when we try to get a perspective on the Negro, we get a distorted perspective' (in Thomas & Sullen 1972: 45). What this observation points to is that the command to see slavery, crime or juvenile delinquency for what negro (black person) means suggests that the term 'negro' (black) is synonymous with crime, slavery or delinquency. Therefore, to say that I am black (negro), means I have committed a crime. I am black; I know what the problem is with my black body. It exists. I exist, therefore I *am* crime. This means that as a black person, I am sentenced even before I have committed a crime because I am crime personified. In Sartre's play '*The Respectful Prostitute*', a white racist declares: 'A nigger has *always* done something...Niggers are the Devil.' Commenting on the lynch mob's pursuit of

The Negro in that play, Fanon says, "Sin is Negro (black) as virtue is white. All those white men in a group, guns in their hands, cannot be wrong. I am guilty. I do not know of what, but I know that I am no good' (1967a: 139). In such a racial hierarchical society, a black accused need only be 'seen' to be considered guilty of an offense he did not commit. His colour is the evidence. He is guilty of blackness.

Consciousness (self-consciousness)

In his *Phenomenology of Spirit*, Hegel pays serious attention to the concept 'consciousness' in the first three chapters and 'self-consciousness' in the fourth. It is these chapters that drew the attention of Biko and his comrades. Pityana recalls how he and his Black Consciousness comrades benefitted from Hegel's idea of consciousness: 'Looking back in time, it interests me that Hegel had become a very influential philosopher and sparring partner for those of us who were seeking answers, and out of which even more questions were raised. The very idea of *consciousness* is very Hegelian' (2012: 5 – italics in original). Aided by Fanon's chapter 'The Negro and Recognition', especially the section The Negro and Hegel, they began to understand the philosophical significance of the *state of being* black. They began to understand that self-consciousness is only possible if there is another self-consciousness to give it recognition. The identity of self-consciousness is possible only through a necessary encounter and interaction with another self-consciousness. This, therefore, meant that Hegel's master/slave dialectic reflected their lived experience of the *baas/kaffir* (master/slave) condition.

Black Consciousness is a form of *consciousness*. This fact situates Black Consciousness within the ambit of phenomenology precisely because (to recall the account in the previous chapter), phenomenology is the study of phenomena as they appear to consciousness – that is, reality as constituted by consciousness in the sense in which consciousness is understood as always consciousness *of* something. Consciousness understood as always consciousness *of* something is referred to in phenomenological terms as 'intentional'. In addition to this intentional feature of consciousness is the phenomenological rejection of theories positing a disembodied consciousness. If phenomenology deals primarily with consciousness as a universal neutral phenomenon, Black Consciousness shifts this universal imaginary of a neutral embodied consciousness to a particularised consciousness of racialised bodies. Black Consciousness becomes particularised self-consciousness produced by and forced upon black people by the constant invocation of the supremacy of white consciousness. Hence, a person with a body designated as black or white in a racist world has a black consciousness or a white consciousness.

What distinguishes human beings from things and objects is their possession of self-consciousness. In fact, human beings do not possess consciousness in the sense of possessing a quality; they *are* consciousness. However, unlike other conscious creatures, human consciousness, while in its intentionality it is consciousness of something other than itself, must at the same time be aware of itself as being conscious of an object in order to be able to relate to itself in its immediate future. Put differently, while a consciousness directly focuses its attention on an object (that is, conscious of the objects), it is simultaneously aware of itself as being aware of that object. For if a consciousness were to be unaware of itself as being aware of an object, it would be a consciousness unconscious of itself as such (that is, the absurd situation of an unconscious consciousness). At another level, such a consciousness would be an animal consciousness, which is a sentiment of self rather than self-consciousness. So every act of consciousness of something is simultaneously an act of self-consciousness. It is this self-consciousness that constitutes human reality as different from other creatures. Indeed, Hegel also uses the term 'self-consciousness' to refer to the human being; a being different from other conscious beings in that it is aware of its individuality, dignity and value.

What then is this self that is conscious of itself? The fundamental structure of human existence is the primordial consciousness of being-in-the-world. The self is that consciousness which is conscious of itself as conscious of the world. Self and world are correlated aspects of existence. Without the self, there is no world; and without the world, there can never be a self. As being-in-the-world, the self experiences the world as an environment that reveals itself through utensils or tools and nature. However, this is not the only mode whereby I existentially experience the world. The world also appears to the self as a world of others (that is, the world is a social world shared by various other selves). Added to these is the third dimension of a self in the world as related to itself.

A self is that being that is conscious of itself as itself in relation to the three dimensions of its existence: world, others and self. In the words of Kierkegaard, the nineteenth-century Danish existentialist philosopher, 'the self is a relation that relates itself to its own self'. To be a self, is to be able to look at ones's self, to love one's self, become alienated from one's self, critical of one's self, anxious about one's self. For Sartre selfhood is constituted by what he calls the 'reflective consciousness', a consciousness that is able to reflect about itself as consciousness of something (that is, mediated consciousness). To say that I am conscious, given the fact that consciousness is always consciousness of something, makes sense insofar as I can say or identify what I am conscious of. At the basic ontological level of pre-reflective or non-positional consciousness, consciousness is merely consciousness of

Being (that is, there is neither black nor white consciousness, there simply exists a consciousness). How then does black or white consciousness come into being?

Black Consciousness

While at the level of pre-reflective (immediate) consciousness there is simply a consciousness of Being in general, black consciousness and white consciousness as particular consciousnesses occur at the level of reflective consciousness – a consciousness that is able to reflect upon itself or position itself in relation to the situation at hand. Black consciousness, then, is a consciousness that is aware of something, namely its blackness. People who are regarded by others and/or regard themselves as black often speak of having a black self-consciousness (that is, a black self which serves to identify or distinguish them from others who consider themselves non-black). We are now already in the realm of the combined product of the two concepts of 'black' and 'consciousness', namely Black Consciousness.

The proponents of Black Consciousness described their consciousness-in-the-world as a 'black' consciousness. Since consciousness is always consciousness of something, since self-consciousness is consciousness of the self as itself, since the self of consciousness is not a disembodied Cartesian 'I' but a consciousness in the flesh or an embodied and incarnated consciousness, and since the body is always a particular body (contingently black or white or yellow or red), in a colour-conscious society (especially in a white hegemonic antiblack world), people of a colour regarded as 'black' are likely to face Fanon's question: 'What and who in reality am I?' The answer to this question is fundamentally a statement about humanity and self-identity. Black Consciousness is a consciousness of one's self as a black human being. The consciousness of a black person is an awareness of one's personhood as significantly different from the bodily appearances of other persons not designated black. The basic traits, therefore, which constitute the foundation for a black consciousness are those that racially identify a person as being black. In a racially white supremacist world, the consciousness of a person designated black invariably becomes a consciousness of a being whose humanity is perpetually an issue – or stated differently, a black person in such a world is a being such that because of its very blackness, its being is always in question.

The symbolism which debases and demeans blackness and elevates whiteness inevitably affects the consciousness of every black person and every white person, and the consequences are a generated black self-hatred and an exaggerated white narcissism (observed and pointed out by Manganyi). In their experience of slavery, colonialism and racism, black people in Africa, South and North America, the Caribbean islands and Europe constantly confronted a hostile antiblack existential reality. This reality defined them not only as evil; ugly; savages; criminals;

irrational and non-rational; children; beasts of burden; animals; subpersons lacking in intelligence, morality and civilisation – in short, subhuman beings, those inhabiting the zone of non-being – but also and because of this conception, deserving of brutal non-human treatment, domination and exclusion from the realm of the human. Hegel exemplified this attitude in declaring:

> The Negro...exhibits the natural man in his completely wild and untamed state. We must lay aside all thought of reverence and morality, all that we call feeling, if we would rightly comprehend him; there is nothing harmonious with humanity to be found in this type of character...Among the Negroes moral sentiments are quite weak, or more strictly speaking, non-existent...Slavery is itself a phase of advance from the merely isolated sensual existence, a phase of education, a mode of becoming participant in a higher morality and the culture connected with it. (1952a: 196–197, 198)

This existential reality of antiblackness – through its political, economic, religious, legal, cultural and social institutions – succeeded in suppressing the consciousness of black people as human beings and thereby produced in them a consciousness of themselves correlative to the demands of each of these oppressive realities, the historical reality associated with being-black-in-an-antiblack-world, namely: slavery, colonialism and racism. In other words, slave consciousness, colonial consciousness and racist consciousness became the correlative products of black self-image, consciousness and reality.

First, how does a slave consciousness emerge? As Hegel reminds us, it is because of the fear to risk or stake one's life, the absolute fear of death that brings about servitude. Because of the fear of death, a slave consciousness remains immersed in life as something too dear to lose. A slave consciousness, therefore, is a consciousness that is shaped by the conditions of slavery. Just as the Nazi concentration camps produced the personalities, perceptions and attitudes of the Jewish prisoners who survived, so did slavery alter the personalities, perceptions and attitudes of the black slaves in America and on the Caribbean islands. In these slavish conditions, the slave developed a slave consciousness. By slave consciousness, I mean the black slaves' interiorisation of the white master's attitudes towards the slaves, an attitude founded on the slave owner's belief in the assumed subhumanity, docility, irresponsibility, criminality, immorality, unrestrained sexuality and irrationality of black people. To the racist white slave owner, black people are a lower form of organism, biologically more primitive; mentally, socially, morally, culturally and religiously inferior; emotionally underdeveloped; insensitive to pain; incapable of learning and animal-like in behaviour. In short, black people belong to a different order of humanity than the white slave owner, if indeed they are human at all. For this reason, the black slave has no justification to exist, except to serve and admire the white master.

A black person who internalises these myths and stereotypes about black people and acts in accordance with their demands has a slave consciousness or, in popular terms, is an 'Uncle Tom' or what Malcolm X referred to as the 'House Nigger'. Of course, not all slaves were House Niggers or Uncle Toms. Malcolm X also correctly identified what he called the 'Field Nigger'. In other words, not all slaves have a slave consciousness. Some slaves, for example Frederick Douglass, rejected slavery while being slaves themselves and thus were not possessed of a slave consciousness.

The colonial consciousness (mentality) is a consciousness that constitutes the coloniser as the splendid model to be imitated in every aspect of existence. It is a consciousness that desires and strives to resemble the white coloniser to the point, as Albert Memmi (1965) notes, of disappearing in him. In its admiration of the coloniser, the colonial consciousness of the black colonised becomes an implicit approval of colonisation. This attitude, besides making the colonised perfect candidates for assimilation into the white colonial world and value system, is also a perfect expression of self-hatred and love of the oppressor. Put differently, a colonial consciousness is a self that wants to tear itself away from its self. Since for the colonisers, the natives' religion is pagan, heathen, savage and primitive, and their culture, morals and values uncivilised, the colonial consciousness of the colonised abandons its religion, morals, culture and values – its civilisation – in favour of the coloniser's, even to the point of outstripping the coloniser himself. The colonial consciousness, as Fanon aptly describes it, is a typical expression of 'Black Skin, White Masks'.

Since the most salient features of colonialism and its predecessor slavery were racism and white supremacy, a racist consciousness persists into the post-slavery and post-colonial situations. Both slavery and colonialism, insofar as they applied to white people vis-à-vis black people, were predicated on the assumption of white superiority and black inferiority. The slave mentality and the colonial mentality continued into the post-slavery and post-colonial situations in the form of white supremacy, apartheid, and institutional and individual racisms. Alexis de Tocqueville acknowledged this fact: 'There is a natural prejudice that prompts men to despise whoever has been their inferior long after he has become their equal...Although the law may abolish slavery, God only can obliterate the traces of its existence' (in Silberman 1964: 78). In an antiblack world, therefore, the black person who immerses himself in the idealisation of everything white and thereby despises his own kind is an example of a slave, colonial or black antiblack racist consciousness. Such a consciousness is one that Black Consciousness advocates is called a 'non-white' consciousness. According to Sartre, it is one that engages in complicitous reflection – that is, a consciousness that accepts the racist status quo and hence the values and fixed beliefs of that social environment.

In the oppressive conditions of slavery, colonialism and antiblack racism, when the self-consciousness of black people is appropriated by the self-consciousness of white people to serve the interest of white people, an impure or accomplice black consciousness is far more common and sometimes seems even 'natural'. For example, in a colonial situation, the coloniser attempts to control the consciousness of the colonised, the result of which is the colonised seeing themselves through the hegemonic consciousness of the coloniser. As Ngũgĩ wa Thiong'o attested during the Steve Biko Memorial Lecture at the University of Cape Town on 12 September 2003: 'The colonising presence tried to mutilate the memory of the colonised and where that failed, it dismembered it, and tried to remember it to the coloniser's memory: his way of defining the world, including his take on the nature of the relations between the colonised and the coloniser.' An accomplice consciousness is one that goes along with the consciousness of the slave master, the coloniser or the antiblack racist who seeks to obliterate the consciousness of its victim. Under slavery, colonialism or a system of white hegemony, whiteness is a value black people are forced to seek. An accomplice consciousness surrenders to this demanded value by seeking to attain the impossible goal of whiteness. This complicitous consciousness very often turns into a conscious or unconscious black antiblack racism.

The common feature of black slavery, African colonialism and antiblack racism puts into serious question the humanity of black people, the idea that 'there is nothing harmonious with humanity' to be found in black people, that black people belong to a different order of humanity than white people, if they are human at all. Black Consciousness as an idea thus emerged from the questions 'What am I?' and 'Who am I?' It was in reaction to slave, colonial and antiblack racist consciousnesses that Black Consciousness came into being – an attempt to liberate the black person from the alienated state of an afflicted, buffeted and unhappy double consciousness. It is here that we have to ask the seemingly belated questions arising from the background about the words 'consciousness' and 'blackness': What then is Black Consciousness? And why then did the Black Consciousness founders choose 'black' as a tag of identity?

The meaning of Black Consciousness

Given the negative connotations attached to the word 'black', why would one wish to constitute one's identity in terms of this negativity? First, no word comes into being invested with an already inherent, fixed, immutable and predetermined meaning. The meaning of a term changes with different locations, significations, values, beliefs, power, historical epochs and usage. Take for example the label 'liberal'; it has undergone numerous changes in connotation despite the fact that it denotatively refers to a single phenomenon. Secondly, Black Consciousness was a response to the Manichean divide that painted the world in white and black as good and evil, civilised and barbaric, self and Other. It sought to overturn the Manicheanism embedded in white/black relations. To this extent, Black Consciousness was aimed at reversing the white definition of black people and, through that very act, change the limits set to black possibilities for existence.

There is, however, another dimension connected with the word 'black', namely the power of naming. Naming is a critical aspect of language and signifies a form of power. To appropriate this power requires renaming that which is named or appropriating the very named and possessing it. To use the word to name is to bring something into existence and reclaiming of a word also constitutes a decisive aspect of the struggle. Some white people were surprised at the adoption of the presumably negative word 'black' and asked: How can anyone choose a negatively charged identity of blackness? In the SASO Nine trial, Judge Boshoff also feigned surprise at the use of the word 'black'. Interrogating Biko, the judge asked: 'But now why do you refer to your people as black?...you use black which really connotes dark forces over the centuries?' (in Biko 1996: 104). Many white people do not realise black people's resistance to imposed values. In other words, many white people do not understand the two-fold reality black people face in their dealings with white culture and white normativity. As Lewis Gordon attests, the hero of white popular culture, for example, is often someone who in the end is the enemy of black people. For example, in the movie *Frankenstein*, the mad scientist Dr Frankenstein (the main protagonist) is depicted as the creator of the evil monster Frankenstein who at the command of his creator kills people. What white people do not realise is that black people identify with Frankenstein the monster rather than the protagonist with whom white consciousness calls them to identify. Another example of this resistance to white normativity is offered by the poet and radical musician Gil Scott Heron: 'When I saw *Jaws*, I was rooting for the shark. He belongs in the water. What we call the beach, he calls the supermarket' (in Gordon 2006: 121). The theme of naming by its very nature in an oppressive situation is a dialectic phenomenon. Because the conditions for the voice of the oppressed to be heard is suppressed or ignored – or not heard at all – by the oppressor, the very fact that they have no say concerning their historic portrayal or identification forces them to take on the identification given to them (black) and transfigure it to mean the direct opposite of what their oppressor intended it to be. If for white people, 'black' means ugly, for black people – by means of a conscious reversal – 'black' means beautiful.

The care with which black people must work with the oppressor's language is a double-edged process. It is, as Lewis Gordon observes, '[t]he language by which he

(Black) was made into the monstrosity he is attempting to overcome, and it is also the language by which he is attempting to overcome it' (2006: 126). The comedian Richard Pryor, for example, opened the door for the now all-pervading use of the term 'nigger' within hip-hop culture. The hip-hoppers use a semantic slippage to make words acquire a different meaning from the conventional one. In one of their early songs, the rap group Run DMC explained to outsiders that when the word 'bad' is used in rap music, it is 'not "bad", meaning "bad" but "bad" meaning "good"'. 'Bad meaning good' is singularly powerful because it turns a negative into a positive. Hence the hip-hoppers (just like the Black Consciousness Movement's activists in relation to the word 'black') reclaimed the word 'nigger' as a word of affection, using it in resistance to its noxious historical use. The aim is to throw the slur 'nigger' back at the white racist by defiantly appropriating it and changing its meaning and value from a negative insulting slur into a positive term.

In the SASO Manifesto, tabled by Biko and Alex Mhlongo at the General Students Council Conference held from 4 to 10 July 1971, Black Consciousness is defined as 'an attitude of mind, a way of life'. This definition resonates perfectly with Nyerere's description of *Ujamaa* (African socialism) as a 'way of life', a worldview, an existential attitude. Nyerere's book *Ujamaa: Essays on Socialism* begins with the declaration 'Socialism, like democracy, is an attitude of mind' (1968: 2). This definition of socialism focuses on the subjective. The point of departure is the recognition by Nyerere (in like manner as the founders of Black Consciousness recognised about apartheid) that colonialism created new subjectivities with a slave, colonial and racist consciousness. So his call for re-education – conscientisation in Black Consciousness terms – is an attempt at decolonising the mind or re-appropriating the alienated consciousness. Describing the Black Power Movement in the USA, James Cone (one of the most influential figures of Black Consciousness in South Africa) declared in almost the same manner as Nyerere and the founders of Black Consciousness that Black Power 'is an *attitude,* an inward affirmation of the essential worth of blackness', and: '[I]t means that the black man will not be poisoned by the stereotypes that others have of him. This is Black Power, the power of the black man to say Yes to his own "black being", and to make the other accept him or be prepared for a struggle' (1969: 8). For the Black Consciousness founders Nyerere and Cone, Black Consciousness was fundamentally an existential attitude that required constantly making existential choices. An existential choice is a choice not of a goal but of oneself. One can, in this instance, existentially choose oneself as an activist of a movement.

If there is some definitional similarity with Nyerere's *Ujamaa* and Cone's conception of the Black Power Movement in the USA, a further foundational connection may be found in the conceptions of Negritude. Sartre defined Negritude in terms that could easily have been a definition of Black Consciousness.

Negritude, in his view, is a descent into the black self. It is an existential attitude, a 'becoming' and (to use Manganyi's or Heidegger's expression) a mode of being-black-in-the-world. Black consciousness is 'a shimmer of being and of needing-to-be' (Sartre 1988: 326). In this existentialist context, we could say that Black Consciousness is a chosen mode of being-in-the-world, a way of experiencing. Put differently, it is an affirmation of *being*, of the being of the black person, and indeed of black subjectivity, an awakening of consciousness of the black subject from an alienated consciousness. Odera Oruka captures the essence of Black Consciousness when he defines it as: '(1) a black man's [sic] awareness or realization that the world is infested with an anti-black social reality, (2) the black man's recognition of himself as black, as a Negro and to be proud of the fact, (3) the black man's urge to explain away or annihilate this social reality, and (4) move toward the creation of a new reality, a fair social reality as a condition for universal humanism' (1990: 71). Since apartheid had denigrated and rejected as inferior the black world, reality and its values, the first reaction of the founders of Black Consciousness was to develop and affirm a sense of self-pride, self-respect, self-worth and self-love in the consciousness of black people. To use Nietzsche's concept, in a significant sense, Black Consciousness became a 'transvaluation' of all white values about blackness. It naturally became an acceptance of and responsibility for black destiny and pride.

The blackness of Black Consciousness

What then is the meaning of blackness to the advocates of Black Consciousness? Blackness in South Africa, just like in Britain and the USA, has been intensely contested both inside and outside the Black Consciousness Movement. First, there is the conception of black people as a race that shares common distinguishable biological and somatic features and cultural characteristics different from other races. Second, there is the notion of black people as a group with common experiences of racism and oppression. In this sense, blackness is assumed to be a political category. Finally, I suggest a third meaning, that of *everyday people* (that is, the existential meaning of blackness or the 'lived-experience' of blackness).[11] For now, I distinguish between the first two meanings and reserve the last meaning of blackness for later discussion because of its overlap with the two meanings.

Biologically, a black person is a human being who racially belongs to the negroid race with distinguishable phenotypical characteristics such as kinky hair, a broad nose, thick and full lips, and dark pigmentation, and is descendent of people originating from sub-Saharan Africa or Africa South of the Sahara. In this sense, black people (persons of negroid stock) as a race 'share, more or less, biologically transmitted physical characteristics that, under the influence of endogenous cultural and geographical factors...contribute to the characterization of the group as a distinct, self-reproducing, encultured population' (Outlaw 1996: 136). In terms of this conception, therefore, biologically transmitted phenotypical traits conditioned by and together with geographical factors constitute a race. This conception of race was a feature of South African political traditions – white, Indian, coloured, African – and even non-racial parties such as the South African Communist Party (SACP) before the Black Consciousness Movement. These traditions conceived of race as biologically given, even though its significance is something they disagreed upon.

For physical anthropologists, races are the various subspecies of *Homo sapiens* characterised by certain phenotypical and genotypical traits. For social scientists, race refers to 'a human group that defines itself and/or is defined by other groups as different from other groups by virtue of innate and immutable physical characteristics' (Van den Berghe 1978: 9). For the layperson, race refers to a human group that shares certain phenotypical, somatic visible and distinguishable physical features and cultural characteristics (for example, language or religion).

Two ideas about race emerge here, namely: that race refers to the differences among groups of human beings, and that these differences are attributable to either physical or biological characteristics and/or cultural differences. In many instances, 'race' refers to physical attributes of which skin colour and physiognomy are the supposed visible signs. In his working definition of race, Marcus Singer arrives at the same conclusion about physical characteristics as indicative of race. According to him, the term 'race' refers to distinguishing characteristics of human beings that are '(1) *inherited* or believed to be inherited, (2) shared by fairly large numbers of people (but not by all), and (3) readily *apparent* to ordinary sense perception, especially the sense of sight' (1978: 155). It is evident from this definition that the word 'race' is normally used to refer to different groups of people characterised by certain physical traits sufficiently distinctive to indicate or identify the various groups. In this sense then, blackness may be a racial category referring to a distinct racial group with common phenotypical, genotypical and physical characteristics, especially the colour of the skin (black), the texture of the hair, the shape of the nose and the size of the lips – with the latter two described as flaring baboon nostrils and swollen lips and so on. A variant of this conception treats black identity not only in terms of biological characteristics, physical traits or ancestry, but also as constituted by shared or common cultural practices, values and beliefs (that is, a shared way of life) locatable in the culture of that biological group or ancestors.

Politically, blackness does not refer to racial affiliation physical characteristics that are biologically transmitted but strictly by political considerations. In short, blackness has nothing to do with phenotype, chromosomes or the colour of the skin; rather, blackness, in an antiblack political and social world, is used as a unifying tool to combat political oppression of those who are not white (there are many shades and phenotypical characteristics of those who are not white). The political sense of blackness concerns a consciousness of the fact that racialisation is calculated to promote and sustain certain power relations in society. On this understanding, one becomes conscious of the fact that to be black inevitably locates one in an inferior oppressive socio-political position and to be white invariably locates one in a position of power and superiority. Black is therefore adopted by the dominated presumably inferior groups to symbolise resistance against oppression and domination; it is used as a form of 'counterhegemonic activity aimed at dismantling the racial categories in question' (Johnson, in Yancy 2005: 178).

The SASO Policy Manifesto is a classic example of the adoption of the colour 'black' as a political instrument. It defines 'Black people as those who are by law or tradition politically, economically and socially discriminated against as a group in South African society and identifying themselves as a unit in the struggle towards the realisation of their aspiration' (1973). Among Black Consciousness adherents, blackness was an oppression-centred phenomenon understood in terms of one's vulnerability to apartheid racism. In this sense, SASO's conception of blackness resonates well with what Clarence Sholé Johnson refers to as the 'transgressive counterhegemonic' (2005: 179) sense of blackness. Those in the Black Consciousness Movement who promoted the category of black as inclusive of Africans, coloureds and Indians insisted that notwithstanding all the differences among these groups, there is a need for unity and solidarity of all those subjected to the oppressive political machinery of apartheid racism. Part of the major reason for adopting a political blackness, therefore, was to foster the politics of solidarity among the three oppressed groups.

Political blackness thus provided the organising principle for a new politics of collective action and resistance. This political meaning of 'blackness' is an example of what Tommie Shelby refers to as the 'Common Oppression Theory' which states that 'Blacks should unite and work together because they suffer a common oppression; and they can overcome or ameliorate their shared conditions only through black solidarity' (2002: 232). A classic example of this theory comes from the pen of Douglass, the nineteenth-century black American former slave. In an editorial of the *North Star* (3 December 1847) entitled 'To Our Oppressed Countrymen', Douglass wrote: 'We are one with you under the ban of prejudice and proscription – one with you under the slander of inferiority – one with you in social and political disenfranchisement. What you suffer, we suffer; what you endure, we endure. We are indissolubly united, and must fall or flourish together' (in Shelby 2005: 20).

In a seeming echo of Douglass's sentiment, Strinivasa Moodley (a prominent member of SASO and the Black Consciousness Movement) articulated the basis and the necessity for black solidarity: 'We have come together on the basis of our common oppression and do not separate on the basis of superficial cultural differences' (1972). What both Douglass and Moodley suggested, is that the common oppression expressed by the term 'black' constitutes an organising principle of political struggle. The term 'black' therefore had to become part of an organised practice of struggle requiring the strengthening of black resistance as well as the development of new forms of black consciousness.

Blackness became not only a signifier of oppression but was also distinguished from the term 'non-white'. In *Why Race Matters in South Africa*, Michael MacDonald interprets Biko and the Black Consciousness Movement's concept of non-whites as referring to 'those who were discriminated against but did not resist' (2006: 118). In his reading of Biko, to be black meant 'to be *militantly* black, openly, proudly, and defiantly'. This is a problematic interpretation of the movement and its philosophy because it locates in the category of 'non-whites' a wider range of black people who were not regarded as 'non-whites' by the movement. Three categories of black people can be distinguished from SASO and Biko's statements: (i) the *real* black person, (ii) the black person and (iii) the non-white person. The 'real black person', for Biko, is 'militantly black, openly, proudly, and defiantly' and actively participates in the opposition to racism 'conscious of the urgent need for an understanding of what is involved in the new approach – "black consciousness"' (1996: 27). The 'black person' is one who while suffering from apartheid oppressive machinery, recognises his blackness from a detached position, neither supporting the system nor openly resisting it. Such black people constitute a category which, through conscientisation, is amenable to change from an uncommitted blackness to a radical position of social, political and philosophical commitment to the Black Consciousness ideology. The term 'non-white', on the one hand, was a term used by the apartheid regime to distinguish all groups not of European descent. It was an umbrella term referring to Africans, Indians, coloureds and in some cases Asians (Chinese, Malaysians or Japanese). For the Black Consciousness proponents, on the other hand, 'non-white' was a derogatory word reserved for those who consciously and willingly supported and participated in apartheid-created structures such as the bantustans (ethnic homelands) and/or Urban Bantu Councils, mostly for their own material benefit. 'Non-white' was a word specifically reserved for those who were regarded or perceived as collaborators or puppets of the racist regime; those, in Biko's view, 'who, like the Bantustan leaders have sold their souls to the white man' (1996: 82).

In certain instances, the term was reserved for those who had a tremendous desire to be white, those who were not proud of their blackness but who proudly aped white values, the educated elites and intellectuals who sought to distance themselves from their own people whom they perceived as 'backward' – indeed, those who tried their utmost to imitate everything Western with the desperate hope of being accepted by the racist white society and its value system. 'A non-white' writes Baartman, 'is an existence with a coloured...pigmentation but wasting his life trying to be white' (1973: 4). In this context then, for Black Consciousness, a non-white was the equivalent of Malcolm X's House Nigger or Uncle Tom.

The Black Consciousness Movement comrades spoke of and deployed the word 'black' as a multi-inflected signifier of oppression and resistance. The redefinition of black identity was an empowering signifier of the African–coloured–Asian alliance against apartheid exclusionary practices and oppression. However, the solidarity which was the fundamental project of Black Consciousness met with some resistance from a significant number of Indian and coloured people who were unwilling to consider themselves black and adopt that negative identity. This unwillingness was an indication of veiled underlying apartheid-induced racist sentiments against Africans who, even before the emergence of SASO, were considered black people by everyone. Concerned about the possibility of being subsumed under and overwhelmed by the African majority, conservative Indian and coloured people appealed to cultural and religious differences among the oppressed to reject solidarity moves. Heribert Adams observes:

> The solidarity of 'Black Consciousness' that includes all three designated racial groups is based on the political factor of common discrimination, not common cultural affinities. The weakness of the shared movement lies precisely in this abstract political bond, not backed up by shared experiences of everyday perceptions, save political exclusion.
> (1985: 173–174)

It seems that a variegated group such as the Indian, coloured and African people makes it extremely difficult to speak of a shared experience of oppression, common sensibility or unified political outlook. In the face of these realities, political mobilisation along presumed 'racial' lines becomes a problematic project indeed.

Biko's enthusiastic and overambitious inclusion of African, Indian and coloured people under the political conception of 'blackness' was not without problems and resistance from members of all three groups. Indeed, he recognised the deeply embedded apartheid suspicions and attitudes of superiority found in the Indian and coloured communities against the African people, and the equally resentful responses of Africans to such attitudes. Referring to how the apartheid system had conditioned Indians to see themselves as superior, Biko laments: 'I must admit I say this with a pain in my heart...Coloured people harbour secret hopes of being classified as 'brown Afrikaners' and therefore meriting admittance into the white laager while Indian people might be given a vote to swell the buffer zone between whites and Africans' (1996: 36). The tensions became evident in a *SASO Newletter* article by Biko entitled 'Ugandan Asians and the Lessons for Us' (1972). Referring to the article, the editor wrote:

> Here in South Africa this [the Ugandan Asian Issue] has a special meaning for the Indian people. Basically, Indians in South Africa believe they are 'one better than the Africans'...Some Indians go to the extent of saying, 'I'd rather have the Nationalist Government ruling me than the African'. And I have heard this particular statement being echoed in various sectors of the Indian community. SASO believes that this kind of statement proves how far Indians refuse to identify with the other Black people. (*SASO Newsletter* 1972)

The fundamental problem in Biko's concept of blackness is its restriction of racism to white supremacy, to a white–black binary phenomenon. As a consequence, much of the racism that occurs in-between, what Lewis Gordon refers to as 'Black anti-black racism', is reduced to the invisible. This blanket categorisation of oppressed identity allows exaggerated and false claims for a common racialised experience, thus ignoring the cracks, internal divisions, charges of racism and ruptures within the 'black experience' itself.[11]

The Black Consciousness concept of blackness that is predicated on the notion of the common experience of oppression calls to mind Sartre's notion of the *look*. According to this concept, the essential condition for one consciousness to be united with another is for both individuals to be subjected to the objectifying *look* of the Third. However, the Sartrean *look* of the Third brings about an external unification of individuals (groups: Africans, coloureds and Indians) that temporarily freezes antagonistic and conflictual relations brought about by cultural, social, economic, religious and existential conditions within an apartheid society. In such relations, the condition of conflict between individuals is momentarily suspended because solidarity is expressed through notions such as Us-object and We-subject, relations that generate an external unification of individuals or groups. But this solidarity as external solidarity lacks cohesion and interiority, and thus is extremely fragile when the Third disappears. It is a solidarity which does not take the form of a free relationship, but is rather imposed from the outside by some sort of foreign and external power and results from common oppression. So the Black Consciousness Movement's conception of 'blackness', as an identity and a foundation for solidarity, faced insurmountable obstacles.

Self-definition

Given this scenario about blackness, people who regard themselves and are regarded by others as black were confronted with the thorny existential question

'Who am I?' Fanon describes the negation of the humanity of black people through systems such as colonialism, slavery and racism: 'Because it is a systematic negation of the other, a resolute decision to refuse the other all the attributes of humanity, colonialism compels the dominated people constantly to ask the question: In reality, who am I?' (1968: 300). The question 'Who am I?' is an expression of a concern about myself, a manifestation of my concern for my being. It is an attempt by the self to relate itself to itself. The word 'I' in the question is that whereby consciousness affirms its reality. The appropriate answer to the question about my identity would be 'I am this kind of consciousness' or 'My consciousness is this kind of consciousness'. Such an answer is a self-definition and a statement about self-identity. Among black people, several answers have emerged but all of them point to a single concern: the denied humanity of black people. In his popular novel *Invisible Man*, Ralph Ellison's response is: 'I am an invisible man.' He writes: 'I am a man of substance, of flesh and bone, fiber and liquid – and I might be said to possess a mind. I am invisible, understand, simply because people refuse to see me' (1995: 3). Invisible though I may be, Ellison suggests, I am nevertheless a man, a human being. To James Baldwin, the reason why he asks the question 'Who am I?' is simply because 'Nobody Knows My Name'. Indeed, in an antiblack world, black people do not have names. Since 'all Niggers look alike' to most white people, they either do not call them by their names – as 'The Negro' in Sartre's '*The Respectful Prostitute*' – or they give them collective names such as 'Sambo'. In fact, over the centuries, black people have been called various names by white people, names which did not portray their being: savages, negroes, niggers, kaffirs, natives, non-whites, coloured people, Bantus and so on.

What was the response of the advocates of Black Consciousness to these external definitions? Forced to experience a radical conversion, the Black Consciousness activists (just like the Negritudinists), in a moment of 'new self-discovery', authentically acknowledged their blackness and began to define themselves accordingly. As Sartre observed: 'Thus he has his back against the wall of authenticity: having been insulted and formerly enslaved, he picks up the word 'nigger' which is thrown at him like a stone, he draws himself erect and proudly proclaims himself a black man, face to face with white men' (1988: 296). So, in line with SASO's principle not to allow the racist white establishment to define them with all sorts of degrading labels such as 'natives', 'Bantu', 'non-white', 'plurals' or 'kaffirs', the black students passed a resolution at the beginning of the General Students Council (GSC) of 1972, urging all newspapers to refrain from using these degrading labels and simply call them 'blacks'.

Let us be clear about what was at stake here. At the heart of the matter was an issue of authority, the authority of black people to describe reality as they perceived it and to define themselves as they saw fit within that reality. This demand to be the authority in one's self-understanding and self-definition brings to mind the conversation between Humpty Dumpty and Alice in *Alice in Wonderland*:

> 'When I use a word, it means just what I choose it to mean, neither more nor less.'
> 'But the question', Alice asked, 'is whether you can make words mean so many different things?'
> 'No', replied Humpty Dumpty, 'the question is: Who is to be the master?' (Carroll 1992: 45)

What is at stake is the power and authority to define. Is the white person to be the sole definer of reality, including black reality? By asserting a positive meaning to the term 'black' for their identity, the Black Consciousness Movement seized the power of defining and naming; thus they invalidated the stigmatising meaning of blackness and the implicit and explicit definition of it as deviance in relation to the norm of whiteness.

Conclusion

There are phenomenological implications that derive from the conception of Black Consciousness. That Black Consciousness is a form of *consciousness* immediately locates it within the realm of phenomenology and thus becomes, as Lewis Gordon would say, 'a subject rich with phenomenological significance' (2002). This is because phenomenology is concerned with meaningful reality as constituted by consciousness which is always understood as consciousness *of* something (that is, intentionality as a defining characteristic of consciousness). The consciousness that manifests itself in Black Consciousness is that of black reality within an antiblack apartheid world. But blackness is a contingent function of embodiment. Thus, not only is the notion of the intentionality of consciousness a significant feature of phenomenology, but added to that is the phenomenological injunction against Cartesian conceptions of disembodied consciousness or *cogito*.

Black Consciousness has always, with and sometimes without justification, been referred to as a philosophy. Hence expressions such as 'the philosophy of Black Consciousness' or 'Black Consciousness as a philosophy' were regularly made by the founders of the movement, and by its followers. If philosophy (as Hegel contends) is consciousness come into its own existence, then by that very fact Black Consciousness is not only a mode of philosophising but also a philosophy. For, in terms of the movement's definition, Black Consciousness is the black person's coming to consciousness of herself as black. More than this, Black Consciousness has as its primary concern questions arising from the phenomena of race and racism as will be evident in the later stages of this book, racism (especially antiblack racism) questions the humanity of black people. When one's personhood or humanity is called into question, concerns about one's humanity or identity take centre stage in one's existence. The centring of human existence constitutes an important aspect of an area of thought known as philosophical anthropology.

Notes

1   A substantial number of writings on Black Consciousness focus mostly on the historical and political dimensions of the movement and none on its philosophical foundations. See, for example, Fatton's *Black Consciousness in South Africa* (1986); Pityana et al.'s (Eds) *Bounds of Possibility: The Legacy of Steve Biko and Black Consciousness* (1991); CRD Halisi's *Black Political Thought in the Making of South African Democracy* (1999); Thomas Ranuga's 'Frantz Fanon and Black Consciousness in Azania' (1986); Chris Nteta's 'Revolutionary Self-Consciousness as an Objective Force Within the Process of Liberation' (1987); Gibson's 'Black Consciousness 1977–1987: The Dialectics of Liberation in South Africa' (1988); and Sono's *Reflections on the Origin of Black Consciousness in South Africa* (1993).

2   Mandaza I, *City Press*, 12 September 2004.

3   'Azania' is the name political formations such as the Black Consciousness Movement, Azanian People's Organisation, PAC and other aligned formations outside the ANC and its allies have given to South Africa. In this book, it is used interchangeably with the name 'South Africa'.

4   According to Pityana, the apartheid regime's Schlebusch Commission (also called the Commission on Certain Organisations) was intent on condemning SASO and the Black Consciousness Movement as subversive organisations deserving to be banned. According to Pityana, it 'found that the ideology, strategy and finance of Black Consciousness organisations were imported from America. Steve Biko and myself were accused of propagating Black power ideas verbatim'. Even the racist Judge Boshoff, looking for a way to convict the SASO Nine on charges of an attempt to overthrow the state through violent means, insisted during the trial that Black Consciousness was a clone of Black Power.

5   On Black Consciousness and culture, see Siloane's 'The Development of Black Consciousness as a Cultural and Political Movement (1967–2007)' (2008) and Andries Oliphant's 'A Human Face: Biko's Conceptions of African Culture and Humanism' (2008).

6   See Young's book *White Mythologies: Writing History and the West* (1990) and his preface to Sartre's *Colonialism and Neocolonialism* (2001).

7   See Lewis Gordon's *An Introduction to Africana Philosophy* (2008) for a fuller description of the concerns of phenomenological enquiry.

8   See Martin Luther King Jr's *Where Do We Go from Here: Chaos or Community?* (1967) for a critique on Black Power.

9   For a detailed account, see Johnson's '(Re)Conceptualizing Blackness and Making Race Obsolescent' (2005).

10   A vast amount of literature now exists on the racist views of the dominant figures of Western philosophy. See, for example, my article 'African Philosophy Revisited' (1996)[?] [unclear] Eze's (Ed.) *Race and the Enlightenment: A Reader* (1997) and *Achieving our Humanity: The Idea of a Postracial Future* (2001), Léon Poliakov's *The Aryan Myth: A History of Racist and Nationalist Ideas in Europe* (1974) and Cornel West's *Prophesy Deliverance! An Afro-American Revolutionary Christianity* (1982).

11   On this distinction, see Lewis Gordon's *Bad Faith and Antiblack Racism* (1995a). The Indian issue has a long history in South Africa, made prominent by Mohandas Gandhi's denegration of Africans as 'Kaffirs' and opting to join the white colonialists against Africans during the Zulu wars against British settlers. The 1948 violent racial confrontation between Indians and Africans highlights the unhealthy relations predicated on race. Also, the lived

experiences of Africans at the hands of Indians, who were legally positioned at a higher hierarchical racial level than the Africans, created relations of superiority and inferiority based on race. Discussing the racial situation of South Africa in the 1950s in *The African Image*, Mphahlele wrote: 'Thus the white man, the Indian, and the Coloured, each in his peculiar compensatory response – often a neurotic one – has through the years driven the African into a defensive position' (1962: 70). Also writing as early as 1963 about Afro-Indo relations, Modisane concluded: 'Thus it is that the social relationship between the Africans and the Indians is not so different from that between black and white; far less different than is supposed by the politicians. There is very little social contact, except on the master and servant level. The Indians reject and segregate against the Africans, who are refused attention – or at best tolerated – in the swank Indian-owned milk bars, restaurants and cinemas; where the Indian patrons refuse to share tables and seating arrangements. In the cinemas, particularly in Johannesburg and Durban, African patrons are humiliated, treated with impatience and relegated to inferior seats. If there is a big Indian, Coloured and Chinese crowd at the box-office, the house-full sign goes up for Africans' (1986: 132–133).

Even in the face of such anti-African evidence, Heribert Adam and Kogila Moodley in their book *The Negotiated Revolution: Society and Politics in Post-Apartheid South Africa* (1993), create the impression that Africans (particularly the SASO group) were anti-Indian and even anticoloured and that some advocated African nationalism with racist overtones. This is a defenceless position in the face of South African existential racial realities. The reaction in the SASO camp was the product of suspicion based on the history of Indo-African relations. The fact is also that many Indian and coloured people, for a number of reasons, resented being categorised as black people, a position represented in the UK by Tariq Madood.

There were therefore serious disagreements in SASO's ranks regarding the thorny issue of the role of the Indian and coloured people, not only in student politics but also in the liberation struggle as a whole. The pro-PAC group led by Mokoape held that Indian and coloured people should not be included in the concept 'black' since historically their interests in relation to Africans lay in the maintenance of white political and economic power.

For similar instances of 'black antiblack racism', see Lewis Gordon's *Bad Faith and Antiblack Racism* (1995a) and 'Critical "Mixed Race"' (1995c). See also Scott's 'The Re-Enchantment of Humanism: An Interview with Sylvia Wynter' (2000) for information on Afro-Indo Caribbean race relations.

3

Philosophy contextualised

IN THE PREVIOUS CHAPTER, I made the claim that Biko's awareness of the urgent
need for a new consciousness became a catalyst for a philosophy that would
eventually give birth to *what-ought-to-be*. In other words, Biko was not only a
philosopher but also a philosopher of change. Indeed, the Black Consciousness
Movement in South Africa, of which Biko was the leader – according to
Millard Arnold, its 'brilliant political theorist' and described by Themba Sono
its 'formidable and articulate philosopher' – conceived of its position as a
'philosophy' and a 'way of life'. From a particular perspective, this is a curious way
of understanding philosophy and brings into sharp contrast the conception of
philosophy from an academic point of view, philosophy as an academic discipline
and a philosopher as *homo academicus*. Philosophy as a way of life (non-professional
philosophy) and philosophy as a professional occupation, while similar in many
respects, differ in their conception of the *telos*, utility and significance of philosophy.
To bring out these differences, I briefly deal with problems related to what
philosophy is variously understood to be by different philosophical traditions, and
discuss its foundations and Black Consciousness's position in all of this.

A matter of definition

The question 'What is philosophy?' has been asked before, and even today it is the
most important philosophical question. We know that chemistry is the study of
the chemical reactions of certain liquids or matter; history is the study of events
of the past and their interpretation; sociology is the study of social arrangements
in different communities or collectivities of human beings; logic is the normative
study of the correctness or incorrectness, validity or invalidity, of arguments.
Philosophy? The greatest controversy in philosophy has hitherto been its
definition. The debate rages on in the present, involving in the process exclusions
or inclusions of philosophical discourses by self-appointed gatekeepers. For this

reason, the very question about what philosophy is is itself a philosophical question (metaphilosophical) without a definite intelligible answer. Philosophy, as Paulin Hountondji asserts, 'can be regarded as the most self-conscious of disciplines. It is the one discipline that involves by its very nature a constant process of reflection upon itself' (1983: 7). This claim may seem puzzling to most people. One of the peculiar features of philosophy, as Hegel acutely observed, is that it is a discipline with the capacity to define everything else except itself. Its complexity, breadth, width and nature render it extremely difficult – if not impossible – to define. Consequently, any attempted definition of what philosophy is is itself a philosophical issue subject to interrogation, reflection, criticism, analysis and so on. At best, such definitions are either an expression of one's philosophical affiliation or preference for a branch, field or part of the philosophical enterprise as a whole. An all-encompassing definition of philosophy, as such, is thus impossible. However, the fact that philosophy is comprehensively indefinable does not necessarily mean that we cannot proffer a general definition of it nor define parts or sections or aspects of it at all. Furthermore, it does not mean that we cannot recognise philosophy when we are confronted with philosophical issues, questions, discourse, texts or activity. Just because we cannot define the colour red or green (or any other colour) does not mean that we cannot recognise red objects or green ones, nor does it mean that we cannot distinguish one colour from another on a particular thing. Although an inexhaustible discursive field which cannot be comprehensively defined, philosophy can nevertheless be recognised. Hence, a number of general definitions have been attempted in the past and will continue to be offered in the future, even though they may be contested for various philosophical, cultural, ideological or hegemonic reasons.

For example, for some, philosophy comes from a sense of wonder. But then this would make all people philosophers since everyone at one time or another in life is gripped by a sense of wonder about so many mysterious phenomena. For others, philosophy is the love of wisdom. But what kind of wisdom: individual or collective? For others still, philosophy is 'thinking thinking itself' or a no man's land between science and religion. For the phenomenologists (one of the many schools of thought or movements in the philosophical field), philosophy is the study of phenomena as they appear; for analytical philosophers, it is the analysis of the logical geography of concepts and our conceptual scheme; for the existentialists, it is the study of human existence-in-the-world; and for Marxists, it is an instrument of ideology. All these different attempts at a definition of philosophy are meant to indicate the contestations over philosophy and the near impossibility of an all-inclusive definition of this enterprise. No one, therefore, can legitimately claim to own the right to declare his philosophy to be the only appropriate conception of what philosophy is. Whatever is ultimately offered as a definition of philosophy ends up in the final analysis to be a definition of a particular tradition, branch, school of thought, perspective or philosophical doctrine – as will be evident later when I attempt a definition of existentialism, Africana philosophy or any other philosophical doctrine. However, whatever philosophy is conceived to be, a common thread in all kinds of conceptions is that it involves critical, reflective and rational thinking (that is, thinking that subjects assumptions to conditions of rational evidence and assessment). Rationality, therefore, is the cornerstone of all philosophical theorising and practice.

By the very nature of the discipline, philosophers are entitled to debate the methodologies and boundaries of their discipline. However, this debate on the definition of philosophy became even more paramount when the issue of African philosophy emerged. Western philosophers questioned the ontological status of African philosophy, with questions such as 'Is there an African philosophy?', 'What is African philosophy?' and 'Does African philosophy exist?' Such questions were generated in the late-1960s by the publication of Tempels' groundbreaking book *Bantu Philosophy*, first published in French in 1945 and in English in 1959, even though Césaire and Senghor had already introduced the Negritude philosophy in their writings in the 1930s. Normally, questions of the type 'What is...?', 'Is there such and such?' or 'Does such and such exist?' are standard philosophical questions. Why then would questions of the same sort about Africa generate more heat than mere philosophical curiosity? Are such questions not as much philosophical as other questions of a metaphysical or ontological nature? If such questions about Africa and the African are simply standard questions, why are questions of the same kind not asked about British, German, French, Indian, Chinese, American and other philosophies? What is common in the philosophies of all other peoples but is supposedly lacking among Africans? Is it a question of the written text? If so, what about Socrates – presumably one of the greatest philosophers ever – who never wrote anything down? Besides, Cheik Anta Diop (1974), Molefi Asante (1990), Theophile Obenga (1989), Martin Bernal (1991) and others have demonstrated the presence of the written text in Africa long before the birth of Christ. There is, therefore, clearly more to the questions about the existence of African philosophy than simply philosophical innocence (More 1996a). As Oluoch Imbo argues: 'the question: Does African philosophy exist? is highly coded...it is a question that cannot be answered satisfactorily without an understanding of the often implicit ideological assumptions' (1998: 43).

In an attempt to justify the existence of African philosophy, African philosophers themselves got entangled in the perennial question 'What is philosophy?' Different conceptions of the definition, not only of African philosophy but also of philosophy itself and who an African philosopher is, emerged. Accompanying these conceptions were the distinct trends or schools of thought identified by Oruka (1990) as *ethno-philosophy, professional philosophy, nationalist-ideological philosophy* and *philosophic sagacity*. Oruka later added another trend: *hermeneutical-historical philosophy*. The leading voices of the professional philosophy school (Hountondji, Kwasi Wiredu, Peter Bodunrin and others) accused the ethno-philosophy represented by Senghor's Negritude, Nyerere and Nkrumah's African socialism, Tempels' Bantu philosophy and so on as communal and undocumented (unwritten) worldviews not deserving of the name 'philosophy'. For them, philosophy is an expression of personal critical reflection rather than collective thought. In a neo-positivistic Eurocentric manner, Hountondji and Wiredu declared that philosophy has to be as rigorous as science in the way it is practised in the West. This position in effect excludes discursive systems such as ubuntu, Negritude and Black Consciousness as philosophies. Oruka (taking a middle position) launched a critique against professional philosophy, stating that his philosophical sagacity is an attempt to uncover an 'authentic African philosophy' (1990: 36) shorn of Western colonialist influences and appropriation.[1]

I suggested above, and will suggest below, that what is actually at stake in the questioning of the ontological status and legitimacy of African philosophy is the attempt to call into question the humanity of African and African-descended people, a humanness 'defined by the reigning Greek-*cum*-European philosophical anthropological paradigm centred around the notion of "rationality"' (Outlaw 1992/1993: 65).

Philosophy, rationality and human nature

Western philosophical tradition from the pre-Socratic period to Plato and Aristotle, Rene Descartes and Kant, Hegel and beyond defined itself and its activity in terms of 'Reason'. Because of the central position that the concept of rationality occupies in the history of philosophy, notions of the universe, society, state and the human being hinge fundamentally upon it. The view of a rational world order, of an external world possessing a logical order, a universe with a rational *telos*, is an established metaphysical and epistemological principle held to be sacrosanct. Since philosophy is a human product, this conception necessitated questions dealt with within the field of philosophical anthropology (that is, the question about the nature of the very being who philosophises – the human being).

Basic to narratives about human nature (essence) is the attempt to deal with the perennial philosophical-anthropological question 'What is a human being?' Answers to this question are usually purported to be descriptive, but more often than not they are normative and thus determine moral, social and political arrangements and relations. The concept 'nature' (essence) in this context refers to that feature, characteristic or attribute that is permanently necessary for something's being or continuance. If the necessary attribute is absent or lacking, the thing cannot be itself (that is, the feature is one without which the thing cannot be what it is). The nature of X, for example, is what makes X an X and not a Y. X's nature prevents it from being a Y. The notion of human nature, therefore, refers to the conception of an attribute that is distinctively or typically human and without which a being cannot be human. What then is this distinctive attribute that makes human beings human?

Heraclitus asserted that '[r]eason belongs to all' and by 'all' he meant all human beings. Plato affirmed the superiority of reason over the senses, reason whereby the rulers or philosopher kings could gain access to true knowledge. A human being, declared Aristotle, 'is a rational being'. In other words, those beings who do not meet the criterion of rationality (those who lack reason) are slaves or animals of burden. It was Descartes who gave rationality its modern respectability. Affirming Aristotle's conception of human nature, Descartes asserted that since humans are thinking beings (*res cogitans*), the distinctive and paramount feature of humanness is thought. Descartes' dictum 'I think, therefore I am' became one of the cornerstones of rationalism as a philosophy. Notwithstanding his empiricism, Locke claimed that human beings are free by virtue of equal possession of rationality. Hence, a person who behaves 'irrationally' is a brute or animal which deserves to be kept in servitude. Rationality, Locke averred, is a mark of human subjectivity and therefore a condition of the necessity for the extension of full moral treatment. Human beings are free because they are equally endowed with rationality. Hence, freedom and rationality are the basic features constitutive of human nature.

The influence of Plato, Aristotle, Descartes and Locke on the Enlightenment became expressed in Kant, who laid the philosophical foundations for a purely formalistic rationalism. His philosophical anthropology is grounded in the belief that the human being is a rationally unified consciousness (that is, reason and understanding unify our experience). This contention means in short that, for Kant, a person is a rational being. Grounded on the primacy of reason, Kant's moral philosophy is thus perhaps the most explicit and influential example of a philosophy which grounds morality on reason. Despite his rejection of Kant's moral doctrine, as enshrined in the universalisability principle, Hegel – like Kant – maintained that what constitutes human beings, society and history is rationality and freedom rather than feelings and inclinations. For him, 'thought is, indeed, essential to humanity. It is this that distinguishes us from the brutes' (Hegel 1952a: 156). In terms of this conception, a human being is a thinking being (*homo rationalis*) distinguishable from everything else by the capacity to think. Human beings, according to Hegel, are essentially 'spirit' or 'reason' and spirit (reason) is necessarily and above all else universal. Universality means thinking in terms of universal principles. Hence, for Hegel, all that is real is rational and all that is rational is real.

Critique of traditional philosophy

It is at this juncture when Hegel's notion of reason seemed to have been dominant that there arose one lone voice that screamed: 'NO!' This cry of protest came from Kierkegaard (1813–1855), who reacted strongly against this whole tradition of philosophical thought and specifically against Hegel's system. To be precise, he rejected Hegel's identification of thought and existence. According to Hegel's conception, existence is the same as thinking about it – that is, 'What is rational is actual, and what is actual is rational' (1952b: 6). But, Kierkegaard argued, one cannot think existence. By doing this, Kierkegaard objected, Hegel reduced existence to pure thought. Insofar as the existing individual is a thinker, she is eternal and infinite in the sense that she is universal and lives through change. Insofar as the thinker exists, she is immersed in the discontinuity of the world of space and time and is thus subject to the becoming that characterises this world. The result, according to Kierkegaard, is that there is a genuine distinction between the rational and the real. Thought is abstraction and therefore infinite, universal and atemporal; however, existence is finite, temporal and particular. In the Hegelian system, Kierkegaard further argued, individuals disappear into humanity. 'You and I,' he wrote, 'any particular existing individual, cannot become visible' (1941: 313). The consequence of this abstraction and disregard for the existing individual is that individuals are absolved from personal responsibility for the solution to their existential problems since they are left to history, necessity, reason and logic.

Thus to claim, as the rationalist of traditional Western philosophy does, that a human being is fundamentally a rational being as expressed in the Cartesian 'I think, therefore I am' is misleading because according to Kierkegaard, I must exist first in order to think. In other words, for Kierkegaard, the rationalist is mistaken in thinking that the ultimate reality is universal reason and that the aim of philosophy is knowledge of this universal. The striving for the universal, which ultimately boils down to striving for objectivity, is for Kierkegaard the denial of the particular and the taking away of our subjectivity. Kierkegaard's ultimate judgement against Hegel is that through his identification of thought and being, Hegel forgot existence. Following in the footsteps of Kierkegaard, the German existentialist philosopher Heidegger, in his monumental work *Being and Time* (1962), also rejected the Cartesian postulation that the task of philosophy is to determine indubitable assertion about the self and the world. For him, the task of philosophy is rather to provide an interpretation of what it means to exist as a human being – that is, what is the Being of human being (*Dasein*).

Kiekegaard's idea that human beings have to exist first before they can think set the groundwork for nearly every theme of what came to be known as existentialism. Hence, existentialism has simply been described as a philosophy of existence. Since by existence is meant the lived-reality of individual human beings, existentialism may also be viewed as a philosophy of lived-reality.[2] However, this is a simplistic – and thus problematic – definition because of its broadness. For example, if it is correct that existentialism is a philosophy of human existence, what then differentiates it from most traditional philosophy? Is it not the case that traditional philosophy has as its fundamental focus the human being? After all, the history of philosophy is the history of questions about human life and existence. Is it therefore not the case, as we have seen above, that traditional philosophy has posed questions such as 'What is a human being?' or 'What am I?' as fundamental questions of its focus? What then distinguishes existentialism from traditional philosophy as it has been practised throughout history?

Furthermore, consider the scientific world and its relation to human existence. All sciences, in one way or another, have as their object of study human existence. Mathematics may simply be defined as the study of human capacity to understand abstract space and quantity; chemistry is concerned with the chemical reactions and actions of certain chemical substances in the human being; physics is concerned not only with the physical environment that affects human existence immensely, but also with the physical make-up of the human being herself. Biology deals with the biological aspects of human existence, while botany deals with the flora or plants that affect (negatively or positively) human existence; zoology deals with animals that may or may not sustain human life; and anatomy is concerned with the anatomical structure of human beings. What then is the difference between existentialism as a philosophy of human existence and the various sciences whose subject matter implicitly or explicitly involves human beings and their existence?

By way of response, let me appeal to what is referred to as existential phenomenology. Most prominent existentialists such as Heidegger and the French Merleau-Ponty and Sartre were also phenomenologists because they adopted the phenomenological method made famous by the philosopher Edmund Husserl. In contrast to the rationalists who viewed reason as the sole means whereby reality can be comprehended, the phenomenologist believes that reality is given to us not through reason but through experience. Simply stated, phenomenology is a method in terms of which phenomena are made to appear, disclose or reveal themselves to consciousness. Phenomenology then, following Kant's claim about the constituting nature of consciousness, focuses on the active role of consciousness in the constitution of the world and its meaning. For the phenomenologist, the self or human consciousness is a meaning-giving entity; it analyses that which appears in its sphere – phenomena. As such, the organising principle of phenomenology in the manner of Husserl and Sartre is that of 'intentionality'. Any act of consciousness, from a phenomenological point of view, is always directed at something. When we desire, we desire something; when we love, we love something or someone; and when we perceive, we perceive something. Thus, as noted earlier in the preceding chapter, consciousness is always consciousness of something.

As a method of existentialist philosophy, phenomenology seeks to disclose, reveal and describe the phenomena of human consciousness as they present themselves in actual experience of everyday existence. Consider the human body: in the sciences of biology, physiology or anatomy, my body is an object of different parts (such as the heart, kidneys, tissues, blood, muscles, veins, nerves, skin, epidermis and a host of others) and how these parts relate to one another. My body is thus an amalgamation of different components of factual objects. My lips and mouth are accordingly composed of skin, nerves, muscles, tissues, blood and so on. From a scientific point of view, a smile is a certain contraction of the nostrils and of the muscles and tissues that form the corners of the mouth. For the optic sciences, my eye is a lens; it has a cornea and retina. The fact that it is a lens situates it in the realm of optic geometry. In the sciences, therefore, the human body is viewed – thanks to Descartes' rationalistic philosophy – as an object of investigation. While existential phenomenology does not dispute the scientific perspective of the human body as an object of study, it deals with the lived subjectivity of the human body, the body as you and I exist and experience it in everyday life. The body as I live it is not the object of anatomical, physiological or biological investigation. It is an existential lived body imbued with meaning and significance. A kiss is definitely not one set of lips (flesh) merely coming into contact with another set of lips (flesh), nor are my eyes and yours two pairs of lenses facing each other. In human everyday experiences, a kiss is a meaning-giving expression of love, understanding and respect; a look is a meaning-giving expression of hatred, love, sympathy, understanding, amazement, surprise and so on. In short, a kiss or a look constitutes a mode of communication between existing human beings.

Existentialism is thus a philosophy about the lived-reality of human existence. From Kierkegaard's response against Hegel's system, it can be said that, strictly speaking, existentialism is a reaction or a series of philosophical revolts against traditional philosophy's attempt to reduce human existence to abstract propositional terms and to incorporate and imprison the individual human being in an absolute universal system. For the existentialist thinker, philosophy must begin from the subjective because the self and its anguish, happiness, anger, suffering and so on cannot be known through detached observation and contemplation, but must be inwardly appropriated.

In general, existentialism was a reaction against the distorted overcommitment to rationality as the defining feature not only of human beings but also of reality in general. In light of the liberals and empiricists' denouncement of existentialism as irrational, it should be noted that existentialist critique of modern philosophy is not a critique of reason *per se* but of the manner in which rationality has been made the absolute attribute of the human to the almost total exclusion of the other complementary attributes such as passions. For the existentialist, a human being is not simply a rational being; a human being is equally an emotional and spiritual being, among other things. In fact, most existentialists believe that a human being is to begin with *nothing*. Human beings first exist and thereafter define who they themselves will be – in Sartre's famous dictum, 'existence precedes essence' in human reality. The project of existentialism ultimately amounts to the rejection of human-nature discourses in favour of those grounded on the notion of the human condition. Thus, the traditional conception of the human being as absolutely a rational animal is considered fundamentally flawed, seriously misleading and dangerous. The danger comes when such a view is used to deny the humanity of others on the basis that they do not demonstrate the capacity for rationality and reason, and that because of this incapacity to think such beings (their humanoid structure, upright posture and appearance notwithstanding) are either non-human or subhuman. Western philosophy is replete with examples of such misleading and dangerous conceptions.

Rationality and racism

Antiblack racism by philosophers, including the so-called philosophers of the Enlightenment, has been an integral part of the discursive practice known as Western philosophy. Since from the philosophical anthropological viewpoint of Western philosophy, a human being is fundamentally and primordially a rational being, any being lacking rationality cannot be human. Since black people are, according to Western philosophers, devoid of rationality, it follows that they are scarcely human. Examples of this kind of reasoning, belief and attitude abound; suffice it here to mention only a few. In his *The Spirit of Laws*, Montesquieu makes the following biting remark (a remark bordering on the absurd and the comical) about black people:

> Sugar would be too dear if the plants which produce it were cultivated by any other than slaves. These creatures are all over black, and with such a flat nose that they can scarcely be pitied. It is hardly to be believed that God, who is a wise Being, should place a soul, especially a good soul, in such a black ugly body...It is impossible for us to suppose that these beings [blacks]

should be men; because if we suppose them to be men, one would begin to believe we ourselves were not Christians. (1952: Book 15, Chapter 5)

Voltaire, one of Europe's leading voices for the equality of human beings and denouncer of the evil system of slavery, was more forthright in his antiblack racist sentiments. He declared that 'bearded whites, fuzzy negroes, the long-manned yellow races and beardless men are not descended from the same man...[White people] are superior to these Negroes, as Negroes are to apes and the apes to oysters' (in Poliakov 1974: 176). In *The People of America*, Voltaire wrote:

> The Negro race is a species of men as different from ours as the breed of spaniels is from that of the greyhounds. The mucous membrane, or network, which nature has spread between the muscles and the skin, is white in us and black or copper-colored in them...If their understanding is not of a different nature from ours, it is at least greatly inferior. *They are not capable of any great application or association of ideas and seemed formed neither for the advantages nor the abuses of philosophy.* (in West 1982: 62 – italics added)

Elsewhere he wrote the following about black people: 'Their round eyes, squat noses, and invariable thick lips, the different configuration of their ears, their woolly heads and the *measure of their intellects,* make a prodigious difference between them and other species of men' (in Mbembe 2017: 70 – italics added). It is clear from the above that for Voltaire, black people did not even belong to the human race. This sentiment is echoed by Hegel claiming that in black people, one finds nothing that suggests human kind: 'there is nothing harmonious with humanity to be found in this type of character' (1952a: 196–197).

The Scottish Enlightenment philosopher David Hume, in a now famous footnote to his essay 'Of national character', states:

> I am apt to suspect the negroes and in general all the other species of men (for there are four or five different kinds) to be naturally inferior to the whites. There never was a civilized nation of any other complexion than white, *nor even any individual eminent either in action or speculation.* No ingenious manufacturers among them, no sciences. On the other hand the most rude and barbarous of the white, such as the ancient Germans, the present Tartars, have still something eminent about them, in their valour, form of government or some other particular. *Such a uniform and constant difference could not happen in so many countries and ages if nature had not made an original distinction betwixt these breeds of men.* Not to mention our colonies, there are negroe slaves dispersed all over Europe, of which none

ever discovered any symptoms of ingenuity; though low people without education will start up amongst us and distinguish themselves in every profession. (in Eze 1997: 33 – italics added)

For both Voltaire and Hume, negro inferiority was a product of negro lack of 'understanding', 'association of ideas', 'speculation', 'ingenuity' and 'learning' – in short, lack of 'rationality'. Hume's racist theories became widespread and had a tremendous influence, for example on Kant. In *Observations on the Feeling of the Beautiful and Sublime*, Kant wrote:

> Mr Hume challenged anyone to cite a simple example in which a negro has shown talents, and asserts that among the hundreds of thousands of blacks who are transported elsewhere from their countries, although many of them have even been set free, still not a single one was ever found who presented anything great in art or science or any other praiseworthy quality, even though among the whites some continually rise aloft from the lowest rabble, and through superior gifts earn respect in the world. So fundamental is the difference between the two races of man, and it appears to be as great in regard to mental capacities as in color. (in Eze 1997: 55)

What Kant effectively says here in affirmation of Hume's theory is that Africans have contributed absolutely nothing to justify them being treated as human beings. Therefore, their life is worthless and dispensable compared to Europeans, whose justification for existence is supported by their creativity and 'civilisation'. Indeed, for Kant, a person's skin colour determines their rationality: "this fellow was quite black from head to foot, a clear proof that what he said was stupid' (in Eze 1997: 57). By virtue of their blackness, black people are excluded from the realm of the rational and civilised.[3]

Hegel's racism is perhaps better known within black philosophical discourse than in Western philosophical circles, where it is mostly unacknowledged.[4] Even the supposedly left Marxist philosophers prefer to be silent about it. In *The Philosophy of History*, Hegel claims that the African is wild and untamed ('[t]he negro exhibits the natural man in his completely wild and untamed state'), cannibalistic ('the devouring of human flesh is altogether consonant with the general principles of the African race'), undialectical ('a succession of contingent happenings and surprises. No aim or state exists whose development could be followed'), ungodly or without a religion (they 'have not the idea of a God'), and intractable and without history because they are incapable of any historical development or culture ('What we properly understand by Africa is the unhistorical, undeveloped spirit, still involved in the conditions of mere nature') (1952a: 196–199).

Kant presumably supporting slavery, counselled that a split bamboo cane be used instead of a whip so that the 'Negro' would suffer a great deal of pain, but without dying because of the 'Negro's thick skin'. Following in the footsteps of Kant, Hegel expressed a view on 'Africa proper' that contains colonialist ideological bases. In defence of African slavery in particular, Hegel states: 'Slavery is itself a phase of advance from the merely isolated sensual existence, a phase of education, a mode of becoming participant in a higher morality and the culture connected with it. Slavery is in and for itself *injustice*, for the essence of humanity is *freedom*; but for this, man must be matured' (1952b: 199 – italics in original). Slavery, as it becomes evident in *The Philosophy of Right* (1952b), is necessary for the possible emergence of 'ethical life' in the context of modernity. Hegel here in effect questions the humanity of Africans. For him, Africans are not human enough to deserve freedom and respect because they lack what is fundamental about existence, namely rationality.

From a philosophical point of view, one would think that since human capacity to reason is used as justification for racism, rationalism is the philosophical theory best suited to the promotion of racism than, for example, empiricism. However, classical empiricism not only fails to offer conceptual barriers to racism but also facilitates racism's articulation.[5] In fact, nowhere is the ideological primacy of reason a more dominant factor than in the liberalism articulated by the empiricists Locke, James Mill and John Stuart Mill. When we remember that the essential attributes of liberalism are individualism, equality, progress and – most importantly – the belief in 'reason', we become aware of liberalism's complicity in racism. Reason, according to liberals, is the common core residing in all individuals (that is, what is common among all human beings is the capacity not only to reason but also to be moved by reason). In his *Treatises of Government*, Locke, for example, argues that human beings are free and equal by virtue of their endowment with reason. Yet he did not only in practice participate in the slave trade by investing in it, but also defended slavery as justifiable in a just war. In his *Second Treatise on Government*, Locke defends slavery as follows:

> But there is another sort of servants, which by a peculiar name we call *slave*, who being captives taken in a just war, are by the right of nature subjected to the absolute dominion and arbitrary power of their masters. These men having, as I say, forfeited their lives, and with it their liberties, and lost their estates; and being in a *state of slavery*, not capable of any property, cannot in that state be considered as any part of *civil society*; the chief end whereof is the preservation of property. (1980: 45–46 – italics in original)

The *Fundamental Constitution of Carolina*, which the founding liberal Locke helped to draft, provides that every freeman (meaning white people) '[s]hall have absolute power and authority over his negro slaves'.[6]

What is evident from the above account is that human nature – whether construed as 'reason', 'rationality', 'morality', 'civility', 'culture' or in some other way – is fundamentally racialised since it is implicitly alleged to be a property exclusive to European males and not to black people. Whatever their differences, Montesquieu, Voltaire, Hume, Kant and Hegel all agreed that Africans and people of African descent are either subhuman or not human at all because of their putative lack of reason (*'logos'*, *'nous'* or 'rationality'). In short, the humanity of Africans – wherever they are – is either put into question or completely denied. Africana philosophy is to a large extent the philosophical articulation of a response to this denied humanity of African peoples. It is a response, especially by African and African-descended people, to the Westerners' (particularly the Enlightenment philosophers') constant calling into question of African humanity. It is this questioning of the humanity of people of African origin – as exemplified by, among others, Voltaire, Kant and Hegel – that animates the tradition of the philosophising enterprise known as Africana philosophy.

Africana philosophy

The phrase 'Africana philosophy' was coined and popularised by Lucius Outlaw as: 'a "gathering" notion under which to situate the articulations (writings, speeches, etc.) and traditions of the same, of African and peoples of African descent collectively, as well as the sub-discipline – or field-forming, tradition-defining, tradition-organizing reconstructive efforts which are (to be) regarded as philosophy' (1996: 76). As the gathering of practices and traditions of discourse, it is not only the philosophising of African and African-American thinkers, but also embraces the philosophy of all the people of African descent, wherever they are. In other words, for Outlaw, Africana philosophy is an 'umbrella' term 'under which can be gathered a potentially large collection of traditions of practices, agendas, and literature of African and African-descended peoples' (1996: 77). Under this umbrella may thus be included literature such as poetry, political writings, philosophical texts, art, proverbs and so on of Africans on the continent and Africans in the diaspora. It is an intertextually embedded philosophy that draws from a multiplicity of sources of black intellectual production. What unifies these diverse traditions into an Africana philosophy is not a set of symbols or geographical space or, for that matter, strictly racial or ethnic affiliation but rather the agendas, norms and practices that result from 'the effort to forge and articulate new identities and life-agendas by which to survive and to flourish in the limiting situations of racialized oppression and New World relocations' (Outlaw 1996: 89).

Outlaw is, however, quick to point out that Africana philosophy also includes the work of those who are neither African nor African-descended people but 'who recognize the legitimacy and importance of the issues and endeavors that constitute the philosophizing of persons African or African-descended and who contribute to discussions of their efforts, persons whose work justifies their being called "Africanist"'(1996: 76). A case in point is Sartre. I pay attention to the contributions Sartre made to Africana philosophy in the following chapter. Suffice to mention here that he has been hailed by various Africana and Western thinkers as a significant contributor to Africana philosophy in general.

Africana philosophy embraces a whole range of philosophical discourses and traditions such as African philosophy, African-American philosophy, black philosophy, Africana existential philosophy, black philosophy of existence, Afro-Caribbean philosophy and other traditions that have emerged from the socially transformative discourses and shared concerns of African and African-descended people in their resistance and struggle against slavery, imperialism, colonialism, racism and oppression in general. Such a philosophy, as Lewis Gordon explains, 'addresses problems across a wide range of philosophical and social issues' (1997b: 6). What unifies all these traditions under the umbrella of Africana philosophy is fundamentally shared concern over the dehumanisation or the denied humanity of African and African-descended people by systems such as slavery, colonialism and racism, which are given philosophical justification by the philosophical anthropologies of the dominant figures in philosophy that we witnessed above. The preoccupation with the systems that are quintessential expressions of antiblack humanity compels Africana philosophy to assume the mantle of a philosophical anthropology. This means that the starting point of Africana philosophy is neither metaphysics nor epistemology, but philosophical anthropology – the problem of the human being.

Philosophical anthropology, Lewis Gordon argues, should not be conceived of as bad anthropology. Etymologically, 'anthropology' means the science of 'man' or the study of human beings. However, many sciences besides anthropology claim that the study of 'man' is their main focus and concern, and many of them claim exclusiveness in varying degrees in this subject. Philosophical anthropology, unlike anthropology's descriptive approach, is a critical reflection not only on the human subject but also on the truth-claims of the various sciences which have the tendency to universalise the conclusions emanating from their particular focus into explanations of the total human being. Positively, it is the study of what is peculiar to humans as human beings. In short, philosophical anthropology has as its main focus the human condition. The existentialist Martin Buber defines philosophical anthropology as a systematic method which deals with the concrete, existential characteristics of human life in order to arrive at the wholeness and uniqueness of the human being:, 'Even as it must again and again distinguish within the human race in order to arrive at a solid comprehension, so it must put man in all seriousness into nature, it must compare him with other things, other living creatures, other bearers of consciousness, in order to define his special place reliably for him' (1967: 123).

A question arises here: What is this human being with which philosophical anthropology is so concerned? For Buber, a human being is a being whose existence is constituted by her participation in time and her existential relation to the cosmos, destiny, death, things and other similar beings. Buber's emphasis on the 'wholeness' of the human being is his existentialist rejection of the notion of traditional philosophy (as discussed above) that reason is the distinctive human characteristic. He writes: 'The depth of the anthropological question is first touched when we also recognize as specifically human that which is not reason... Human reason is to be understood only in connexion with human non-reason. The problem of philosophical anthropology is the problem of a specific totality and of its specific structures' (1967: 160). Since the dominant question of philosophical anthropology is 'What does it mean to be a human being?', and since the primary mission of Africana philosophy is concern over the humanity or personhood of beings whose humanity has been denied or called into question, philosophical anthropology becomes an important part of Africana philosophy.

The concern about lost humanness, about the denial of the person of certain people, is what Mills describes as the concern about 'subpersonhood'. According to him, a subperson is neither an inanimate object nor a non-human animal but 'an entity which because of phenotype, seems (from, of course, the perspective of the categorizer) human in some respects but not in others. It is a human (or, if this word already seems normatively loaded, a humanoid) who, though adult, is not fully a person' (Mills 1998: 6). Historically, this subpersonhood (often non-personhood) resulted in the treatment of humans – shall we, following Lewis Gordon as stated above, say – as 'property (slavery), as waste to be eliminated (genocides and holocausts) and as subhuman or animal (racism)' (2008: 13). When a similar question as the dominant philosophical anthropological question above is couched in the terms 'What does it mean to be a *black* human being in the world?' or 'What does it mean to exist, appear, live or emerge as a *black* human being in the world?', we move into what is known as Africana philosophy of existence or 'Africana existentialism'– which I have occasion to discuss in the subsequent chapters of this book. As lived-experience of black people in an antiblack world, Africana philosophy becomes not only a theoretical endeavour but also (as the Black Consciousness exponents conceived it) 'a way of life'. To this extent, Africana philosophy and Black Consciousness philosophy as 'an attitude of mind and a way of life' (Biko 1996: 91) become indistinguishable and consonant.

Philosophy as a way of life

As I suggested above, there is simply no single, determined and unquestioned way to appreciate the meaning and purpose of philosophy. One way may be to view it from two different and distinct perspectives, described by Hadot (1995) as philosophy for itself (discourse about philosophy or metaphilosophy) and philosophy in itself (lived philosophy). Sartre's notions of reflective (positional or thetic) consciousness and pre-reflective (non-positional or non-thetic) consciousness capture this distinction perfectly. As reflective philosophy becomes philosophy about philosophy, a pre-reflective philosophy *is* existence itself. Philosophy as taught at universities (academic philosophy) is constituted by several branches such as metaphysics, ethics, epistemology and logic, which form part of philosophical discourse or philosophy as a discipline about philosophy. This means that philosophy as taught becomes a theory of metaphysics, a theory of ethics or a theory of knowledge. According to this view, philosophy becomes scholastic in the sense that it becomes a discipline constituted by those who profess to be experts training those who want to be experts, 'professors who train professors, or professionals training professionals' (Hadot 1995: 270). In this sense, philosophy is indissolubly linked to the university, a precedence set by university professors such as Kant, Hegel, Husserl and Heidegger. This institutionalisation of philosophy has rendered those who operate outside the academy suspect philosophers (if indeed they are regarded as such) or not philosophers at all if they do not subscribe to the academic requirements of studying and obtaining degrees in philosophy, publish in esoteric journals meant specifically for 'experts', or write texts which can be taught in academic philosophy classes. Hadot explains: 'Modern philosophy is first and foremost a discourse developed in the classroom, and then consigned to books. It is a text which requires exegesis' (1995: 271). Consequently, discourse or professional philosophy has turned out to be 'the construction of a technical jargon reserved for specialist'. In terms of this view, therefore, the Black Consciousness philosophy and Steve Biko would not qualify as philosophy or philosopher respectively.

Many professional philosophers from the academy fail to make the transition from pure disinterested philosophical reflection (theory) to action (praxis). This amounts to what Yancy calls 'the historical process of "academicizing" philosophical practice' (2002: xi), the immediate results of which are the removal of philosophy from immediate existential problems of everyday life. Academic philosophy has become an insulated, abstract and obscure practice, a specialised study focused on discourses of technical problems. This approach to philosophy fosters 'the illusion that philosophers are pure minds capable of standing nowhere, free to understand the tremendous mystery and complexity of our presence here, our existence, how we come to know, what there is to know, and what we cannot possibly know' (Yancy 2002: xii).

Concerned about this professionalisation and institutionalisation of philosophy, Yancy poses a number of disturbing but relevant questions:

> Have professional philosophers become prisoners of the philosopher as *homo academicus*, where they are simply entertained by semantic and conceptual games played within academic space?...Is philosophy a cerebral game engaged in by those who deem themselves clever because they can formulate the most abstract and logically coherent arguments?...Is it about attempting to see the world from nowhere, peeling back, as it were, one's gender, race, historical situatedness, and biography? Is philosophy a lived existential project, a project that has profound implications for who we are and how we live as persons in the world? Indeed, is philosophy a way of being in the world where the entire self, the engendered, classed, sexed, racialized, and abled self with all of its idiosyncrasies is called upon? (2002: xvi–xvii)

From these questions, it is evident where Yancy's sympathies lie; they are located in philosophy as lived experience, philosophy-in-itself, philosophy as a way of being or (as Black Consciousness thinkers describe it) philosophy as 'a way of life'.

Philosophy as a way a life is independent of the academy because it develops outside the university environment. It does not indulge in exegeses or training students to be experts in philosophical discourse, but has as its fundamental project the radical and concrete transformation of the being of the individual, the bringing about of a certain way of being human. It does not attempt to construct a technical and obscure jargon reserved for specialists but proposes to communicate with the being of individual persons in their own lived-experiential language, the everyday-world language of ordinary people. As a way of life, philosophy thus means that philosophical reflection does not occur outside the social, political, historical and cultural contexts but is something that is fundamentally situated.

The American pragmatist philosopher John Dewey, emphasising the social and critical function in his philosophy, stated outright that his philosophy was fundamentally a result of his personal experiences – that, more than anything, it had emerged from people he had encountered and situations in which he had found himself. If philosophy emerges from the lived experience of the individual philosopher rather than from pure theoretical reflection, it simply becomes a way of life. Plato's portrayal of Socrates' life is a classic example of philosophy as a way of life. Socrates' life was exemplary precisely because of his 'existential practice of the norms that constituted his philosophy in the face of Athenian authority' (Yancy 2002: xvi). His life and philosophy were inseparable and synonymous, the one feeding on and becoming the other. From this perspective, as Yancy aptly observes, 'the life of a philosopher [is] internally related to his or her philosophy, [and] a philosopher's philosophy is also internally related to his or her life. On this score, life and philosophy constitute a symbiotic relationship' (2002: xvi).

It is through this very Socratic conception of philosophy as a way of life that Black Consciousness assumes its philosophical mantle. For the advocates of Black Consciousness, philosophy is not merely seeing the world from nowhere or with no point of view, but a way of being in the world in which the whole racial and classed self with all its perculiarities is involved. More fundamentally, Black Consciousness philosophy offers itself as a therapeutic philosophy, a philosophy intended to cure the black person's existential anguish. It offers itself as a way for achieving inner freedom and political independence, a consciousness where the ego depends only upon itself as expressed in the popular declarative 'Black man, you're on your own'. It emphasises the awareness of the power of the black self to free itself from everything oppressive.

Although often operating within the realm of academic philosophy, existentialism has been the closest philosophy to Black Consciousness's way of philosophising. In contrast to traditional Western philosophy's valorisation of rationality over existence, existentialism emphasises the lived experiences and lived reality of human existence here and now. From Kierkegaard's critique of Hegel's rationalistic system, it can be said that strictly speaking, existentialism is a reaction or a series of philosophical revolts against traditional philosophy's attempt to reduce human existence to abstract propositional terms and to incorporate and imprison the individual human being in an absolute universal system. For the existentialist thinker, philosophy must begin from the subjective, because the self and its anguish, happiness, anger, suffering and so on cannot be known through detached observation and contemplation, but must be inwardly appropriated. Hence, for existentialism, philosophy is not a purely intellectual pursuit but *a way of life*, a mode of being and experience. This Kierkegaardian conception is articulated by Sartre's attempt, in his existentialist approach, to deal more with the concrete and particular than with the purely abstract or universal. In an interview published as 'The Purpose of Writing', Sartre said:

> Today I think that philosophy is dramatic in nature. The time for contemplating the immobility of substances, which are what they are, or for laying bare the laws underlying a succession of phenomena, is past.

Philosophy is concerned with man – who is at once an *agent* and an *actor*, who...lives the contradictions of his situation, until either his individuality is shattered or his conflicts are resolved...It is with this man that philosophy, from its own point of view should be concerned. (1974b: 11–12 – italics in original)

For Sartre, therefore, philosophy is not abstract self-reflection and aloof contemplation but complete involvement in the drama of existence, the everydayness of lived experience. In this context, the philosopher surpasses philosophical speculation and becomes one with the activity of philosophising through her intense involvement with the problems at hand. Contrary to the contemplative approach of Western traditional philosophy, captured by a disinterested Cartesian spirit of reason as standing apart, Sartre – in line with the main tenets of existentialist philosophy – held that contemplation alone impoverishes the world and deprives it of its human richness and meaning. Philosophy – Sartre insists – is engagement, participation, involvement and commitment to, in, with and through the world. Hence, in his view, 'it is not in some hiding-place that we will discover ourselves; it is on the road, in the city, in the midst of the crowd, a thing among things, a man among men' (1970: 45). It is this contingent world of the existents, the world of things and human beings, which Sartre wants to grasp and uncover and disclose. As I later demonstrate, it is precisely this conception of philosophy as 'a way of life', as participation, involvement and commitment to, in, with and through the world that Steve Biko and the Black Consciousness Movement pursued and realised.

Because of their situatedness in a white supremacist world, Africana philosophers (both professional and non-professional, and including Black Consciousness thinkers) have hitherto grappled with the philosophical significance of being-black-in-an-antiblack-world. Hence traditional philosophical problems of ontological, epistemological, metaphysical or axiological nature are viewed in the context of the social, political and cultural problematic of existing in a white supremacist universe. In other words, Africana philosophy is a philosophy that is engaged much more in the particular lived experiences of African and African-descended people than with presumably universal and ahistorical philosophical views. Because of this particularity in blackness, Africana philosophers (as Mills observes) have been accused of being too preoccupied with race rather than with metaphysical and grand epistemological problems that have been the central pre-occupation of Western traditional philosophy.

Black Consciousness philosophy

Every philosophy originates from the conflict between what *is* and what *ought* to be. Some systems of philosophy prefer to maintain and defend what *is*, while others are desirous of changing what *is* to what *ought* to be. For some philosophies, what *is* counts as the most real; while for others, what is real is that which *ought* to be (that is, the 'ought-to-be' constitutes 'the most real reality' and therefore has to be brought into being because it is what matters most). Even in Hegel, what matters and ought-to-be is the self-realisation and self-consciousness of the German spirit; in Plato, what matters is the 'Philosopher King'; in Heidegger, what ought-to-be is authenticity; in Camus, it is the recognition of the absurdity of existence; in Sartre, what matters is 'freedom'; in Fanon, what ought-to-be is decolonisation; and in Nyerere, what ought-to-be is *Ujamaa*. What ought-to-be, therefore, stands in a dialectical relationship with what *is*. This means that what *is* and what *ought*-to-be do not stand in a purely external relationship with each other; neither what *is* nor what *ought*-to-be can exist without the other. The what *is* generates what *ought* to be, and what *ought* to be is a response to and a negation of what *is*. The upshot is that any philosophy that seeks to realise what ought-to-be has the function of helping rational human beings through rational thought to realise that reality.

The *is–ought* problem

I have just committed a putatively cardinal sin in philosophy, particularly in analytical philosophy, which is the logical question of the *is–ought* gap. The accepted 'truth' in analytical philosophy, especially in meta-ethics, is that one cannot derive an *ought* from an *is* – an issue known as the fact/value problem. Is it logically valid to draw an ethical value judgement from a purely factual (ontological) given? Put differently, is it permissible to deduce a value conclusion from purely factual premises? Made famous by Hume, the issue is that we cannot deduce imperatives from indicatives of the way the world is. Both Sartre and Heidegger seem to subscribe to this view. Sartre, for example, claims in *Being and Nothingness* that his phenomenological ontology is not and does not produce ethics: 'Ontology itself cannot formulate ethical precepts. It is concerned solely with what is, and we cannot possibly derive imperatives from ontology's indicatives' (1956: 625). In his book on ontology, *Being and Time,* Heidegger also disavows the connection between ontology and ethics or politics despite the fact that some of the concepts he uses in his ontology are morally encumbered. The problem with the *is–ought* question (also referred to as 'Hume's guillotine') is that it often brings about a 'cult of neutrality' according to which the philosopher's task is not to prescribe or make judgements but simply, in the manner of Wittgenstein, to analyse the logical geography of concepts and as such 'leave everything as it is' (Wittgenstein 1953: 49). From a political point of view, 'leaving everything as it is' simply becomes acquiescence with the status quo. Biko and the Black Consciousness philosophy went against the grain of conventional philosophy's acceptance of 'Hume's guillotine'. For Biko, what *is* can logically and politically lead to what *ought-to-be*, and what *ought-to-be* can in turn be derived from what *is*. Apartheid as a fact of life (as what *is*), for Biko, necessitates and demands its own overcoming into what *ought-to-be*: an apartheid-free society. This means that one can deduce political consequences from ontological concerns. For the Black Consciousness Movement, concern with the category of 'being' was also a political concern which could be called 'ontology of freedom'.

Agnes Heller (1984) offers an instructive metaphoric characterisation of philosophy, namely 'homesickness'. According to her, philosophy is homesick because it longs for truth and goodness. In other words, it longs for a world in which it will be home. Since every philosophy is a pursuit of truth and goodness, every philosophy assumes a rational utopia which becomes a home longed for. However, the moment that utopia (what ought-to-be) is realised, that particular philosophy has arrived home. This arrival signals the end of that philosophy's journey because in such a world, this philosophy is at home. Put differently, the transcendence of philosophy is the realisation of that which it longs for, and this realisation renders it unnecessary. Like desire, philosophies kill themselves on their satisfaction.

Like every philosophy, the Black Consciousness philosophy as a quest for true humanity would be fulfilled in a world where true humanity would be realised, a world where race would disappear and no one's humanity would be called into question. In such a world, the Black Consciousness philosophy would be superfluous and unnecessary. Indeed, in such a world this philosophy would disappear precisely because its journey would have ended since it had arrived home. In this respect, the Black Consciousness philosophy – like all other such philosophies – is a creator of a world, a philosophy that demands that the world become a home for humanity. Since by its very nature this philosophy maintains a healthy balance between theory (thought) and praxis (political action), its demand becomes the will of the people so that – as Heller puts it – it can be said, '[i]t did happen'. It is this movement from thinking to acting that makes the Black Consciousness philosophy a *radical philosophy*. It enjoins its adherents not only to think but also to act. While the thinking is directed to philosophical reflection (theory), the acting is aimed at political and social action. Together, theory and praxis are fundamentally connected to the rational utopia (what ought-to-be), with changing, altering or transforming society.

What do I mean by 'radical'? The word 'radical' comes from the word '*radicalis*', which means foundation or roots. However, in contemporary usage 'radical' refers to a total critique of an exploitative, hierarchical, racial, sexist and generally oppressive society. To say, therefore, that a philosophy is radical involves a number of propositions and functional expectations as set out by Heller (1984):

- Radical philosophy attempts to raise consciousness about relationships of domination and oppression and, in light of this conscientisation process, creates space for a critique of society. This critique should not only be total but also be in defence of its rational ideal and vision that seeks to substitute the existing oppressive one.
- Radical philosophy has to develop a social theory to enable it to determine the possibilities of what ought-to-be and how what ought-to-be is to be accomplished or made possible.
- Radical philosophy has to include the perspective of philosophical anthropology. Any philosophy usually constructs its system from an ideal of humanity. It has to investigate the social nature of human beings for it to counterpoise its philosophical anthropology with the dominant ideology.[7]

It is this last characterisation of radical philosophy as philosophical anthropology that animated the adherents of the Black Consciousness philosophy to ask the frightening and yet most fundamental question, 'What does it mean to be human in an antiblack society?' They raised this question because their humanity had been systematically called into question for over 300 years by the major authorities in philosophy, science, religion, mass media, culture and the vicious legacy of white supremacy.

The recognition of what ought-to-be constitutes the core function of philosophy – which in Césaire's phrase is the 'coming into consciousness' – and for Black Consciousness, the coming into consciousness was the achievement of freedom in an egalitarian society free from racism, oppression and sexism. But every philosophy has a representative. Ludwig Feuerbach represents materialism; Hegel represents, among others, idealism; Marx dialectical materialism; Nkrumah consciencism; Nyerere *Ujamaa*; West prophetic pragmatism; and so on. For Black Consciousness, Biko stands out as its most articulate representative. The representative of philosophy is the philosopher. However, every philosopher is a child of her time – even when such a philosopher vehemently rejects and attacks the needs, judgements, knowledge or prejudices of that very historical period. In rejecting the values and prejudices of her time, the philosopher simultaneously creates a new consciousness.

Conclusion

If any conclusion has to be drawn from the above exposition, it is that there is no one absolute philosophy or a single all-encompassing, universally agreed upon definition of philosophy. Hence, there also cannot be a single way or mode of philosophising or specific problems peculiar to philosophy. There are various and sometimes contradictory modes of philosophising, such that it actually becomes 'unphilosophical' to exclude any of them by dogmatically clinging to a narrow ideologically inflected arbitrary definition of what philosophy is.

The many disputes about the nature of philosophy are themselves a perpetuation of philosophy. For the existentialist, the philosophers of the past ignored fundamental problems of human existence. The logical positivists, however, accuse existentialists of uttering and making nonsensical meaningless propositions and statements. Alfred Ayer, a leading member of the logical positivist movement, for example refers to the doctrines of Heidegger and Sartre: 'Whatever may be the effective value of these statements, I cannot but think that they are literally nonsensical'; he continues about existentialism: 'What is called existentialist philosophy has become very largely an exercise in the art of misusing the verb "to be"' (1945: 15). Africana philosophy, on its part, accuses philosophy and philosophers of advancing a false universalism that in fact excludes the particularity of being-black-in-an-antiblack-world.

The above exposition does not in any way exhaust the vastness of philosophical doctrines, schools of thought, problematics and concerns. The intention was merely to familiarise the reader with the philosophical arena in which Biko is grounded.

Notes

1   For more information on the issues connected to the contestations in African philosophy, see for example Tempels' *Bantu Philosophy* (1959); Senghor's *On African Socialism* (1964) and 'Negritude' (1974); Cheik Anta Diop's *The African Origin of Civilization: Myth or Reality* (1974); Asante's *Kemet: Afrocentricity and Knowledge* (1990); Bernal's *Black Athena* (1991); Obenga's *Ancient Egypt and Black Africa* (1989); Bodunrin's 'The Question of African Philosophy' (1981); Hountondji's *African Philosophy: Myth or Reality?* (1983); Wiredu's *Philosophy and an African Culture* (1980); Oruka's *Trends in Contemporary African Philosophy* (1990); Tsenay Serequeberhan's *African Philosophy: The Essential Readings* (1991); and Ramose's *African Philosophy Through Ubuntu* (1999).

2   See Lewis Gordon's introduction to *The Edinburgh Encyclopedia of Continental Philosophy* (Glendinning 1999) for 'varieties of existentialism'.

3   In 'Physische Geography', Kant anticipates Hegel when he claims that black people are lazy, passive (note that for Hegel, they are not only passive but at the same time 'wild'), callous and thick skinned (in Neugerbauer 1991: 59). For a recent thorough engagement on Western philosophy's involvement in antiblack racism, see Achille Mbembe's *Critique of Black Reason* (2017).

4   For a critical discussion on Hegel's antiblack racism, see for example Outlaw's 'The Future of Philosophy in America' (1991), Asante's *Kemet: Afrocentricity and Knowledge* (1990), Ramose's 'Hegel and Universalism: An African Perspective' (1991) and Tsenay Serequeberhan's 'The Idea of Colonialism in Hegel's *Philosophy of Right*' (1989). On Hegel's racist views about South Americans and other Third World people, see Jorge Larrain's *Ideology and Cultural Identity* (1994).

5   For the connection between empiricism and racism, see for example Harry Bracken's 'Philosophy and Racism' (1978), Noam Chomsky's *Reflections on Language* (1975), Martin Baker's 'Racism and Empiricism' (1983) and David Goldberg's *Racist Culture: Philosophy and the Politics of Meaning* (1993). For a defence of empiricism against charges of racism, see Kay Squadrito's 'Racism and Empiricism' (1979).

6   For a useful account of Locke's involvement in slavery, see Wayne Glausser's 'Three Approaches to Locke and the Slave Trade' (1990) and David Goldberg's *Racist Culture: Philosophy and the Politics of Meaning* (1993).

7   For a sustained description of what radical philosophy is, see Agnes Heller's *A Radical Philosophy* (1984).

4

Biko and philosophy

The thing about Biko that appealed to me is that he doesn't conform to the standard Freedom Fighter image. Mandela might have been more topical but... he is very much in the tradition of Kenyatta or Nyerere, leaders of political movements. Steve Biko was much of a philosopher
— Richard Fawkes, *Sunday Star*, 31 May 1992

Biko the political philosopher.
— Xolela Mangcu, *Sunday Times*, 7 February 1999

DESPITE THE EPIGRAPH BY Fawkes locating Nelson Mandela primarily within a political leadership category, he also found his way into the philosophical terrain through the mediation and efforts of Derrida and Tlili's *For Nelson Mandela* (1987) and Presbey's *Fanon on the Role of Violence in Liberation: A Comparison with Gandhi and Mandela* (1996).[1] Although the Fawkes epigraph might be correct about Mandela and Kenyatta to some extent, it definitely misses the point in its exclusion and silencing of Nyerere from the philosophical realm of thought. However, in affirmation of the epigraph's assertion about Biko, this chapter (following in the footsteps of those whose philosophical efforts have been to locate Fanon within the philosophical space), is aimed at baptising Biko into and affirming his place within that terrain to be part of what Parry describes as 'the battle to disclose the dead victim's...[philosophical] claims' (1996: 12).[2] I believe that part of my mandate as a practitioner, interpreter, producer and engager in philosophical labour is to think about traditions of philosophical thought that grapple with what Anthony Bogues calls 'dead and erased bodies which speak' (2012: 34). In short, this chapter is an attempt to listen to and hear the voices or writings of those who have not only been silenced but also been excluded. In the previous chapter, I pointed out that every movement and every philosophy has a representative. I contend that more than anyone in the Black Consciousness Movement, Biko emerged as and took the mantle of the movement's philosopher.

As noted in the introductory chapter of to this book, Lewis Gordon points out that there is an ongoing tendency in certain quarters to lock black thinkers and their productions in the biographical moment and political activism. Biko also suffers as a result of this conception.[3] But, as I have argued in another publication (2008),

Biko was simply more than an activist; he was also a thinker. In the epigraph, Sono counts as an example of those who recognise Biko as 'a formidable and articulate philosopher', a philosopher not in the usual academic sense of a university professor but more precisely a man of theory and action, an 'organising philosopher', perhaps a sort of social and political lay philosopher. Mangcu repeatedly refers to Biko as a political philosopher. In Mangcu's view, 'Biko was a public philosopher in the tradition of Jean Jacques Rousseau, Mahatma Gandhi and Julius Nyerere'.[4] But to merely describe someone as a philosopher as Sono, Mangcu and Richard Fawkes do in the epigraphs is merely to state a generality without specificity. My aim in this chapter is to locate Biko within a specific philosophical tradition, namely Africana existential philosophy (black existentialism). I thus make the claim that Biko was a philosopher even though some people would regard this as a flight of fancy on my part. One reason for such scepticism is the modern conception of what constitutes a philosopher.

Who and what is a philosopher is a controversial issue which continues to be a problem for philosophy itself. In 2014, a symposium with the theme 'Who is a philosopher?' was held in South Africa.[5] It is often the case (especially at universities) that a philosopher is regarded as someone who holds some qualification(s) in philosophy, in particular a doctorate in philosophy. A referee of one of my journal articles on Biko objected that Biko can never be considered a philosopher in any imaginable sense since he could not have been formally trained as a philosopher while he was a student at the University of Natal's Medical School. But is philosophy practised only by those who have taken courses or have degrees in the discipline? As Lewis Gordon correctly points out, a person with a doctorate in philosophy is not necessarily a philosopher but may sometimes be correctly regarded as a scholar or even a teacher of philosophy instead of a philosopher (2000). A philosopher is an individual who has the capacity to make an original contribution to the development of philosophical thought and to the world of ideas irrespective of his training in the discipline. It comes as no surprise then that philosophers, in terms of this conception, are few in number and the majority of them do not possess a doctorate in philosophy. For example, a number of 'great' philosophers in the West hardly possessed doctorates or other qualifications in philosophy. Among these were St Augustine, St Thomas Aquinas and George Berkeley (priests); Descartes (a mathematician and physicist); Locke (a physician); Hume (a lawyer); Hegel (a theologian); Nietzsche (a philologist of Greek classics); Alfred North Whitehead, Bertrand Russell and Husserl (mathematicians); Du Bois (a sociologist); and Fanon (a psychiatrist). Indeed, most philosophers (for example Sartre, De Beauvoir, Karl Jaspers, Alfred Schutz and Kierkegaard) did not hold doctorates in philosophy or teach at universities.

Great philosophy appears to grow outside academic boundaries. Most academicians (particularly academic philosophy's gatekeepers) are guilty of what Lewis Gordon characterises as 'disciplinary decadence' or the 'ontologizing or reification of a discipline' (2006: 4). In this case, a decadent philosopher criticises all for not being philosophical, a decadent historian criticises others for not being historical, a decadent scientist criticises the humanities for not being scientific, and so on. As a response to this decadence, Lewis Gordon proposes what he calls 'teleological suspension' – that is, 'when a discipline suspends its own centring because of a commitment to questions greater than the discipline itself' (2006: 34). Ironically, the above-mentioned philosophers did exactly what Lewis Gordon suggests: effected a teleological suspension of their disciplines by going beyond the boundaries of the disciplines in which they were trained. Even though he was a medical student, Biko – just like the philosophers mentioned above – ventured beyond the limits of medical knowledge into the realm of philosophy. His writings and speeches are full of philosophical ideas, theories and fragments, though his concern was not specifically with theoretical abstractions but with the concrete and existential struggles which shape human (especially black) existence, alienation, self-consciousness, bad faith, dialectics, moral responsibility, identity, authenticity, freedom, African humanism and critique of liberalism. These problematics are the subject matter and concern of that tradition of philosophising known recently as Africana existential philosophy, which is a branch of Africana philosophy.

Intellectual and political influence

Philosophical doctrines and theories do not simply emerge in a vacuum. Every philosophy and philosopher emerges within a certain philosophical context or social milieu that leaves indelible marks on that philosophy or philosopher. Hence every philosopher is to some extent a product of being directly or indirectly influenced, positively or negatively, by some other philosophical doctrine or philosopher(s). A philosopher, therefore, is always affirming, opposing, modifying or transcending another philosopher's position – who in turn is doing or did do the same with his predecessors. So too is the case with Biko. The philosophy of Black Consciousness as articulated by Biko may be traced from a long line of black philosophical orientations and traditions such as Garvey's black nationalist movement, the Universal Negro Improvement Association; Du Bois and George Padmore's Pan-Africanism; Negritude; Nyerere's African socialism; and the Black Power Movement. Similarly, Biko's existentialist orientation may also be traced from the dominant figures in that tradition, such as Hegel, Césaire, Sartre, Jaspers, Fanon, Freire and Cone. Since most of these influences were dealt with in an earlier chapter, here I deal with only with those whose philosophical influence on

Biko is much more evident, namely Hegel, Sartre and Fanon. To understand Biko's philosophy, we have to first understand the philosophies of those whose influence on his philosophical outlook was significant.

Hegel

Sartre's influence on Biko and some members of the Black Consciousness Movement was through the mediation of Hegel's conception of consciousness. I have indicated how Pityana acknowledged the contribution of Hegel's conception of consciousness to the self-understanding of Black Consciousness adherents. Hegel, as Pityana points out, had become a very influential philosopher for Biko and his comrades: 'The very idea of *consciousness* is very Hegelian' (2012: 5). More than simply being a philosopher of consciousness, Hegel was for Black Consciousness members also a philosopher of freedom: 'Consciousness in the Hegelian construct is freedom, because it raises the capacity of willing the impossible to become possible, to think out of the box and to shape one's destiny' (Pityana 2012: 5). Biko, as Pityana recounts and indeed as it is evident in his writings, was fascinated by Hegel's dialectical principle of the identity of opposites – or put differently, the synthesis of opposites. For Pityana, it is this engagement with philosophy (regrettably unacknowledged) that 'brought into sharp relief the depravity of the environment we sought to challenge' (2012: 7). Hegel has a special place in black freedom struggles, his anti-African views notwithstanding. His master/ slave paradigm has captivated black revolutionaries' attention all over the world. It is to this paradigm that I now briefly turn to establish some of the significant philosophical nuances of Biko's thought.

   Hegel's philosophy is worked out in its most elaborate and sophisticated form in *Phenomenology of Spirit*. The importance of this for Biko was Hegel's articulation of the concepts 'consciousness', 'dialectic' and 'alienation', and the famous master/ slave dialectic. Hegel's conception of self-consciousness made Biko understand that it is consciousness of self as self that often generates the declaration and affirmation of one's own identity and deep commitment. According to Hegel, self-consciousness is precisely what distinguishes a human being from any other conscious being such as animals. Human beings as self-consciousnesses are conscious of who they are – their individuality, value and dignity. But, since self-consciousness refers to human reality and human reality in turn is primordially social, it is logical that 'self-consciousness achieves its satisfaction only in another self-consciousness' (Hegel 1977: 110). In other words, self-consciousness requires recognition from another self-consciousness in order for it to attain true self-consciousness. It desires recognition from another self-consciousness in order for it to be.

A dialectical process begins to emerge. By dialectic, Hegel means the pattern of development through inner conflict. For Hegel, it refers to a relationship that embodies opposition and interdependence at the same time. As a principle of change, dialectics proceeds through a three-stage logical process, what Hegel calls 'thesis, antithesis and synthesis'. He believes that reason, history and even nations follow this dialectical process in their development. It begins by laying down a positive thesis which is at once negated by its antithesis, and then a further combination of the two produces a synthesis. It follows a pattern of affirmation, denial and integration (pose–oppose–compose). The driving force behind dialectics, Hegel says, is the power of the negative, the antithetical moment. It is the pressure to overcome negativity which provides the dialectical process with its potency. The transcendence of the negative moment is accomplished through the act of negating the negation which ultimately constitutes the synthetic moment.

The first stage of the Hegelian dialectic is the encounter of two self-consciousnesses, each seeking recognition from the Other while simultaneously negating each other. It is, as Sartre would put it, 'a reciprocal relation of exclusion' (1982: 255). Each consciousness, in order to gain recognition, has to assert itself as the subject and impose itself on the Other. This situation turns into a bitter confrontation: 'The relation of the two self-conscious individuals is such that they prove themselves and each other through a life-and-death struggle' (Hegel 1977: 113–114). Dialectically overcoming this struggle results in the emergence of the master/slave relationship which ultimately, through its synthesis, ends in the disappearance of both the slave and the master – and thus of slavery as an institution. The relevance of this formulation to Biko's opposition to antiblack racism becomes clear. Antiblack racism is fundamentally the negation of black peoples' humanity. Black Consciousness as antiracism becomes a negation of the racist negation of black humanity (that is, a negation of the negation). The synthetic moment, which is the unity of opposites, would thus become an absolute affirmation of humanity – which in turn would bring about the disappearance of Biko's 'quest for humanity'.

Sartre

Sartre's name featured a number of times in the preceding chapters. His significance in the development of Biko's thought came, directly and indirectly, through the mediation of Fanon and Cone. Sartre's name and those of other existentialists feature quite regularly in the writings of Biko and the other Black Consciousness advocates. The attraction to Sartre was expressed by one of the leading Black Consciousness activists, Mandla Langa, in an interview with Lindy Wilson. According to Langa, 'we read the existential philosophers such as Jean-Paul

Sartre' (in Pityana et al. 1991: 29). Sam Nolutshungu observes that there was an evident 'interest in existentialism, phenomenology, and philosophical psychology... with explicit citation of Sartre' (1983: 156–157). Pityana states that Biko 'laid his hands on some philosophical writings like *Jean-Paul Sartre and made ready use of them*' (October 2002 – italics added). Indeed, Biko's characterisation of Black Consciousness in Hegelian terms distinctly and deliberately recalls Sartre's essay 'Black Orpheus' in which Negritude is described as an antithesis, the weak upbeat of a dialectical progression, a negative moment responding to the thesis white racism; in short, an 'antiracist racism' (Sartre 1988: 296). Certainly alluding to Sartre's essay 'The Republic of Silence', written during the German occupation of France, and its implications for speaking out without fear, Biko notes: There is no freedom in silence, Sartre discovered this to his dismay' (1972: 10). For both Biko and Sartre, silence in an oppressive society is not only a question of fear but also an indication of disengagement from radical political participation and thus the legitimisation of existing injustices. 'Our attitude is that the longer the silence, the more accustomed white society is going to be to that silence. And therefore the more stringent the measures are going to be against anybody who tries to undo that situation' (Biko, in Mngxitama et al. 2008: 29).

In a brief dialogue with Sartre and his concept of freedom, Biko states: 'We have to imprison ourselves in the ideal of humanity. Humanity is beyond freedom. To be human is to be more than free. Freedom is subservient to humanity, although Sartre believes that man is *condemned* to freedom; but I would hastily add that he is condemned to responsibility too, which is a human attribute' (1972: 7 – italics in original). As it will be evident later, Biko engaged several themes from Sartre's existential phenomenology: consciousness, dialectical understanding of racism, bad faith, moral responsibility, radical conversion, authenticity and so on. He used their insights to understand and explain the condition of black people in an apartheid society. Judging by the primacy of the concept of 'consciousness' in Biko's thought, Sartre's influence is unmistakable. In fact, Sartre provided conceptual tools, philosophical insights and political vision that played a key role in shaping the antiracist, anticolonial and anti-oppression thinking of black thinkers and activists in general. His philosophy became a source of personal, philosophical and political inspiration for most Third World radical black thinkers. As a result, he has been variously described as an 'African philosopher', a 'negro philosopher' (Mudimbe), 'the African philosopher' (Young) or 'Africana Philosopher', and a 'Third World philosopher' (Gordon). Finally, and significantly, Fanon describes Sartre as 'a friend of the colored peoples' (1967a: 133).[6] These descriptions are not accidental, imaginary or unfounded. Sartre was indeed one of the very few European philosophers who made colonialism and antiblack racism central concerns of his work. Unlike many white philosophers of his time and even after,

Sartre (together with De Beauvoir) lent a sympathetic ear to the voices and writings of black thinkers.

Through philosophy, literature, political essays, public speeches and political action, Sartre radically engaged some of the critical and vexing problems of his century: freedom, responsibility, authenticity, capitalist exploitation, colonial repression and racial oppression. He took measures to provide both a theoretically reasoned attack on these forms of oppression and domination and a practical means to combat them. Some of his major philosophical texts and political and social essays consequently became major influences on the leading political and social theorists of the Third World. Satre – mediated through prefaces to Fanon's *The Wretched of the Earth* (1968), Memmi's *The Colonizer and the Colonized* (1964) and Senghor's *Anthologie de la Nouvelle Poésie Nègre et Malgache de Langue Française* (1977); essays such as 'The Political Thought of Patrice Lumumba' (1963) and 'Colonialism is a System' (2001); the political and literary journal *Présence Africaine*; and a host of media publications about the colonial situation in Algeria and even in apartheid South Africa, South Africa – played a major role in placing racism, colonialism and other forms of oppression on the political, social and moral terrain and also on the philosophical landscape. Hence his contribution to anticolonial, anti-apartheid and antiracist struggles around the world. Among his direct contributions to antiblack racism are 'Black Orpheus' (1988); '*The Respectful Prostitute*' (1989); 'Black Presence' (1974c); 'Return from the United States: What I Learned about the Black Problem' (1997); Appendix II 'Revolutionary Violence' in his posthumous *Notebooks for an Ethics* (1992); and, closer to us, a statement at a press conference of the French Liaison Committee against Apartheid: 'Those Who Are Confronting Apartheid Should Know They Are Not Alone' (1966).

One of the reasons why Sartre regarded racism as a philosophical problem to be confronted had to do with his conception of the methodology and the content of philosophy, and what it should and can do. This conception, as articulated by its outstanding proponent the German philosopher Husserl, is known as phenomenology. In phenomenology, Sartre found a method which has an existential basis in everyday life. While Husserl 'brackets' judgements about the necessity of the world's existence, Sartre places existence (especially human existence) at the centre of his phenomenological inquiry precisely because, in his view, there can be no 'bracketing' of existence. While he agrees with Husserl's notion of 'intentionality' (that is, the notion that consciousness is always consciousness of something), Sartre rejects the Husserlian concept of intentionality in its cognitive sense. Instead, he imbues it with the concept of 'lived experience'. For Sartre, phenomenology without being a philosophical doctrine is in fact simply a method with which human existence may be described and examined. What he wants to achieve, therefore, is to 'reveal' or 'disclose' by means of the phenomenological method the 'being' of the human existent itself, to make manifest and to elucidate the phenomena of human experience or consciousness as they appear in their existential immediacy. This approach became known as 'phenomenological ontology' or existential phenomenology. As István Mészáros asserts:

> Having successfully liberated himself from the shackles of academic philosophy…Sartre is determined not to get involved in some other kind of academic operation which might turn out to be merely an intellectual method, a complicated erudite methodological procedure preserved for the few. He is looking for a method which has an existential basis in everyday life and is thus open to all. (1979: 104)

The contemplative approach leads to yet another overemphasised element in Western philosophical anthropology which Sartre questioned: rationality as a determinant of human nature. Western philosophy (in the manner in which the dominant voices of Plato, Aristotle, Descartes, Kant, Hegel and even Husserl conceived it) has always moved from what may be called, in a very broad sense, the standpoint of rationalism – the belief that the universe is rationally ordered, that it follows clearly formulated rational laws and that this rational world is inhabited by essentially rational beings who comprehend it. Hence the practitioners of philosophy have been rendered pure contemplators of a phenomenal world, thereby generating the dichotomy of knower and known, subject and object. The human knower (the subject) becomes constituted as essentially a rational being. Whereas Western philosophical anthropology looks for the human being in an *a priori* or presupposed definition of what constitutes the human, Sartre's philosophical anthropology moves from the standpoint that human existence comes before the definition of the human – put differently, in human reality, 'existence precedes essence' (1948, 1956).

Theories of 'human nature', as indicated in an earlier chapter, have been used to justify racism and racial inequality. Voltaire, Hume, Kant, Hegel and Locke all used the notion of rationality to question the humanity of black people. Sartre's existentialism proffers one of the widely known critiques of human nature and the legitimation of racism. The major premise of Sartre's *Being and Nothingness* is: There is no human nature. While the human person as conceived by traditional Western philosophy is a rational being who exists in a rationally ordered world, both the world and the human person are contingent for Sartre. The human person as consciousness, to start with, is nothing. It is not what it is because it is not any *thing* at all. In other words, Sartre inverts the Cartesian dictum from 'I think, therefore

I am' to 'I exist, therefore I am'. This rejection of the notion of human nature was simultaneously a rejection of determinism and an affirmation of human freedom. A consequence of this view is that if human nature is not given, then racism (as derived from this concept) is equally not given but a social construct intended to deal with or evade the contingency of our existence. This evasion of contingency constitutes a perfect example of what Sartre calls 'bad faith'.

The seeds of Sartre's antiracism were already planted by the time he wrote *Being and Nothingness*. His sensibility to the racial problematic is made manifest by the numerous examples involving raciality in the text. In Chapter 1 'Being and Doing: Freedom' of Part 4 of the text, no less than 10 references to or examples of 'race' and 'oppression' are used. In Section III, Chapter 3 'Being-With' (*Mitsein*) of Part 3, the 'We' is effectively a phenomenological account of group oppression that can easily refer to antiblack oppression and racism in general. Indeed, most of the categories applied in the text may validly have more explanatory power when applied to the lived experiences of black people as a group in an antiblack world, rather than specifically to intersubjective relationships. Consider, for example, how the notions of 'Us-object' and 'We-subject' translate to 'us' and 'them' categories in a racist society. Sartre's concepts of the 'Look', 'Otherness', 'the body', 'sadism', 'hate', 'situation', 'bad faith' and a host of others readily present themselves as tools for understanding antiblack racism. His statements that '[c]onflict is the original meaning of being-for-others' and '[h]ell is – other people' make profound sense within the context of group relations in an antiblack racist society. It is therefore not surprising that during the decade when *Being and Nothingness* was written, Sartre applied the ontological categories of that text to various other texts dealing with racism.

Consciousness as freedom

The central focus of Sartre's existentialism in *Being and Nothingness* is human freedom or consciousness as freedom (that is, the freedom to choose the form of self-creation and self-definition). The relation between human consciousness and objects is one of negation and this is partly because they are different modes of being. In other words, consciousness lacks the properties of objects and is therefore a lack of being. As a lack of being, consciousness is nothing (that is, empty), a sort of Locke's *tabula rasa*. This emptiness of consciousness suggests that consciousness is nothing more than intentional activity. Intentional activity or 'intentionality' is understood in the sense that every act of consciousness is always an embodied consciousness of something (an object) outside of itself, 'out there in the world'. A black consciousness is a consciousness that is conscious of its blackness or of its body as black in an antiblack world. Since consciousness is nothing (not an object), it is incomplete, unfulfilled and thus full of possibilities and free. A human being as consciousness – unlike things, objects or substances – possesses possibilities and the freedom to choose, act and define herself. For Sartre, the lack of being which characterises consciousness is synonymous with desire, and what consciousness lacks and desires is to be an object, since objects or things do not have freedom and as a consequence also lack responsibilities. In its desire to be like an object, consciousness wants to flee from its freedom and the responsibility that goes along with being free – and hence plunges into bad faith. Simply put, bad faith is the attempt by consciousness to avoid it being free by constituting itself as an object without freedom; it is a flight from one's freedom, from self and from others. But since human beings are freedom itself, we cannot escape from the reality and necessity of our freedom. We are, as Sartre says, 'condemned to be free'; in other words, 'we are not free to cease being free' (1956: 439).

Awareness of our freedom, Sartre argues, takes the form of anguish: '[I]t is in anguish that man gets the consciousness of his freedom, or if you prefer, anguish is the mode of being of freedom as consciousness of being; it is in anguish that freedom is, in its being, in question for itself' (1956: 29). In anguish, I find myself confronting myself as freedom and facticity ('facticity' is the word Sartre adopts to refer to a whole range of given facts which apply to me in the world, including my birth place, date of birth, socioeconomic status, height, hair texture, physical condition and skin colour, and the shape of my nose – in short, my racial constitution). In anguish, I realise that I constitute myself and that I am responsible for myself. In fact, *anguish is indistinguishable from a sense of responsibility* (Sartre 1974a: 159). But freedom, responsibility and anguish are unbearable. This discomfort necessitates a flight from my freedom, from confronting myself. It requires seeking comfort in certain untruths; it is, paradoxically, 'anguish-in-order-to-flee-anguish within the unity of a single consciousness' (Sartre 1956: 45). The attempt to avoid confrontation with anguish is doomed to failure precisely because in order to flee or hide, one must be aware of the anguish from which one is fleeing or hiding. This evasion of our freedom and responsibility, this refusal to confront ourselves, this flight from anguish, this attempt to achieve self-identity or self-coincidence in the manner of objects and things, Sartre named 'bad faith' (*mauvaise foi*). In simple terms, bad faith is a form of self-deception, consciousness lying to itself about its freedom.

In response to the question 'What is a human being?', Sartre (following Heidegger) argues that this question is *sui generis* or unique because it involves the questioner being the questioned. A human being, according to him, is 'a being such that in its own being, its being is in question' (1956: 47). However, in the act of questioning ourselves, we *change*. So the answer to the question 'What is a human being?' is not found already given in our nature. It is an answer we must *give* to ourselves. If human nature were given, it would be easy to construct a science of the human being capable of establishing human essence.

The look

A vexing problem Sartre had to deal with was the old philosophical problem of the existence of other human beings. The problem assumes the following form: How can I know that there are other conscious beings and not simply sophisticated high-tech humanoids inhabiting the world? Arguments purporting to establish the existence of other minds are, in Sartre's view, untenable precisely because they are based on epistemological claims and arguments from analogy. Most of them (notably the Cartesian, Hegelian, Husserlian and Heideggerian positions) are problematic because the Other is posited as an object of knowledge, which implies that the Other's existence can only be inferred through analogy with us, thus rendering them epistemologically probable (Sartre 1956: 233–252). According to Sartre, we do not experience other human beings as objects of knowledge but we have an immediate and direct experience of them through the *look* (*le Regard*). This does not pretend to be proof of the existence of other beings because if it was, it would constitute a theory of knowledge. On the contrary, the existence of the Other is established intuitively through the consciousness of being looked at. I encounter the Other through the *look*. The Other's *look* causes an immediate modification of my being. Through the *look*, the Other annihilates my subjectivity by making me an object, a thing, a mere body. Indeed, through the Other's *look*, I experience myself as an object that is looked at and seen by the Other. The Other, therefore, holds a secret about me which I have no privilege of accessing. The Other knows me better than I know myself. In short, the Other's *look* does not only strip me naked but also strips me of my freedom. This situation produces in me not only a sense of alienation but also acute shame. Shame, Sartre argues, is shame of *self*. 'In being ashamed I recognize the fact that I am indeed that object which the Other is looking at and judging. I can be ashamed only as my freedom escapes me in order to become a *given* object' (Sartre 1956: 261). In order to regain my subjectivity and my freedom, I have to return the *look* of the looker. Only in this way can I avoid being reduced to a perpetual thing in the eyes of the Other. This means that my subjectivity is dependent on my reducing the Other to an object while he, at the same time, attempts to do the same to me.

Sartre's understanding of the *look*, however, is a very special one – a look that can only be understood properly as '*the look*' or, more appropriately, the '*gaze*' or '*stare*'. Such a *look* can never be forgiving, sympathetic or loving. It is a condemnatory *look*, one that is objectifying, dehumanising, oppressive or hateful. It is the *look* that does not accept me as a subject but reduces me to a thing. It is clear then that Sartre cannot be referring to the look in general, but to a particular type of *look*. As we shall see later in this chapter, racism makes productive use of the dehumanising and objectifying *look*. Thus, in an antiblack world, *the look* that the racist directs at black people is best described by the Sartrean *look*. Through the Other's *look*, I discover my body, my racialised body. The Other's *look* constructs my body in its nakedness, 'causes it to be born, sculptures it, produces it as it is, sees it as I shall never see it. The Other holds a secret – the secret of what I am' (Sartre 1956: 364). It is precisely this special *look* that made Fanon complain: 'I am being dissected under white eyes, the only real eyes. I am fixed...I had read it rightly: It was hate; I was hated, despised, detested, not by the neighbor across the street or any cousin on my mother's side, but by an entire race (1967: 116, 118). It is this horrifying *look,* therefore, that Linda Alcoff refers to as 'fully justifying of all Sartre's horror of the Look' (2000: 31).

The existentialist categories enunciated above from Sartre's famous philosophical text are applied in three other texts dealing specifically with anti-Semitism and antiblack racism, namely: *Anti-Semite and Jew*, 'Black Orpheus' and *The Respectable Prostitute*. It is these texts that had tremendous influence on Third World thinkers, particularly black thinkers such as Fanon and later Manganyi, Biko and other Black Consciousness proponents.

In *Anti-Semite and Jew*, Sartre weaves categories of *Being and Nothingness* such as *choice, subjectivity, objectivity, bad faith, situation, authenticity* and above all *freedom* to deal with three portraits that emerge within the context of anti-Semitism: the anti-Semite, the liberal democrat and the Jew. Sartre gives attention to the following questions: What is anti-Semitism? Who and what is an anti-Semite? What is a Jew? What is an authentic or inauthentic Jew? His response to the first question is simultaneously a response to the second, a characterisation of the anti-Semite; for, in his view, the explanation of anti-Semitism must be sought not in the nature of the Jew but in the consciousness of the anti-Semite. His portrait of the anti-Semite is accordingly a sustained phenomenological description of the anti-Semite's adoption of certain evasive strategies to overcome the brute contingency of his existence.

I do not wish to pay much attention to this text except to say that as a book on anti-Semitism as racism, it had a tremendous impact not only on Biko's thought but more importantly on Fanon's book *Black Skin, White Masks*. Substitute the word 'Jews' with people', and then Sartre's existential phenomenology carries serious weight in the analysis of black people in apartheid South Africa and the diaspora. It was Fanon who actually successfully did the substitution and located it within an antiblack world, particularly the situation of black people in racist France.

'Black Orpheus', written in 1948 as a preface to Senghor's *Anthologie de la Nouvelle Poésie Nègre et Malgache de Langue Française* (a collection of poems by black people espousing a black outlook known as Negritude) demonstrates Sartre's ability to use poetic tools to give expression to philosophical insights and categories of *Being and Nothingness*. I here briefly consider two such categories (namely *otherness* and its correlate the *look*) and the dialectic. It is this philosophical orientation of the text that many Sartrean critics ignore or fail to grasp when discussing it, and therefore it justifies revisiting these categories. In a sense, the essay is fundamentally a text about the dialectics of black otherness in a white world.

Working on the myth of Orpheus, Sartre argues that the black person in the midst of slavery, racism and colonial alienation must continuously descend into the depths of his soul to reclaim his blackness. Earlier we noted how, for Sartre, the Other's *look* intuitively makes us aware of his existence; how this very *look* robs us of our subjectivity; and how, in order to regain this subjectivity, we must objectify the Other by returning the look. The opening paragraph of 'Black Orpheus' is an address to white people in which Sartre, with his usual dramatic fashion, applies the notion of the *look* to enact the significance of the destructive look of Orpheus. He remarks:

> Here are black men standing, looking at us, and I hope that you – like me – will feel the shock of being seen. For three thousand years, the white man has enjoyed the privilege of *seeing without being seen*; he was only a look – the light from his eyes drew each thing out of the shadow of its birth; the whiteness of his skin was another look, condensed light. The white man – white because he was man, white like daylight, white like truth, white like virtue – lighted up the creation like a torch and unveiled the secret white essence of beings. Today, these black men are looking at us, and our gaze comes back to our own eyes. (1988: 291 – italics added)

The reference to '*seeing without being seen*', I suggest, was not accidental but designed to recapture the themes articulated in *Being and Nothingness*, namely: the *look*, Otherness and the impossibility of the fundamental project to become God in the face of contingency. First, there is the suggestion that the white person has attempted to be God, to possess the qualities and properties ascribed to God, the Other *par excellence*, the unlooked-look or the uncaused-cause *causa sui* (cause or generated of itself). But if the white person assumes the role of God, the 'unseen-seeing', then the reaction of black people will be that of perpetual shame and collective objectness. In shame, Sartre argues, I am ashamed of what I am. In other words, in shame, I recognise that I am as the Other sees me. Therefore, shame is shame of myself before the Other who looks at me.

Since to be God is to be one's own foundation, one's existence needs no justification. But to have one's existence justified and necessary, to be one's own foundation, is to be superior to those whose existence is superfluous, without foundation and lacking something. Indeed Sartre's statement, directed against white people but of course including himself as a white man, is a clear reference to the failure of the project to be God: 'We think we are *essential* to the world... European with divine right, [yet] *we are accidental*...eaten away by these quiet and corrosive looks' (1988: 291 – italics added).

In 'Black Orpheus', Sartre is actually saying to his white audience that the 'chips are down' and the game is over, that whatever exists (including himself) need not be as it is, need not be at all. No one, no thing, exists by right – even divine right – or by necessity. No human being *is* existentially justified precisely because no human being is God. Since the *look* has been reversed, white people are no longer the 'unlooked-look'; they have been seen and exposed by the black *look*. The *look* has been returned because Negritude or 'Blackness has been rediscovered' (Sartre 1988: 298). Because the black *look* is a returned gaze, a *look* against a white *look*, it assumes the character of negation – an antithetical quality. It is this conception that explains Sartre's unfortunate and controversial description of Negritude as the antithetical moment, a weak upbeat of a dialectical progression in the face of white supremacy, an '*antiracist racism*' (Sartre 1988: 296). For him, Negritude 'appears like the upbeat [unaccented beat] of a dialectical progression: the theoretical and practical affirmation of white supremacy is the thesis; the position of negritude as the antithetical value is the moment of negativity' (1988: 327). However, Negritude cannot only be frozen at the antithetical moment because it is not an 'arrival at' but a 'crossing to', a simple 'going-beyond-itself'. This going-beyond is the synthetical moment which is the 'realization of the human being in a raceless society' (1988: 327). Put differently, Negritude aims at its own destruction at the moment of synthesis; it kills itself on its realisation of a raceless society.

An authentic black person, just like an authentic Jew, must recognise his facticity at the same time that he recognises his transcendence. He must recognise the fact that he is black and proclaim himself black: 'Having been insulted, and formerly enslaved, he [the black man] picks up the word "nigger" which was thrown at him like a stone, he draws himself erect and proudly proclaims himself a black man, face to face with white men' (Sartre 1988: 296). The burden of the black person, therefore, is to '*oblige those who have vainly tried throughout the centuries to reduce him to the status of a beast, to recognize that he is a man*' (1988: 296 – italics added). The first necessary step towards liberation from racial oppression, according to Sartre, is the achievement of a Black consciousness; the black person '*must first of all become conscious of his race*' (1988: 296 – italics added). This is not just a self-recovery project but also the recognition by black people that they are oppressed first as black people. What this recognition requires is an act of black solidarity as separation from the oppressor group, a moment of negativity, of separation, of Black consciousness, of black solidarity or negritude – in short, 'antiracist racism'. All these insights, as we will see later, are found in Biko's philosophy and often constitute the foundation of his thought.

Fanon

Lewis Gordon quite rightly points out that what is significant about Sartre is that he speaks to black thinkers in a way that no other white thinker does or has done. His phenomenological account of freedom as a fundamental characteristic of the condition of being human, of the contingency of human existence; the centrality of the concept of consciousness and its incompleteness; his focus on the necessity of freedom, of existing authentically in an oppressive racist situation – these immediately appealed to and made his thoughts attractive to those whose existence and humanity are/were either denied or called into question. We should be careful, however, not to assume that black existential philosophy is a fundamentally Sartrean phenomenon. Sartre merely stands as an uncommon catalyst in black philosophy of existence. For this reason, Lewis Gordon's warning makes a lot of sense:

> [A]lthough there are Africana philosophers who have been influenced by both Sartre and European thought, it would nevertheless be fallacious to assume that that influence functions as the cause instead of the opportunity. Africana philosophers already have a reason to raise existential questions of liberation and questions of identity...by virtue of racial oppression...Africana philosophers' choice of European thinkers through whom to consider these questions is, therefore, already existentially situated. To place European thinkers as cause would be to place the proverbial cart before the horse. (2000: 9–10)

To appreciate Biko's philosophical orientation, a brief account of Fanon's work and ideas is appropriate. It is true that Biko cites Fanon's *The Wretched of the Earth* extensively, but it is Fanon's first book – *Black Skin, White Masks* – which in my opinion had a greater impact on Biko's philosophical position and its relevance to Black Consciousness as philosophy. Because it contains philosophical (especially existentialist) and psychoanalytical insights and references, most readers of the latter text consider it very difficult and indigestible. As David Macey points out, Fanon's materials when he wrote *Black Skin, White Masks* 'were the phenomenology of Sartre and Merleau-Ponty, the cultural discourse or tradition of negritude...and the fragments of psychoanalytic theory' (2000: 162–163). Indeed, the existential phenomenology of Sartre's *Being and Nothingness* and *Anti-Semite and Jew*, Merleau-Ponty's *Phenomenology of Perception* and Hegel's *Phenomenology of Mind* provided Fanon with the necessary analytic tools. Macey is definitely not off the mark when he declares that of all the theories available to Fanon in the Paris of the 1940s, existential phenomenology turned out to be 'the most useful and most concrete' (2000: 163). So, one could make a case that the text is a phenomenological work; however, as Lewis Gordon notes, one would have to add that the existential imports in it make it an existential phenomenological work. Though the work may be classed an existential phenomenological text, there are differences between Fanon's phenomenology and that of the German philosopher Husserl (considered by many to be the father of phenomenology). While Husserl talks of the primacy of the Transcendental Ego, Fanon talks of the lived experience – especially the lived experience of black human beings.

To be sure, the main categories in Fanon's text (for example, the notion of otherness, the white 'look' and black invisibility, and black bodily presence in the world – in short, being-black-in-the-world) resonate with Sartre's and Merleau-Ponty's existentialist ideas. Fanon readily acknowledges his relationship to Sartre. After completing *The Wretched of the Earth,* Fanon reportedly wrote a letter to his publishers asking them to speed up the publication of the book and to ask Sartre to write the preface:

> The state of my health having improved slightly, I have decided to write something after all. I must say that I was asked insistently to do so by our own people...Trusting that you'll satisfy my request, I would like to ask you to speed up the publication of this book: we need it in Algeria and Africa... Ask Sartre to write a preface. Tell him that each time I sit down at my desk, *I think of him who writes such important things for our future but who as yet has found no readers...at all.* (in Cohen-Solal 1987: 433 – italics added)

Another biographer of Sartre, Ronald Hayman, reports that although having been diagnosed with leukaemia, Fanon took a short break from writing the book to travel to Rome where he met with Sartre and De Beauvoir to discuss the introduction which Sartre enthusiastically agreed to write for *The Wretched of the Earth.* Fanon and Sartre reportedly spent 40 hours non-stop in discussion until De Beauvoir complained about Sartre's lack of sleep. Fanon's response was, 'I don't like men who hoard their resources'. Subsequently, Fanon told Claude Lanzmann: 'I'd give twenty thousand francs a day if I could talk to Sartre from morning till night for two weeks' (in Hayman 1987: 384–385). The attraction of Sartre's existential phenomenology was, for Fanon, 'its immediacy and its concentration on the category of experience. It was also a philosophy of freedom' (Macey 2000: 163–164). Even then, existential phenomenology had to be adapted to the 'lived experience' of black people.

Existential phenomenology (lived experience)

Fanon studies have recently been characterised into several developmental stages by Lewis Gordon, namely: reactionary, biographical, colonial (anticolonial and post-colonial), social and political, and pragmatic.[7] To this, I would add the existential phenomenological approach of Lewis Gordon, in which I locate Biko. This stage finds the most articulate expression in *Black Skin, White Masks*, which Francis Jeanson described as a hymn to human freedom. This is not to say that the other three texts by Fanon lack a philosophical orientation; their impact in this tradition is minimal compared to the first work. The entire book, from Chapter 1 to Chapter 7, is a phenomenological description of the consciousness of a black person existing in an antiblack world. In this world, black people are told in various ways (language, interracial relationships, psychology, psychopathology, philosophy and their existential lived experiences) that since they are not white, they are not human. In any attempt – through each of these ways – the black subject makes to simply live as a human being, he soon discovers that being human actually means being white. The black subject, therefore, ultimately finds himself locked in a 'zone of nonbeing' (Fanon 1967a: 8). In other words, antiblack racism constructs whiteness as the 'normal' mode of 'humanness'.

This basic existentialist concept of a 'zone of nonbeing' is applied as a phenomenological description of the conditions of black self-consciousness in the face of negative reflections of blackness. In doing this, Fanon simultaneously appropriates and deploys the language of the philosophical tradition of both Sartre and Hegel. For example, he inherits Sartre and Hegel's distinction between 'being-in-itself' and 'being-for-itself' and also Heidegger's notion of 'human reality' popularised by Sartre. In a passage that had an impact on Biko, the manner in which he lived his life and the manner in which it was ended in conflict, a life whose fundamental aim was to 'go beyond the life toward a supreme good', Fanon wrote: 'Thus human reality in-itself-for-itself can be achieved only through conflict and through the risk that conflict implies. This risk means that I go beyond life toward a supreme good that is the transformation of subjective certainty of my own worth into a universally valid objective truth' (1967a: 218).

In the introduction to *Black Skin, White Masks*, Fanon spells out his intentions in writing the book: to liberate the black subject from the 'zone of nonbeing' imposed by the racist society. Since the black subject is regarded as non-human, 'I propose' Fanon declares, 'nothing short of the liberation of the man of color from himself' (1967a: 8). Why is this liberation from the self? Because the black self desires to be white. Why does the black self desire to be white? Because '[t]here is a fact: white men consider themselves superior to black men' (1967a: 10). The black subject's internalisation of this fact forces Fanon to conclude: 'For the black there is only one destiny. And it is white' (1967a: 10). This destiny is precisely what Fanon wishes to disclose and destroy. He then proceeds to inform us that the last two chapters of the book will be '...an attempt at a...philosophical explanation of the *state of being* a Negro' (1967a: 13); in other words, the ontological status of being black. It is here that Fanon questions the applicability of Sartrean ontology to black people. He wonders whether the phenomenological description used by Sartre or Hegel is appropriate for dealing with the ontological status of the black person. Put differently, he questions the explanatory power and efficacy of ontology for the situation of black people in an antiblack world. His answer is that such an ontological analysis of the mode of being-black-in-the-world is inadequate and inappropriate: 'Though Sartre's speculation on the existence of The Other may be correct (to the extent, we must remember, to which *Being and Nothingness* describes an alienated consciousness), their application to a black consciousness proves fallacious. That is because the white man is not only The Other but also the master...' (Fanon 1967a: 138, footnote). Furthermore, Fanon writes:

> As long as the black man is among his own, he will have no occasion, except in minor internal conflicts, to experience his being through others. There is of course the moment of 'being for others' of which Hegel speaks, but every ontology is made unattainable in a colonized and civilized society...In the *Weltanschauung* of the colonized people there is an impurity, a flaw that outlaws any ontological explanation...Ontology – once it is finally admitted as leaving existence by the wayside – does not permit us to understand the being of the black man. For not only must the black man be black; he must be black in relation to the white man. (1967a: 109–110)

This, however, is not to say that Fanon rejects ontology in itself. His point is that classical or traditional ontological descriptions cannot explain the existential dimensions of black people. While the main object of Fanon's criticism is Hegel, it may erroneously be assumed that it applies with equal force to Sartre, whom Fanon describes as a 'born Hegelian'. For Fanon, Hegel's ontology is speculative and without reference to the actual existential situations of concrete living human beings, especially black people. This ontology leaves 'existence by the wayside', and thus makes it impossible for us to understand the existential situation of the black person. This critique of ontology is definitely not critique of any and all ontology. It is criticism of this particular Hegelian ontology. When Fanon describes Sartre as a 'born Hegelian', the reference is not in relation to ontology but to Sartre's appropriation of Hegel's dialectic which Fanon himself uses. What Fanon – indeed Sartre as well – objects to, is traditional or Hegelian classical ontology. Both believe that being human is neither ontology nor ontological. Being human *is* the critique of traditional ontology; it positively raises the negative. It is this ontology that Fanon endorses in his final prayer, 'O my body, make of me always a man who questions!' (1967a: 232).

One of the most formidable chapters in *Black Skin, White Masks* which to my mind captivated Biko's attention is Chapter 5: 'The Fact of Blackness' – a translation that is contestable in view of its original French title '*L'expérience vécue du Noir*', which could also be correctly translated as 'The Lived Experience of the Black Person'.[8] The chapter is a phenomenological description of being black in an antiblack world. In an autobiographical mood, Fanon explains that he 'wanted to come lithe and young into a world that was ours and to help to build it together... All I wanted was to be a man among other men', but this desire was frustrated by the fact of his blackness in an antiblack world. Here, recounting his experiences during an encounter with a little white boy, Fanon echoes Sartre's theory of '*The Look*'. On seeing Fanon, the young boy exclaimed in horror to his mother: 'Look Negro!'...'Mama see the Negro! I'm frightened!' Fanon's description of his self-consciousness at that moment is similar to Sartre's description of being seen in *Being and Nothingness*: 'I am being dissected under white eyes, the only real eye, I am fixed...My body was given back to me sprawled out, distorted, recolored, clad in mourning in that white winter day. The Negro is an animal, the Negro is bad, the Negro is mean, the Negro is ugly...I found that I was an object in the midst of other objects' (Fanon 1967a: 109, 113, 116). Recall that, for Sartre, the Other's *look* causes an immediate modification of my being. Through the *look*, the Other annihilates my subjectivity by making me into an object, a thing, a mere body. Indeed, through the Other's *look*, I experience myself as an object that is looked at and seen by the Other. In short, the Other's *look* strips me of my freedom. This situation produces in me not only a sense of alienation but also acute shame. Shame, as we noted above, is for Sartre shame of *self*. Being ashamed of myself is recognition that indeed I am the object the Other is looking at. In an antiblack world, Fanon argues, the black person is only black in the eyes of the white person; he loses his blackness to the white person. In rebellion, the black person has to reclaim his blackness, hence Fanon declares: 'I resolved, since it was impossible for me to get away from an *inborn complex*, to assert myself as a BLACK MAN. Since the other hesitated to recognize me, there remained only one solution: to make myself known' (1967a: 115 – italics in original).

Being the object of the Other's look is a classic example of Sartre's notion of 'being-for-others'. Fanon suggests that in an antiblack world, Sartre's third ontological dimension of the body (that is, the consciousness of one's body as a body-for-others) dominates black bodily experience. The disequilibrium between the body-for-itself and my body as a consciousness of being known as a body for the Other is made manifest to Fanon by the little boy's proclamation. As seen and known by the white Other, Fanon realises that his body is of a different (dark) skin colour. His consciousness of his body as seen by the Other thus became a consciousness of blackness. This mediation between our interiority and exteriority, between the way we live and exist, our bodies and the way others see them, is precisely what is unique to racialised identities as opposed to, for example, ethnic identities. From the child's remarks, it becomes evident that the concepts of race and racial identity are predicated on the kind of body one is. For Fanon, the body for black people thus necessarily becomes central in an antiblack world in a way that it does not for white people (even for white Jews), since this is the visible marker of black invisibility. For black people, it is actually not their bodies or the colour of their skin in and by itself that matters; it is the meaning and significance attached to the colour 'black' that is at issue. Since the colour 'black' cannot exist in and by itself, since it has to be the colour of something (in this case the body), the body assumes an existential significance without which racism cannot be understood. Liberation from the objectifying look of the Other rests on re-appropriating my subjectivity and freedom from the Other by a return of the look. However, more is needed for a black person than just merely returning the gaze.

Resonating with Sartre's prescription of black liberation through Negritude and black solidarity, and Jews through Jewish authenticity and solidarity, Fanon insists that to transcend their overwhelming sense of alienation and to regain their dignity and self-esteem, black people must undergo what in the previous chapter I referred to as the 'radical conversion'. They must not only liberate their consciousness from sedative Western values but must also learn to accept their blackness in an authentic manner: 'I resolved...Since the other hesitated to recognize me, there remained only one solution: to make myself known' (Fanon 1967a: 115).

Fanon's engagement with Sartre is also evident not only in his application of some of Sartre's insights into anti-Semitism but also in his severe criticisms of the ontology of Sartre's *Being and Nothingness* and Negritude. In 'Black Orpheus', Sartre characterised Negritude as an 'antiracist racism', a negative moment in a dialectic whose synthetic moment would be a universal humanism, a situation or society in which the colour of one's skin would be considered purely contingent or accidental. It is this location of Negritude at the moment of negativity in the dialectic to which Fanon objects. Although Sartre correctly pointed out that Negritude was a response to white racism, Fanon argues that Sartre's view should be rejected for several reasons. First, Fanon rejects Sartre's suggestion that black people must be the only ones to renounce their race pride in favour of the synthetic moment: universal humanism. Second, he thinks that Sartre failed to grasp the lived experience of black people and the dimensions of their need for liberation. In other words, Sartre failed to understand the embodied nature of black experience: 'Jean-Paul Sartre had forgotten that the Negro suffers in his body quite differently from the white man' (Fanon 1967a: 138). Third, Sartre's dialectic implied that the meaning black people chose in confronting white racism was predetermined by that very white racism. Even in the act of resistance, the theme of the action of black people is already created by white people. Thus black antiracism is purely a reactive response to an agenda already determined. A serious question to this kind of objection is: What else should it be? Fourth, while agreeing with Sartre's ultimate vision of depoliticising identity, he objects to the fact that Sartre's final utopia seems to exclude black identity. Lastly, what seems to agitate Fanon more than anything is the fact that in the phrase 'antiracist racism', a concentrated focus is on the term 'racism' – which implicitly is intended to point an accusatory finger at the victims of racism as the ironic perpetrators of that to which they are victims: racism. It is this appearance of blaming the victim that seems to enrage Fanon.[9]

Furthermore, Fanon's reaction is directed towards the one-sidedness of Sartre's account of consciousness and Negritude. For Sartre, negativity describes the being of consciousness as freedom. Since consciousness constitutes itself as a lack of being, it therefore 'arises in the world as a *Not*; it is as a Not that the slave first apprehends the master' (Sartre 1956: 47). In Fanon's view, however, human consciousness is not simply a NO – a negation; it is also equally a YES – an affirmation of being, of life, of existence. Negritude, as described by Sartre, is not simply a NO to the degrading look of racism but also a YES to and an affirmation of black humanity. Therefore, it is strange for him to portray it as simply a negation, an antithetical moment. As Fanon points out: 'Man is not merely a possibility of recapture or of negation. If it is true that consciousness is a process of transcendence, we have to see too that this transcendence is haunted by the problems of love and understanding. Man is a *yes* that vibrates to cosmic harmonies...But man is also a *no*...No to the butchery of what is most human in man: freedom' (1967a: 8, 222 – italics in original).

Fanon's criticism of Sartre should not be simply taken as a rejection of Sartre's dialectical explanation. To be sure, he applies Sartre's dialectic in two distinct ways: economic and psycho-existential. First, the dialectic applies to the economic exploitation Africans suffer at the hands of Europe. The thesis is European economic exploitation; the antithesis is the African social revolution; and the synthesis is a new social and economic order – socialism. In its latter form, Sartre's influence becomes evident. The thesis is white racism, the antithesis is Negritude (or what Fanon calls 'white mask'); and the synthesis is a new humanism in a world where racism has disappeared. Akin as this is to Sartre's dialectic, there is disagreement about the synthesis. For Sartre, a socialist society is by definition a humane society without racism. For Fanon, however, the new humanism of the synthetic moment is not necessarily a socialist humanism. To put it differently, a revolutionary decolonisation does not necessarily lead to a socialist society; it may or it may not.

As suggested earlier, we should be careful not think that Fanon's ideas have their origin in Sartre's philosophy. Although he was influenced by Sartre, it will nevertheless be an error to assume that this influence functions as a 'cause' rather than a consequence; Fanon is not Sartrean. His writings, especially *Toward the African Revolution, A Dying Colonialism* and certainly *The Wretched of the Earth*, testify to his intellectual originality. Besides, his lived experience of racism in Paris had already provided him with sufficient grounds to raise existential questions of being-black-in-the-world, black identity, authenticity or black liberation independent from Sartrean influences. Furthermore, a number of other important thinkers such as Freud, Marx, Jacques Lacan and Césaire, may just as well claim to have had an influence on him. Césaire, for example, occupied a special place in Fanon's life. Fanon's discovery of his being-black-in-the-world (Paris) and his acceptance of this factical condition, suggests the influence of Negritude on him, especially in *Black Skin, White Masks*. Paying tribute to his former teacher, Fanon admits that Césaire taught him 'that it is fine and good to be a Negro'. Rather than merely being influenced by these thinkers (especially Sartre, Césaire and Hegel), Fanon seriously confronted, interrogated and engaged their ideas in relation to the situation of the black subject in an antiblack context. While he appropriated the Hegelian master/slave paradigm, as well as Marx's concept of alienation and Sartre's notion of consciousness and the Other, he considered Sartre and Hegel's ontological views inadequate when applied to the situation of black subjects and, in the tradition of black radical thought, questioned Marx's class analysis in the colonial context.[10]

A glance at Biko's *I Write What I Like* and his numerous interviews indicates the importance of Fanon's thought in Biko's philosophical development. Besides the numerous references to Fanon in the book, some of the chapter titles directly echo Fanon. For example, 'Black Souls in White Skins', 'Black Consciousness and the Quest for Humanity' or 'White Racism and Black Consciousness' clearly reiterate and resonate with the Fanon of *Black Skin, White Masks*. As I indicate in my article 'Locating Frantz Fanon in (Post)Apartheid South Africa' (2017), many of the philosophical issues such as racism, alienation, identity and racial consciousness raised in Fanon are reworked and applied within the South African context.

Even though this chapter situates Biko within the existentialist philosophical tradition, it does not suggest that there were no other traditions that had an influence on him. From the point of view of political philosophy, the early influence of liberalism is evident even though liberals and their distinctively South African liberalism came under serious critique from Biko. African humanism (as propounded by leading thinkers in Africa such as Nkrumah, Kaunda and even Banda) and Marxist socialism, especially its African variant as articulated by Nyerere's African socialism and Amílcar Cabral's culture as an instrument of struggle, had a direct or indirect influence on Biko's formative thought. I now turn to Biko and philosophy, particularly the existentialist tradition.

Africana existential philosophy in South Africa (Azania)

In South Africa, what I earlier referred to as 'Africana philosophy' has been systematically rendered invisible by years of the apartheid regime's repressive censorship machinery. What this invisibility has prevented from being disclosed is that there *have been* and there *are* Africana philosophers in South Africa, just as there are on the rest of the African continent and in the diaspora. Africana existential philosophy in South Africa is not only the product of the actual common historical experiences of Africans but also a product of five distinct intellectual forces, namely: (i) the early *Drum* magazine writers (urban African social thought) such as Mphahlele, Lewis Nkosi, Modisane, Henry Nxumalo, Sepamla, Mongane Wally Serote; (ii) the work of Afro-Caribbean thinkers such as Garvey, Fanon, Césaire and Damas; (iii) African thinkers such as Senghor, Nyerere, Nkrumah, Cabral and Oginga Odinga; (iv) African-American thinkers such as Du Bois, Baldwin, Carmichael, Charles Hamilton, George Jackson, Cleaver, Malcolm X, Cone and Davis; and (v) the European tradition of existentialism which culminated with Sartre, De Beauvoir, Camus, Victor Frankl and others. Africana existential philosophy in South Africa seems to be as much an attempt to rethink and thereby reclaim a tradition of existential analysis which definitely appears more powerfully at work in the writings of Fanon, Cone and Carmichael than anyone else. Thus Sartre and the other existentialists were more catalysts for, rather than the 'founders' of, Africana existential philosophy. Africana existential thought builds upon problems of existence produced by the problematic historical experiences of black people. The problems of existence encountered by black subjects are mainly, but not exclusively, problems regarding their racialised being and antiblack racism. Together these problems, as Lewis Gordon notes, 'posed the problem of black suffering and the sustained black concern with freedom/liberation and what it means to be human' (2006: 22).

In his 'Existentialism: A Clarification', Sartre emphasises: '*Existentialism is no mournful delectation but a humanistic philosophy of action, effort, combat, and solidarity*' (2013: 91 – italics in original). This means (as Charles William Ephraim indicates about his philosophy of redemption) that to philosophise about the encumbrance of being-black-in-an-antiblack-world means far more than mere passive speculative, contemplative and abstract theorising about the brutal experiences of black people. Philosophy, on this account, is an *activity* and not passive cognition about reality. In his view:

...properly philosophic engagement with any issue yields concrete action and points to results in the real world. It points to the *oughtness* of the world with respect to the possibility of universal human improvement. Thus construed, philosophy is a very dangerous activity, which is why, for example, Nietzsche considered his work as 'philosophizing with a hammer'. (2003: 417 – italics in original)

It is indeed such philosophical engagement that characterises Biko as a philosopher of action whose philosophy was considered a threat and a danger to white hegemony in Azania.

By virtue of the historical fact of racial oppression, colonisation and slavery, Africana philosophy (as noted above) raises existential questions of identity and liberation by focusing on the reality that African people are black people and hence are affected by the significance of race and racism. These questions, concerned about self-image and self-determination, constitute the two most basic challenges confronting black people. The raising and articulation of these existential questions of identity and liberation within the context and framework of the situation of black people structure the foundations of what has been named 'Africana philosophy of existence' by its leading exponent Lewis Gordon,[11] or sometimes in a more general meaning 'black existentialism' as captured in the title of Gordon's ground-breaking *Existence in Black: An Anthology of Black Existential Philosophy* (1997a).

As part of Africana philosophy, Africana existential philosophy also raises questions primarily about two themes: identity and liberation. Questions of identity raised by this discursive field are in the form of 'Who are Africana (black) people?' or 'What are Africana people?' In other words, at the subjective level, the questions combined may become 'Who or what am I?' The *who* of identity, Lewis Gordon argues, generates questions about selfhood: 'Who am I?' The *what* of identity takes on an ontological demand about questions of *being* or *essence* and the existential question of meaning 'What am I?' This is the ontological question about black identity in an antiblack world. If the black subject at a certain stage of existence is compelled to ask the question 'Who am I?', it is precisely because his identity as a person or human being has been challenged or questioned.

Black people are certainly not the only ones with an identity problem. A lot of contemporary post-industrial middle-class people suffer from neuroses generated by an uncertainty about the answer to the question 'Who really am I?' However, black people living in an antiblack world have historically suffered more serious and unique problems of identity than any other people, especially white people. Elijah Muhammad, the leader of the Nation of Islam (Black Muslims) in the USA, articulated this black problem as follows:

The Negro wants to be everything but himself. He wants to be a white man. He processes his hair. Acts like a white man. He wants to integrate with the white man, but he cannot integrate with himself or his own kind. The Negro wants to lose his identity because he does not know his own identity. (in Silberman 1964: 71)

Put in Kierkegaardian terms, Muhammad is saying that the black subject is a relation which fails to relate itself to its own self. This failure of the self as a relation to relate itself to its own self is what Kierkegaard identifies as alienation. Black identity in an antiblack environment has always come from without; that is, black people have always had their identity defined by someone else, determined externally, always given to them. As Silberman attests, 'every Negro must grapple with the universal "who am I?" in a way no white man can ever know. For always the Negro must come up against the knowledge of the white world's distaste for him, and so always there remains a lingering doubt' (1964: 109).

Liberation, however, is purposive or teleological in nature (that is, what-*ought-to-be*). Its concerns are directly connected to the demands of 'ought' or 'why'. Accordingly, Gordon insists, whatever we may be, the point is to focus energy on what we ought to become and 'what-ought-to-be'. There is, therefore, a convergence between questions of identity and questions of liberation; they intersect at the question '*Who* is to be liberated?' Put differently, an epistemological turn constitutes the intersection between the ontological and the teleological. To know what we ought to do requires knowing who we are, and to know who we are, we frequently have to discover what we ought to be doing. These concerns, Lewis Gordon explains, are symbiotic concerns which 'point values at the heart of *being* and forms of being at the heart of value' (2000).

Although European existentialism and Africana existential philosophy may share certain common characteristics such as concerns about freedom, responsibility, anguish, bad faith, authenticity or death, they nevertheless differ in that the former (as Lewis Gordon indicates) is an ideology which in its particularism purports to be universalistic – that is, it is a 'fundamentally European historical phenomenon' (Gordon 1997a: 3) dealing with the history of European literature. Hence Fanon's insistence that whenever black thinkers deal with existentialism, and even Marxism for that matter, they need to stretch it beyond its boundaries. By contrast, Africana existential philosophy does not claim universality but deals with issues of the emergence of black selfhood, black suffering, embodied agency, freedom, racism and liberation, the concept 'situation'; in short, it deals with being-black-in-the-world. For example, while for Heidegger the most important question is 'What does it mean to exist?', Africana existential philosophy attempts to address the concern 'What does it mean to exist as a *black* human being in the world?' – which in Du Bois' words is: 'How does it feel to be a problem?' These questions of problematic existence and suffering, in Lewis Gordon's view, animate the theoretical dimensions of black intellectual existential production (2000: 8). Africana existential philosophy, therefore, consists in reflections, rooted in black experience, on the boundaries of human existence, and using such reflections for challenges confronting African and African-descended people in the diaspora. To an extent, Africana philosophers appropriate Heidegger's notion of philosophy as phenomenological description and interpretation of what it means for African and African-descended people who – as a consequence of an active engagement in the world infused with racism, colonialism, slavery and oppression – reconstitute their past, make a choice in the now and envisage possibilities for the future.

Manganyi's work serves as a paradigmatic example of Africana philosophy and he occupies a special place within Africana philosophy of existence. As a pioneer in Africana existential philosophy in this country, he has over the years articulated a humanist existentialism that found its most profound expression in his seminal book *Being-Black-in-the-World* (1973). He brings forth a mixture of Fanon's phenomenology of blackness, Sartre's existential phenomenology, Frankl's logotherapy, Camus' notion of absurdity and suicide as existential realities, Heidegger's ontology and Césaire's Negritude (More 2006). Like Fanon, Manganyi uses phenomenological and existential psychoanalysis to understand the complex effects of racism on the personality and identity of the oppressed black subject. His fundamental point of departure, *being-black-in-the-world*, incorporates Fanon's phenomenological interpretation of the 'lived experience' of the black person bodily being in an antiblack society. Indeed, the very title of his text *Being-Black-in-the-World*, besides invoking Heidegger's existentialist notion of 'thrownness', is in many ways a rephrase of Fanon's climactic fifth chapter in *Black Skin, White Masks*, of which the literal translation is 'The Lived Experience of the Black Person'.

Creatively using Camus' notion of the absurdity of existence, Manganyi comes close to identifying the cause of racism in contingency. He declares: 'The racist belongs to the class of "absurd" man; he suffers from existential frustration and a sense of helplessness' (1977: 46). However, he claims that this condition of absurdity does not apply to the black person or the Jew. Their exclusion from the category of the 'absurd man' is because as victims of racism within an antiblack or anti-Semite world, their situation is a predetermined one, a socially constructed situation that constitutes their presence-in-the-world to be existentially and essentially different from that of the racist. The absurd man, Manganyi suggests, is led to absurdity by the metaphysical question 'Why?' in the face of the contingency of existence. The consciousness of one's lack of necessity, of the meaninglessness of existence, leads the absurd man to suicide, racism or fascism among other evasive, bad-faith infested reactions. The reason for suicide or racism is that while suicide for white people is a product of the contingency of existence or 'existential frustration' (Manganyi), or the feeling of existential absurdity (Camus), suicide is a product of white presence for black people. Black people do not contemplate suicide as a flight from contingency; their very existence in the world is suicidal. In agreement with Manganyi, Lewis Gordon argues that black suffering emanates not from Camus' metaphysical 'Why?', but from the derivative question necessitated by their situation in an antiblack world: 'Why do black people go on?' Death for black subjects is for both Manganyi and Lewis Gordon – indeed even for Biko – a forever-present event. In describing the situation of the black person vis-à-vis the white person in relation to Camus' question about existence, Manganyi states:

> A further difference has been that we [black people] have not had any difficulties in identifying the source of our nausea – of our suffering. We have been compelled to recognise that unlike the white man we live with the originators of our absurdity. The source of our suffering may be identified in the streets of Pretoria and Johannesburg. Should it surprise anybody that the problem of suicide recognised by Camus as the most important problem of philosophy should be recognised as a paltry matter by us? The fact of the matter is that we live suicide and are too involved in living to contemplate it. (1973: 47)

What is important to note here is that Manganyi's articulation of his Africana philosophy of existence occurred within the context and realm of the Black Consciousness philosophy. In fact, it is the very articulation of that philosophy.

It is within this discursive field of Africana existential philosophy that Biko claimed his philosophical space. As a philosopher, his concern was not with theoretical abstractions but with the concrete and existential struggles which shape human, especially black people's, existence – what Fanon refers to as the '*l'expérience vécue du noir*'. We have noted that Nolutshungu ascribes to the Black Consciousness Movement led by Biko a philosophical preoccupation with existential phenomenology, particularly with the notions of consciousness, being and social guilt as articulated in the works of Sartre and Jaspers. Unfortunately, as in the epigraphs, Nolutshungu's claims about Biko, Black Consciousness and philosophy were mere assertions rather than demonstrations of the philosophical content of Biko's ideas. Following on the insights of my earlier articulation of Biko's philosophy (More 2008), I here attempt to tease out some of these existentialist categories from Biko's writings.

I have thus far located Biko's views and the Black Consciousness philosophy within the Africana existential philosophy. Biko's philosophical articulations have been shown to be dependent upon a particular philosophical anthropology which asserts that a human being is best understood as a free being and that any denial of this freedom is by that very fact a denial of the humanity of that being. This denial assumes various forms, among which are exploitation, oppression and (in Biko's perspective) white racism. Since as consciousness, human beings are free and in Sartre's words 'we are condemned to be free' and consequently are not free not to be free, the denial or questioning of the humanity of black people through antiblack white racism constitutes a condition which restricts or negates the exercise or realisation of the fundamental and basic feature of what it is to be human – freedom. Conditions constituting the denial and questioning of the fundamental being of black people – and of any group of people for that matter – are conditions which must of necessity be eradicated. Biko set himself the task of eradicating and eliminating the insidiousness and dehumanising project of antiblack racism in South Africa, negating the negation of black humanity through the quest for a true humanity that would embrace every human being living in an envisaged future Azania.

But what does Biko mean by freedom? Freedom, he declares, 'is the ability to define oneself with one's possibilities held back not by the power of other people over one but only by one's relationship to...natural surroundings' (1996: 92). The presence of the notion 'possibilities' suggests that one is always faced with a number of possibilities and that such possibilities are the grounds for making choices; and choice by its very nature is a fundamental expression of freedom. Biko then points out that it is these 'natural surroundings' that present themselves as conditions for the testing of possibilities. 'On his own, therefore, the black man wishes to explore his surroundings and test his possibilities – in other words to make his freedom real' (1996: 92). When Biko offers us this basic conception of freedom, it becomes abundantly clear that his conception is much more an expression of the existentialist conception of freedom than the liberal notion of it as some commentators want us to believe. In his view, freedom is more than simply the absence of external constraints; it requires the presence of a liberated consciousness. This consciousness is not another's to give; it is a state of mind that must be chosen. For, without a change from within, the changes without are superficial; after all, 'the most potent weapon in the hands of the oppressor is the mind of the oppressed' (Biko 1996: 92). To be sure, freedom for Biko amounts to self-consciousness precisely because 'we cannot be conscious of ourselves and yet remain in bondage' (1996: 49).

The 'natural surroundings' which in existentialist terms refers to the givenness of the world, its facticity, may limit my freedom, my possibilities, while simultaneously constituting themselves as the very condition of my freedom. The value of freedom, as Sartre insists, discloses itself when it confronts obstacles and limiting natural conditions – that is, freedom reveals itself in the act of resistance. It is through my resistance to my limiting situation that my freedom is meaningfully given to me. Biko's 'limiting situation' and 'natural surroundings' are another way of expressing what Sartre calls 'facticity'. Facticity, paradoxically, limits freedom while also constituting the conditions against which freedom can manifest itself; it both limits my freedom and makes it possible in the first place. As human subjects, we always encounter resistance and obstacles in our lives, resistances and obstacles which we have not created but which acquire meaning only in and through the free choices we make. 'Thus freedom can be truly free only by constituting facticity as its own restriction...Without facticity freedom would not exist – as a power of nihilation and of choice – and without freedom facticity would not be discovered and would have no meaning' (Sartre 1956: 495–496). In this sense, the natural surroundings are the source and necessity for freedom. Hence, Sartre's paradoxical statement about freedom in oppression, a statement with direct implications for conditions reminiscent of existence in apartheid:

> Never were we freer than under the German occupation. We had lost all our rights, beginning with the right to speak. We were insulted to our faces every day and had to remain silent. We were deported en mass, as workers, Jews, or political prisoners. Everywhere – on the walls, on the movie screens, and in the newspapers – we came up against the vile, insipid picture of ourselves our oppressors wanted to present to us. Because of all this, we were free. Because the Nazi venom seeped even into our thoughts, every accurate thought was a triumph...Every second, we lived to the full the meaning of that banal little phrase: 'Man is mortal!' And the choice each of us made of his life and being was an authentic choice, since it was made in the presence of death, since it could always have been expressed in the form: 'Better death than...' All those among us with any snippets of information about the Resistance...asked ourselves anxiously, 'if they torture me, will I be able to hold out?' In this way, the very question of freedom was posed, and we were on the verge of the deepest knowledge human beings can have of themselves. For the secret of a human being is not his Oedipus complex or his inferiority complex. It is the very limit of his freedom, his ability to resist torture and death. (Sartre 2013: 83–84)

The value of freedom, Sartre insists, discloses itself when it confronts obstacles and limiting conditions (that is, freedom exhibits itself in the act of resistance). It is through my resistance to my limiting situation that my freedom is given meaning. It thus becomes evident in his existentialist conception of freedom that Biko initially focuses on subjective freedom as a prerequisite for objective freedom. Subjectively, 'if one is free at heart' Biko argues, then 'no man-made chains can bind one to servitude' (1996: 92). Put differently, subjective freedom is ontological while objective freedom is ontic. This is a distinction that most people often neglect when dealing with existential phenomenology. A distinction should be made between freedom and liberty (emancipation).

It should be remembered here that Fanon, in a similar manner as Biko, makes a distinction between external freedom and internal freedom. Freedom that is given as a gift without struggle may make an external difference to the situation of the oppressed. However, it does not internally free the oppressed from his slavish consciousness or inferiority complex. Though freed, the individual remains with an inferiority consciousness precisely because this freedom is not a consequence of a struggle for liberation but a result of being acted upon from without by the oppressor. The suggestion here is that freedom is more than the absence of external limitation or obstacles. Anticipating Biko and the Black Consciousness Movement, for Fanon freedom involved a liberated consciousness; without freedom from within, freedom from without means virtually nothing.

Many people fail to take into account Isaiah Berlin's notion of freedom 'to' and freedom 'from'.[12] Liberty *from* or external freedom is what one is able to do without constraints (that is, the presence or absence of limitation or obstacles), while freedom *to* involves how an individual makes choices and assumes responsibility for those choices. What this distinction points to is that one can be free where there is no liberty at all or one can enjoy liberty without being free. The one does not necessarily entail the other. Hence Fanon contends: 'The liberation of the individual does not follow national liberation. An authentic national liberation exists only to the degree to which the individual has irreversibly begun his own liberation' (1967b: 103). For Biko, therefore, true liberation occurs at two levels: first and foremost, at the subjective level as an act of freeing the consciousness of the black subject from the fear of white people, the inferiority complex and the tendency of self-hate; second, at the physical and political levels as an act of emancipation from oppressive apartheid machinery.

Both Biko and Fanon echo the belief long held by some black antiracist, anticolonialist and antislavery thinkers that black people need to free themselves psychologically before they can succeed to liberate themselves politically. Cone puts the matter in this fashion: 'Freedom is what happens to a man on the inside; it is what happens to a man's being. It has nothing to do with voting, marching, picketing or rioting, though all may be manifestations of it. No man can give me freedom or help me get it' (1969: 28).

At this juncture, it is important to note that since the appearance of my article 'Biko: Africana Existentialist Philosopher' (2004a, reprinted in 2008 and 2012), there has been a growing interest and acceptance of Biko as a philosopher. In 2015, the newly established Centre for Phenomenology in South Africa hosted a lecture series in honour of Biko entitled 'The Steve Biko Lectures in Philosophy'. It is significant that one of the speakers was Robert Bernasconi, an existentialist philosopher whose focus on racism in his work locates him within Africana existential philosophy in the same manner as Sartre. The aim of the lecturer series, according to the centre's advertisement, was:

'to continue [the] interrogation and critique of modernity from the epistemic standpoint that Steve Biko's life and thought represents and symbolizes. This is a standpoint that is at once developed inside the hierarchy of the system, colonized by its norms, and yet formulates a perspective outside of it as the oppressed other'.

This legitimation of Biko's position in the philosophical world is not only a recent South African phenomenon, but one that has been articulated by black philosophers the world over.

Notes

1   See Derrida and Tlili's *For Nelson Mandela* (1987); Kalumba's 'The Political Philosophy of Nelson Mandela: A Primer' (1995); and Presbey's 'Fanon on the Role of Violence in Liberation: A Comparison with Gandhi and Mandela' (1996).

2   See for example Lewis Gordon's work on Fanon, particularly *Fanon and the Crisis of European Man: An Essay on the Philosophy and the Human Sciences* (1995b), and Gibson's *Fanon: The Postcolonial Imagination* (2003).

3   A substantial number of writings on Biko focus mostly on the political aspect of his thinking and a few on his thoughts on culture and politics. See for example: Fatton's *Black Consciousness in South Africa* (1986); Pityana et al.'s *Bounds of Possibility: The Legacy of Steve Biko and Black Conciousness* (1991); Halisi's *Black Political Thought in the Making of South African Democracy* (1999); Ranuga's 'Frantz Fanon and Black Consciousness in Azania' (1986); Nteta's 'Revolutionary Self-Consciousness as an Objective Force Within the Process of Liberation: Biko and Gramsci' (1987); Gibson's 'Black Consciousness 1977–1987: The Dialectics of Liberation in South Africa' (1988); Hemson's 'The Antinomies of Black Rage: A review of *I Write What I Like* by Steve Biko' (1995); Ahluwalia and Zegeye's 'Frantz Fanon and Steve Biko: Towards Liberation' (2001).

4   Mangcu X, We must go back to Steve Biko for inspiration, *Sunday Times*, 7 February 1999. See Sono's *Reflections on the Origin of Black Consciousness in South Africa* (1993). For a philosophical debate about Biko's views on violence, see Lötter's 'The Intellectual Legacy of Stephen Bantu Biko (1946–1977)' (1992); Teffo and Ramose's 'Steve Biko and the Interpreters of Black Consciousness: A Response to Lötter' (1993); and Lötter's 'On Interpreting Biko and the "new" South Africa: A Reply to Teffo and Ramose' (1993). See also my chapter 'Albert Luthuli, Nelson Mandela and Steve Biko: The Philosophical Bases of their Thought and Practice' in *Philosophy and an African culture* (Wiredu 1980).

5   The 4th Annual Wild Coast Philosophy Symposium, theme 'Who is a philosopher?', Crawford's Beach Lodge, Cintsa, 25 October 2014. This symposium was graced by international names such as Lewis Gordon's and was hosted by the University of Fort Hare. Represented also at the symposium were Rhodes University, the University of Johannesburg, the University of KwaZulu-Natal and the Nelson Mandela Metropolitan University.

6   See Valentin Mudimbe's *The Invention of Africa: Gnosis, philosophy, and the order of knowledge* and Young in Sartre (2001: vii). For a detailed description of Sartre as an Africana philosopher, see Lewis Gordon's paper 'Sartre in Africana Philosophy' (2001).

7   See Lewis Gordon's introduction Gordon et al.'s (Eds) *Fanon: A Critical Reader* (1996).

8   See Ronald Judy (in Gordon et al. 1996: 53), for a discussion on this translation.

9   Blaming the victim is excellently discussed in a text of the same title by William Ryan, *Blaming the Victim* (1976).

10 For a detailed account of black radical thought, see for example Cedric Robinson's *Black Marxism: The Making of the Black Radical Tradition* (1983).

11 See his *An Introduction to Africana Philosophy* (2008).

12 For an informative distinction between freedom 'from' and freedom 'to', see Berlin's 'Two Concepts of Liberty' in his book *Four Essays on Liberty* (1969).

5

Biko's Africana existentialist philosophy

I INDICATED IN THE last chapter that Biko was concerned with the concrete and existential struggles for freedom which shaped human – especially black – existence. But more than the concern for black existence as such was the understanding that philosophy as 'the love of wisdom' involves two notions, namely: the 'True' and the 'Good'. Put differently, philosophy is the constant pursuit of the unity between true human knowledge and good human conduct: 'The unity of the true and the good is the highest value in philosophy' (Heller 1984: 8). Is philosophy, among other things, not the search for truth? Is Plato's *Metaphysics and the Forms* not an explanation of reality as absolute truth? Is his definition of knowledge as 'true justified belief' not an inquiry into the nature of truth? Is Hegel's *Phenomenology of Spirit* not a treatise on the truth and certainty of spirit or consciousness? Is Sartre not in pursuit of existential truth in *Truth and Existence*? Philosophers want not only to know but also to pursue the True (truth) and the Good (justice). Generally, therefore, philosophy is understood as the project to gain knowledge of what is true – more precisely, to say and speak that which is true, to understand *what* is true and say *why* it is true.

In the same spirit of philosophers, Biko's consciousness of the importance of truth made him intransigent to anything less than the truth, as the title of his column *Frank Talk* suggests. In his foreword to Biko's *I Write What I Like*, Lewis Gordon states: 'The clarity of Frank Talk is a demand for truth...[Biko] reveals here a unique, double relationship blacks have with European civilizations: blacks face a world of lies in which they are forced to pretend as true that which is false and pretend as false that which is true' (2002: viii). For Biko, truth is truth and therefore must be duly recognised as such. However, truth is not only an epistemological category; it is also an existential reality. As such, truth becomes the revelation of concealed or unrevealed Being. Because the unconcealedness of reality, of Being, means the revelation of existential reality, not only to the philosopher as such but also to others. In his view, the dehumanising effects of apartheid on black people was to be confronted head on, its unpalatability notwithstanding. The evilness of this system on black people was so devastating that it has completely dehumanised them to a point where they were complicit in their own dehumanisation. 'This *is* the first truth, bitter as it may seem, that we must acknowledge before we can start on a programme designed in changing the status quo' (Biko 1996: 29). In other words, a serious and truthful confrontation with what *is* will facilitate a clear conception and vision of what *ought-to-be*. Thus he adds, 'it becomes more necessary to see the truth as it is if you realise that the only vehicle for change are these people who have lost their personality' (Biko 1996: 29). For most black people, to hear this was painful, devastating; but it was nonetheless the truth, and those who understood, accepted it. Biko's Africana philosophy, to use the words of Serequeberhan, is therefore 'engaged in articulating the *truth* of its lived present. This "truth" is, furthermore, nothing more than its own reflexive self-representation on the plain of philosophy, in the service of fulfilling the emancipatory hopes and aspirations inscribed in our "common history, tradition, [and] universe of discourse" as...Africans' (1994: 120 – italics in original).

The truth of Biko's lived experience was white racism. But (as Lewis Gordon noted above) in Biko's apartheid world, 'blacks face a world of lies in which they are forced to pretend as true that which is false and pretend as false that which is true'. In this way, black people were coerced to fall into the trap of bad faith. To coerce anyone into the abyss of bad faith is by the same stroke to be in bad faith yourself because it is an indication of the fear of truth on your part. In fact, racism is in many ways the fear of truth. In the *Anti-Semite and Jew*, Sartre puts his finger on the pulse when he describes the anti-Semite as one in bad faith because she fears not only herself but also suffers from the 'fear of truth'. Since truth involves reasoning about *what is*, the racist adopts a mode of passion in which reasoning and the pursuit of truth play only a subordinate role. In pursuit of the truth, Biko demands that the racist should think – should use the very same *reason* she denies black people – in order to arrive at the truth and avoid being guilty of bad faith.

When a society bases itself upon lies, the genuine philosopher, in defence of truth, readily becomes the revealer of the lies. Since in apartheid South Africa black people had been lied to, the real challenge for Biko was to reveal the lie by exposing things as they really were. Hence the constant reference to apartheid lies by Biko in his writings and speeches. 'To get the right answers' he argued, 'we must ask the right questions...we have to find out whether our position is a deliberate creation of God or an artificial fabrication of the truth by power-hungry people whose motive is authority' (1996: 87). The white people's lie, constituted by the belief in the inferiority of black people, emanated from the tradition 'that whenever a group of people has tasted the lovely fruits of wealth, security, and prestige, it begins to find it more comfortable to believe in the obvious lie and to accept it as normal that it alone is entitled to privilege. In order to believe this seriously, it needs to convince itself of all the arguments that support the lie...To make the lie live even longer, Blacks have to be denied any chance of accidentally proving their equality with white men' (Biko 1996: 88). In a society built on such lies, the deceived buy into the lies and thus begin to accept the lie as the truth. This requires that the truth about their complicity and acceptance of the lies be revealed. The revelation, for Biko, would have to be in the form of what he called conscientisation to the truth of their situation, to awaken their consciousness to the truth that without freedom there is no truth. This indeed is the task of a serious and committed philosopher, one who speaks for humanity. In such circumstances, the genuine philosopher (as mentioned in the previous chapter), questions what *is* from the point of view of what *ought-to-be*. Through the philosophical system of existential Africana philosophy and the philosophical attitude of Black Consciousness, Biko strove to lead black subjects from what *is* to what *ought-to-be*.

As an existential Africana philosopher, the following existentialist and political problematics are evident in and extractable from Biko's thought: freedom, alienation, self-consciousness, bad faith, dialectics, moral responsibility, identity, authenticity, African humanism, the critique of liberalism and so on. These concerns justify his location within the matrix of Africana or Black existential philosophy. Linking all these existentialist categories is the foundational problem in Biko's thought: *white racism*. In Africana philosophy, special attention is paid to 'the reality that Africana people are a black people and hence are impacted by the significance of race and racism' (2000: 6). What then actually unifies all the traditions under the philosophy known as Africana philosophy is fundamentally the shared concern about the dehumanisation or the denied humanity of African and African-descended people by invidious systems such as slavery, colonialism and racism, which have been given philosophical justification by the dominant figures of Western philosophy. The serious concern with racism induces Africana philosophy to assume the responsibility of philosophical anthropology. This means that the starting point of Africana philosophy is neither metaphysics nor epistemology but philosophical anthropology, the problem of the human being (in this case, that of the black human being).

The problem of racism

In his definition of Black Consciousness, Biko isolates the fundamental problem black people constantly faced in the antiblack racism of apartheid South Africa: 'In terms of the Black Consciousness approach we recognise the existence of one major force in South Africa. This is White Racism' (1996: 50). In the same text, critiquing white liberals' view that South Africa's problem is 'a black problem', Biko states:

'There is nothing the matter with blacks. The problem is WHITE RACISM and it rests squarely on the laps of the white society' (1996: 23 – upper case original). This immediately indicates that for Biko, race – rather than class – was the fundamental and primary problem in South Africa. However, Biko did not completely ignore class distinctions, particularly among black people. He recognised the existence of class divisions as important impediments to black solidarity.

Since Africana existential thought builds upon problems of existence produced by the problematic racial historical experiences of black people, and since the problems of existence encountered by black people concern mainly but not exclusively problems having to do with their racialised being and antiblack racism, Biko's Black Consciousness becomes embedded in Africana existential philosophy. In the same manner as Africana existential philosophy, the philosophy of Black Consciousness does not claim to deal with universal problems but deals with issues of the emergence of black selfhood, black suffering, embodied agency, freedom and liberation, and the concept of situation – in short, it deals with the problem of antiblack racism insofar as it determines being-black-in-the-world.

Let me first deal with the popular charge that black philosophers, including Biko, are primarily obsessed with racism (which is a specific issue) rather than with problems of metaphysical or epistemological universal significance. The implicit suggestion is that white philosophers can easily marginalise racism as a terrain for black philosophers only, as something 'they' (the black Other as black philosophers) should have as their philosophical responsibility. Not only does this absolve white philosophers from taking racism as a philosophical problem seriously, but also effectively keeps racism easily and expediently on the margins and out of sight for them. First of all, this accusation indicates serious ignorance of the diversity of philosophical discourse among black philosophers. Skin pigmentation, as Stephen Brookfield remarks, does not produce philosophical unanimity (2005). In fact, a look at the texts produced by black philosophers indicates what, in Yancy's words, is 'a complex set of philosophical positionalities and thoughts exhibiting areas of commonality and diversity' (1998: 10).

It is however also true that black philosophers, within the context of worldwide antiblack racism, share a certain *Othered* experiential reality or social ontology that shapes aspects of their being-philosophically-in-the-world. This means that even if one chooses to be a philosopher, one's choice within certain contexts is sometimes – though not always – influenced by the existential or social situation one finds oneself in. In an antiblack world, the racial context or situation may determine to a large extent the kind of philosopher a black subject becomes and the kinds of problematics such a philosopher deals with in her philosophising endeavours. In such a world, I for example, as a black existentialist philosopher, primordially perceive the world and the world sees me through the contingent fact and historical narrative of my skin colour: *my blackness*. As a consequence, philosophy (as Nkrumah advisedly asserts) often arises from an existential situation. Within the context of racialised antiblack reality, therefore, it is possible to talk of 'black philosophy' and 'white philosophy'. Put differently, it is possible to exist as being-a-black-philosopher-in-the-world as opposed to being-a-white-philosopher-in-the-world. In other words, it is almost impossible to ignore our racial modes of being and perceiving, which are a function of our thrownness in the world.

What sorts of problems are likely to take centre stage in the black philosopher's life? Responding to this question, Mills argues that black philosophers can ill afford to engage in metaphysical or epistemological questions and problems such as universal or global scepticism precisely because as subordinated people, they cannot doubt the existence of the world of oppression and their oppressors. For Mills, '[i]f your daily existence is largely defined by oppression, by *forced* intercourse with the world, it is not going to occur to you that doubt about your oppressor's existence could in any way be a serious or pressing philosophical problem; this idea will simply seem frivolous, a peck of social privilege' (1998: 8).

This explains why many black philosophers living in countries such as South Africa, the USA, Britain, Brazil, the Caribbean islands and many antiblack societies give pride of place to racism as a philosophical problematic and category. Indeed, many white philosophers have contemptuously pointed out that for black philosophers to make race their primary subject is in the long run detrimental to their image and success as genuine philosophers. In fact, some white philosophers even go to the extent of rejecting race and racism as legitimate philosophical problematics and instead assign them to sociological or anthropological investigation. Mills points out that 'impressive work on race and racism by Black philosophers has tended to be Ghettoized and not taken up in what (by conventional criteria) are judged the trend-setting sectors of the [philosophy] profession' (2008: 138). True enough, some black philosophers are indeed 'pre-occupied' with race. But, first, this is because of the 'whiteness' of philosophy and its practitioners in the academies and outside. Black people do not only not appear in Western philosophical canons – except as objects of ridicule from the racism of the leading figures in the white Western tradition such as Aristotle, Hume, Kant, Locke, Voltaire, Montesquieu, Hegel, Marx, Fredrick Engels and so on – but are also invisible. When Western white (even Asian) philosophers speak about the human condition as a philosophically universal category of utmost importance, they do not include black people in the category of 'human', the putative universality and generality of their theories notwithstanding.

Second, the primary concern of the black philosopher is the relations of human beings in society as opposed to the place of the human being in the universe.

People who are rooted, who find it worthwhile to pursue abstract metaphysical entities in the universe, belong to the dominant white group and they enjoy a certain kind of security about their position in society. That is not so easy for black dehumanised people, the outcasts and denigrated people. Sartre, for example, argues that the social, economic and psychological security of white philosophers gives them the leisure and freedom to focus on metaphysical and epistemological problems with ease and alacrity. This is not so simple for an oppressed, denigrated and dehumanised people. Since the social milieu of black people (slavery, colonialism, racism, apartheid, general oppression and poverty) is different from that of white people, their respective philosophical predicaments are quite different. Indeed since slavery, poverty, colonialism and apartheid are products of racism, race plays a more dominant role in the philosophising activities and practices of those who suffer from racism than in the activities of those who practise racism and also benefit tremendously from it. As an example, Sartre – in response to the question 'For whom does one write?' – mentions the case of the African-American novelist Richard Wright:

> If we consider only his condition as a *man*, that is, as a Southern 'nigger' transported to the North, we shall at once imagine that he can only write about Negroes or Whites *seen through the eyes of Negroes*. Can one imagine for a moment that he would agree to pass his life in the contemplation of the eternal True, Good, and Beautiful when ninety per cent of the negroes in the South are practically deprived of the right to vote?...If we want to go further, we must consider his public. To whom does Richard Wright address himself? Certainly not the universal man. The essential characteristic of the notion of the universal man is that he is not involved in any particular age and that he is no more and no less moved by the lot of the negroes of Louisiana than by that of the Roman slaves...He is a pure and abstract affirmation of the inalienable right of man. But neither can Wright think of intending his book for the white racialists of Virginia or South Carolina whose minds are made up in advance and who will not open them. (1988: 78 – italics in original)

This, however, does not mean that metaphysical or epistemological concerns do not deeply interest black philosophers; rather, it is that the social and human questions tend to be predominant concerns. The dilemmas of a black philosopher are in a significant way different from the dilemmas of a white philosopher.

Third, racism is one of those phenomena a black philosopher as human being experiences almost every day in her lived experience. Racism does not distinguish one black person from another in terms of class, intelligence, wealth or religiosity.

'All niggers, look alike', the racist saying goes. It does not matter whether you have a doctorate (PhD or DLitt et Phil) in Philosophy, Chemistry or Physics. In an antiblack world, there are PhDs in Chemistry, Mathematics or Philosophy; medical doctors; engineers; millionaires; women; men; and so on – *and* there are also Black PhDs in Chemistry, Mathematics or Philosophy; black medical doctors; black engineers; black millionaires; black women; black men; and so on. As a norm, whiteness is not mentioned, only blackness – which is the absolute Other to whiteness (the norm, the standard, the benchmark) – has to be identified. So, black philosophers as black people do not escape the viciousness of racism in their lives. Race, therefore, has been an important philosophical issue for black philosophers and will continue to be so in the future.

Du Bois made one of the most prophetic predictions of the twentieth century when he declared, 'the problem of the Twentieth Century is the problem of the color line' (1969: xi). True to Du Bois' prediction, the twentieth century was indeed plagued by the racial problem. In fact, racism refuses to die. It is alive and thriving, not only in its crude biological form but also in its veiled and new perverted frameworks of exclusion in terms of 'culture', 'behaviour' and 'standards'. Racism still parades our landscape in different configurations, shapes and disguised forms adapted to new circumstances or camouflaged in new clothes of 'non-racialism', 'colour-blindness' and even 'multiculturalism'.

The problem of the so-called obsession with race and racism of black philosophers rests squarely on the hegemony and normativity of whiteness vis-à-vis blackness. The question is: Is it possible to talk of black identity without talking about it within a white hegemonic context? In other words, could it have been possible to talk of blackness during a pre-colonial context before the black person met the white colonising person? This question also touches on a significant difference within African thought – that is, between most African philosophers on the African continent and the African and African-descended philosophers in the diaspora, a difference which simultaneously posits itself as a rebuttal of the charge that black philosophers are obsessed with racism to the total exclusion of metaphysical or epistemological issues. Most African philosophers on the African continent, except of course in South Africa, do not privilege racism as a primary issue of their philosophising practices. The simple reason for this lack of interest in race matters is that within the context and milieu of their post-independent philosophical world, racism is practically absent. After independence, the colonial master returned to the colonial metropolis. As a consequence, very few white people remained as settlers and thus constituted a very insignificant section of the population. In most African states today (perhaps with the exception of, for example, Zimbabwe, Namibia, Algeria and Kenya), it is possible to spend a week or more without running into a white settler except maybe tourists. In some rural areas, it is possible to go for days on end without running into a white person or farmer. Therefore, concrete and immediate white hegemony is virtually immediately absent in most African countries other than South Africa. South Africa is still the most visible white dominated country, black political administration notwithstanding. Consider, for example, some of the African national sport teams (especially at the Olympic Games); they are virtually constituted by black athletes or participants. Not so with South African national teams in sports such as cricket, rugby, hockey or swimming (except for slow-paced progress in cricket and rugby); they are all almost entirely white, as if they are from Europe. In fact, the French national soccer team would more easily qualify as an African team than the South African one. So the racial problematic is almost absent in most African states and this explains the paucity of racial discourse among black philosophers from such contexts.

Fanon, describing racism as a system of unreason in *Black Skin, White Masks*, declares that there is 'nothing more neurotic...than contact with unreason' (1967a). He states:

> As long as the black man is among his own, he will have no occasion, except in minor internal conflicts, to experience his being through others... The black man among his own...does not know at what moment his inferiority comes into being through the other...And then the occasion arose when I had to meet the white man's eyes. An unfamiliar weight burdened me. The real world challenged my claims. (1967a: 109–110)

Emmanuel Eze, the late Nigerian philosopher who taught in the USA, captures this Fanonian observation in an insightful passage:

> It wasn't until I came to the United States and England that I became black. In Nigeria, I grew up believing that I belonged to the Igbo 'tribe', so that when the Igbo had conflicts with other equally 'tribal' groups...the language for articulating intergroup tension and grievances was that of tribalism...
>
> The idea of tribe or ethnicity in Africa has little or nothing to do with the color of skin, eye or hair. In Nigeria all the peoples who belong to the various tribes and ethnicities may be said to be considered racially 'black' only because, as I and other Africans growing up in the modern world have discovered, one can be black – with those special and overdetermined meanings attaching to the label – without knowing or choosing it. With the exception of the very educated individuals who travel to South Africa, Europe, and the Americas, or who have read extensive *literature produced by Africans and African-descended peoples in these parts of the world,* Nigerians do not routinely identify themselves racially. In fact, the language of race

and the vocabulary of racism as means of initiating and conducting intra- or intergroup conflicts are practically absent in most parts of contemporary Africa. With the exceptions of the Republic of South Africa, Zimbabwe, or Algeria, which have had large settlements of white populations, these observations apply to most of Africa's modern nations. Thus, despite travels in West and Central Africa where my status as 'foreign' was always on display either through my physical features or inability to speak the local languages, it is outside of Africa that I learned the modern meanings of 'blackness' as a racial identity. (Eze 2001: 216, 218 – italics added)

In an interesting piece entitled 'This Prison Called My Skin: On Being Black in America', the Nigerian philosopher Olufemi Taiwo (who had never experienced racism and considered himself simply a Nigerian and a Yoruba man) explains: 'As soon as I arrived in the United States of America, I underwent a singular transformation, the consequences of which have circumscribed my life since. I BECAME BLACK!...as soon as I entered the United States, my otherwise complex, multidimensional, and rich *human* identity became completely reduced to a simple, one-dimensional, and impoverished *nonhuman* identity' (2003: 42 – italics in original). Indeed, many post-colonial African philosophers learn about their blackness on arriving in antiblack societies.

The argument above does not suggest that neither some black philosophers outside South Africa nor some white philosophers take an interest in race matters. Since colonialism was a direct product of racism, most African peoples have at one time or another in their history experienced racism. Since racism and its product colonialism were evil practices against other human beings, some white people felt they could not participate in evil practices and therefore made their voices heard against this human scourge. One such white philosopher was, as indicated above, the most celebrated twentieth-century French existentialist Jean-Paul Sartre.

Understanding racism

As noted in Chapter 3, when a philosopher of the 'Age of Enlightenment' such as Hume declares that 'Negroes...are naturally inferior to whites'; when one of the most outstanding figures in the history of Western philosophy, Immanuel Kant, declares that blackness is 'a clear proof' of stupidity; or when Hegel or Voltaire makes similar derogatory statements about Africans, we say that they are racists or that they express racist attitudes or feelings. These judgements, attitudes or statements are expressed every day against black people by extraordinary intelligent as well as ordinary people. There are even jokes and cartoons that are used simply to ridicule, humiliate or insult black people. When such jokes are passed or caricatures appear, we often refer to them as antiblack racist humour. Certain books and films are sometimes said to perpetuate, stimulate or promote racist beliefs and feelings. What then is the racism which Biko found problematic? When is a person said to be acting in a racist manner? Philosophical approaches to the phenomenon of racism may take any of the following forms: first, a search for rational arguments for racist beliefs and the testing of their cogency and, second, an analysis of the logical geography or functions of the concept of racism and its related notions. Let us begin with the latter approach.

The problem of racism is difficult to analyse without recourse to or investigation of its roots. It is unfortunately derived from the equally confusing term 'race'. Anthropologists, biologists, geneticists, phrenologists and physiognomists themselves do not agree on what the concept 'race' is and what it denotes. Consequently, vagueness and confusion accompany its usage and application. For Van den Berghe, for example, the confusion is as a result of the concept's different connotations. First, for physical anthropologists, races are 'the various subspecies of *Homo sapiens* characterised by certain phenotypical and genotypical traits'; second, the word 'race' has been used by lay subjects 'to describe a human group that shared certain cultural characteristics such as language or religion…'; third, 'race' has been used as a synonym for species; and, lastly, it has been employed by social scientists to refer to 'a human group that defines itself and/or is defined by other groups as different from other groups by virtue of innate and immutable physical characteristics' (Van den Berghe 1978: 9). Two ideas about race emerge here, namely that race refers to the differences among groups of human beings and that these differences are attributable to either physical or biological characteristics and cultural differences. In many instances 'race' refers to physical attributes, of which skin colour and physiognomy are the supposed signs (that is, the human body plays a fundamentally significant role in the determination of a person's race). Singer arrives at the same conclusion about physical characteristics as indicative of race in his working definition of race: 'The term 'race'…is to be taken as referring to *distinguishing* characteristics of human beings that are (1) *inherited* or believed to be inherited, (2) shared by fairly large numbers of people (but not by all), and (3) readily *apparent* to ordinary sense perception, especially the sense of sight (1978: 155 – italics in original). It is evident from this definition that the word 'race' is normally used to refer to different groups of people characterised by certain physical or biological traits which are sufficiently distinctive to indicate or identify the various groups. This observation is expressed lucidly by Outlaw's conception of 'race'. In his view, 'race':

> …refers to a group of persons who share, more or less biologically
> transmitted physical characteristics that, under the influence of

endogenous cultural and geographical factors as well as exogenous social
and political factors, contribute to the characterization of the group as a
distinct, self-reproducing, encultured population. (1996: 136)

This means that biologically transmitted physical factors, conditioned by and
along with cultural process and geographical factors, come together to form a
race. These recognisable characteristics have led scientists, anthropologists and
others to categorise human beings into different races. Even in this context,
disagreements persist. For example, in 1684, the French physician François Bernier
divided humankind into basically four races: Europeans, Africans, Orientals and
Lapps (West 1982: 55); Johann Friedrich Blumenbach (1752–1840) recognised
Caucasians, Mongolians, Ethiopians, Americans and Malays; and Georges Cuvier
(1769–1832) distinguished only Caucasian, Mongol and Negro (Okolo 1974: 5). In
contrast, technology (particularly in modern genetics) has put into question the
view that there are separate human races. It is believed that characteristics such as
skin colour and physiognomy, which are popularly regarded as indicators of race,
are genetically very superficial and suspect. This view is articulated by physical
anthropologists such as Jacques Barzun and Ashley Montagu. For Montagu, race is
a 'myth' and a 'fallacy' (1965); whereas for Barzun, race is 'a modern superstition'.
According to Barzun, 'the notion of race is a myth which all intelligent people
should discard' (1937: 8). But this does not alter the fact that people of different
skin colour and physiognomy exist, that some people are conscious of these
differences, and that these differences influence their behaviour toward other
people and other people's life chances.

Let me now attempt to answer my original question: When is a person said to
be acting in a racist manner? Put differently: What is racism? The words 'racist'
and 'racism' are derived from the word 'race'. Does it then mean that a person
who studies races or regards races as given is by that very fact a racist in the same
way that a person who studies the physiological make-up of living organisms *is* a
physiologist? The same cannot be said of a racist. Unlike a physiologist, a person
who studies human races is not strictly speaking a 'racist'; she is an ethnologist.
However, a physiologist ceases to be one when she transcends the realm of her
discipline by making aesthetic or value judgements about the object of her study.
Similarly, an ethnologist ceases to be one and becomes a 'racist' when, in addition
to the facts about the objects of her study, she goes on to draw value and moral
conclusions from these given factual differences of the races. Hence, according
to Singer, an ethnologist for example would be said to be a 'racist' if, in addition
to the three points mentioned above in his working definition, she moves to the
conclusion that '(4) these visible characteristics determine or accompany other less
apparent physical, mental, emotional or cultural traits, and (5) that these inherited

physical – so-called racial – traits are therefore relevant to how a person or a group should be treated or regarded – to status in the society' (Singer 1978: 156). Thus, according to (4) and (5), a 'racist' would be a person who – from the fact that there are different races – believes in addition and regards this fact as always relevant to how some race ought to be treated; and a person acts in a racist manner when she practises, engages in or encourages race prejudice, exclusion, domination and oppression.

Michael Philips (1984) defines a racist act from the point of view of the victim and calls this the *act-centred* theory, as against the *agent-centred* theory. According to this theory, a racist act R is performed by person X when:

* X does R in order to harm P because P is a member of a certain racial group; or
* (regardless of X's intentions or purpose) X's doing R can reasonably be expected to mistreat P as a consequence of P being a member of a certain racial group (Philips 1984: 77).

This account focuses mainly on what X's act means for its victim. The significance of this conception is that it covers certain acts of racism which are not intentional on the part of the actor, but which may nevertheless harm, hurt or even mistreat the victim. This latter kind of racism is known as 'visceral racism'.

From the above account of 'racist' acts, we may now proceed to define racism. Okolo defines racism as 'a "mental or psychological attitude", "outlook", "mood" or "temper" that regards one race (usually one's own) as essentially superior to another, often, on the basis of skin color or cultural achievement' (1974: 6). Note that in terms of this definition, Hume's declaration cited above constitutes him as a racist. Furthermore, Okolo's definition brings out certain features associated with racism, namely: (i) that racism mostly involves attitudes or feelings rather than reason (an argument which is highly contested) and (ii) that it also involves a hierarchical ordering of races, with one (usually the racist's race) superior to the other – which is accordingly regarded as inferior. Perhaps a look at other definitions may bring other features. Marvin Glass regards racism as '[t]he assertion that a group of people – usually identified by national, religious or physical characteristic (such as skin color) – is innately inferior to other segments of the population'. He adds: 'Biologically inherited characteristics, it is claimed, are the chief determinants of intellectual ability and thus the environment is not a major factor with regard to intellectual contrasts between groups of individuals' (1978: 564). This latter part of Glass's conception of racism captures Kant's racist view that black people lack rationality and are therefore stupid. The inferiority–superiority dichotomy is also a feature in Glass's conception. A further feature of this conception is that racism is not only an attitude or feeling, but also a claim or assertion – something that constitutes it as a doctrine or ideology.

According to Kurt Baier, a racist doctrine comprises three types of propositions. First, there is a 'taxonomic theory dividing mankind (the species *Homo sapiens*) into sub-species or races which differ from one another in certain specifiable characteristics' (1978: 123). In my account of a 'racist', the taxonomic theory of races would not constitute racism. That there are different distinguishing characteristics of human beings is a fact, and that these differences are readily apparent to ordinary sense perception, especially the sense of sight, is also a fact. Therefore, a person who classifies or studies these differences or who holds a taxonomic theory cannot rightly be called a racist or be said to espouse racism. At worst, she could be called a racialist, a person who simply believes in the existence of different groups of the human species. The second type of racist doctrine, according to Baier, is *'evaluative racism*, that is, views on where these different races are to be placed in a hierarchical ordering of all races' (1978: 123 – italics in original). This approximates my understanding of racism because a person who classifies races in a hierarchical order would frequently place her own race at the top of the hierarchy (although this need not always be so), thus making a claim of superiority. In other words, she would be making an implicit or explicit value judgement about the essential superiority or inferiority of one race against another. The last type of doctrine, Baier asserts, is normative racism. This is a normative theory which offers principles about how members of one race should treat members of other races regarded as inferior. It is alleged that the superior race has a moral right to dominate, subjugate or enslave the putative inferior races. It also claims that superior and inferior races should not intermarry, because race mixture is not only against nature but can also lead to the lowering of standards and racial degeneration of the superior race. Montagu explains this theory in this way:

> The 'races' that have achieved most are obviously biologically 'superior', so it is reasoned, to those who have achieved less. There is, therefore, so the argument runs, a natural hierarchy of 'races'. Racists – that is to say – *persons who believe or subscribe to such ideas* – feel that certain discriminations are necessary in order to protect themselves from the contaminating effects of social or biological admixture with members of 'inferior races'... (in Singer 1978: 175 – italics in original)

It is precisely at this hierarchisation point, with the implicit power relations involved, that the question of race acquires a serious dimension and becomes racism.

As the term is commonly used, 'racism' implies 'prejudice' and 'discrimination' and is always associated with them. As a state of mind, a belief or attitude, 'racism' is associated with the term 'prejudice'. Etymologically, the term 'prejudice' refers to a 'pre-judgement' or an evaluation or decision made before the facts of a case can be properly determined and weighed. It differs from strict 'pre-judgement' in the sense that errors of pre-judgement are capable of being easily rectified in light of new evidence coming to the fore. A prejudiced person, on the contrary, is emotionally resistant to all evidence that threatens her belief or attitude. Thus a person who stubbornly commits herself to a position or belief in the face of overwhelming counter-evidence could be called a prejudiced person. An appropriate example of prejudice is that of a magistrate or a jury making up her or its mind about the guilt or innocence of an accused person before hearing all the relevant evidence about the crime.

Prejudice may take on a negative or positive form. People may be prejudiced *against* or *in favour* of others. Thus a jury that has made up its mind about the innocence of an accused person before all the evidence is led is prejudiced in favour of the accused. Parents normally react in this manner about their children. But when the jury reacts negatively toward the accused person before all the relevant facts have been produced, it is prejudiced against the accused. In this context, the judgement – whether favourable or unfavourable – is determined by pre-conceived opinions or notions about the accused. When a person's physical characteristics or traits, her cultural background or her membership of a particular race is made the grounds for such prejudice, we talk of racial prejudice. Allport defines racial prejudice as 'an antipathy based upon a faulty and inflexible generalization. It may be felt or expressed. It may be directed toward a group as a whole or toward an individual because he is a member of that group' (1954: 9). The net effect of prejudice thus defined, according to Allport, is to place the object of prejudice at some disadvantage not merited by her own misconduct. The word 'antipathy' in the above definition is meant to cover a wide range of negative attitudes, including hatred, aversion, dislike, enmity, and various other hostile and unfavourable feelings. Hence racial prejudice is 'mostly negative' (Allport 1954: 6). My interpretation of prejudice is also one that is based on negative feelings, tendencies or beliefs that arise against human beings by virtue of the status they occupy or are perceived to occupy as members of a group. It includes the following elements or dimensions: (i) negative beliefs or stereotypes, (ii) negative feelings or emotions, and (iii) the tendency to discriminate against others.

Although the word 'racial prejudice' is often used interchangeably with the word 'racism', certain significant distinctions can nevertheless be made. Whereas racial prejudice connotes individual or group feelings of antipathy toward a particular racial group, these feelings *may* or *may not* involve assumptions about the inferiority of the other group. Racism, however, posits the biological, intellectual, aesthetic, moral and/or cultural superiority of one race against another. A further distinction between the two is that while racial prejudice cannot be readily categorised as an ideology of racial domination, racism can easily be categorised as such. Notwithstanding these differences, the effects of both racism and racial prejudice are the same on the consciousness of their victims.

When racial prejudice is translated into action, it leads to racial discrimination. Okolo understands it well when he avers:

> ...racism or a biased mental attitude leads to selective responses in thought and action...When responses to another are selective in action (on the basis of skin color or permanent racial characteristics), it is known in everyday language as discrimination. When responses in thought are selective and are codified or formulated into laws which in turn become the permanent basis for exploiting and oppressing members of a particular race, they are known as discriminatory or racist laws. (1974: 7)

Care should, however, be exercised when dealing with the concept 'discrimination'. The term 'discrimination' can be used in two senses, namely: a non-moral or neutral sense and a moral or normative sense. In the former sense, discrimination simply means making distinctions or differentiations between two entities. For example, a person who is not colour-blind can discriminate one colour from another, or a person who is not tone-deaf can discriminate between different sounds. In its moral connotation, discrimination entails making distinctions on arbitrary or unjustifiable grounds either by discriminating *against* or *in favour of* someone or some group. In this context, it involves differential treatment of persons or groups of persons on irrelevant grounds such as sex, race or religion. For example, sexual discrimination involves differential treatment of individuals solely on the basis of their sex; racial discrimination involves treating individuals differently because of their racial affiliation or membership usually epitomised by the colour of the skin and/or hair texture. In these examples, sex and race are both taken to be the arbitrary or unjustifiable grounds of differentiation based on prejudice.

From what has been said about racism and its derivatives, racial prejudice and racial discrimination, I am now in a position to suggest a general definition of the phenomenon. *Racism may be defined as the attitudes, feelings, beliefs or doctrine that one group of people with common physiological characteristics (referred to as a race) is biologically, morally, intellectually and/or culturally intrinsically inferior to another race; this presumed inferiority justifies and prescribes domination, oppression, unfair treatment or exclusionary practices of one racial group by another which wields the power to carry these actions out.* In terms of this definition, there are four dimensions to racism: biological, moral, intellectual and cultural. All of these posit the innate or inherent inferiority of one race to another and an implicit justification for racial domination of the supposedly 'inferior' by the putative 'superior' and powerful race. Implied in this definition is the notion that racial prejudice, racial discrimination and racialism are different from racism. Racism (as used here and is evident in Biko) has as its foundational ingredient, in addition to prejudice or discrimination, the conception of power.

Racism is either individual or institutional, overt or covert. Individual racism refers to a power invested in an individual person's set of attitudes, beliefs, feelings or prejudices about the inferiority of another racial group and how that presumed inferior racial group should be treated. When such attitudes and beliefs are codified and formulated into legislation or laws governing the political, social, economic, organisational and even religious relations of different racial groups in a given society, we talk of 'institutionalised racism', or we might say that that society is governed by a 'racial ideology'. By racial ideology is meant:

> Racial domination that incorporates beliefs in a particular race's cultural and/or inherent biological inferiority. It uses such beliefs to justify and prescribe unequal treatment of that group...It is not merely a vague feeling of racial superiority, it is a system of *domination* with structures of domination – social, political and economic. (Boesak 1983: 3)

From the above definition, we notice that racism becomes an ideology when as a set of beliefs or ideas it is connected to the power structure and power relations of a given society. Hence Boesak characterises it as 'a system of domination'. The element of domination or power relation that defines racism is captured clearly in Carmichael and Hamilton's conception of racism. In their view, racism is 'the predication of decisions and policies on considerations of race for the purpose of *subordinating* a racial group and maintaining control over that group' (1967: 25 – italics in original). Ambalavaner Sivanandan defines racism so that the focus is on practice and power: 'It is the acting out of racial prejudice and not racial prejudice itself that matters...Racism is about power not about prejudice' (1983: 3).[1]

Biko on racism

Central to Biko's thinking is first and foremost the problem of white racism in general, but in particular the apartheid type. Indeed, true to Nkrumah's statement that the social milieu affects the content of philosophy, Biko's thought was affected by the apartheid racist social and political milieu; Biko, through his antiracist philosophy of Black Consciousness, sought to affect the socio-political milieu by opposing it. Just as Marx was 'created' by capitalism, Lenin by the Russian aristocracy, Gandhi by British imperialism and Fanon by French colonialism and the colonised 'Wretched of the Earth', Biko was a product of apartheid racism. To mention a commonplace, Biko was a child of his time and a bearer of the judgements and prejudices of his historical period. His thoughts on racism reflect the reality of apartheid and should be understood within that context.

Apartheid

Very few political, social and economic systems in the latter half of the twentieth century generated so much controversy as apartheid in South Africa. Because of its complexity and wide-ranging significance, apartheid has variously been defined from religious, cultural, political, ethical, economic, social and racial perspectives and its origins theoretically ascribed to these various aspects. The breadth and width of the apartheid phenomenon makes it literally impossible to attempt a comprehensive articulation of its varied and complex manifestations here. What follows is merely a humble scratch on the surface of a fundamentally deep and complex oppressive system.

To most people who did not live under it, experience it or become direct victims of it, apartheid means something different than it does to those who lived it. To give us a sense of what apartheid really was, Derrida describes it as 'an untranslatable idiom' of racism, 'the worst...racism par excellence', 'the most racist of racism' and 'the ultimate racism in the world' (1985: 291). Indeed, the numerous apartheid laws represented 'racism's last word' (Derrida 1985: 290). In addition, apartheid was the only racism 'on the scene that dare[d] to say its name and to present itself for what it [was]' (Derrida 1985: 292). Literally, the word 'apartheid' is the Afrikaans equivalent of 'apartness' or simply the state of separateness, but in reality it was much more than mere separateness. Introduced in an Afrikaans newspaper in 1943, it became the official doctrine and policy of the white Afrikaner Nationalist Party in 1948.

But one cannot simply say 'apartness' or 'separateness' in a vacuum. 'Separateness' is a relational concept that refers us to two or more entities or phenomena distanced from one another. When one uses the word 'apartness', one has to indicate *what* is separated from *what*. As a concept, 'apartheid' functions much like 'consciousness'. One cannot simply be 'conscious' without being conscious of something. Consciousness is always already consciousness of something; it is intentional. The apartness of apartheid is the separation of races of people. *Prima facie*, the doctrine of 'apartheid' holds that each race has a unique destiny, history, religion, culture and values; and that for this reason, they must be kept apart. This then might be taken to mean the separation of the different racial groups and their right to self-determination. However, in practice and theory, apartheid was a colonialist, capitalist, religious and racial ideology designed to ensure the domination and subjugation of the majority of black people by the minority white European settlers – what Mbembe aptly captures as the 'theory of Blacks as "humans apart"' (2017: 86). There is a widespread tendency to conflate apartheid with racial prejudice or discrimination, both of which are reducible to individual moral deficits. The fact is that apartheid was neither simply racial prejudice nor racial discrimination; it was, as Biko and his Black Consciousness comrades correctly claimed, 'an absolutely evil system' put in place by the Dutch and British settlers long before the Afrikaner Nationalist Party introduced the word when it came into power. In fact, the doctrine emerged – at least in its practical manifestation – as a strategy of strengthening and perfecting an already historically extant system of racial domination and white supremacy long before its enactment by the Afrikaners. Rooted in the values of Europeans abroad and in South Africa, apartheid was a refined and fine-tuned British colonial policy of 'Native Segregation'. Sartre graphically describes the operation of the system:

> [Y]ou begin by occupying the country, then you take the land and exploit the former owners at starvation rates. Then, with mechanization, this cheap labour is still too expensive; you finish up taking from the natives their right to work. All that is left for the [natives] to do, *in their own land*, at a time of great prosperity, is to die of starvation. (2001: 39 – italics in original)

Apartheid was the enforcement by a minority of Europeans of a policy designed to keep in conditions of slavery or neo-slavery the majority of the population consisting of black people. Committed to establishing and intensifying absolute white supremacy, the apartheid Nationalist Party government enacted a series of racially discriminatory laws, including the Group Areas Act, mandating residential segregation; the Reservation of Separate Amenities Act, requiring segregated public facilities; the Immorality Act, forbidding sexual liaisons across the colour divide; the Prohibition of Mixed Marriages Act, forbidding interracial matrimony; the Population Registration Act, the pillar of apartheid legislation which classified people according to their race and ordering; the Bantu Education Act, enacting separate and unequal education for different racial groups; the Prevention of Illegal Squatting Act, preventing unemployed African work seekers from living in white cities and towns; the Native Resettlement Act, for the coerced removal of Africans to the bantustans; the Land Act of 1913, the appropriation of African land, giving 87 per cent of the total land to white people and 13 per cent to Africans; the Influx Control Act, regulating the influx and labour of Africans in the white urban areas. All these Acts – together with thousands of proclamations, regulations, by-laws and government notices – were collectively a method of compartmentalising the settlers and the natives, forcing apart the racial groups and instituting white supremacy in South Africa. In the apartheid world, therefore, race made all the difference, because it determined one's mode of being and perceiving; one's being-for-others; one's relation to objects, space and time; and one's opportunities – in short, one's being.

Through these and a myriad other apartheid laws, South Africa became a quintessentially colonial racist society, a society violently compartmentalised into races ruled by a Manichean psychology. These laws legalised the separation of the races in almost every sphere of existence. Forced separation became the norm, from unequal separate hospitals to separate cemeteries, from separate beaches to separate swimming pools, from separate toilets to separate transport systems, from separate territorial areas to separate residential areas, from separate churches to separate jails, from separate sports to separate types of jobs – existential separation in full flight not excepting work, as even there, the facilities were separate. For example, in terms of the Influx Control Act, Africans were divested of political rights and were required by law to carry the much-hated *passbook* (an identity document Africans euphemistically called '*dompas*' meaning 'stupid/dumb pass') to justify their presence in various places. The restrictions and laws pertaining to passbooks were so dehumanising and demanding that it was almost impossible to comply with all the requirements at any given time, reducing Africans to potential candidates for police harassment, arrest and imprisonment. Black people had neither economic nor cultural rights. Economically, they could not own property and were confined or supposed to be confined to 13 per cent of the land, with the rest owned by white people. Concentrated or cooped up in 'concentration camps' called urban townships, black people were allowed out – only with the pass or permit – to go and work in the white cities and return to the townships every night. Africans who were born in the township of a city, who lived there without interruption (that is, in possession of what was called the Section 10(1)(a) rule, which allowed Africans to be in the urban white space) would in terms of Regulation 17(1)(v), Chapter II, on black labour, loose the right to return and stay more than 72 hours if they left the township for 2 weeks. This meant that they forfeited their status as a resident of the township and, in terms of Section 10(1)(b), had to possess a permit to be in the township longer than 72 hours. Arrest for infringement of the pass laws meant deportation to a bantustan, even if the violator had no connections whatsoever with the purported homeland. Furthermore, an African who was born in a township and lived there without interruption did not have the right to let her married daughter and son who was older than 18 years or her grandchildren stay in her house if they had not been born there. Such draconian laws put Africans in constant encounter with the wrath of the police and perpetually landed them in prison to be sold to the farmers as quasi-slaves.

The basis of apartheid as individual, institutional, state, cultural, legal and/or religious racism was essentially the claims to white supremacy, white domination and racial separation. According to its fundamental principles, the culture, customs, values and daily life of the white race had to be preserved and protected against adulteration or contamination by African people believed to be alien savages, biologically and mentally inferior, undeveloped, lazy, irresponsible and dangerous. To achieve this project, each racial group had to live, work and develop as much apart and separated from one another as political, social, economic, religious and cultural circumstances permitted. Hence the ruling white Nationalist Party's first official statement on assuming power reads: 'In our attitude toward the Natives the fundamental principle is the supremacy of the European population in a spirit of Christian trusteeship utterly rejecting every attempt to mix the races' (in Leatt et al. 1986: 77–78). Incidentally, European aversion to Africans and their attempt to put as much separation and distance between themselves and Africans were not peculiar to or new to the apartheid system. Indeed, this separation has been a distinguishing feature of colonial experience in Africa. According to Jane Gordon, eighteenth-century colonial France also associated 'blackness with servitude and corresponding efforts to assure that blacks and whites remained separated' (2014: 22). To ensure that this separation was maintained, 'a series of theoretical and legal measures were enacted with the aim to shore up national and racial boundaries'. These boundaries were designed to keep Africans (natives) 'out of sight and mind in safely distant offshore locations' (2014: 23).[2] Fanon makes the same point when he describes this apartheid colonial world as '...a narrow world strewn with prohibitions...a world cut into two...The zone where the natives live is not complimentary to the zone inhabited by the settlers. The two zones are opposed, but not in the service of a higher unity. Obedient to the rules of pure Aristotelian logic, they both follow the principle of reciprocal exclusivity' (1968: 38–39). Apartheid geography also followed a Manichean logic. The town where white people lived, is described as:

> ... strongly built town, all made of stone and steel. It is a brightly lit town; the streets are covered with asphalt, and the garbage cans swallow all the leavings, unseen, unknown and hardly thought about. The [white people's] feet are never visible, except perhaps in the sea, but there you're never close enough to see them...The [white] town is a well-fed town...its belly is always full of good things...
>
> The native town [township] is a place of ill fame, peopled by men of evil repute. They are born there...they die there. It is a world without spaciousness; men live there on top of each other...The [township] is a hungry town, starved of bread, of meat, of shoes, of coal, of light...The

native town is a town on its knees, a town wallowing in the mire. (Fanon 1968: 39)

This apartheid world cut into two, this compartmentalised world, was 'inhabited by two different species' and what differentiated this compartmentalised world was 'to begin with the fact of belonging to or not belonging to a given race, a given species'. In such a world, 'the economic substructure is also a superstructure. The cause is the consequence; you are rich because you are white, you are white because you are rich' (Fanon 1968: 39–40). In short, the apartheid world was a Manichean world, 'a motionless Manicheistic world' of the good white person and the evil black person in which 'the native is hemmed in' (1968: 51–52). Apartheid, for Fanon, is to be understood as a paradigmatic case of the logic of colonial antagonism, an existential prohibition fixed in space, coercive segregation and a relation of social closure. In this racially fractured colonial society, this 'racial polity' (to use Mills' phrase), the daily occurrence of violence against the natives was normal. Hemmed in and brutalised by the apartheid policing system, the Africans subjected to continuous state violence struggled for survival, ironically in the midst of the euphoria generated by the independence of many erstwhile African colonial countries. It is these regular and constant occurrences of murder and violence that with the Sharpeville massacre of 1960, drew attention to the brutality of the apartheid condition. Fanon states: 'The murders of Sharpeville shook public opinion for months. In the newspapers, over the wave-lengths, and in private conversations, Sharpeville has become a symbol. It was through Sharpeville that men and women first became acquainted with the problem of apartheid in South Africa' (1968: 75).

It was within this racial polity, this motionless Manicheistic world, this world which was the embodiment of 'racism par excellence' and 'the most racist of racism', that Biko was born, created and nurtured. In his words: 'Born shortly before 1948, I have lived all my conscious life in the framework of institutionalised separate development [apartheid]. My friendships, my love, my education, my thinking and every other facet of my life have been carved and shaped within the context of separate development' (1996: 27). It was this world that inexorably situated him within the Africana existential philosophy whose *leitmotif* is the concern with racial problematics. Lewis Gordon could not have put it better when he wrote of Africana philosophy: '[R]acial problems serve a dominating role. In Africana existential philosophy, this reality has meant detailed explorations of this dominating factor in the lived experience of African people. It has meant an exploration of their lived experience of blackness' (2000: 8).

With this in mind, let us return to the question of racism. What is racism for Biko? He defines racism as 'discrimination by a group against another for the purpose of subjugation or maintaining subjugation' (1996: 25). First, to 'discriminate' involves acts of exclusion and inclusion (that is, certain practices) in this case, discriminatory practices. Accordingly, it is not enough to characterise racism as simply ideological. And to 'subjugate' entails the notion of power.[3] Power in itself is an empty notion. Words like 'power' or 'force' are simply ways of talking about phenomena that are able to generate the emergence of other things (that is, to put other things into being). For example, a person who has power is one whose actions and choices can affect the world. Her physical presence is not necessary for there to be some change in the location of her power. It is this ability to have an effect on the world that constitutes power. In terms of this conception, Lewis Gordon defines power as 'the ability to live outwardly, to make choices that would initiate a chain of effects in the social world that would constitute the set of norms and institutions that would affirm one's belonging in the world instead of stimulating a flight from it to an infinitesimal, inwardly directed path of madness and despair' (2006: 105).

To have power, therefore, is to have power or control over someone or something, both of which are predicated on or originate in separation. Power, Goldberg notes, 'involves control that can be exercised – at least in principle – over a person(s) or over resources – often over the former to effect the latter, or vice versa' (1995: 13). A definition of this kind is obviously one that indicates in a racial context that power by controlling and dominating establishes and maintains exclusionary relations of superiority and inferiority: racism. What is invidious about racism is that apart from dehumanising the racial object, it fundamentally rejects the humanity of other groups of human beings. Since racism is dehumanisation, it gets situated as a form of oppression. Oppression is often understood as the imposition of power on unwilling victims. Taken within the context of apartheid and the extant power relations between black people and white people within that oppressive system, Biko's definition restricts all acts or expressions of racism to white people. Racism, therefore, is not discrimination or simple prejudice alone but also the imposition of one's power on the lives of those one regards as inferior. This power found its concrete exercise in apartheid white subjugation of black people through acts of control, domination, conquest and defeat. In all these acts, power was also exercised in the promotion, execution and maintenance of discriminatory practices.

What this actually means is that an individual or a designated racial group A treats an individual or a designated group B in a racist manner only if (in addition to A's attitude and feelings of biological, moral, intellectual and social superiority over group B persons), A holds and exercises power over B. Since in South Africa white people held and exercised power over black people, only white people could be racist, and black people could not because the latter lacked power. This conception of racism is objectionable to some people on the basis that '[t]he bitter, solitary old [white] bigot, alone in her room, is a racist for all her powerlessness' (Garcia 1997: 13). The appropriate response to this objection is the question: Powerless in relation to whom and as a member of which group? If she belongs to the dominant group, powerless as she may seem to be at that particular time, she belongs to a group designated as a race which at that particular point in time possesses power. Therefore, the power she wields is the power derived from her membership in the powerful and dominant group. Being a white person renders being-in-the-world a reality of political, economic, aesthetic, social, cultural and religious dominance.

Of course, Biko's conception of racism raises the following question: 'Can Blacks be racist' in an antiblack world? For him, the answer is NO! Racism, in his view, is about power; hence, '[o]ne cannot be a racist unless he has the power to subjugate' (1996: 25). A number of people, particularly liberals, are very critical of this conception of racism that excludes black people from being racists. In his book (the title of which is revealing in its focus) 'I'm Not a Racist, But...' The Moral Quandary of Race (2002), Lawrence Blum argues that black people – indeed everyone – is a racist. He objects to the view that racism is prejudice plus power. In his view, since black people also have power in certain subinstitutions such as municipality or government institutions, they therefore can also be racists. Insofar as his conception of 'Blacks' includes Latinos, Mexicans, Japanese, Chinese, Koreans and Indians, a little concession can be allowed. In terms of power relations, Japanese, Chinese, Mexicans and so on can be racists against Africans and African-descended people. For example, in 1986, the then prime minister of Japan Yasuhiro Nakasone said that because of its black population, the USA was less intelligent than Japan. Indeed, many Japanese laws are, as Wolferen argues, racist.[4] But his argument cannot hold if, for him, the word 'Blacks' refers only to Africans and African-Americans. First, in citing these examples as racism, Blum inadvertently recognises the element of power as constitutive of racism and therefore cannot deny its significance. Second, he seems to have a limited conception of power which does not include global white supremacy. A striking example of white power or 'white supremacy' which Blum does not take into account is provided by Margaret Mead in a discussion with Baldwin on racism in their book A Rap on Race (1971). She recounts her experience of white supremacy as an anthropologist doing research in New Guinea. The following is her account of her experiences as a member of the dominant and powerful group:

I've been on a plantation in New Guinea where I was responsible for a labor line. Now, they weren't slaves. They were indentured laborers; they were grown men. You have two hundred men out of the bush...

Now when I was temporarily alone, I had to run that labor line. I had to give them orders based on absolutely nothing but *white supremacy*. I was one lone white woman. Any one of them could have killed me...If anything had happened to me, maybe twenty of them would have been killed...This was a fine exercise of sheer white supremacy, nothing else. (1971: 21–22 – italics added)

In response, Baldwin says, 'Yes. Of course, at the root of all this is power, isn't it?' (1971: 23). In another register on Malcolm X, as if adding to the conversation with Mead, Baldwin asserts that power is the terrain where racism is played out and because of this fact, '[t]he powerless by definition, can never be "racist", for they can never make the world pay for what they feel or fear except by the suicidal endeavour which makes of them fanatics or revolutionaries, or both' (in Marable & Felber 2013: 494–495). White power in an antiblack world means that the life of a single white woman is worth more than two hundred black lives. This is precisely what racism means for Biko, that one single white woman can control and have the power of life and death: the blood of one single white farmer in Zimbabwe, for example, is reflected on TVs throughout the world rather than the blood of a thousand black workers in the same country simply because black lives do not matter. In short, Biko's concept of power translates into a demand by a single white woman that the black Other justifies her existence. Her existence is justified by the existence of the black Other whose existence depends on her. In other words, she is her own justification, her own foundation, an in-itself-for-itself, God. As a demonstration of the significance of power in racism, Albert Memmi poses the following question: 'How else can one explain how... a handful of often arrogant colonizers [white people] can live in the midst of a multitude of colonized?' His answer is that the colonisers know very well that if their lives were to be in danger, 'their lonely position would quickly be changed. All the resources of science – telephone, telegraph and airplane – would be placed at their disposal and within a few minutes, terrible weapons of defense and destruction. For each colonizer [white person] killed, hundreds or thousands of the colonised [black people] have been or would be exterminated' (1964: 93).

In a racist society, power relations are not necessarily between individuals; rather, as Donna-Dale Marcano explains, those individuals are 'representatives of groups with...power'. We thus have to take seriously 'the consciously or unconsciously felt security of belonging to a group in power...In other words, group empowerment is a relevant source of empowerment for individuals as representatives of that group' (2009: 22). White power in an antiblack world, as Mead's example makes clear, therefore entails that the life of a single white woman is worth more than the lives of twenty or more black people. Racism as domination, Biko suggests, has as its equivalent the psychological phenomenon of sadism. Sartre argues that sadism is an attitude that constitutes other human beings as mere objects in the world. Such an attitude is ultimately responsible for the emergence of the master/slave, dominator/dominated, exploiter/exploited or subject/object relation. From this point of view, the main ideas in Biko's definition of racism – racial 'discrimination' (exclusion/inclusion), 'subjugation' (domination, control) and so on – and Sartre's characterisation of sadism fit pretty well with the theory and practices of the very architect of apartheid whom Biko fundamentally rebelled against, Prime Minister Hendrik Verwoerd. In his sadistic attempt to justify apartheid (or 'separate development' as he preferred to call it), Verwoerd said:

> Reduced to its simplest form the problem is nothing else than this: We want to keep South Africa White...'keeping it White' can only mean one thing, namely White *domination*, not 'leadership', not 'guidance', but 'control', 'supremacy'. If we are agreed that it is the desire of the people that the white man should be able to protect himself by retaining White *domination*, we say that it can be achieved by separate development. (Bunting, in La Guma 1971: 28 – italics added)

Verwoerd's justification of apartheid racism expresses one significant element of a racist consciousness: the idea of the 'opposite race'. In his racist consciousness, the black race is believed to be the absolute Other, an enemy and threat to the white race (*swart gevaar*/black threat) against whom all white people must unite. It was in the context of such racist consciousness, as will be evident later, that Biko – in a similar fashion as Sartre in relation to Negritude – articulated his conception of Black Consciousness in terms of the Hegelian dialectic of thesis, antithesis and synthesis.

Biko's definition therefore, without pretension to universality, captures apartheid racism as articulated by Verwoerd in the statement cited above. The basis of apartheid, in Verwoerd's view, was white supremacy, white domination and racial separation. Hence the ruling National Party's first official statement after winning the election in 1948 reads: 'In our attitude towards the Natives the fundamental principle is the supremacy of the European population in a spirit of Christian trusteeship utterly rejecting every attempt to mix the races.' One of the spokespersons of apartheid declared: 'The more radically racial segregation is carried through, the better it will be; and the more consistently we apply the policy of apartheid, the more efficient our purity of blood and our unadulterated European racial survival will be guaranteed' (in Leatt et al. 1986: 77). The words 'carried through' and 'we apply' in the citation are indicative of the possession of 'power to do'.

The fundamental categories in Biko's thinking, therefore, are *racism, freedom, blackness, consciousness, responsibility* and *authenticity*. These categories are interwoven in a set of ideas that came to be called the Black Consciousness philosophy. Biko's position can be explained in terms of two types of consciousness, namely pre-reflective and reflective consciousness. On the one hand, there is the primordial human being-in-the-world pre-reflective consciousness, a consciousness immersed and engulfed in the reality of the world, a consciousness that is one with the world. Reflective consciousness, on the other hand, is not consciousness of the world but consciousness of consciousness of the world. It is consciousness that posits itself as its own object, a consciousness that stands out of itself and looks at itself from a distance and reflects upon itself. Put differently, pre-reflective consciousness is similar to what Gilbert Ryle calls 'first-order-statements', the function of which is to refer us directly to phenomena, entities and events in the world of experience; whereas reflective consciousness could be 'second-order-statements' whose function is not to refer us directly to the world – they are statements about statements about the world. Arising from this ontology are two modes of human existence in an antiblack world such as South Africa which are products of reflective consciousness: being-white-in-the-world (white consciousness) and being-black-in-the-world (black consciousness). These two modes of being and perceiving – or 'ways of life' – are dialectically related in such a way that they are contradictory yet dependent upon each other for their existence. Through various means (economic, religious, social, political and legal), white self-consciousness subjugated and destroyed black self-consciousness – thus denying black people their existential freedom. Since human reality as consciousness is (in Sartre's view) freedom, the emergence of Black Consciousness was therefore a response to a white consciousness that sought to appropriate and dominate a black consciousness and thus the freedom of black people. It was and still is a struggle for a new consciousness; a re-awakening of self-consciousness; a re-appropriation of black self-consciousness from the clutches of an appropriative and dominating white consciousness; a rediscovery of the black self which lay buried beneath white consciousness imposed on black people through cultural, political, economic, linguistic and religious domination. It is, so to speak, an 'affirmative action' on the self by the self, an affirmation not from the Other but from and by the self.

The existential ontology of Black Consciousness

One of the primary tasks of philosophy has hitherto been the analysis of the problem of 'being'. To be precise, the preoccupation with being is the fundamental concern of the branch of philosophy known as ontology and, by extension, philosophical anthropology. Ontology has unfortunately suffered the disrepute that has befallen metaphysics. Hence Heidegger's lamentation in his classic text *Being and Time* that contemporary philosophy has forgotten 'being'. For, according to Heidegger's ontological conception, '[t]he essence of *Dasein* [the human being] lies in its existence' – put differently, '[t]he essence [*wesen*] of this entity [human being] lies in its "*to be*"' (1962: 67). From this Heideggerian point of view, ontology becomes the basic interpretation of the human way of being. It is this lament by Heidegger, I have insisted elsewhere (2012), to which Biko and the Black Consciousness Movement of South Africa in particular – indeed the entire Black world in general – responded. The response was mainly in the form of a concern for the category of being, especially the being of the black subject in an antiblack world. My point here, as I have argued elsewhere (More 2012), is that the interest in the concept of being shown by Black Consciousness adherents was born not only of struggle, but also of the politics of being (that is, the politics of black being in an antiblack apartheid world). As a seeming response to Heidegger's lamentation of philosophy's forgetfulness of being, Black Consciousness thinkers resurrected being as a central concept of their political philosophy. Unlike Heidegger, the question of black being was for the movement inherently a political question. For them, politics operated as a midwife in the process of bringing to life the problem of black being. For this reason, Black Consciousness is a philosophy born of struggle and a movement animated by what Sartre characterises as a '*needing-to-be*'.

Most publications on Black Consciousness, and Biko in particular, either ignore or are oblivious of the self-evidently philosophical foundations of the movement. This philosophical grounding, particularly as a concern for the ontological category of being, was first articulated by Chabani Manganyi (a leading Black Consciousness existentialist of the time) and later noted by Nolutshungu, who made the observation that there was 'a philosophical preoccupation with "being"' (1983: 156–157) in the Black Consciousness Movement of South Africa. An overview of the articles appearing in the main publication of Black Consciousness, the *SASO Newsletter*, reveals a definite and determined concern with being. Black South Africans, SASO president Barney Pityana asserts, were motivated not only by the struggle for survival in an antiblack apartheid world but also and fundamentally by 'a determination TO BE and to assert one's humanity' (1971:

8). In characteristically existentialist language, Sono states: 'The Black man is Negritude because...he cannot hate his being without ceasing to be. Being cannot be non-Being, Black cannot be Non-White' (1971: 18). Elsewhere, the same SASO president declares: 'Blackness is the *beingness* that characterizes oppressed people in this country' (Sono 1972: 11). The reference to Negritude, both the Senghor and Césaire's variants, indicates how the concern with being was not only a political or philosophical preoccupation of Black Consciousness but also its cultural dimension. The poetry of Black Consciousness advocates (especially the *SASO Newsletter, Staffrider* and *New Classic* contributors Mafika Gwala, Serote, Oswald Mtshali, Don Mattera, Sepamla, Mbulelo Mzamane and others), replete with reference to black being and humanity, bears witness to this concern.

Even though Sartre's contribution to the ontological framework of the Black Consciousness Movement is considerable, Fanon counsels that whenever we deal with Sartre's ontology in relation to black people, this ontology has to be revised or turned on its head. This is so because at the reflective consciousness level, the being of the black subject as a particular mode of being in an antiblack world differs radically from the ontological facticity of the white subject. In other words, the phenomenological description employed by Sartre (and even Hegel), though fundamental and informative, is inadequate to deal with the ontological state of being black. For example, in Sartre's ontological phenomenology, the being that is human is a being who interrogates being; a being who asks the question 'What does it mean *to be*?' But more fundamentally, the being that is human is a being such that in its own being its very being is always already in question. This is true of all beings that are human at the level of pre-reflective consciousness. However, while Sartre declares that, pre-reflectively, the very same human being who questions is 'the being which is to itself its own lack of being' (1956: 565) in order that there might be being, Pityana – approvingly citing Fanon and responding from a reflective consciousness point of view – declares: 'My Negro consciousness does not hold itself out as a lack' (in Van der Merwe & Welsh 1972: 180). What Pityana and Fanon are saying here is that the reality of the black being is a being who *is constituted* as lack and thus overdetermined from without. Put differently, the reality of being black is that of a being whose being as human is perpetually questioned.

When Sartre's human being asks 'What does it mean *to be*?', Black Consciousness adherents ask 'What does it mean *to be a human being*?' While Heidegger and Sartre ask 'What is the meaning of being?', Black Consciousness raises the question 'What is the meaning of the being of a black person in an antiblack world?' What binds the two questions is a philosophical anthropology whose central question is: What does it mean to be a human being? However, Black Consciousness's philosophical ontology goes further than both Sartre and

Heidegger by dedicating itself to the understanding of beings whose humanity has been called into question. The consequences of a questioned and denied humanness – of being treated as subhumans, subpersons or animals – invariably lead to the profound experience of existential dread and anguish in the face of non-being. This feeling, in turn, generates the problem of identity and thus the question 'Who am I?' Since questions of identity naturally imply the being's relation to itself, they ultimately become ontological questions of being, essence and meaning which then take the form 'What am I?' This engagement with philosophical anthropology suggests that the adherents of Black Consciousness understood that in order for philosophy to respond meaningfully to apartheid racism, colonialism and oppression, it must take seriously how these phenomena affect human beings (including what it means to be human).

Ontology and antiblack racism

A necessary condition for the presence of racism (according to Memmi's definition of the phenomenon) is the justification of present or possible privilege, hostility or violence. This condition suggests the exclusion of black people from the moral community – that is, from the group of people such as white people to which privilege, kindliness and peace apply. In other words, this group enjoys civil, social and political rights from which other groups such as black people are excluded. If a group is situated outside the moral community, this translates into social, moral and political death. Consequently, the exteriority justifies violence, oppression and even genocide against the excluded group. But to exclude a group of people from the moral universe is essentially to dehumanise them, to consider its members as non-human, simply as objects. Indeed, one of the many issues connected with antiblack racism, as Lewis Gordon defines it, is not only the self-deceiving belief that one's race is superior to another race but also – and I may add mainly – the belief that 'one's race is the only race qualified to be considered human' (Gordon 1995a: 2). In this sense, racism is a form of dehumanisation and dehumanisation is a form of bad faith because it involves lying to oneself about something of which one is aware. Racism as dehumanisation does not entail self–Other binary relations but rather involves the self-not-Other or Buber's 'I–It' binary relations. Buttressing Fanon's thesis that Sartre's conception of Self/Other (and even Hegel's master/slave) is flawed when applied to white/black relations, Lewis Gordon argues that '[i]mplicit in Other is a shared category. If one is a human being, then the Other is also a human being...Dehumanization takes a different form: here one finds the self, another self, and those who are not-self and not-Other' (2000: 85). While for the black person, the white person is another human being, the structure of antiblack racism is such that for the antiblack racist, the black person is not another human being. Thus, antiblack racism finds itself in a paradoxical context of 'being a human relation of inhumanity. It is a human act of denying the humanity of other groups of human being' (Gordon 2000: 85). But this paradox is constitutive of bad faith precisely because to dehumanise someone involves first recognising her humanity in order to be able to dehumanise her. Any act of dehumanisation is paradoxically an acknowledgement of the humanity of those whom one attempts to reduce to the status of the non-human. Indeed, one cannot dehumanise a stone; the concept would not be appropriate at all. Winthrop Jordan affirms this observation when he explains the Englishmen's attitudes toward Africans: 'They knew perfectly well that Negroes were men, yet they frequently described the Africans as "brutish" or ""bestial" or "beastly"' (1974: 14). Hence the reference to Africans as 'beastlike men'.

The implication of such a situation is that the below-Otherness existence of black people locates their existence in Fanon's 'Zone of Nonbeing', which means the invariable suspension of ethical relations. In such a zone, where the dialectic of self–Other does not exist but is supplanted by the dialectic of self-not-Other, the moral realm vanishes and every act becomes permissible. In such a situation, the racist does not have any serious moral obligations toward an object or even some animals. Any shocking treatment is permissible. This situation then forces black people to struggle for the achievement of Otherness in order to position themselves in the realm of the ethical. In Sartre's play 'The Respectful Prostitute', for example, a white Southerner in defence of his cousin who has murdered a black man says: 'He shot a dirty nigger; so what? You do things like that without thinking; they don't count [in the Southern white moral universe]' (1989: 256–257). Think again of the apartheid Minister of Justice James (Jimmy) Kruger's remarks on the death of Steve Biko: 'Biko's death leaves me cold'; and Hegel's remark 'Among the Negroes moral sentiments are quite weak, or more strictly speaking, non-existent' (1952a: 198). In such a racist world, 'all is permitted' when it involves white actions towards black people.

It is precisely this character of antiblack racism which distinguishes it from other racisms such as anti-Semitism, anti-Asian racism or anti-Arab racism; racisms which, although recognising the humanity of their racial victim, nevertheless consider that humanity as a different kind of humanness.[5] For example, as Mills (1998) reminds us, the classic racist stereotypes of Jews and black people differ crucially in that Jews are generally credited with (sometimes supernormal) intelligence; whereas black people are traditionally represented as bestial, animal-like or subnormal. While white settlers in North America regarded Native Americans as 'savages', they nevertheless recognised them as falling within the pale of humanity. Indeed, De Beauvoir's notion of woman as the absolute Other makes the point that although fundamentally different from men, white women are nevertheless still human. Their humanity is not called into question; she remains the man's mother, sister or daughter. In most instances of oppression, the victim is simply considered an Other. However, with antiblack racism, the concept of 'The Other', as Fanon contends, 'proves fallacious'. Wynter captures this non-beingness in a phrase she uses with devastating effect in most of her writings about the dehumanisation of black people, namely: 'No Humans Involved' (N.H.I.).[6]

Biko demonstrates profound understanding of the dehumanising effect of apartheid racism when he points out that this racism has managed to produce 'a kind of a black man who is man only in form. *This is the extent to which the process of dehumanisation has advanced*...All in all the black man has become a shell, a shadow of a man...a slave, an ox bearing the yoke of oppression with sheepish timidity' (1996: 28, 29 – italics added). The reference to black people in terms of animal imagery is significant here. For the essential problem with antiblack racism is that, among its various purposes, it is a concerted effort to not simply deny the humanity of black human beings but also to equate them with and treat them as animals.[7] Reduced to the *what* mode of animalhood, Douglass recalls an incident during an auction of slaves in the USA: 'We were all ranked together at the valuation. There were horses and men, cattle and women, pigs and children, all holding the same rank in the *scale of being*' (1983: 89–90 – italics added). Nowhere else is the denial of black humanity as evident as in the thoughts of the philosophers and scientists of the Enlightenment period.

Denial of black humanity

A popular approach to race and racism has been to associate these phenomena with primitive, backward, unenlightened people and – by extension – with people who reject modernity. Within this reasoning, the Enlightenment as a project to free people from their backwardness and primitive beliefs was expected to be free from superstitions and ignorance about race and racism. Yet it is the very same Enlightenment period and its Western dominant philosophers who proliferated racist theories and views in the name of civilisation. The African, Hegel declares, 'is an example of *animal man* in all his savagery and lawlessness. And if we wish to understand him at all, we must abstract from all reverence and morality... There is nothing harmonious with humanity to be found in this type of character' (1952a: 198 – italics added). From this, Hegel concludes: 'At this point we leave Africa, not to mention it again. For, it is no historical part of the world...What we properly understand by Africa, is the unhistorical, undeveloped spirit, still involved in the conditions of mere nature' (1952a: 199). Hegel's exclusion of Africans from both the historical process and the dialectical negation that moves history ahead leaves the African as non-being or non-Other. Since history is a human phenomenon, beings without history cannot be human. History makes human beings and human beings make history. Almost at the same time, Cuvier, giving his claims some scientific veneer, declared that black people's morphological and cranial characteristics evidently suggest their proximity 'to the monkey' (in Eze 1997: 105) – a racist slur that, as we shall see later, has survived the years.[8] The 'animality of the blacks' thesis found further propagation in the views of the German philosopher Christoph Meiners, who opined that black people 'display so many animal features, and so few human, that they can scarcely be described as men' (in Poliakov 1974: 179). It is thus this philosophical stereotyping or reasoning that frames African people as non-human and justifies their oppression and exploitation. But this justification paradoxically raises a metaphilosophical question of philosophy's self-justification. How can philosophy truly and honestly justify itself as truly a rational endeavour when philosophical reason is employed to rationalise the inhumanity of African people?

Hegel uses philosophical rationality to claim that the African person is in every respect the opposite of the white person, the human being. While Europeans and Asians have history manifested in reason, Africans are simply unhistorical because they are steeped in nature; while Europe is the symbol of morality, beauty, good, religiousness and civilisation, Africans are a symbol of immorality, ugliness, evil, cannibalism, savagery and/or bestiality. If rationality, morality, civilisation, virtue and godliness are essences of the (truly) human, then by that very fact, a lack of these essential attributes relegates one to the subhuman or the non-human. In other words, Hegel divides the world of African and white people such that from a logical point of view, Africans appear to white people not as subalterns (Others) but both as contraries and contradictions of the Venn diagrammatic syllogism. This syllogistic divide is, according to Lewis Gordon, 'not one of Being and less-Being, but instead one of Being and *no-Being*. Its divide is absolute. It is a divide between Being and Nothingness' (1997b: 28).

It is these attitudes, views and conceptions about the animality of black people that found their greatest expression in apartheid racism. This supposed 'animality of the blacks' animated ontological questions about the being of black people in the Black Consciousness Movement. In a *SASO Newsletter* piece, Pityana declares: 'The history of black and white people from the days of colonialism displays a concerted attempt by white people at repudiating the humanity of the black man' (1970: 9). Black people (in South Africa and elsewhere) have variously been depicted either as animals or as animal-like – 'pigs', 'porch monkeys' or 'yard apes', '*bobbejane*' (baboons) and so on – and therefore not full human beings endowed with rights. According to Janet Smith, the black journalists who covered the funeral of Eugene Terre'Blanche – the racist *Afrikaner Weerstandsbeweging* (AWB) leader – were called 'kaffirs' and 'baboons'. One black farm worker complained to her: 'They [white farmers] think we are nothing but baboons.'⁹ The association of Africans with apes has a long history dating back to the early sixteenth century when, according to Jordan, the English in particular came into contact with West Africans, even though they were highly influenced by 'speculations derived from traditions which had been accumulating in Western Culture since ancient times' (1974: 15). Certain character traits of the apes were imputed to Africans. 'Men that have low and flat nostrils are libidinous as Apes' and loved the company of women because their 'genital member was greater than might match the quantity of [their] other parts' (in Jordan 1974: 16). It is hardly surprising that William Cornwallis Harris, a British military officer visiting South Africa, admonished the British government for not dealing effectively with the Xhosa people in the Eastern Cape. According to him, the British government should 'not long ago have seen the imperious necessity, dictated alike by reason, justice, and humanity, of exterminating from off the face of the earth, *a race of monsters*, who, being the unprovoked destroyers, and implacable foes of Her Majesty's Christian subjects, have forfeited every claim to mercy or consideration' (in Thompson 1985: 89 – italics added). Harris' genocidal desire is indicative of the viciousness of racism and its intention to stop at nothing when it comes to its victims. The case of Saartjie Baartman (the Hottentot Venus) is a paradigmatic instance of the dehumanisation of African people. This animalisation did not even escape Nelson Mandela, who in his own defence at the Rivonia Treason Trial accused white people of dehumanising Africans: 'The lack of human dignity experienced by Africans is the direct result of the policy of White supremacy...Because of this attitude, Whites tend to regard Africans as a separate breed. They do not look upon them as people...' (1995: 437).

Despite the fact that Mandela for obvious reasons became the darling of white South Africa, that did not stop them from regarding him and his people as animals, his earlier protestations to the contrary notwithstanding. The year 2016 opened with a flurry of dehumanising antiblack racism in our country. Penny Sparrow, a white woman trapped in virulent apartheid consciousness, publicly reduced black people to animals by calling them monkeys. In a tweet posted on New Year's Day, Sparrow reacted to the presence of black people on the beaches of South Africa during the festive season as follows:

> These monkeys that are allowed to be released on New Year's eve and new years day on to public beaches towns etc obviously have no education what so ever so to allow them loose is inviting huge dirt and troubles and discomfort to others [read 'white people']. I'm sorry to say I was amongst the revelers and all I saw were black on black skins, what a shame. I do

know some wonderful black people. This lot of monkeys just just don't want to even try. But think they can voice opinions about statute and get away clear, oh dear. From now I shall address blacks of South Africa as monkeys as I see the cute little wild monkeys do the same pick drop and litter. (2 January 2016, 1.30 pm)

This was not the first time she equated black people with monkeys. On Twitter on 8 December 2014 at 9.21 pm, after complaining about how both South Africa and Zimbabwe have degenerated since black people took over the governments, she endorsed her stepdaughter's dehumanisation of black people: 'Now as my step daughter said were actually living on THE PLANET OF THE APES.'

The irony of this kind of thinking is that it is so incompatible with notions of universal rights, human dignity and equality espoused by the European Enlightenment. Indeed, this irony was particularly acute with Voltaire, Hume, Locke, Mill, Kant and even Hegel – the great defenders of universal equality and human dignity for whom Europe was the archetype of humanity and history. But more importantly, as Sartre keenly observed, to treat another human being as a dog is ironically to recognise her humanity. This being the case, how can black people fail to engage in existential and ontological self-interrogation? In *I Write What I Like* (1996) and the interviews he gave, Biko persistently argues that in apartheid South Africa, black people are constantly posing and demanding answers to the questions 'Who am I?' and 'Who are we?'[10] Referring to Césaire's letter of resignation from the French Communist Party, Biko states: 'At about the same time that Césaire said this, there was emerging in South Africa a group of angry young black men who were beginning to "grasp the notion of (their) peculiar uniqueness" and who were eager to define *who they were and what*' (1996: 67 – italics added).

The posing of this question by 'young black men' of the Black Consciousness Movement who found 'themselves at the mercy of white definitional power' is, as Yancy points out, 'an existential, ontological and historical question that white supremacy solicits' (2005: 237). Indeed, the racism of apartheid by its very nature was inclined to challenge its victims to constantly ask the question 'In reality what am I?' If any black human being is constantly told that she is not fully human yet she constantly finds herself struggling with human problems of life and death, freedom and unfreedom, justice and injustice, and so on, Black Consciousness becomes the moment of critically engaging the human being through so-called non-human beings' struggle for their humanity.

As I indicated above, at the primordial level, black people are not the only ones to confront and deal with the question 'Who am I?' The rapid technological developments of the twentieth and twenty-first centuries have indeed rendered this question an everyday source of anguish. Subjectively, such concerns about identity problems and experiences of alienation are common features of the contemporary world. However, at the objective collective level, there is certainly no other racial group that has always faced the problem of identity more seriously than black people. No other group has, in addition to 'Who am I?', asked the question 'What am I?' In other words, no other group of people has had its humanity questioned as black people have; no other group in the world has been demanded to justify its very being as human as black people have.[11] Black people's humanity is not only questioned but denied because they are considered to belong to a completely different species.

If a person's humanity is questioned or denied, what else can that person do except assert her humanity? How could it be otherwise? When asked 'What do Blacks want?' black spokespersons from Douglass to Sojourner Truth, Garvey, Harriet Tubman, Du Bois, Malcolm X, Nelson Mandela, Winnie Mandela, Helen Khuzwayo, Sobukwe, Lumumba, Fanon, Angela Davis, Kwame Ture, Wynter and so on have always responded: Black people want to be treated as human beings. As Cedric Robinson (1983) demonstrated, the demand to be treated as human beings constituted a fundamental feature of the black radical tradition. In response to the ever-present ontological questions 'Who am I?' and 'What am I?' black people have historically declared, 'I am a human being!' Malcolm X, perhaps the fiercest defender of black humanity against white racism in all its overt and covert manifestations, expressed this important desire by black people: 'In essence it only means we want one thing. We declare our right on this earth to be a man, to be a human being, to be respected as a human being, to be given the rights of a human being in this society, on this earth, in this day, which we intend to bring into existence by any means necessary' (1970: 56). Césaire wrote a poem entitled 'I am also Human!' Finally, for Biko, to think along the precepts of Black Consciousness, 'makes the black man see himself as a being, entire in himself, and not an extension of a broom or additional leverage to some machine' (1996: 68).

In human terms, to live under the threat of non-being is to live in what existentialists call a condition of finitude, the constant possibility of disintegration and death and therefore anguish and anxiety. The fundamental source of anguish is the ever-present possibility of death. Apartheid racism is misanthropy, total and complete hate of the human – the hatred of the being of black subjectivity. The original project of hate is the total suppression of the Other's consciousness; it is the desire to annihilate and kill the Other. To hate, Sartre tells us, is fundamentally to pursue the death of the Other. Hussein Bulhan (1985) and Ruth Gilmore (2006) describe apartheid and racism in terms of death. Both argue that apartheid and racism definitely promote the premature death of the victims of their violence, what Abdul JanMohamed calls the 'Death-Bound Subject' (2005).[12] Thus, in a dehumanising apartheid world, each individual black person lived with the consciousness of imminent death – police brutality, township violence, structural violence, poverty, disease, torture and so on – all characterised being-black-in-the-apartheid-world. Hence Biko's insightful observation that because of the constant threat of death, '[o]ne need not try to establish the truth of a claim that black people in South Africa have to struggle for survival. It presents itself in ever so many facets of our lives' (1996: 75). In fact, he even prophetically predicted his death. In the chapter 'On Death' in his book, Biko constantly refers to the reality of his own imminent death. Before Biko, Fanon made the observation that the existential reality of black people in an antiblack world is fundamentally 'a permanent struggle against an omnipresent death. This ever-menacing death is experienced as endemic famine, unemployment, a high death rate, an inferiority complex and the absence of any hope for the future' (1965: 128). In apartheid South Africa, blackness – racially and historically conceived – literally became Heidegger's 'being-towards-death'.

The encounter with one's ownmost non-being as ever-present threat of death generates anguish or existential *angst*. Anguish discloses the reality of human freedom and the possibility of authentic being. Freedom, in turn, allows the individual the conscious decision whereby she defines herself. It is this consciousness of one's freedom in the face of non-being that animated the advocates of the Black Consciousness Movement to question their condition in an apartheid world whose singular *telos* was to question their humanity. But this consciousness required some courage (that is, Tillich's 'courage to be'). Courage is the principle which enabled Black Consciousness adherents to recognise the fact of their enforced non-being and to affirm and define their own being. When such an ontological self-affirmation in the face of non-being is realised, the anguish of death becomes diminished and a radical conversion has occurred. How do black people deal with racist dehumanisation? What are the individual and social effects of an invidious racist system such as apartheid? 'What is the being...of human reality in an antiblack world?' Lewis Gordon asks. The answer, he declares definitively, is *bad faith*.

Bad faith

Of utmost importance to Black Consciousness is the problem of bad faith and its necessary consequence, alienation. The concept of bad faith, popularised by Sartre and adapted to the black condition by Lewis Gordon in his path-breaking book *Bad Faith and Antiblack Racism* (1995a), refers to the attempt by a human being to choose herself as a being who is incapable of choosing. In other words, since a human being as consciousness is a free being, and since freedom is the capacity to choose, any attempt to avoid choosing as a possibility becomes a futile attempt to escape one's freedom and what one is. The attempt not to choose fails precisely because the choice not to choose is itself a choice. Simply stated, bad faith is the attempt to flee the anguish of freedom and responsibility. What this amounts to is that such an individual is in a sense involved in what can loosely be termed 'self-deception', a state in which the deceiver and the deceived are one and the same person, a phenomenon that happens within 'the unity of a single consciousness' (Sartre 1956: 89). Since freedom, according to Sartre, implies assuming responsibility for one's choices, the attempt to flee from one's freedom in bad faith is at the same time an attempt to evade the responsibility that goes with making choices. In bad faith, one attempts to make excuses for one's choices, to constitute oneself as determined and thus not blameworthy for one's choices or actions. Bad faith, according to Sartre, may be committed in various ways, some of which are the attempt to consider oneself as purely transcendence or subject (*being-for-itself*) or purely as facticity or object (*being-in-itself*). This attempt on the part of human reality to emphasise transcendence to the exclusion of facticity or facticity to the exclusion of transcendence constitutes bad faith because human reality is simultaneously transcendence and facticity. By privileging one aspect to the exclusion of the other, one disregards the reality of human existence which is constituted by the ambiguity of being both transcendence and facticity.

From another angle, bad faith amounts to an attempt to evade the truth by concealing it from oneself. It is a refusal to face the truth by positing it either as falsehood or non-existent. As Sartre puts it: 'To be sure, the one who practises bad faith is hiding a displeasing truth or presenting as truth a pleasing untruth' (1956: 89). In this form, bad faith is almost similar to lying to oneself. In short, therefore, bad faith refers to different modes of human existence characterised by self-deception, self-evasion, flight from one's freedom and responsibility, and the acceptance of values as pre-given. To understand the concept of bad faith within the context of the apartheid world, Lewis Gordon's book mentioned above provides better insights. Gordon's text primarily explores through existential phenomenology the relevance of Sartre's concept of bad faith to racism of a special kind, antiblack racism. Gordon basically understands bad faith as 'lying to ourselves', 'irony of belief', 'flight from anguish', 'spirit of seriousness', 'transcendence and facticity' and 'flight from displeasing truths about the body'. Reduced to its fundamental level, bad faith is – for Gordon, just as it is for Sartre – an attempted flight from and an evasion of freedom.

Why bad faith? For Lewis Gordon, racism is a form of self-deception and can only be understood in terms of the concept of bad faith. He defines racism as 'the self-deceiving choice to believe either that one's race is the only race qualified to be considered human or that one's race is superior to other races' (1995a: 2).

Embedded in this definition is the idea that racism involves choice (rational) of a kind which is deceptive, not to an external other (deceived) but to the one who makes that choice. Accordingly, the core assumptions of self-deception (bad faith) are: 'that human beings are aware, no matter how fugitive that awareness may be, of their freedom in their various situations, that they are free choosers of various aspects of their situations, that they are consequently responsible for their condition on some level, that they have the power to change at least themselves through coming to grips with their situations...' (1995a: 5). The fact that the belief in the superiority of one's race is a choice means that this alleged superiority is not a given, a fact, but merely an opinion. As Sartre says in another register, an anti-Semite is one who 'holds anti-Sematic opinion' (1965: 5). Gordon poses the incisive question, 'What is the being...of human reality in an antiblack world?' The answer, he declares in a single phrase, is *bad faith*. In this antiblack world, bad faith is an 'effort to evade one's humanity' by asserting this 'humanity as what it is not' (Gordon 1997b: 124) – that is, as either black or white consciousness. Furthermore, located within the context of an antiblack world, bad faith is 'an effort to deny the blackness within by way of asserting the supremacy of whiteness. It can be regarded as an effort to purge blackness from the self and the world, symbolically and literally' (Gordon 1995a: 6). Bad faith, therefore, has to do with self-identity in the sense of one's reflective consciousness of who one is and what one is like. Such reflection is, however, unavoidable given that a human being is 'a being such that in its own being, its being is in question' (Sartre 1956: 47).

A society such as apartheid South Africa, one embedded in antiblack racism which compels black people to constantly pose the question 'In reality, who and what am I?', is certain to spawn seeds of both bad faith and authentic responses to the question. In such a society, black people suffer from ontological insecurity, what Ronald Laing refers to as a 'divided self' and Du Bois as 'double consciousness'. Laing claims that whereas the ontologically secure individual (for example, white people in apartheid society) generally experiences her being as real, alive and whole, and in ordinary circumstances has no questions about her identity (Who am I?) and autonomy, the ontologically insecure person such as a black individual may in ordinary circumstances 'lack the experience of his own temporal continuity...He may feel more insubstantial than substantial, and unable to assume that the stuff he is made of is genuine, good, valuable. And he may feel himself as partially divorced from his body' (1965: 41–42). The consequence of this alienated state is that a black person desires to escape from the self. She longs to be other than what she is and so plunges in a senseless flight from the self. From a psycho-existential point of view, this vain attempt at flight from self signals a kind of 'self-hatred' which Biko was at pains to eradicate from black people.

Apartheid racism, Biko emphatically declared, was absolutely *evil*. However, according to him, the tragedy is that the victims of this vicious system (black people) not only acquiesced to it but also participated in their own oppression. In this, Biko is nowhere near doing what liberals normally do – that is, 'blaming the victim'. By blaming the victim, I mean (following on William Ryan's excellent book with the same title) the tendency to blame the victim of oppression for the condition in which she finds herself when that very condition is not of her own making but that of the oppressor. For example, white South Africans blamed black people for not being educated and civilised when they in fact, through apartheid policies such as Bantu education, were the ones who not only made it impossible for black people to be educated but also fundamentally denied them education. In other words, you deny someone education and you go on to accuse her of being uneducated. Here is an example from Ryan: 'Slavery...was justified – even praised – on the basis of a complex ideology that showed quite conclusively how useful slavery was to society and how uplifting it was for the slaves' (1976: 26). Biko is certainly not guilty of this kind of phenomenon which is prevalent among liberals. He is not saying that black people must pick themselves up by their bootstraps. He is aware that in the first place for them to do that, they need to have some boots. Biko understands that black people do not *have* boots, let alone the straps that are necessary for the pulling up. What he is simply saying is that black people should not willingly accept the condition of being bootless; they must fight for the boots with straps in order for them to be able to pull themselves up. As long as black people accept their slavish condition as given, as divinely ordered, as their essence or nature, they will remain in bondage. A master *is* a master if and only if there is a slave who makes masterhood possible. Bad faith is the black subject's appropriation of herself as naturally suited for the condition in which she is confined. She is in bad faith because she is aware that this is not the way things ought to be, that what *is* can be changed to *what-ought-to-be*.

It is this melting away of everything solid and stable in black people that Biko decries, for it renders them impotent to fight for their freedom: 'How can people be prepared to put up a resistance against their overall oppression if in their individual situations, they cannot insist on the observance of their manhood?' (1996: 76). Biko derides most black people for emulating Hegel's slave who preferred a life of servitude rather than risk death. According to him, 'You are either alive and proud or you are dead, and when you are dead, you can't care anyway' (1996: 152). The point, as he puts it, is to transcend and conquer the personal fear of death.[13] He takes from Fanon and Sartre the insistence that oppression is not only a phenomenon that is simply imposed from without, but it is also an introjection of domination by the oppressed at the psychological level. This introjection, Biko argues, takes the form of a morbid fear of white people by black people. The implication of this view is that black people have an investment in their oppression because it represents the already-known that is taken as divinely given, however unbearable the conditions of everyday existence are. This is because they deceive themselves into believing in the naturalness and givenness of their situation. After all, as De Beauvoir indicates, 'one cannot revolt against nature' (1994: 83). 'What makes the black man fail to tick?' Biko asks in earnest. Because 'reduced to an obliging shell, he looks with awe at the white power structure and accepts what he regards as the "inevitable position"' (1996: 28). However, deep inside, the black subject knows that he is lying to himself for '[i]n the privacy of his toilet his face twists in the silent condemnation of White society but brightens up in sheepish obedience as he comes out hurrying in response to his master's impatient call' (1996: 28). This act of lying to oneself is exactly what constitutes bad faith.

Someone may argue that this attitude does not represent a clear case of bad faith but simply a consciously assumed survival mechanism. In a repressive apartheid environment, in fact in any antiblack oppressive society, black people learned to act and react in certain ways for the sake of staying out of trouble and keeping alive. They perfected the art of hiding their anger behind the mask of servility. This attitude was observed among the Southern States slaves by Kenneth Stampp '...to be sure, there were plenty of opportunists among the Negroes who played the role assigned to them, acted the clown, and curried the favour of their masters in order to win the maximum rewards within the system' (in Silberman 1964: 79). For reasons of survival, black people learned to play the game accordingly. Baldwin coldly confessed, 'I have spent most of my life, after all, watching white people and outwitting them, so that I might survive' (1993: 217). Most black people turned fawning and flattery into arsenals of self-protection. For example, often in the presence of the white person, the black person assumed an attitude of pure facticity. She played the role assigned to her by the master. She lived her situation by fleeing it; she chose either to deny it or to deny her responsibility. This attitude constitutes the double relationship black people have with European civilisation; 'blacks face a world of lies in which they are forced to pretend as true that which is false and pretend as false that which is true' (Gordon 2002: viii). Besides being a paradigmatic example of bad faith, the attitude of brightening 'up in sheepish obedience as he comes out hurrying in response to his master's impatient call' is also known as masking.

The point to note here is that whether or not masking is a survival mechanism, it remains a form of bad faith. The phenomenon of masking among black people is a problem long articulated by thinkers such as Du Bois with his notion of the 'double consciousness' that afflicts black people in their relation with white people. The white world and the black world are divided by a thick wall – what Du Bois calls a 'veil' which demands that black people should wear a mask or play-act rather than engage in authentic interaction with white people. In playing a role, black people 'must not be too frank and outspoken and must never fail to flatter and be pleasant in order to lessen white unease and discomfort' (West, in Gates & West 1996: 86–87). The consequences of wearing a mask and playing a role in the white world is that one ends up with a double consciousness which, according to Du Bois, 'is a peculiar sensation...this sense of looking at one's self through the eyes of others, of measuring one's soul by the tape of a world that looks on in amused contempt and pity' (1969: 45).

A similar phenomenon is described by Stanley Elkins and the sociologist Orlando Patterson. Elkins argues that quite a sizable number of slaves in the American South developed the Sambo personality, the main characteristics of which included docility, clowning and fawning as a means not only of survival but also of saving self-respect, salvaging one's dignity constantly undermined by the system. Patterson points out that the same Sambo personality was found among the slaves in the West Indies, where it was known as the 'Quashie' character. The Quashie is, in fact, neither docile nor a comedian but merely pretending to be; such a person 'both disguises his true feelings (which it was his cardinal principle never to reveal since no one, least of all the master, could be trusted) and had the psychological satisfaction of duping the master' (Patterson 1973: 44)[14]

Masking is a survival strategy adopted by slaves or black people in their relation with the master or the white racist person. In masking, the black person pretends to be exactly what the white person expects her to be, in order to gain acceptance or approval from the white person or even reprieve from impending or potential harm. Masking is much like play-acting, except that in black role-play, the play-acting is done as an essential mechanism for survival. This situation is forced on black people by circumstances which require them, for safety's sake to adopt the role of 'yes-man', to conform to a pattern of behaviour and response determined by the dominant racial Other or risk serious repercussion. Jane Watts asserts: 'The adoption of the humble yes-baas role is not a matter of choice, or personality or belief: it is not the refuge of the passive, subservient nature. It is a prerequisite for survival: the compulsory disguise both for the placid and the rebellious, if they are going to have any hope of staying out of prison' (1989: 26). The survival element of masking notwithstanding, it still is a form of bad faith motivated by the desire not to be who one really is. It is playing at being a Sambo or Quashie in the manner of not being it (that is, one plays at being a Quashie while fully conscious that one is not one). The Quashie pretends that she has no choice and finds an excuse for acting the way she does. There is certainly a choice to be made: survival or harm, or even death. Some black people, like Biko himself, did not choose survival in the face of degradation or the possibility of death.

The masking phenomenon exhibited by South African black people is captured with lucid clarity by Modisane in his book *Blame me on History*:

> The African needs to be a master in the art of chicanery, for only the simple and the very proud are arrested on trifling offences...Africans have discovered – and this by way of self-protection – that the white South Africa is hopelessly and fanatically susceptible to flattery, a weapon which the Africans use with vicious enthusiasm to express their sincerest contempt... In the presence of South African [white] friends I could wear a mask, be the eternal actor in a make-believe world of tinsel reality revealing the face, the profile which photographed the best. (1986: 73, 90, 91)

Having to choose between pride or butter, between dignity or survival, imprisonment or degradation, self-respect or servility and submissiveness, black people under apartheid conditions were normally forced to opt for the second alternatives: butter, degradation, insults, submissiveness, servility – in short, survival. If black people chose pride, dignity and self-respect, they had a greater chance of consequential trouble, imprisonment and sometimes death. Offering a justification for behaving obsequiously and appearing to be stupid towards his white boss, Modisane says:

> I thought of my job, the idea of losing it; the nightmare of the Pass Office, the long queues, the emasculating medical examination; fresh permits for seeking employment, the permission to work; I thought of my family, the food, the rent, the school fees for the children. These are the evaluations I had to make at that moment of crisis. This is my kind of cowardice. My self-respect is derived from a knowledge of fidelity to my responsibility. If I had been civilised, with a highly-developed sense of honour, I would have spat on the boss, told him to go to hell and probably kicked his teeth in. (1986: 227)

Modisane had to suppress any assertion of self in order to hold on to his job, indeed his life. He had to become a person with two personalities in order to survive. Acknowledging its debilitating effects, whether it is called discretion or cowardice, Modisane confesses that this mastery of form, this servile attitude is 'solely responsible for the white arrogance which is aware of the motives behind the legendary good-naturedness of the African' (1986: 227). But the most humble good-natured black person can in reality be someone who hates the white people and persuades them, however unconsciously, to serve her. Indeed, what Modisane and later Biko are saying, is that there is a double occurrence of bad faith here.

First, is the bad faith of the black subject '[b]eing what he is not', reducing himself into an object in the same way as Sartre's waiter does; second, there is the bad faith of white racism.

The phenomenological argument for the attainment of a particular consciousness of self, and thus a particular self, has been the *leitmotif* of Biko's lifelong philosophical and political project. What Biko is suggesting is that human beings constitute themselves into what they make of themselves. However, he is not blind to the fact that – as Hegel demonstrates – we *fashion* each other. For example, a human being is neither ugly nor beautiful; it is the opinions of others that constitute her beautiful or ugly. A human being is not generous or courageous or shy or thin, except in the context of and in relation to other people and what they say about her. For some of us, to be called stupid or inferior is exactly what we become. 'I am...as I appear to the Other' Sartre insists (1956: 339). This, for Biko, is only one side of the issue. The other side is that I am 'for myself', in Sartre and Hegel's terms. This means that at some point in certain situations, I can reject the ascription and labels others put on me. When the apartheid system reduced people to 'non-whites' and 'kaffirs', they responded by rejecting these ascriptions and calling themselves black people. This reaction was an assertion of the black self, a reaction of the concept self-imposed by others which is unacceptable because it is derogatory. It is this assertion of the self that Biko tried to instil in the consciousness of black people. When he derides them for accepting the labels forced upon them, for internalising the inferiority complex inculcated in their consciousness by the racist apartheid regime, Biko simultaneously urges them to assert themselves, to define themselves in the manner in which they perceive themselves and not through the perceptions and eyes of others. Black consciousness, in Biko's mind, is a consciousness that exists for itself.

What Biko was driving home in his seeming accusation of black people of bad faith was, in fact, to explore the ways in which they failed to be authentic and how this inauthenticity damaged their lives and the lives of those they affected. Since inauthenticity is similar to bad faith and their opposite mode of existence is that of authenticity, what then should blacks do to be authentic and avoid bad faith? Of what does authentic existence consist? Does it mean being true to the person you really are? Is it identification with a fixed or essential self? Does it mean resisting social pressures to conform to the goals and values of society? Does it entail our commitment to think, speak and act in a particular manner? Is it really the recognition or recollection of what it is to be a human being, a person? These are the questions dealt with in the following chapters.

Notes

1 For more on racism as power, see Carmichael's (Kwame Ture) *Stokely Carmichael Speaks: From Black Power to Pan-Africanism* (2007). For liberals, racism is simply racial prejudice or discrimination – both of which are reduced to individual moral shortfall.

2 For a recent detailed articulation of the colonial system of racial separation, see Mbembe's *Critique of Black Reason* (2017).

3 Indeed, Biko enjoys a lot of good company in restricting racism to the powerful, Carmichael, Manning Marable and Sivanandan among others. In an interesting book entitled *Racial Paranoia*, John Jackson Jr defines racism in a similar manner as Biko: 'Racism is characterized by hatred and power; the hate people express for other racial groups and the relative power they possess to turn that hatred into palpable discrimination or material advantage' (2008: 4).

4 See Karel von Wolferen's *The Enigma of Japanese Power* (1990) and Michael Adams' *The Multicultural Imagination* (1996: 182 onwards) on Japanese antiblack racism.

5 For an insightful discussion on the difference between anti-Semitism and antiblack racism, see Fanon's *Black Skin, White Masks* (1967a), especially pages 115 to 117 and 162, and Chapter 4 of Mills' *Blackness Visible* (1998).

6 See for example her articles 'No Humans Involved: An Open Letter to My Colleagues' (1994: 42–73) and 'On How We Mistook the Map for the Territory, and Re-Imprisoned Ourselves in Our Unbearable Wrongness of Being, of *Désétre*: Black Studies toward the Human Project' in *Not Only the Master's Tools: African-American Studies in Theory and Practice* (edited by Lewis Gordon and Jane Gordon, 2006), as well as Scott's 'The Re-Enchantment of Humanism: An Interview with Sylvia Wynter' (2000).

7 Cone also sees racism as a dehumanisation phenomenon. 'White racism denied the humanity of black people, with even theologians debating whether blacks had souls. Some said blacks were subhuman "beasts"' (www.crosscurrents.org/cone.htm).

8 Recent European antiblack racism manifested as 'monkey chants' at European soccer games. In the Spanish *La Liga*, the Cameroonian Barcelona striker Samuel E'too had bananas and peanuts thrown at him while playing and monkey chants were heard every time he touched the ball. The same happened to many black players, including stars such as the Frenchman Thiery Henry, Mark Zoro from the Ivory Coast and the Cameroonian Carlos Kameni. The latter remarked in a television documentary about racism, 'When I see a banana on the field I think I'm not a monkey, I'm a human'. For more details on the animalisation of Africans, see Mbembe's *Critique of Black Reason* (2017).

9 *Sunday Times*, 11 March 2010.

10 Biko gave several interviews in his lifetime, among them: Gerhart (1972); Zylstra's 'Steve Biko on Black Consciousness in South Africa' (1993); BBC (transcript in *Umtapo Focus*, November 1987: 7–8; and 'Steve Biko interviewed by Greg Lanning, 5 June 1971' in *Steve Biko: Voices of Liberation*, compiled by Derek Hook.

11 As Ali Mazrui also attests: 'The African people may not be the most brutalized people in modern history, but they are almost certainly the most humiliated. The most brutalized people in modern history include the indigenous peoples of the Americas and those of Australia, who were subjected to genocidal attacks by white invaders. Also among the most brutalized in recent times were the Jews and the Gypsies in the Nazi Holocaust...On the other hand, no groups were subjected to such large-scale indignities of *enslavement* for several centuries in their millions as the Africans were. No other group experienced to the same extent such indignities as *lynching*, systematic *segregation*, and well-planned *apartheid* as the Africans were' (in Kiros 2001: 107 – italics in original).

12 For discussions on racism and death, see, for example Bulhan's *Frantz Fanon and the Psychology of Oppression* (1985: 166 onwards); Gilmore's *Golden Gulag* (2006); Goldberg's *The Threat of Race: Reflections on Racial Neoliberalism* (2009, especially Chapters 1 and 2); and particularly JanMohamed's *The Death-Bound-Subject: Richard Wright's Archaeology of Death* (2005).

13 For a lengthy discussion on Biko and death, see my article 'Biko and Douglass: Existentialist Conceptions of Death' (2016).

14 For example, the black actor of the early-1930s Stepin Fetchit, while personifying this buffoonish and fawning character in the movies, worked hard for the cause of black freedom off the movie screen/in real life.

6

The problematics of liberalism

> *There is no place in the movement for the white liberal. He is our affliction.*
> – James Baldwin (in Newfield 1964: 5)

ONE OF THE KEY figures under attack in Sartre's *Anti-Semite and Jew* is the liberal democrat. Much like Sartre, Biko pays special attention to liberals – particularly white liberals and their attitudes to black people and racism in general. The term 'liberal' in South Africa has a very elusive referent. It refers to those individuals who believe in liberalism as an ideology. However, it also refers (from the point of view of the Black Consciousness adherents and most black people for that matter) negatively to any white South African, particularly the English-speaking white people who were presumably 'Friends of the Natives' and opposed to the Afrikaner Nationalist Party's domination and apartheid policies yet still enjoyed the privileges of whiteness. Such individuals – the liberals – also rejected the policies of the SACP and black nationalist organisations such as the PAC and were thus regarded not only as reactionaries but also as 'in the closet racists'. To a large extent, the term has lost its political and moral meaning, rendering it difficult to define let alone offer a conclusive set of values characterising liberalism. Even liberals themselves at times appear uncertain of what they really are or represent. In the past, political leaders who were unquestionably liberals were often unwilling to be called liberals because of the negative connotations associated with the term. A fairly recent book captures the ambiguity of liberalism in South Africa in its title: *Watchdogs or Hypocrites? The Amazing Debate on South African Liberals and Liberalism* (Husemeyer 1997).

It is something truly peculiar when people of a certain ideological persuasion throughout history are constantly accused of and criticised for hindering the liberation of some people. Biko was not the first to mount an attack on liberals. Liberals have persistently been criticised for preventing black people from standing on their own feet, from exercising their full humanity. The history of black radicalism in antiblack societies has been a history of unrelenting confrontation, not only with the avowed racists (for example the Ku Klux Klan,

AWB, *Afrikaner Broederbond*, the National Front in Britain and so on) but also with the liberals and liberalism. Garvey's Universal Negro Improvement Association fought for independence from white liberals through self-improvement and self-determination. The first editorial of the first negro newspaper, *Freedom's Journal* (1827), expressed resentment against those white liberals who assumed the role of spokespersons for black peoples' problems. From Du Bois, to the NAACP, the Student Non-Violent Coordinating Committee (SNCC), Baldwin's statement in the epigraph, Malcolm X, Carmichael, Cone, Sobukwe and so on, white liberal patronage and hypocrisy have been a thorn in the flesh of black radicals. Consider, for example, the comments by several radical black intellectuals in a 1964 panel discussion with white liberals: 'It is impossible to carry on a dialogue with the white man...There is no point in even seeking help or support from the white liberal', declared Paule Marshall; 'How many white liberals will desert our ranks when we assert our right of self-defense?' John Killens enquired: 'We are wasting our time talking to these white liberals...The *New York Post* represents an understanding of reality that debases the world every day', pronounced LeRoi Jones (aka Amiri Baraka), (in Newfield 1964:5). Carmichael eloquently captures the problem with liberals: 'The liberal is so preoccupied with stopping confrontation that he usually finds himself defending and calling for law and order, the law and order of the oppressor...he finds himself politically aligned with the oppressor rather than with the oppressed' (2007: 170). In the face of all these condemnations, perhaps a brief description of the larger tradition of ideas and principles that constitute the foundation of political liberalism will clarify why white liberalism has historically been such a problem to black people – and Biko in particular.

Liberalism is a European ideology imported by British colonisers to South Africa and other British colonies. Basically, it is a political philosophy or ideology whose primary focus is the protection and enhancement of individual liberty or autonomy. What is termed 'classical liberalism' gives priority to individual liberty, human rationality and the ability of such rational beings to order their own lives without unnecessary interference from anyone or the state, and the rule of law. Since all human beings are rational moral agents guided by universal rational principles, such morally equal individuals possess equal rights and dignity. In short, liberalism's core set of principles are: (i) a commitment to an individualism which considers as basic the political, moral and legal claims of the individual over and against groups; (ii) the belief in reason as constitutive of human nature and therefore the basis for human quality; (iii) freedom of choice; (iv) individual privacy; and (v) individual autonomy without undue prescriptions or limitations from outside; (vi) tolerance; (vii) our capacity to use all our individual rational faculties that give us (as individuals) the right to freedom; and (viii) the rule of law and order.

The philosophical foundations of liberalism have been extremely varied such that individual philosophers have differed in their emphasis of what constitutes the primary principle of liberalism. The reason for this is that there are a number of varied forms of liberalism. For some, individual autonomy is the primary metaphysical and ontological basis of liberalism. Describing himself as a modern liberal, Appiah states: 'We believe...that individual autonomy is at the heart of political morality' (1997: 79–80). For some, equality is the highest political and social goal; while for others, reason, freedom of speech and thought are the highest political *telos*. Kant, for example, believed that individuals are equal in their capacity for autonomy and that moral responsibility and human dignity both rest on the capacity to reason. The key figures in classical liberalism (Locke, Hume, Kant, Adam Smith, John Stuart Mill and Jeremy Bentham), though diverse in emphasis, were all committed to the flourishing of the individual. Liberalism promotes certain distinctive values, including individualism, egalitarianism, universalism, tolerance, rationality, constitutionalism, the rule of law, autonomy and private property. There are a number of competing different types within liberalism: utilitarian liberalism (Mill and Bentham) versus contractarian liberalism (Locke, Rousseau and Thomas Hobbes), property and self-ownership liberalism (Locke) versus personhood-respecting liberalism (Kant), left-wing progressive democratic liberalism versus conservative neo-liberalism, and so on.

Liberalism and racism

Mills describes liberalism as a political and moral ideological position that has historically been predominantly racial. 'Racial liberalism, or white liberalism', he contends, 'is the actual liberalism that has been historically dominant since modernity: a liberal theory whose terms originally restricted full personhood to whites...and relegated nonwhites to an inferior category, so that its schedule of rights and prescriptions for justice were all color-coded' (2008: 1382). The key terms of this white liberalism have been reshaped and changed by race such that a different set of rules for members of different races have been generated. This means that some members of other races do not satisfy the criteria set to constitute a human being, although they meet the criterion of individuality. Such liberalism may, for example, explicitly represent black people as lesser creatures not deserving of equal treatment or rights, but deserving to be dominated by white people. A look at the dominant figures in the history of liberalism support Mills' claim. As noted in an earlier chapter, Locke (popularly referred to as the father of liberalism) justified the expropriation of Native American land, had investments in African slavery and helped to write the Fundamental Constitution of Carolina in which the rights of slaveholders over their slaves were recognised while those of the slaves were not. Kant, the liberal theorist, turned out to be one of the forerunners of what later came to be known as scientific racism. In Chapter 3, I noted how Kant used reason as an essential human feature to exclude black people from humanity. John Stuart Mill was an employee of the colonial British East India Company. Though he criticised slavery in the USA, this changed (as noted above) when he turned his attention to British colonies in Africa. Now, if liberals believe in the equality, autonomy and the dignity of the individual, we have to question a lot of philosophers and people normally known as liberals. Was Locke or Kant or Mill a liberal? If the answer is 'no', the question becomes 'Why then does Locke continue to be called the father of liberalism?' or 'Why is Kant or Mill labelled liberal?' If the answer is 'yes', then it becomes impossible to sustain the putative definition of liberalism as the promotion of individual autonomy and human equality – precisely because of Locke's involvement and justification of slavery and colonialism. Nor can we take Mill or Kant at their word. In fact, according to Domenico Losurdo in his thought-provoking book *Liberalism: A Counter-History*, if we look at what leading liberal theorists did and said, all we notice is their complicity in gender subordination, racial oppression, white supremacy, and even class divisions and white male working-class exploitation. Thus, as he remarks about Locke's position, this was a 'love of liberty and legitimation or revindication of slavery' (2011: 5). Is there a contradiction lurking in the theories and practices of these liberal philosophers? Indeed, a popular response has hitherto been to accuse them of being guilty of a major contradiction.

Contrary to this popular view, I want to suggest that there is certainly no contradiction between the theoretical views of these philosophers and their apparent racist practices and views or justification of slavery as such. A possible third answer to the question, I think, would be that we do continue to call them liberals because as liberals, their conception of what it is to be a human being excludes slaves or negro people, Africans or black people. For liberals, a human being is essentially a rational self-determining autonomous being. Recall that for Kant, the human being is a rationally unified consciousness (that is, reason and understanding unify our experience). We also noted that in support of Kant's view, Hegel held that 'thought is, indeed, essential to humanity. It is this that distinguishes us from the brutes'. In terms of this conception, a human being is a thinking being (*homo rationalis*), distinguishable from everything else by the capacity to think. If this is the liberal definition of what it is to be human, and if reason or rationality is at the heart of liberal philosophy, those beings who putatively lack rationality cannot qualify to be human and therefore liberal principles such as equality of human beings, individual autonomy and human dignity can simply not apply to them. When we revisit what Kant, Mill, Hume and a host of other liberals say about black people and their capacity to reason, the seeming contradiction in liberalism vanishes. To be denied rationality is, therefore, to be denied humanity because reason distinguishes human beings from nature and other creatures. Furthermore, to posit *a priori* that human nature entails the possession of a mind whose distinctive feature is rationality does not in any way commit one to a position where one is unable to deny that certain seemingly human-like groups or 'manlike beasts and beastlike men' (for example, savages or apes) lack this distinctive characteristic. It might just be the case that certain *human* groups (according to the criteria laid down as determinative of that feature) lack the required feature and thus cannot be treated as having or being accorded the same rights, respect or whatever benefit those who fully possess the said features deserve. Mills aptly suggests: 'If X [Kant, Mill, Locke and so on] made pronouncements about nonwhites that are in seeming contradiction to his general pronouncements about "men"/"persons", then we do have to entertain the possibility that he did not mean "men"/"persons" to include them' (2006: 227).

Consider, for example, Montesquieu's insistence that '[i]t is impossible for us to suppose that these beings [black people] should be men'; Voltaire's statement that '[t]he Negro race is a species of men as different from ours as the breed of spaniels is from that of the greyhounds...If their understanding is not of a different nature from ours, it is at least greatly inferior'; Kant's invocation of skin colour to prove the non-rationality of black people, 'this fellow was quite black from head to foot...a clear proof that what he said was stupid'; and finally, Hegel's declaration that in black people, one finds nothing that suggests humankind, 'there is nothing harmonious with humanity to be found in this type of character'. It is clear from these few examples that for Montesquieu, Voltaire, Kant and Hegel, black people do not even belong to the human race. In other words, by virtue of their blackness, they are excluded from the realm of the rational and civilised – and therefore from the human.

The case of Thomas Jefferson, the former president of the USA, is a succinct example of the liberal conception of the difference between humanness and blackness. Having played a major role in the production and writing of the American Declaration of Independence (which reads: 'We hold these truths to be self-evident: that all men are created equal...), Jefferson wrote some fifteen years later in a letter: 'Nobody wishes more than I do to see proof that nature has given to our black brethren talents equal to those of the other colors of men, and that the appearance of a lack of them is owing merely to the degraded condition of their existence in Africa and America' (in Hacker 1992: 25). If it is a 'self-evident' truth that all human beings are equal, why question the humanity of black people unless you regard them as non-human or subhuman? Sadly, as Hacker remarks, 'even for those who allude to blacks as their "brethren" a desire to believe does not always bring that result. Warring within the minds of Jeffersonians, both in his time and ours, is the hope that blacks are equal – accompanied by the suspicion that they are not' (1992: 25). Given all these philosophical views, is it surprising that liberals can love liberty, individual autonomy and human dignity and yet legitimatise or revindicate slavery or even own slaves as Locke and Jefferson did?

Biko and liberals

Liberalism in South Africa, as it was with Jim Crow in America, found itself in the presence of apartheid – a society characterised by racial hatred. Because of this unique situation, it inherited a legacy of ambiguity – especially in relation to race matters. Friedman states: 'Well before its arrival on South African shores, liberalism was ambiguous – a weapon of domination and a route to emancipation' (2014: 34). Questions posed regarding this ambiguity become patently pertinent. For example, 'Is liberalism in South Africa an expression of white bigotry or a recipe for freedom?' (Friedman 2014: 29) or 'Are liberals and liberalism watchdogs or hypocrites?' The answers to these sorts of questions depend on which side of the racial-ideological debate one is. On the one hand, liberals saw themselves as messiahs, liberators or freedom fighters. On the other hand, conservative Afrikaners who supported apartheid labelled liberals propagandists, provocateurs, traitors or agitators; black elite converts to liberalism regarded liberals as emancipators, friends of black people, sympathisers and good-willed white people; radical black people variously labelled liberals racist, hypocritical, arrogant and patronising.

   This ambiguity in racial positioning is the reason why Black Consciousness activists and thinkers attacked and dismissed liberals not only as useless to the cause of black people but also as serious impediments to their liberation. Echoing Baldwin's sentiment about liberals in the epigraph, Biko declares: 'Their presence amongst us is irksome and of nuisance value. It removes the focus of attention from essentials and shifts it to ill-defined philosophical concepts that are both irrelevant to the black man and merely a red herring across the track' (1996: 23). It should however be noted that at the fundamental level, Biko and most Black Consciousness proponents did not critique liberalism per se but directed their venom at the contradictions between the theory and practice of white liberals. Some of the principles attributed to and appropriated by liberalism as its own principles are adhered to by most rational human beings with different ideological orientations. The belief in freedom, equality and human dignity are principles dear to most people outside of liberal ideological circles. One of the main differences between liberalism and Black Consciousness philosophy is liberalism's emphasis on individualism as opposed to collectivism. One of the leading figures in the Black Consciousness Movement, Harry Nengwekhulu, blamed white liberals for retarding the revolutionary progress of black people by instilling mythical solutions such as racial integration or multiracialism to apartheid, thereby arresting black liberation. He states:

> ...white liberals have indeed been criminally responsible for arresting and aborting the struggle by playing the role of a bulwark, a kind of buffer zone between the blacks and the White system which has been oppressing us for centuries. In fact, to us, the white liberal establishment's involvement in the Black struggle is its desire to kill the revolutionary zeal of the Black masses by promising them a 'controlled' change which will result in some mythical, 'mosaic' multi-racialism. (1976: 2)

For Biko, liberals in South Africa were not recipes of freedom for black people but instead hindrances and obstructions to black liberation: 'The limitations that have accompanied the involvement of liberals in the black man's struggle have been mostly responsible for the arrest of progress' (1996: 65). Indeed, their integration myth must be destroyed 'because it makes people believe that something is done when in reality the artificially integrated circles are the soporific to the blacks while salving the consciences of the guilt-stricken white' (1996: 64). Biko's distrust of white liberals has a long history in the struggles of black people the world over. Black people in the Americas, for example, never trusted white liberals. 'Negroes have never really trusted their white allies; they have always had a nagging suspicion that the whites were holding them back, that they could gain more, and faster, if they were only free to act on their own' (Silberman 1964: 213). Carmichael argues in a piece entitled 'The Pitfalls of Liberalism' (2007) that the liberal segment of white society in America has positioned itself as the mediator between black radicalism and white conservatism. For him, the biggest problem with the white liberal everywhere in antiblack societies is that his primary role is to stop violent confrontation between black people and white people. However, instead of talking to the white person who uses violence of every kind on black people, the liberal concentrates his energies on convincing the black victim of white violence to be non-violent. In fact, the liberal ends up being part of the problem rather than part of the solution. Historically, part of the objective of liberals was to 'stem the tide of African radicalisation' (Maloka 2014: 71), hence the persistent drive to infiltrate black organisations and assume leadership positions.

The mistrust of white liberals comes from Biko's awareness of their history regarding race and racism, a history replete with contradictions and ambiguity, a history that moves from a defence of equality to collusion with racism. According to Ramphela, for Biko, liberalism was seriously problematic because it 'lacked a coherent critique of racism' which meant that white liberal politics 'did not interfere with the "real" world of white privilege' (1995: 55). The white liberal hypocrisy may be captured by these examples from a cartoon: When the Afrikaner racists say 'We don't want Kaffirs in our schools and areas', the liberals say 'We believe in the neighborhood concept'. When the Afrikaner racists say 'There must be separate residential areas (Group Areas Act)', the liberals say 'We believe in urban renewal'. When the Afrikaner racists say 'There will never be freedom for Kaffirs', the liberals say 'It will take time'. When the Afrikaner racist beats up a black person and says 'I hate Kaffirs!!', the liberal says 'Nothing personal, you understand!'

For Biko the first instance of liberal hypocrisy in fighting racism was demonstrated when Rhodes University refused to accommodate delegates of different races in the same dormitories during a NUSAS conference in 1968. A motion tabled by Biko to postpone the conference until the white NUSAS executive could find a non-racial venue was rejected by white delegates. 'The response was a simple one: we agree with you but...' (interview with Gerhart 1972: 6); a similar popular response today is 'I'm not a racist, but...'[1] This experience made Biko realise '[t]hat while these guys [white liberals] are adopting a classical liberal stance, saying this is the truth, they are not prepared to work toward the truth in any form whatsoever' (interview with Gerhart 1972: 7). This position is captured by a letter written 24 years later to the editor of the *Sunday Times* (1996): 'Black people have realised that, whereas Afrikaners were straightforward with their colonial mission, white liberals were patronising...and deceived black people into seeing racism only in its manifestation of individual acts of untamed ruthlessness...not in invisible systems and patterns conferring dominance over black people'. Related to this problem is the problem of the difference between Biko and the liberals about the means to achieve an ideal society (an issue discussed later in this book). What then is the position of liberals towards racism?

Historically, liberalism in South Africa 'emerged as a branch of British imperial expansion and settler colonialism...it arose and evolved as an ideology of colonial conquest and control, not as a product of anti-colonial struggle' (Maloka 2014: 5); it was thus not different from the colonial conceptions of racial matters, a conception that led to the practice of racial segregation. Since racism was built into the colonial system, and since South African liberalism arose and evolved as an ideology of colonial conquest, liberalism is tainted with racism. As Sartre emphasised, '[r]acism is ingrained in actions, institutions, and in the nature of the colonialist methods of production and exchange' (in Memmi 1965: xxiv). For example, Rudolf Hoernle, the South African liberal and philosopher who was highly influenced by the dominant figures of liberalism in Europe (Thomas Hill Green, Bernard Bosanquet and so on), applied liberal idealist concepts to the South African condition. In his inaugural lecture as professor of philosophy at the University of the Witwatersrand (1923), Hoernle emphasised the significance of segregation in multiracial societies such as South Africa. Later, in his famous lecture 'South African Native Policy and the

Liberal Spirit' (1939), he argued for the policy of racial separation as opposed to parallelism or assimilation. This prelude to apartheid, as Maloka points out, was a consequence of 'the core assumptions of Cape liberalism...that Africans were inferior to whites and had to be civilised' (2014: 35). In fact, the Cape liberals and the Witwatersrand liberals set the political tone for issues of race and racism in the country, and later provided black revolutionaries and SASO with enough evidence and ammunition against them. While Hoernle was a leading liberal in the country, others of almost equal stature (including Jan Hofmeyer, Leo Marquard, Margaret Ballinger, Helen Suzman and Edgar Brookes) voiced their views on race relations.

Biko, as the letter cited above suggests, had absolutely no doubt who and what the primary enemy of black people was: the apartheid regime (as represented by Afrikaners) and its racist power structures. But, as he pointed out, 'these are not the people we are concerned with' (1996: 20). Adopting the radical black position, he believed that liberalism as practised in South Africa was extremely problematic. Hence, for him, the real target besides the obvious white racist regime was the white liberal. Why? Because Biko moved from the premise that Black Consciousness deals with the totality of the white power structure, yet liberals want to exclude themselves from this totality: 'Basically the South African white community is a homogeneous community. It is a community of people who sit to enjoy a privileged position that they do not deserve, are aware of this, and therefore spend their time trying to justify why they are doing so. Where differences in political opinion exist, they are in the process of trying to justify their position of privilege and their usurpation of power' (1996: 19). Biko here articulates what Carmichael emphasised: that the liberals were preoccupied with stopping any racial confrontation that would disrupt the smooth functioning of the apartheid society and thus interfere with white privilege.

It may be recalled that the fundamental problem in South Africa for Biko was 'white racism'. This means that white people collectively, without exception, were part and parcel of the problem such that even 'the friends of the Natives' were part of the problem rather than part of the solution. Indeed, even though the two main white tribes (the Afrikaners and the English-speaking British descendents), were historically ideologically at odds, their differences dissolved in the face of any possible African threat. They become homogeneous as soon as the threat of what they called the *swart gevaar* (black threat) reared its head. In fact, Biko argued that the Afrikaner ideological project of apartheid sought – and indeed managed – to extend its span and range to include all white people (Afrikaners, English, Portuguese, Jewish and other white groups). All white people, Biko argues, 'collectively recognise in [the Afrikaner Nationalist Party] a strong bastion against the highly played-up *swart gevaar*' (1996: 77). Whiteness in South Africa generated a type of solidarity among white people which Sartre refers to as 'the recognition of one master by another' such that every greeting 'indicate[d] that one is a man by divine right and that one belongs to the privileged race' (1992: 569). That Biko echoed the sentiments of most Black Consciousness followers is a point made with brilliant clarity by Pityana: 'Let it be noted that despite their differences the Afrikaners and the British never allowed their antagonism to disrupt the social order. They manipulated the Blacks for political capital and made common cause against them in defence of White supremacy' (1972: 182). This white conspiracy against black people (what Mills identified as the 'racial contract' in his well-received text with the same title) can be traced, Pityana argues, to the 1913 Native Land Act, the 1936 removal of the Cape Africans from the common voters' roll, and of course the numerous apartheid legislation or statutes. The solidarity is further entrenched by the fact that each white person's recognition of the freedom of the other white person was achieved *against and at the expense of* the black person. The suggested point here is that apartheid was primordially not an ethnic but a racial ideology and project, because there was certainly no fundamental difference among the South African white groups on matters of race and the privileges accruing from whiteness.

Biko here also suggests that apartheid, as a system, was not an abstract mechanism. To use Sartre's formulation, the system exists, it functions; the infernal cycle of apartheid as a system is a reality. This reality is embodied and personified in millions of white South Africans, children and grandchildren of white people 'who have been shaped by [it] and who think, speak and act according to the principles of the...system' (Sartre 2001: 44). The white liberal Donald Woods, in his book *Biko*, ironically gives substance to Biko and Sartre's observations. He has this to say about his background and the influences that shaped his own thinking:

> Like most South Africans, I was born into a home highly conservative on racial issues. My early view of blacks was therefore of backward people... in the grip of extreme superstition dominated by sorcery and witchcraft, one whose effects appeared to be an alarming degree of callousness and cruelty...[notice Hegel's influence]. A white child brought up in these circumstances, being taught at an early age...understandably regarded blacks as inferior and easily accepted the general white attitude that color and race were the determinant of the chasm in cultures.
> My contact with other white children reinforced the generally accepted white version of the black stereotype – that black could never be the same as us; that they did not want to be the same as us; that they were created black because the Almighty clearly intended that they be set apart and should stay

different, with a different color, different smell, different language, different attitudes (all naturally inferior to ours). (1987: 41–42)

Woods' account affirms Fanon's observation that '[t]he racist in a culture with racism is therefore normal' (1967a: 40). Indeed, in antiblack white hegemonic societies, racism is so embedded in what white people consider to be 'normal' attitudes and behaviours that it is in fact a serious problem. Behind this putative normalcy, the white racist remains concealed except of course to the victim, the non-white person.

Who then are liberals for Biko? Building on Cone's ideas and drawing from his own experience in his encounter with white people, especially organisations such as NUSAS, he viewed liberals as: '[T]hat curious bunch of nonconformists who explain their participation in negative terms; that bunch of do-gooders that goes under all sorts of names – liberals, leftists etc. These are the people who argue that they are not responsible for white racism and the country's "inhumanity to the black man". These are the people who claim that they too feel the oppression just as acutely as the black and therefore should be jointly involved in the black man's [sic] struggle for a place under the sun' (1996: 20). The claim here is essentially that liberals are those white South Africans, irrespective of ideological orientation, who alleged to be critical and opposed to the apartheid regime yet had no misgivings about enjoying the privileges the white racist power structure provided; those who deny their complicity in apartheid racism in an attempt to evade moral responsibility for its horrors; those who constitute the chorus of the innocents; those who want to have black people believe that there are good white people (goodwill white) and bad white people, and that it is the fault of the latter that the situation in South Africa is as it is; those who believe in the equality of human beings irrespective of race, colour or creed and, because of this, claim to be colour-blind, to be tolerant of different religions, cultures, belief systems, political or ideological orientation, to believe in the rule of law, freedom of speech and individual autonomy, and to support non-racial meritocracy. In short, for Biko, liberals are those white people who not only 'lacked a coherent critique of racism and its socio-economic manifestations' but are also (un)consciously racists themselves. Liberals are those who also were not spared by the conservative Afrikaner who accused them of being 'negrophilists' or 'kafir-boeties' (nigger-lovers). Hoernle, in recognition of this fact, states:

> For a member of the White group to be concerned about the impact of White domination on the non-European population of the Union, or for such one to plead for fuller knowledge, or more humane consideration,

of non-European needs and interests, is to earn for himself the title of 'negrophilist', *kafir-boetie*, or – most scathing of all – 'liberal'. The White heretic on the subject of race relations is felt by many of his fellow-White to be a traitor to his own group. (1939: vii)

The liberals deservedly earned this antinomy from both sides of the racial fence because of their assumed position as arbitrator between the oppressor and the oppressed. And, as Carmichael points out, one of the pitfalls of white liberalism is the fear of the white liberals 'to alienate anyone, therefore...is incapable of presenting any clear alternative' (2007: 170)

Basically, then, liberalism in the South African context for Biko and others was more than merely the theoretical and abstract belief in certain specific core political principles such as parliamentary and constitutional government, the rule of law, independent judiciary, freedom of the press, equality in the eyes of the law and individual liberty. For Biko, the fundamental problem about liberals was the inherent contradictions not only in the very principles themselves when faced with multiracial antiblack societies but also between liberal theory and practice. To put it in Sartre's words, the liberals just as the colonialists '*do* each day, *in deed*, what they condemn *in their dreams*, and each of their acts contributes to maintaining oppression' (2001: 22). In the everyday lived context, liberals do not live up to their abstract principles of equality, freedom and dignity for all – a point captured beautifully in a different context by Otto von Bismarck: 'When you say that you agree to a thing in principle, you mean that you have not the slightest intention of carrying it out in practice' (in Silberman 1964: 217). Liberal indignation and rejection of apartheid were not always accompanied by action. It was and still is rather a position of principle. Liberals, as Malcolm X would say, preach integration and practise segregation. What kinds of solutions do the liberals offer for the transcendence of racism?

Recall that liberals – classical and modern – conceptualise reason or rationality as constitutive of humanness. The philosophical basis of this human identity is assumed to reside in a common rational capacity within each individual (that is, it lies in their capacity to reason). Human form, some liberals insist, 'is the mark of rationality and by extension of civil liberties, of the capacity to follow the law' (Goldberg 1993: 23). This commitment to, or shall I say 'faith' in, reason has led liberals to exclude those beings whom they regard as lacking in reason from the realm or category of the human. Since black people are assumed to be lacking in rationality, they consequently are deemed to belong at the lowest rung of humanity in the great Chain of Being, relegated to animals, subhumans or savages. On the basis of this conception, liberals feel it to be their moral, political, cultural, epistemological or even religious duty to uplift black people to the status of human being. This attitude (popularly known as the 'white man's burden') called forth all sorts of mechanisms, attitudes and practices to bring the below-human creatures to the level of the human.

Emerging from these attitudes and practices is the liberal's construction of what is called a 'Black problem' or the 'Black question', otherwise called the 'Native problem' or 'Native question' in colonial settings, or the 'Negro Problem' or 'Negro Question' in the USA. However one calls it, the point is that it has to do only with black people. Biko, however, argues that liberals falsely believe that 'we are faced with a black problem. There is nothing the matter with blacks. The problem is WHITE RACISM' (1996: 23 – upper case original). Richard Wright also earlier insisted that the so-called 'Negro problem' was actually not a black problem at all but a white problem. Influenced by Wright, Sartre wrote the book *Anti-Semite and Jew*, in which he argues that in a similar manner no 'Jew problem' exists. Such a presumed problem is simply a problem of anti-Semitism. As he says: 'If the Jew did not exist, the anti-Semite would invent him' (1965: 13). More importantly though, Biko understood that this notion has ontological significance in the sense that it implies that the very existence of black people is in essence problematic. What this assumption amounts to is that white people have a justified right to exist, whereas black people have no justification to exist – and if they do exist, they have to justify their existence which is continually put into question. Hence Du Bois' question, 'How does it feel to be a problem?' Lewis Gordon asserts that the notion of the black problem indicates what Sartre calls 'the spirit of seriousness', which is a form of bad faith on the part of those who regard others as problems: 'In cases of a problematic people, the result is straightforward. They cease to be people who might face, signify, or be associated with a set of problems: they become those problems. Thus, a problematic people do not signify crime, licentiousness, and other social pathologies; they, under such a view, *are* crime, licentiousness, and other social pathologies' (2000: 69 – italics in original).

What Gordon suggests above is that in such instance, an object ceases to signify or stand as a particular meaning; instead, it *becomes* that meaning. Thus in Biko's South African apartheid space, black people *became* the *problem*, translating itself into trouble, absence or that which has gone wrong. Recall the negative symbolism associated with the colour black mentioned in Chapter 2 of this book. In an antiblack world, to be black is to be not only sin and devil but also criminal. I am black; I have therefore committed a crime. I am black; I know what the problem with my black body is. It exists. I exist, therefore I *am* crime. This means that as a black person, I am sentenced even before I have committed a crime because I am crime personified.[2] A black person accused of a crime need only be 'seen' to be considered guilty of an offence he did not commit. His colour is the evidence. He is guilty of blackness. For black people, this guilt is transformed into '*don't*'. Don't do this, don't do that, don't think this or that, don't believe or behave this way or that way, and so on.

Problematic people require attention, guidance and protection. However, the ambiguity of the phrase 'Black problem' solicits the question 'Whose problem?' Guidance can only be offered by those who see them as problems: white people. Having noted that black people, particularly Africans and African-descended people, have been presumed by the Western philosopher to be lacking in rational capacity, mentally underdeveloped, it was agreed, in what – following Pateman's 'Sexual Contract' and Mills' 'Racial Contract' – we can call the 'liberal contract', that they should be relegated to the category of children or subhuman beings. Not only did this belief bring about an air of white condescension towards Africans, but it also brought the resultant white paternalism. There are different kinds and models of paternalism, among which are parent/child, teacher/pupil, and doctor/patient or mentally competent/mentally incompetent.[3] Involved in white paternalistic attitudes towards black people are all the above forms of paternalism, which implicitly are founded on the underlying racist assumption and perception of black people as lacking the ability to do things for themselves, a putting into question their capacity as independent rational agents. This questioning of the rational agency of black people reduces them to less than human or non-humanhood incommensurate with the Cartesian definition of what it is to be human.

The notion of black people as childlike, or 'child-human' as Mbembe calls it, has a long history in the West. Hegel, for example, after whitening Egypt – 'it does not belong to the African spirit' (1952a: 199) – describes what he calls Africa proper: 'that which lies south of the desert of Sahara...*the land of childhood*' (1952a: 196 – italics added). In order to civilise this 'land of childhood', Hegel (as indicated earlier) prescribed slavery as a remedy: 'Slavery is itself a phase of advance from the merely isolated sensual existence, a phase of education, a mode of becoming participant in a higher morality and the culture connected with it. Slavery is in and for itself *injustice*, for the essence of humanity is *freedom*; but for this, man must be matured' (1952a: 199 – italics in original). John Stuart Mill justified British despotism over the races of her colonies that, in his view, were still 'underage' and required to be absolutely obedient in order for their civilisation process by the British to have an effect. For Mill, any means necessary were to be used in educating 'savage tribes'. Like Hegel, he believed that slavery was a necessary stage for transforming savage tribes into workers and thus making them useful to civilisation and progress. The psychologist Stanley Hall believed that Africans, 'like children, are in a state of immature development and must be treated gently and understandingly by more developed [white] people' (Thomas & Sullen 1972: 7). Silberman offers a description by Stanley Elkins of black people in the Antebellum South in the USA: 'The Negro...in his true nature is always a boy, let him be ever so old...He is...dependent upon the white race; dependent for guidance and direction even to the procurement of his most indispensable necessities. Apart from this protection he has the helplessness of a child...' (1964: 75). This conception and attitude of white people toward black people led to Fanon's observation, '[a] white man addressing a Negro behaves exactly like an adult with a child and starts smirking, whispering, patronizing, cozening' (1967a: 31). According to this view, superior races have a moral, political, social and religious duty to protect, civilise and guide inferior races – a mission which functioned as an apology for colonialism.

The metaphor of childhood suggests the infantilism of Africans and is thus used as justification for and rationalisation of white paternalism. It made it possible for white people to talk of 'the white man's burden' – the burden to civilise the heathens and savages; the burden of protecting the savages against themselves; the burden of controlling African lives, desires, actions, attitudes and self-images; the burden of bringing enlightenment through trusteeship, tutelage and patronage. It is this paternalistic attitude – very typical of white South Africans, particularly white liberals – that Biko abhorred, and for which he heavily and constantly criticised and chastised them. For example, he states: 'The role of the white liberal in the black man's history in South Africa is a curious one. Very few black organisations were not under white direction. True to their image, the white liberals always knew what was good for the blacks and told them so' (1996: 20). Furthermore, '[b]lacks are reasserting themselves in a society where they are being treated as perpetual under-16s...I am against the superior–inferior white–black stratification that makes the white a perpetual teacher and the black a perpetual pupil (a poor one at that)' (1996: 21, 240). In 2013, Gillian Schutte made a similar observation about liberals and liberalism, contending, 'liberalism becomes a top down form of paternal humanitarianism that (still) insists that Africans are a childlike people who need to be real human beings'.[4] This paternalistic attitude leads directly to white people assuming the position of being spokespersons for black interest and liberation. According to Biko, '[l]iberals are the "self-appointed trustees of black interest"' (1996: 25).

All the above-mentioned models of paternalism are individually and collectively present among South African white people in general. At various historical periods in South Africa, Africans have been viewed as childlike, stupid and lazy – and thus requiring white guardianship. In an insightful discussion of South African liberalism, Maloka argues that South African liberalism has always been racist despite claims to the contrary by its adherents. This racism found covert expression through the notion of 'civilising mission' paternalism. Maloka notes that this paternalistic attitude did not proceed without challenges. He cites Dr John Philip (arguably the 'father of Cape liberalism'), who in an attempt to confront the challenges, proposed a teacher/pupil, mentally competent/incompetent and doctor/patient model all rolled into one in 1828: 'The first step towards the civilisation of a savage is to rouse the thinking principle. This can only be done by proposing to his mind considerations of sufficient force to overcome his native indolence. These considerations must be addressed to his passions and suited to his capacity' (in Maloka 2014: 36). White liberals have throughout their history held a number of stereotypes about Africans in particular, one of which Maloka suggests is the belief that Africans are children: 'that therefore, they needed to be placed under white trusteeship or guardianship, for their civilisation and indeed for their own good'. He concludes that 'this stereotype was an established view in liberal circles, at least, well into the 1960s' (2014: 56). Modisane (writing in 1963) reports that as a guest in the house gatherings organised by white liberals, he noticed that 'at some point [during the party] there would be the interminable references to the house servants...as "boy" or "girl" (1986: 159). Indeed, which South African of the apartheid period has never heard the words 'boy' or 'girl' directed at a black adult male or adult female?

At first, the Afrikaner Nationalist Party concurred with the liberal trusteeship paternalism. Its first official statement after assuming power in 1948 (as cited above) was: 'In our attitude toward the Native the fundamental principle is the supremacy of the European population in a spirit of Christian trusteeship' (in Leatt et al. 1986: 77–78). However, with the entrenchment of apartheid in the 1950s, the Afrikaner appeared to shift from liberal trusteeship or guardianship paternalism to a declaration of complete control of Africans and separation from them. Prime Minister Hans Strydom declared: 'Our policy is that Europeans must stand their ground and must remain *baas* [master] in South Africa...Our view is that in every sphere the European must retain the right to rule the country and to keep it a white man's country' (Bunting, in La Guma 1971: 27–28). In 1963, the supposed architect of apartheid – Prime Minister Hendrik Verwoerd – clearly expressed the Afrikaner's shift from trusteeship to total domination when he declared: 'Reduced to its simplest form, the problem is nothing else than this: We want to keep South Africa White. Keeping it White can only mean one thing; namely, White domination, not "leadership", not "guidance", but "control", "supremacy" (Bunting, in La Guma 1971: 28). The emphasis on *complete control* notwithstanding, every attitude of superiority contains within itself camouflaged or lurking paternalistic inclinations. That is why a delegate to the Afrikaner Conservative Party of South Africa Congress in 1985 unabashedly declared, 'The black man is a childlike human being' (*Sunday Times* 11 August 1985).

Although white paternalism assumed many different forms, the one form which Biko particularly abhorred was what Alcoff calls 'the problem of speaking for others' (1991). Speaking on behalf of black people by white people of goodwill has always been a major problem for black people struggling for freedom in antiblack societies. As far back as 1827, for example, the opening editorial of the first black newspaper in New York read:

> We wish to plead our own cause. Too long have others spoken for us. Too long has the public been deceived by misrepresentations, in things which concern us dearly. From the press and the pulpit we have suffered much by being incorrectly represented. Men whom we equally love and admire have not hesitated to represent us disadvantageously, without becoming personally acquainted with the state of things, nor discerning between virtue and vice among us. (in Ephraim 2003: 18–19)

Around the same period, Martin Delany rejected white paternalism and urged black people not to allow white people to think and speak for them. Persons from dominant groups who speak for others are often treated as authenticating presences that confer legitimacy and credibility on the demands of subjugated speakers; such speaking for others does nothing to disrupt the discursive hierarchies that operate in public spaces (Alcoff 1991).

According to Alcoff, this is a problem because the 'speaker's location is epistemically salient and also, certain privileged locations are discursively dangerous, i.e. the practice of privileged persons speaking for or on behalf of less privileged persons has actually resulted (in many cases) in increasing or re-enforcing the oppression of the group spoken for' (1991: 10). To see Africans such as Senghor, Nkrumah, Banda, Nyerere or Kaunda speak for themselves was a novelty, an eye-opener, for SASO members who had to learn not to allow white liberals to speak on their behalf. In fact, Biko argues, even before SASO, many people could not see '[t]hat blacks in this last ten-year period had been subjected to so much suffocation by representation by whites, representation by this, by that – that to speak for themselves was a novelty' (interview with Gerhart 1972: 11). SASO thus wanted to encourage a more receptive listening on the part of privileged liberals, a listening practice which discouraged 'presumptuous and oppressive practices of speaking for others' (Alcoff 1991: 8). For in listening is implied the notion of a speaker. If liberals become the listeners, black people assume the role of being speakers speaking for themselves about themselves through themselves to themselves.

In a similar manner as Delany, Biko blamed some black people for allowing white people to speak on their behalf. The African tendency to take the back seat was, in Biko's view, a consequence of the fear of the regime's punitive reprisals and a lack of courage to rebel. 'There was this sort of appalling silence on the part of Africans and this tendency to play kids and hide behind the skirts of white liberals who were speaking for them' (interview with Gerhart 1972: 18). In the extremely oppressive situation of the South Africa of the 1960s in which African political organisations were outlawed, it was safer for an African to be silent than to speak out. The silence, unfortunately, created a situation in which the liberals intensified their role not only as speakers for but also as trustees of black interests. This, according to Biko, constitutes the *locus* of the main conflict with liberals. In the context of a society such as apartheid South Africa, white people speaking for black people was problematic not only for the two reasons that Alcoff mentions but also because of the superiority/inferiority complex and paternalistic relations at play. White liberal paternalism manifested in various forms; underlying all these forms was an assumption of white superiority and African inferiority. In short, white liberal paternalism was and still is predicated on the notion of white supremacy.

Individualism

As noted above, at the core of liberal social ontology is individualism (that is, the autonomy of the individual). Part of Biko's problem with liberalism as an ideology is its overemphasis on the primacy of the individual over and above the collective. For liberalism, individual autonomy is the highest good and thus any act, practice or behaviour (including group interest or group solidarity, or any collectivist arrangement) that threatens this core value, the individual's capacity to make choices and judgements as a rational being, is *a priori* problematic. Very high on the liberal's agenda is individual self-consciousness, which is a product of the liberal doctrine of individual rights and liberties. There is therefore the tendency to think in terms of the individual person rather than collectives or groups, and further in terms of personal merit and demerit as important aspects of one's life. This belief in individualism is responsible for the liberal's rejection of race, ethnic or class identities while espousing an ethic of tolerance that preserves the existence of the very groups they reject. They insist that race is a morally irrelevant category, because it is not earned but an accident of nature. Accordingly, human beings must avoid irrational choices that appeal to contingencies like race. What therefore needs to be done, liberals argue, is to eradicate the evil of irrational and illogical individual prejudices and exclusions based on an irrelevant category such as the colour of a person's skin or the texture of his hair. This sounds very fair and logical, until we dig deeper into the situation of black people vis-à-vis liberal principles.

An appeal to Sartre's concept of series will hopefully provide some insight into one of liberalism's core concepts: atomistic individualism. According to Sartre, a series is a collection of people who are connected only by external closeness or immediacy. Put differently, it is a collection of unselfconscious, isolated, passive, autonomous individuals brought together exclusively by a common product or object situated outside the collective. Since in Sartre's conception of human freedom all relations must be understood in terms of action, a series is a social collective whose members are unified passively either by objects of interest or by the material effects of the actions of others, the practico-inert. Examples of a series include a collection of people listening to a radio broadcast, consumers connected by the market or a number of commuters waiting for a bus. In the bus example, everyone is in the queue for the same reason (transport) and this constitutes them into a collective, albeit they do not have a common or collective goal. No one is interested in the Other except insofar as the Other is a possible competitor for limited seats on the bus. When this happens, scarcity has entered the collective, determining in the process relations between individuals as that of hostile competition. To this extent, each wishes the Other was not there and each becomes Other than himself, penetrated by the scarcity of the material things and how they influence their relation to Others. To avoid imminent conflict, they constitute themselves into an ordered queue – an act that in itself is also recognition of their community. The serial object, the bus for example, not only dictates the seriality of the members of the collective but also renders individual members interchangeable because they are not socially differentiated. For this reason, each member of the serial collective experiences feelings of isolation, passivity, alienation, powerlessness and otherness. As a result, no individual action in the serial group can bring about change or liberation from the serial condition. In fact, seriality renders human beings socially impotent. It pushes the human beings outside of relations with all others. In such a scenario, the individual is left and rendered impotent. Understood as the atomisation of the collective into a diffusion of innumerable individuals who relate to one another through some abstract external mediation, seriality resonates with liberalism's atomisation of the individual as a social unit. Indeed, it is clear that because of its philosophical and moral commitment to the universalist ethos, liberalism wishes to preserve social collectives (if at all) at the level of seriality constituted by atomic autonomous individuals whose only relations to others are alterity.

Liberals are gripped by what Sartre calls 'analytic reason', which is the mode of thought of liberal humanists according to which composite realities must necessarily be reducible to simple elements or atoms whose relations to one another are external relations. In the social and political spheres, human beings (for the analytic spirit) are atomic, solitary individuals whose only concept of solidarity is that of 'a pea in a can of peas: he is round, closed in on himself, incommunicative' (Sartre 1988: 256). Human beings exist as individuals, side by side, without any true unity; their relations are external and their solidarity a passive bond among distinct molecules. Sartre argues that blinded by this mode of reason, for the liberal, 'a physical body is a collection of molecules; a social body, a collection of individuals. And by individual he means the incarnation in a single example of the universal traits which make up human nature' (1965: 55). The liberal humanist rejects claims of racial group identity such as black people and Jews, but recognises only the individual human being who is an incarnation of universal traits of human nature that is constituted by reason. For the liberal humanist, therefore, the black person does not exist. There is no black consciousness or Jewish consciousness; there is only a human consciousness. In this way, the concrete particular is rejected in favour of the abstract universal. What this mode of thought ultimately leaves us with is the idea that there are no black people and therefore there is no racial problem. For this reason, white liberals are antagonistic to and reject any form of group identity, as was manifested by Black Consciousness as a group approach to political, social and racial problems. For them, the 'group' or 'community' has no ontological status at all. Only individual human beings can be rational – and since knowledge, thinking and rational action are attributes of the individual, there is therefore 'no such thing as a collective brain' (Rand 1967: 16). People must be protected as individuals and not as groups, because it is as individuals that they are oppressed. A group, according to liberals, cannot be oppressed; only individuals are oppressed. Opposed to this view is the antiblack racist according to whom there are no individuals; black people simply exist as a group.

Biko realised the deceptiveness of liberal individualism. He became an expression of Fanon's intuition: 'The colonialist bourgeoisie had hammered into the native's mind the idea of a society of individuals where each person shuts himself up in his own subjectivity, and whose only wealth is individual thought.' He goes on to caution us: '*Now the native who has the opportunity to return to the people during the struggle for freedom will discover the falseness of this theory*' (1968: 47 – italics added). Following Fanon's warning, Biko realised that in a serious liberation struggle intended to create a new society and new human reality, individualism should be among the first things to be discarded. He understood that the liberal ideology of individualism serves as a safety valve for white people against the group consciousness of the oppressed black majority, that it opposes the progression and development of group consciousness. Black social and political consciousness and radicalism get restrained by the hope fostered that at least some of them, as individuals, can rise out of the misery and suffering that typifies their existential condition. Thus individualism has the effect of countering the growth of group or class consciousness and hinders the development of a consciousness of the social character of oppression and exploitation. The white liberal, Biko believed, wants to plunge the black person in a liberal 'crucible out of which he will emerge single and naked, an individual and solitary particle, just like all other particles' (Sartre 1965: 57). This means that the liberal is someone who is afraid of the consciousness of the [black] collectivity, someone who wishes to destroy the black person as a black person 'and leave nothing in him but the man, the abstract and universal subject' (Sartre 1965: 57). Hence, among the first tasks undertaken by Black Consciousness was the demolition of the emergent urban black individualism inculcated by liberalism. Biko realised that white liberalism has the effect of preventing black people from standing on their own feet, from being on their own, from exercising their capacity as full human beings. It is this realisation that prompted the slogan 'Black man, you are on your own'. That meant getting rid of black dependency on white liberals and their influence on black aspiration just so that black people can be able 'to rise and attain the envisaged self'. White liberals, Biko argues, have been doing things for black people on behalf of black people and because of black people. Now, echoing Sobukwe, '[t]he blacks are tired of standing at the touchlines to witness a game that they should be playing. They want to do things for themselves and all by themselves' (Biko 1996: 15).

Part of the problem of liberal individualism is its intolerance of group identity, and therefore its disregard of the fact that racist consciousness always operates at the level of collectives. It is this indifference to racist collectivist nature that makes liberals blind to racism's viciousness. The word 'race' itself signifies not a single individual person but a collection or group of people socially distinguishable by certain morphological and phenotypical characteristics, biological, genetic or scientific evidence to the contrary notwithstanding. If, as it is commonly agreed, racism is predicated on the assumption of the existence of races, if race refers to a collective or a group of human beings with certain socially identifiable physical traits, then racism cannot be a phenomenon directed against a single individual; its reference is to a group. Consequently, to the racist consciousness, human beings always exist as collective wholes and their individual identities inhere in those collectives. To such a consciousness, human beings will always appear as black, white or coloured people. A person, according to this logic, is not an isolated being within a collective whole but part of a homogenised crowd. An individual person with a self-identity is unheard of to the racist consciousness because the foundation of being is the racial group or collective.

Since racism is fundamentally not a phenomenon about the uniqueness of an autonomous individual but about collectives (groups, the superiority or inferiority of a presumed racial group), each individual person belonging to that particular collective is replaceable and changeable in the manner of each individual within the Sartrean seriality. This fact is captured by the popular racist phrase 'All Niggers look alike' (that is, they are one and all). Any *one of them* will do. For this reason, it is impossible to fight racism as an autonomous individual. While a single individual can refuse to be broken by racism, while he can act to diminish the extent to which he suffers from racism and can make a significant contribution to the emancipatory effort against racism, he cannot abolish or destroy racism all by himself. Mandela, Martin Luther King Jr, Rosa Parks, Gandhi, Malcolm X and even Steve Biko could not. Racial solidarity is a necessary condition for emancipation from racism. Biko recognised this when he emphatically stated: 'We are oppressed not as individuals...we are oppressed because we are black. We must use that very concept to unite ourselves and to respond as a cohesive group. We must cling to each other with the tenacity that will shock the perpetrators of evil (1996: 97).

Black liberals

What was even more problematic about liberal paternalism, individualism and egalitarianism for Biko was that 'the black people have believed in them for so long' (1996: 20) – that is, some black people bought into and appropriated the liberal ideology, thus becoming representative of this ideology themselves. How could it be otherwise? Liberal politics is couched in terms of kindness and concern for the oppressed that is quite genuine; it is cloaked in a veil of humanism that is quite different from vulgar Afrikaner Calvinism or crude racism of the apartheid era. Besides, leaders of liberalism such as Alan Paton and Suzman indignantly condemned apartheid as a morally bankrupt system requiring to be replaced by reforms such as multiracialism. In this sort of situation, the debilitating consequences of oppression become evident. Some black people, Biko argues, 'have been made to feel inferior for so long that for them it is comforting to drink tea, wine or beer with whites who seem to treat them as equals. This serves to boost up their own ego to the extent of making them feel slightly superior to those blacks who do not get similar treatment from whites. These are the sort of blacks who are a danger to the community' (1996: 23).

Although Biko mainly focuses his criticism on white liberals, he does not spare black liberals from criticism. Who are the black liberals? I suggest that Biko makes a distinction between principled ideological black liberals and opportunistic black liberals. The ideologically committed black liberals were members of the predominantly white Liberal Party. In the first place, political principles associated with liberalism are not the sole property of white liberalism. Africans hitherto had democratic political structures which resonated with certain principles of white liberalism.[5] The ANC, from its inception in 1912, promoted liberal principles of equality, the rule of law, liberty, justice, human dignity, tolerance and rationality. ANC leaders such as Pixley Isak Ka Seme, Dr Alfred Xuma and Albert Luthuli were avowed liberals. Speaking as the president of the ANC, Luthuli declared: 'I welcome the presence of the Liberal Party. It stands for and represents lasting values, values which would make South Africa a country to be honoured. We in the A.N.C. would particularly like to work with the Liberal Party. I must say that we do usually cooperate in those matters where we agree and as the years have gone by we have found ourselves more and more in agreement with the Liberal Party' (in Robertson 1971: 183). The Liberal Party attracted a fair amount of black members who promoted liberal principles and political projects. Prominent individuals such as Jordan Ngubane were members of the Liberal Party.

The other kind of black liberals were the 'intelligent and articulate' few black people who, by virtue of education and political activism, were incorporated into the liberal white social world. They are the 'dull-witted, self-centred blacks [who]...are in the ultimate analysis as guilty of the arrest of progress as their white friends' (Biko 1996: 24). Influenced by the liberal ideology of the rule of law (even if it is the law not of their own making and the law that oppresses them), they are inducted into the theory of gradualism and indulge in 'comfortable politics' demanding 'a move at a pace that doesn't rock the boat' (interview with Gerhart 1972: 27). Ensnared and fascinated by tea, beer and wine parties to which they were constantly invited by white liberals, such black people found themselves engaging in what Heidegger calls 'idle talk'. In other words, Biko accuses black liberals of what Heidegger calls 'inauthentic existence'. Heidegger describes an inauthentic existence as an 'absorption' in the everyday routine, 'dispersion' into modes of being such as idle chatter. By idle chatter, Heidegger refers to that everyday average explanation of existence and the world where any real understanding is not attempted at all. In idle chatter, no real content is communicated and nothing is really understood; attention is merely focused on talking itself, which always already uses conventional phrases and simply repeats what has already been said by someone. These, finally, are the black people who are intent on changing the white person's image of the black person, while the Black Consciousness Movement is concerned with changing the black person's image of himself. Biko offers examples of what happened at the tea, beer and wine parties he attended; in such 'artificial integrated circles', he explains:

> You meet in a comfortable house, and they're [white liberals] going to talk about art and poetry...things you are not exposed to. And the tendency is you sit and listen to these guys analysing these things...But at that moment, during your contact with these whites, it serves to dramatize your inferiority; you blame yourself for not knowing these things. You don't blame the society. Instead of sensitizing you to oppression, it tends to re-emphasize your own inferiority and emphasize their superiority. (interview with Gerhart 1972: 45–46)

The major problem about these artificially integrated circles is their drowning of black people into inauthenticity because 'they are so *far* from the real problem, so far from efforts toward a real solution' (interview with Gerhart 1972: 46). An example of what Biko would classify as black liberal is Modisane who, in his autobiography, expresses the same sentiments.

> I am...insulted with multi-racial tea parties where we wear our different racial masks and become synthetically polite to each other, in a kind of masquerade where Africans are being educated into an acceptance of their inferior position...the African is persuaded to understand that he must be humble if he is not to antagonise 'the growing number of Europeans who are taking an interest in African affairs and welfare'...I said the right things, echoed the appropriately eloquent justification for my social inequality.
>
> I remember that I used to become overpowered by a sense of self-consciousness, I felt that I was a curiosity at most of these tea parties. I was a piece of rare Africana; subject to such illuminations like, 'I've never met an *intelligent* African before – I mean an African who is actually *articulate*.' (1986: 158–159 – italics added)

Black people in such integrated circles, Biko proclaims, are dangerous to the struggles of black people because in heated arguments, 'the people who were protecting whites were mainly not whites but blacks who were in the circle' (interview with Gerhart 1972: 46). Malcolm X famously metaphorically referred to such black people as the 'House Negroes', as distinct from the 'Field Negroes'. The House Negroes were those slaves who protected the master and his property as if it was their own, while the Field Negroes hated and resisted the master. The 'House Nigger' metaphor highlights the tendency among highly assimilated black liberals to valorise whiteness in all its multifarious forms. In one of the speeches he gave prior to his separation from the Nation of Islam, 'Message to the Grassroots', Malcolm X said: 'Just as the slavemaster of that day used Tom, the house Negro, to keep the field Negroes in check, the same old slavemaster today has Negroes who are nothing but modern Uncle Toms, twentieth-century Uncle Toms to keep you and me in check, to keep us under control, keep us passive and peaceful and nonviolent' (in Breitman 1965: 12).

The tragedy about such black liberals who unfortunately valorised and had faith in white liberals, Biko argued, was that they were the 'intelligent and articulate' ones, those who by virtue of their intelligence and expressiveness should have been in a position to lead the struggle and be at the forefront of radical change. But these black liberals refused to see race as a systemic problem; they reduced it to an individual problem which could easily be transcended when one pulled oneself up by one's bootstraps. Because they believed in liberal white non-racialism and were convinced by its individualism, they subscribed to what may be called the doctrine of transcendence. This doctrine asserts that a black individual must transcend his blackness. The black self is de-emphasised or overlooked completely in the determination of who one is. Such a person would make assertions such as: 'I want to be a person (human being), not a black person (human being).' Tiger Woods, responding to a question from a journalist about him being the greatest black golfer ever, said: 'I don't want to be the greatest Black golfer; I want to be the greatest golfer.' The upshot of this assertion here is: Physically black though I may be, I am essentially an individual for whom blackness has no significance. My blackness is irrelevant because I'm simply an individual who is also a Christian, a liberal, a South African, a husband and so on. In short, I am colour-blind. Such black people view themselves as raceless liberals, autonomous, atomic individuals whose identity is not determined by the colour of their skin. We shall return to the notion of colour-blindness later in the text. Suffice to point out here that the problem with black liberals' colour-blindness is that the white racists are colour-conscious.

In addition to the unfortunate claims that Black Consciousness was a replica of the American Black Power Movement, Sono argues that SASO activists were – their vehement critique of liberalism notwithstanding – liberals to the core. This claim renders Biko's critique of liberalism bizarre. In Sono's view, the Black Consciousness Movement had 'its roots firmly located primarily in the African liberals' disenchantment with (white) liberalism, primarily because it was not liberalism *per se* as much as it was *white* liberalism that epitomised political uselessness' (1993: 6). In Black Consciousness, Sono continues, the white liberal has been replaced by 'a more hardnosed new liberal' (1993: 6). Thus Black Consciousness 'was no more than one family member (black liberals) unilaterally declaring independence from the other member (white liberals)' (1993: 7).

Evidently Black Consciousness as a SASO philosophy was not the product of older African liberals as such but a product of a number of young, initially almost politically naïve, students with divergent ideological conceptions. Biko's interview statement – 'I doubt if the movement [Black Consciousness] could claim any staunch member beyond the age say of 40. There's a lot in the range of 35' (interview with Gerhart 1972: 32) – renders Sono's claims absurd.

In the course of this book, I have argued that Black Consciousness is a philosophy of existence and as such it is a form of existentialism. It is a feature of existentialist philosophy not to define freedom in a narrow sense (which liberals do). For existentialists, freedom is distinguishable from individual liberty, which is the core concept of liberal democracy. Many critics and interpreters of the Black Consciousness Movement fail to make the distinction between freedom (internal freedom) and liberty (external freedom) in the manner in which Berlin does with freedom 'to' and freedom 'from'. Put differently, freedom *to* (in Sartrean formulation) is ontological freedom, the idea that in human reality freedom is not a quality or property one possesses but the very being of human reality. 'What we call freedom', Sartre argues, 'is impossible to distinguish from the *being* of human reality' (1956: 25). This ontological freedom places the entire responsibility for human existence squarely upon human shoulders. This of course is not the kind of freedom as individual liberty envisaged and preached by liberals. Indeed, many black thinkers also believed that the oppressed have to realise that freedom is not another's to give or bestow; it must be taken. Formal liberation is meaningless: true freedom (substantive freedom) cannot be conferred upon a people who are not willing to work or struggle, if need be to sacrifice in order to attain it. In the words of Paulo Freire, 'freedom is acquired by conquest, not by gift' (1985: 31). Douglass understood what this means when he stated that without a struggle, there can be no freedom. Biko was no exception to this thinking. Given this conception of freedom, situating all Black Consciousness proponents in liberalism is very problematic indeed.

The fundamental irreconcilable differences between liberalism and the Black Consciousness Movement concerned (i) the politics of race and identity, and (ii) the means for the elimination of racism. How then do liberals conceive of the transcendence of race and identity? Liberals propose a form of antiracism that has become known as race-eliminativism, according to which race as a biological, cultural or social phenomenon is a fiction and therefore requires to be eliminated. This is because race has neither scientific nor ontological foundations at all. Since there is no scientific evidence that races have ontological legitimacy, human beings belong to the same race – the human race. Racism, therefore, is a social construction which will disappear as soon as we (i) eliminate the use of the word 'race' from our everyday dealings with one another, (ii) adopt colour-blindness as an ideology (that is, black people must simply forget that they are black, must simply forego their identity) and (iii) strive for integration as a means to transcend racism. I attend to these liberal approaches to apartheid racism and Biko's response to them in the following chapter. Suffice it mention here that South African liberals fundamentally saw apartheid as a moral problem that required moral solutions, such as appealing to the conscience of the Nationalist regime. Hence, for them, the problem would be solved once apartheid was abolished non-violently and by legal means. The problem would be solved precisely because it was the result of the immorality of racism and not the condition of the black people. In his article on South African apartheid, 'Racism and Moral Pollution', Appiah – as a true representative of the liberal conception of racism – argues that race is not a morally relevant determinant of a person's worth and that 'an ethical system which regards race...as a morally relevant characteristic offends against the Kantian conception of morality' (1986/1987: 186).

Moral responsibility

White liberals, Biko insists, are those 'people who argue that they are not responsible for white racism and the country's "inhumanity to the black man"' (1996: 20). This white liberal denial of moral responsibility and accountability raises a number of vexing questions about ascriptions of moral responsibility for the crimes of apartheid, an issue whose seriousness was expressed by the establishment of what later came to be known as the Truth and Reconciliation Commission during Mandela's presidency. The question of an agent's responsibility for his choice and actions raises a set of questions about moral responsibility and complicity in the evils of apartheid. How, for example, can moral responsibility for the evils of apartheid be assessed? Can we, for example, hold all white people in apartheid South Africa collectively responsible for the racist treatment of black people? Certain white people, particularly liberals and leftists, consider themselves immune from any wrongdoing during apartheid and therefore absolve themselves from moral blame for the atrocities perpetrated by that regime. These white people, Biko argues, claim that 'they too feel the oppression just as acutely as the blacks and therefore should be jointly involved in the black man's struggle for a place under the sun' (Biko 1996: 12).

Fundamental to Biko's argument is the premise (as I indicated above) that Black Consciousness deals with the totality of the white power structure, yet liberals want to exclude themselves from this totality. In a similar vein as existentialists such as Jaspers and Sartre, Biko argues that all those who reproduced, participated or in whatever way benefitted from the system are guilty of wrongdoing and therefore should be held responsible for the atrocities perpetrated in the name of that system. He concludes: 'Thus in the ultimate analysis no white person can escape being part of the oppressor camp' (1996: 23). But how is it possible that white people are collectively responsible for apartheid? What about those who not only spoke on behalf of but worked with the oppressed black masses – that is, those white people like Richard Turner, Neil Aggett, Bram Fisher and Ruth First who paid the ultimate price? What about those who claimed to have been unaware of what was happening in the black townships? Today, very few white people in the 'New South Africa' are prepared to concede that they voted for the Nationalist Party. Indeed, almost every white person today unashamedly blames apartheid for the injustices of the past, as if the system was of its own creation without the people who kept it in existence. What about those who in fact did not vote for the apartheid government but voted for the opposition parties, or did not vote at all? What about those who claim they were obeying orders from the state authorities?

What about those who never touched a living or dead black victim? What about those who emigrated rather than opposed apartheid, those who from a safe distance expressed self-righteous criticism of those who remained? What about those who deserted the apartheid army, those who refused to be conscripted into the apartheid defence force (for example, the End Conscription Campaign of the 1980s)? Put differently: What would it mean for a white South African to fight against apartheid while simultaneously reaping the ontological, social, legal and material benefits of whiteness? How wide can or should the moral responsibility net be cast? (More 1996b, 2008).

Biko's moral net covers a wide range indeed, because he shares with Jaspers the belief that '[t]here exists among men, because they are men, a solidarity through which each shares responsibility for every injustice and every wrong committed in the world, and especially for crimes that are committed in his presence or of which he cannot be ignorant' (Biko 1996: 23). In a similar fashion as Jaspers and Sartre, Biko contends that all those who created, planned and ordered it are responsible for it; all those who carried it out are responsible for it, all those who accepted it and allowed it to happen are responsible for it; all those who were silent about it and pretended not to know are responsible for it. These are those who, in Jaspers' words, 'knew, or could know, yet walked in ways which self-analysis reveals to them as culpable error – whether conveniently closing their eyes to events, or permitting themselves to be intoxicated, seduced or bought with personal advantages, or obeying from fear' (1995: 159). In Biko's view, if white people did not like what was happening to black people, they possessed enough power collectively to stop black suffering. Since they did not, he concludes, '[w]e...have every reason to bundle them together and blame them jointly' (1996: 78). Therefore, as Madhubuti has insisted, 'the one or two White friends or mates [should not] exonerate the crimes of their people' (in Ephraim 2003: xiii).

Robert Fatton maintains that Biko's articulation of Black Consciousness philosophy must be understood as an ethico-political philosophy of action. This ethico-political philosophy, Fatton argues, means that the political manifestations and the moral principle of Black Consciousness are inseparable for 'they expressed the transcendence of the "ethical demand" and the responsibility of human beings for their choice and actions' (1986: 156). It is precisely in this ethico-political realm that the existentialist influence of Sartre, mediated through Jaspers and Fanon, emerges in full and becomes evident in Biko's thinking. Sartre's preface to Fanon's *The Wretched of the Earth*, for example, evidently has resonance with Biko's view on moral responsibility. For it is in that text where Sartre accuses Europeans, especially the French, 'for being the accomplice in the crime of colonialism' (1968: 24). It is also here that Sartre responds to Camus' protestation that he is 'neither executioner nor victim': 'Very well then, if you're not victims when the government which you've voted for, when the army in which your younger brothers are serving without hesitation or remorse have undertaken race murder, you are, without a shadow of doubt, executioners....With us [Europeans], to be a man is to be an accomplice to colonialism, since all of us without exception have profited by colonial exploitation' (1968: 25).

Biko begins his ascription of moral responsibility on this Sartrean note, directed primarily against the white liberals. He wrote: 'It may perhaps surprise some people that I should talk of whites in a collective sense when in fact it is a particular section – i.e. the government – that carries out this unwarranted vendetta against blacks' (1996: 77). In his view, white people are collectively responsible for at least three reasons: First, the apartheid government's 'immorality and naked cruelty are done in the name of white people' (1996: 76). Second, white people are responsible for putting the apartheid regime in power:

> There are those whites who will completely disclaim responsibility for the country's inhumanity to the black man. These are the people who are governed by logic for 4½ years but by fear at election time. The Nationalist Party has perhaps many more English votes than one imagines. All whites collectively recognise in it a strong bastion against the highly played-up swart gevaar [black peril]...Thus if whites in general do not like what is happening to the black people, they have the power in them to stop it here and now. We, on the other hand, have every reason to bundle them together and blame them jointly. (1996: 77–78).

Third, white people remain in the country because they benefit from the oppression of black people. Hence, the very fact that even the so-called 'disgruntled whites remain [in the country] to enjoy the fruits of the system would alone be enough to condemn them at Nuremberg' (1996: 78–79). The similarity between Biko and Sartre is here remarkable, as Sartre's comment indicates: 'But we vote, we give mandates and, in any way we can revoke them; the stirring of public opinion can bring down governments. We personally must be accomplices to the crimes that are committed in our name, since it is within our power to stop them. We have to take responsibility for this guilt which was dormant in us, inert, foreign, and demean ourselves in order to be able to bear it' (2001: 55).

As noted earlier, one of Sartre's main targets in *Anti-Semite and Jew* is the liberal democrat, the supposed friend of the Jew, the champion of equal rights, the 'Rights of Man' and universal human essence. It is the liberal democrat's perverted Western humanism whose principle of universality provides a veiled moral, political and economic justification for racism and pillage that Sartre denounces. The tendency of Western humanism to collude with colonialism and its racist practices led Sartre to conclude that 'humanism is the counterpart of racism: it is a practice of exclusion' (1982: 752). Just like Sartre's liberal humanist, Biko's liberals are those whose 'protests are directed at and appeal to white conscience, [such that] everything they do is directed at finally convincing the white electorate that *the black man is also a man* and that at some future date he should be given a place at the white man's table' (Biko 1996: 21–22 – italics added). Putting aside the 'evil-doers', the normal stubborn white South African racist, it is the white liberal who consistently denies his responsibility for black oppression through what Biko calls 'deliberate evasiveness' or what Sartre famously means by bad faith. In response to these denials Biko argues:

> [O]ne has to come to the painful conclusion that the liberal is in fact appeasing his own conscience, or at best is eager to demonstrate his identification with the black people only so far as it does not sever all his ties with his relatives on the other side of the colour line. Being white, he possesses the natural passport to the exclusive pool of white privileges from which he does not hesitate to extract whatever suits him. Yet, since he identifies with the blacks, he moves around his white circles – white-only beaches, restaurants, and cinemas – with a lighter load, feeling that he is not like the rest. (1996: 65)

But such people cannot escape moral responsibility for apartheid because as members of the white South African community, they enjoyed a privileged position they did not deserve and they are aware of this. In fact, long before the upsurge of theories and literature on 'Whiteness' and 'White Privilege',[6] Biko critiqued whiteness and white privilege in this country. For him, whiteness has historically been used to acquire benefits that white people do not deserve and at the expense of black people. As mentioned above, Biko argues that white privilege constitutes the white community into a single group undeserving of the privilege it enjoys (1996).

Those who created, planned and ordered it, those who accepted it and allowed it to happen, those who voted for the system – all of them are obviously responsible for apartheid's inhumanity. There is equally no excuse for those who carried it out under orders, for they had the choice to either obey or disobey and then face the consequences of their disobedience. Since they chose to obey, they are responsible for their decisions and actions. What about those who were silent and pretended not to know? Biko's response is that no white person in South Africa can truly and genuinely claim that he did not know or was 'unaware' of what was happening in the country. This state of ignorance is what Sartre aptly calls 'the state of false ignorance' imposed on the citizens by the regime, but in which the citizens themselves contributed to its maintenance in order to ensure their peace of mind and quell their consciences. In spite of every effort by the apartheid regime to suppress the truth from reaching the public domain, everybody – through the few courageous media reports – knew about the death in detention of prisoners, torture, the apartheid army's occupation of the black townships, and bombing of so-called terrorists in neighbouring states such as Lesotho or Botswana. If the majority of white South Africans did not read the newspapers or were illiterate, they knew people who read them. Even many of those who had not heard of the atrocities committed in their name, heard the accounts of white soldiers – their brothers, cousins, fathers, uncles, relatives, friends, neighbours and acquaintances – who returned home and spoke about it. The international and public attention on the 1960 Sharpeville Massacre, the 1976 Soweto Student Riots, the death in detention of many activists (including Biko himself) and many other brutal incidents cannot justify or support any claim or excuse of ignorance. Debunking the French citizens' appeal to ignorance during the Algerian war, Sartre comments: 'False naiveté, flight, bad faith, solitude, silence, a complicity at once rejected and accepted, that is what we called, in 1945, collective responsibility. There was no way the German people, at the time, could feign ignorance of the camps...We were right, they did know everything, and it is only today that we can understand because we too know everything' (2001: 60–61).

Similarly, many white South Africans appeal to the argument of ignorance, that they did not know what was happening on the other side of the racial fence, precisely because of the strict racial separation enforced by the apartheid regime. The ignorance claim seems to be a popular escape route form of bad faith even today for most former supporters of apartheid who claim that they were unaware of the brutality of the system. Academics are no exception: Like many of the academics at South African universities, Prof. Sampie Terreblanche (an economics professor at Stellenbosch University and a passionate apartheid regime enthusiast who wrote speeches for government ministers but later became a fierce critic of apartheid) claimed, on noticing that apartheid was a spent force in 1989, that he was unaware of the entrenched poverty and suffering under apartheid (in Leach 1989: 171). It is even more disingenuous for a professor of economics to claim that the reality of social and economic exclusion and discrimination against black people had remained unbeknownst to him. Indeed, the many Germans who supported Hitler's virulent anti-Semitism also claimed ignorance of the genocidal Nazi practices.

Someone may finally ask: What about those who – like Neil Aggett, Bram Fischer and Ruth First or Richard Turner – paid the ultimate price and died through the apartheid machinery in an attempt to fight the system? Of course, there are always exceptions to the rule, but the exception does not eliminate the explanatory force of the rule; it merely indicates that every rule has limits. Put differently, such exceptions (for example, John Brown) are so rare that they become conspicuous exceptions that prove the rule. The one or two good white people, as Madhubuti insists, cannot exonerate the crimes of their people. Unsettling as it may sound, Biko concedes that 'it is a cruel assumption to believe that all whites are not sincere, yet methods adopted by some white groups often do suggest a lack of real commitment...What we are concerned here with is group attitudes and group politics. The exception does not make a lie of the rule – it merely substantiates it' (1996: 65, 51). Whether they like it or not, all white people benefited not only from the system but also by virtue of being members of the dominant white group, 'the colour of his skin – [being] his passport to privilege' (Biko 1996: 26). For example, Richard Turner (a white Sartrean turned Marxist philosophy lecturer at the University of Natal who engaged Biko quite often on the question of race and class and was subsequently assassinated by the apartheid regime) owned a farm and had the opportunity to study philosophy in France, two privileges which Biko could not have because of the colour of his skin. So, despite the fact that they fought against the system, they still are responsible for it all. They are not guilty; they are simply morally responsible. This view finds support from none other than the grandchild of the architect of apartheid, Wilhelm Verwoerd. According to him, even those white people who opposed apartheid benefitted from the system because they belonged to a race that was unjustly privileged at the expense of other racial groups (2000).

Unlike Sartre in the case of the Jews in his portrait of the anti-Semite, Biko's moral net is wide enough to cover the complicity of those black people who participated in their own oppression, those who were 'participants in the white man's game of holding the aspirations of the black people' (1996: 146). These are the 'people who deliberately allowed themselves into an unholy collusion with the enemy' (1996: 81); black leaders who were 'subconsciously siding and abetting in the total subjugation of the black people' (1996: 85); the black subject who had to be constantly reminded of 'his complicity in the crime of allowing himself to be misused and therefore letting evil reign supreme in the country of his birth' (1996: 29). It is this strong position, somewhat shared also by Sartre, I think, that prompted him to say: 'You are either alive and proud or you are dead'. The black policeman and woman, black Special Branch agent, black civil servant, black teacher, and particularly the apartheid created homeland (bantustan) leader were all directly responsible for perpetuating and propping up the apartheid machinery and thus did not escape Biko's moral responsibility net. These then are the people whom Biko and his comrades contemptuously labelled 'non-whites' because of their association and collaboration with the oppressive apartheid system. Barring those like the homeland leaders who consciously, explicitly, deliberately and actively colluded and collaborated with and aided the regime, those who were at once victims and beneficiaries, Biko's net did not leave out '[t]hose Blacks Who Suffered "But"'. They also were equally morally responsible for letting it happen. Here, Biko comes dangerously close to blaming the victim. Interpreted in this strong sense, this might sound like Hegel's justification of colonialism and slavery when he reminds us that to the extent that a slave aquiesces in slavery, he is responsible for the slavish situation: 'If a man is a slave, his own will is responsible for his slavery, just as it is its will which is responsible if a people is subjugated. Hence the wrong of slavery lies at the door not simply of enslavers or conquerors, but of the slave and the conquered themselves' (Hegel 1952b: para. 57A).

One of the major difficulties about Biko's concept of responsibility is that he seems to fluctuate freely between moral or political responsibility and an existentialist conception of ontological responsibility which Jaspers refers to as being 'metaphysical guilty'. It is this conflation of responsibility that accounts for his sweeping ascription of moral responsibility and guilt for the evils of apartheid. Ontological responsibility, as Biko himself recognises, assumes that there is a solidarity among human beings which constitutes each one of us to be responsible 'for every injustice and every wrong committed in the world' against humankind, because in choosing for myself, I am at the same time choosing for all human beings.

Moral responsibility, however, involves blameworthiness and praise for actions performed or not performed when they could have been performed. In other words, moral responsibility involves answerability and accountability for one's choices and actions. To apply criteria for ontological responsibility to cases of moral responsibility, as both Biko and Sartre do, entails overlooking questions about degrees of responsibility which are pertinent in determining moral blame. The responsibility of persons as citizens is not only an ontological fact, but also a social and historical one. To that extent, human beings cannot always be equally responsible for acts performed by their leaders and rulers. Ascription of moral guilt requires differentiating in terms of the degree of involvement or non-involvement. Surely, those who create, plan and order differ in degrees of responsibility from those who execute the orders, or those who merely accept and allow it to happen and those who are silent and fake ignorance or merely indifference to suffering. Ontological responsibility does not allow this moral gradation and thus is subject to the criticism that if everyone is responsible, then no one is responsible.

Conclusion

Biko's critique of liberals and liberalism's response to racism and his ideas on moral responsibility and complicity are interesting, not only for their philosophical significance but also importantly for their relevance to what I call 'post-apartheid

apartheid', which he (together with Fanon) so perfectly predicted. Evidence of his views on moral responsibility can be found in the spurious proceedings and handling of the Truth and Reconciliation Commission led by Archbishop Desmond Tutu. The adoption of neo-liberal policies by the ANC regime points to the still existing antiblack racism similar to and reminiscent of the apartheid era. The liberals' influence on black agency and outlook which Biko so vehemently castigated persists and therefore suggests the continuing significance and relevance of Biko and the Black Consciousness Movement's ideas. Biko's ideas did not go unchallenged by liberals and the leftists. Serious counter-critiques and attacks were mounted against Biko and his comrades. I deal with some of these responses in the following chapter.

Notes

1   See Blum's book *'I'm Not a Racist, But...': The Moral Quandary of Race* (2002).
2   Tshepo Matloga (a black teenager) was murdered by nine white rugby players not because he was allegedly poaching but because as a black person, he simply was 'crime' incarnate. The similarity between the death of Tshepo Matloga and that of Trayvon Martin in the USA is indicative of the persistence of global antiblack racism and the vulnerability or cheapness of black people's lives.
3   See Howard McGary's philosophically insightful chapter 'Paternalism and Slavery' in *Between Slavery and Freedom* (1992).
4   Schutte G, The trouble with liberalism, *Mail & Guardian*, 3 July 2013.
5   See Oguejiofor's *Philosophy, Democracy and Responsible Governance in Africa* (2003), Kimmerle and Wimmer's Eds *Philosophy and Democracy in Intercultural Perspective* (1997) and Kuper's 'Commitment: The Liberal as Scholar in South Africa' (1979) for detailed explanations of African liberalism and democratic practices.

6   See for example Frances Kendall's *White Privilege: Creating Pathways to Authentic Relationships Across Race* (2006), Tim Wise's *White Like Me: Reflections on Race from a Privileged Son* (2004) and Charles Cilliers' *For Whites Only: What Whites Think about the New SA* (2008).

7

Liberalism's transcendence of apartheid racism

IN AN ANTIBLACK SOCIETY such as South Africa under apartheid, negative reactions to any philosophy purporting to advance the freedom of black people were invariably plentiful. Criticism came from as divergent political spectrums and ideological formations as NUSAS, the Nationalist Party, the Inkatha Cultural Organisation, the ANC, the SACP, the Teacher's League of South Africa, the Natal Indian Congress, the Coloured Persons Representative Council and the media that represented these ideological positions.[1] These criticisms may generally be classified within two main traditions, namely the liberal and Marxist critiques. What is, however, interesting about both of them is that they converge in their belief that race has no ontological reality, that it has no objective reality and therefore should be understood as an illusion. Accordingly, the use of racial categories such as 'blackness' or 'whiteness' – as it is done in the Black Consciousness Movement – is a misplaced, dangerous and reactionary response to South African reality. As for the apartheid regime, at first it had a cautious reaction to the emergence of the Black Consciousness Movement, which it initially assumed to be a separatist movement and thus a justification for apartheid. However, the movement later came to conjure up a frightening image of the Black Power Movement in the USA and controversial militants such as Malcolm X who declared 'freedom by any means necessary' or Rap Brown who exclaimed 'Burn, Baby, Burn!' This association provided the regime with the necessary excuses to clamp down hard on the Black Consciousness Movement and its leaders for allegedly attempting to overthrow the government through violent means. This suppression was carried out even though the movement did not pose a violent threat, at least explicitly, to the so-called legitimate violence of the apartheid state.

In both the standard liberal and standard Marxist analyses of the South African apartheid situation, there has been ongoing failure to do theoretical justice to the question of race. Liberal individualistic social ontology and Marxist class ontology consider race an irrelevant explanatory category to the social and political difficulties faced in apartheid South Africa. Captivated by their individualist and class perspectives, both the liberal and the Marxist refuse or are reluctant to acknowledge the primacy of race as a determining factor in an antiblack society such as South Africa, Brazil or the USA. The consequences of this refusal are reductionisms of all sorts, including individualism or class reductionisms. In short, both these positions avoid addressing racism on its own terms. What they want to do is to find a category under which to subsume the problem of racism. For the liberals, racism is individual prejudice based on an illusionary notion of race; for Marxists, racism is an epiphenomenon of class exploitation, a subspecies of capitalist oppression. For black radicals, the problem amounted to finding the proper balanced relationship between a fundamentally racial analysis on the one hand and an essentially class analysis on the other hand. Biko's approach to this problem was beset by ambiguities and shifts that were a consequence of the prevailing political oppression of the time.

Liberalism's critique of Black Consciousness

True to their paternalistic attitude towards black people, white liberals initially complained about SASO's ingratitude to NUSAS and white liberals in general for the support that they offered the movement and the serious sacrifices that they made for the liberation of black people. White liberals seemed to be saying, to use Fanon's words, '[w]e have brought you up to our level and now you turn against your benefactors. Ingrates! Obviously nothing can be expected of you' (1967a: 35). Donald Woods (the then honorary president of NUSAS who later became friends with Biko) paternalistically criticised SASO, this group of unappreciative and ungrateful black people, for letting 'down the members of NUSAS, who have battled so long and so admirably for the cause of non-racial values' (in Buthelezi 1987: 29). In his confessional book on Biko, Woods recounts that he did not only regard Biko's 'argument that black students had to develop their own black identity' as racist, but also regarded the 'foundation of SASO as an act of betrayal of the white liberal commitment' (1987: 54). There is a sense of self-importance and self-justification in Woods' statement that reflects the opinion and attitudes of white liberals toward black people. In so doing, the liberals were simply reproducing the very same paternalistic attitude Biko fought against; they did not realise that *that* is precisely the problem that stifled black liberation. For example, when black students began to adopt the habit of seeing for themselves, hearing for themselves, thinking for themselves and talking for themselves, when they began to realise that they were on their own and started to 'take care of their own business' (Biko 1996: 23), white liberals accused them of being ungrateful, disrespectful and militant. Biko reports that when black people discard their fear and confront the lies thrown at them, they are branded militant and radical ingrates: 'A journalist from a liberal

newspaper like the the *Sunday Times* of Johannesburg described a black student –
who is only telling the truth – as a militant, impatient young man' (1996: 89). The
negative responses against the emergence of the Black Consciousness Movement,
particularly from the liberals, insinuated that black people:

> ...were becoming the ungrateful people that they are known to be by putting
> the liberals out of work...What, in fact, these people [for example NUSAS
> and Woods] were saying was that they have been fighting for the black
> cause for a long time, that it has since become second nature to them, to do
> this pious work. How dare the black people disturb the scheme of things
> by wanting to do the spade-work as well as the dirty work themselves?
> (Manganyi 1973: 17)

As a psychologist, Manganyi insists that these South African white liberals'
reactions were unsurprising because they suffered not only from acute narcissism
but also from its consequence, self-pity – what Ephraim calls 'the white man's
obsession with self-aggrandizement' or '*ressentiment* projection' by Europeans
(2003: 2). Sartre's rebuke of Europeans in 'Black Orpheus' may without alteration
be directed at South African white liberals. He asks: 'When you removed the gag
that was keeping these black mouths shut, what were you hoping for? That they
will sing your praise? Did you think that when they raised themselves up again,
you would read adoration in the eyes of these heads that our fathers had forced to
bend down to the very ground?' (1988: 291).

Given their core principle of the autonomy of the individual (individualism),
liberals are invariably averse to any position that privileges groups or collectives
over and above the individual. This opposition may be phrased in this manner:
for the liberal, the operating dictum should be the Cartesian 'I think, therefore
I am'; while for Black Consciousness, the dictum would read something like 'I
think, therefore we are'. The latter was thus in the line of fire of the liberals, since
it preached group solidarity and that liberation cannot be an individual problem
but is a group problem. By virtue of the presence of the word 'black' in the
Black Consciousness philosophy and the fact that the movement excluded white
people collectively from participation, liberals accused Biko and his comrades of
racism. For them, Black Consciousness was simply divisive, fanatical, dangerous,
conflictual and racist. This is hardly surprising since liberal political philosophy is
hostile and averse to anything resembling what it regards as nationalism or racial
solidarity. For liberals, the fact that the Black Consciousness Movement excluded
white people from its ranks and adopted the word 'black' as an identity tag was in
itself an act of racism, pure and simple. In other words, the very use of an ordinary
racial category such as 'black' is racist, essentialist and a form of black nationalism.

A typical example of this criticism is advanced by Donald Woods in his book *Biko*. He states: 'Black Consciousness...had in my view too many overtones of black racism' (1987: 62), and he repeatedly describes Black Consciousness as 'anti-white hatred', 'racial exclusivism in reverse' and so on. In the 'Editorial Opinion' of his newspaper *The Daily Dispatch* (1971) of East London, Woods (at the time a hard-core white liberal): 'The promoters of Black Consciousness are wrong in what they are doing. They are promoting apartheid. They are entrenching the idea of racial exclusivity and therefore are doing the Government's work...If SASO believes it will achieve more through exclusivity, it betrays a sense of unreality quite equal to those who believe apartheid has a future' (in Buthelezi, 1987:29). In his confession, Woods explains: 'As one of a tiny band of white South African liberals, I was totally opposed to race as a factor in political thinking, and totally committed to nonracist policies and philosophy' (1987: 54). The point Woods is driving at here is that the racism of Black Consciousness is equivalent to apartheid racism (that is, that there is a logical equivalence between the two). I cite Woods for the simple reason that not only was he a vociferous enemy of Biko and the Black Consciousness Movement, but also because he later came to understand and embrace Biko's philosophical position and became his 'spokesperson' after his death, as evidenced by the book he wrote on Biko which was later released as a movie. Woods' critique fundamentally boils down to this: Biko and his Black Consciousness comrades are racists to the core. The Black Consciousness philosophy preaches 'racism in reverse'. In other words, Black Consciousness was reduced to a black equivalent of apartheid racism, a logical move whereby the victims of racism are accused of racism the moment they attempt to fight racism. Since black people have been fighting against white racism, the argument goes, is black racism in the form of Black Consciousness not as bad as the other? Racism is racism no matter what it is called, white or black.

I want to pay particular attention to two intertwined – and obvious liberal – critiques of Black Consciousness, namely: (i) the charge that Black Consciousness is a racist philosophy and (ii) the anticollectivist or antisolidarity critique. I shall, however, attempt to contextualise these issues within the philosophical realm by paying particular attention to Appiah's critique of similar ideological formations as the Black Consciousness Movement – that is, political movements such as Du Bois and Crummell's Pan-Africanism, not only for its philosophical sophistication but also because of its close liberalistic resonance with the position of the white liberal critics of the Black Consciousness Movement. I suggest that in Appiah, we have what is perhaps the most articulate expression of white South African liberalism.

It is particularly noteworthy that Appiah's concerns were initially a response to Du Bois' 'The Conservation of Races', a paper Du Bois delivered on the occasion of the formation of the American Negro Academy in 1897. Races, according to Appiah, do not exist – 'The truth is that there are no races' (in Gates & West 1996: 35) – and since this is the case, the use of the word 'race' becomes problematic. For him, any belief or claim that human races have ontological status is *ipso facto* racist, even in the absence of any value judgement being made about the superiority or inferiority of the races or hierarchising them according to physical, moral or intellectual traits. He finds support for this claim in scientific findings of biology and genetics. Appiah is not alone in this liberal conception of race. Naomi Zack also argues that races do not exist. 'The general thesis of this book', she states in the introduction to her book *Race and Mixed Race*, 'is that black and white racial designations are themselves racist because the concept of race does not have an adequate scientific foundation' (1993: 3–4). In an almost similar argument as that of Appiah, Zack asserts that (i) since there are no races, race-talk is morally dangerous because it gives birth to racism or renders it possible; (ii) race-talk invariably gets reduced to bad biology even though it has no scientific status; and (iii) the meaning of the word 'race' can equally be conveyed and thus replaced by the word 'ethnicity'.[2] The upshot of both Appiah's and Zack's conception of race (similar in almost every detail with South African white liberals' conception) is that there are no black people and white people, no differences among people, no particular identities at all, but simply the universal human being. The requirement here is therefore that one looks beyond what has been regarded as *'accidental'* differences, such as raciality and gender, to the essence constitutive of the human species that is common to all. The colour-blindness thesis emerges from this universalistic conception and is consequently used as justification by liberals to deny the need for race-based solutions to extant racism.

In support of his claims, Appiah posits two kinds of racisms: extrinsic and intrinsic. Extrinsic racism is a belief that people of different racial groups possess certain characteristics that warrant differential treatment. It involves the belief that one's race is superior to another race which is in itself inferior. However, extrinsic racists are amenable to rational persuasion and can therefore change their beliefs and attitudes on provision of evidence to the contrary (that is, through exposition of the falsity or invalidity of their position). Intrinsic racism, however, involves loyalty to and preference of one's own racial group without rational bases at all. Hence, intrinsic racists are not amenable to rational persuasion or dissuasion. The preference or loyalty given to one's racial group is not based on the other group's essential racial inferiority but simply on racial solidarity. Appiah's intrinsic racism is thus fundamentally an attack on racial solidarity. He argues that intrinsic racism presupposes the existence of races (racialism), yet races do not have any ontological reality. Thus having given a lengthy argument that races do not have a biological or scientific legitimacy, Appiah insists that racial solidarity should be rejected not only on the grounds that it is predicated on a falsehood but also – equally important – because it involves treating an irrelevant (accidental) factor (morphological characteristics) as a basis for being concerned about one's group rather than about another. In short, because he holds that races do not exist, Appiah concludes that race is an unworthy basis for identity and political liberation. Indeed, anyone who preaches solidarity on the basis of race is a racist. In an article written for *The Atlantic Monthly* (1997) entitled 'My Race Problem – And Ours', Randall Kennedy takes up this black solidarity problem arising from racial identity. According to him, notions such as racial pride, racial kinship, racial patriotism, racial loyalty and racial solidarity – all synonyms of racial exclusiveness – should be rejected because they become burdensome for an unencumbered liberal self as he is, a self 'animated by a liberal, individualistic, and universalistic ethos that is sceptical of, if not hostile to, particularisms' (1997: 56) such as black racial kinship. Race must not matter in solidarity formations. Both Appiah and Kennedy, it should be noted, are not seriously antisolidarity but simply against the solidarity predicated only on race.

What I think informs these positions is the adherence to liberal values and ideals, particularly the principle of the autonomy of the individual. There is definitely no mistaking Appiah's liberalism, which he outrightly proclaims, and his antipathy to any collectivism that puts individuality in jeopardy. Behind his views on race and racism is strict adherence to liberalism's core set of general principles, namely: (i) commitment to an individualism which considers as basic the political, moral and legal claims of the individual over and against groups; (ii) the belief in reason as constitutive of human nature and therefore the basis for human equality; (iii) freedom of choice; and (iv) individual autonomy without undue prescriptions or limitations from outside. Liberalism insists that race is a morally irrelevant category because it is not earned but an accident of nature. Accordingly, human beings must avoid irrational choices that appeal to contingencies like race. What therefore needs to be done, liberals argue, is to eradicate the evil of irrational and illogical prejudices and exclusions based on an irrelevant category such as the colour of a person's skin or the texture of her hair. It is this belief in the irrelevancy of race that constitutes the foundation of the principle of colour-blindness or what in South African parlance is known as 'non-racialism'.

Biko was acutely aware of these objections and accusations, and attempted to confront them upfront. He refers to these objections several times in his writings and interviews. As early as his tenure as the president of SASO, Biko responded: 'The fact that the whole ideology [Black Consciousness] centres around non-white students as a group might make a few people to believe that the organisation is racially inclined. Yet what SASO has done is simply to take stock of the present scene in the country and to realise that not unless the non-white students decide to lift themselves from the doldrums will they ever hope to get out of them' (1996: 5).

Again he observes: 'Some will charge that we are racist' (1996: 97). The charge of racism opens up a plethora of issues and problems surrounding the concept of racism itself. In Chapter 5 of this book, I analysed the concepts of race and racism and showed how varied conceptions of them are. Now I need to show how the different conceptions are often in conflict with one another. Let me put this charge in another register: 'First, can the struggle against racism avoid being racist?' In other words, is Black Consciousness not a racist organisation? And 'second, can the achievement of Black liberation avoid the elimination of the black race?' (Gordon 1995a: 4).

To the first question (Can the struggle against racism avoid being racist as charged by the liberals?), Biko's answer is affirmative; Black Consciousness, in his view, is not a racist philosophy. Two reasons account for this. First, liberals lack an understanding of what racism is and thus they are unable to offer a coherent critique of it. For him, the defining feature of liberalism is an antiracist attitude that coexists with support of racist results. Liberals reject discriminatory exclusions on the basis of race and colour, and detest the subjugation and domination of groups on racial grounds; but the very same liberals uphold and defend systems that are complicit in the reproduction of racist effects. They do so in the name of some principle regarded as much loftier and 'urgent' (for example, individual autonomy, equality, or human and constitutional rights in a democratic society) than remedying racial oppression. As a consequence, liberals want to transcend race through their rejection of racialised perspectives on racism on the grounds that such perspectives are a kind of reverse racism. In doing this, they sacrifice the historical aspect of racism for the 'rational' aspect.

His second response to this question echoed his conceptualisation of racism as predicated upon power relations of superiority and inferiority, of domination and subjugation. Biko (recall from Chapter 5 of this book) defines racism as 'discrimination by a group against another for the purpose of subjugation or maintaining subjugation'. In terms of this conception, racism is about power; hence, in his view, '[o]ne cannot be a racist unless he has the power to subjugate' (1996: 25). This controversial definition locates Biko's conception of race as fundamentally political. In other words, the grounds for the separation and classification of human beings into distinct races are the power relations constituting people into the subjugating group and the subjugated group in a particular society. This political theory of race is not the only one that Biko espouses; there is also the cultural theory of race.

Contrasted with the Bikoian theories of racism is the liberal moral conception theory of racism according to which racism is restricted to individual racial prejudices or racial discrimination (that is, making moral distinctions between different races or among individuals based on an irrelevant criterion such as their 'race'). According to this conception, racism offends moral rationality because it is based on an irrelevant feature (race) for making a distinction in dealings with others. In fact, racial prejudice and racial discrimination are often used interchangeably in South African white liberal discourse. They look at racism as some sort of social ignorance, a phenomenon characteristic of the irrationality of the individual that can be transcended through education, racial tolerance, democratic procedures or integration. There is, however, a huge difference between racial prejudice/discrimination and racism (as indicated in Chapter 5 of this book). Racial prejudice describes negative attitudes or beliefs of one individual against another on the grounds of race. Racism, as understood by Biko, involves the imposition of one's power on the lives of those whom one regards as intrinsically racially inferior to oneself. As noted earlier, Biko enjoys a lot of good company in restricting racism to the powerful: Carmichael, Marable and Sivanandan, among others, also privilege power as a necessary condition for racism. In a revealing article entitled 'I was a White Liberal, and Survived', Margaret Legum defends Biko's conception of racism in this manner: 'Racism is not only about actions based on negative personal attitude. It is the result of generations of control by one "race" of people over another, such that the culture, norms, theories and practices of the dominant group have become at least partly internalised by both groups' (in Husemeyer 1997: 124). Hacker explains that the same sentiment was echoed by the former mayor of Detroit, Coleman Young, who argued that racism can only be a product of those who wield the power to produce suffering. The suggestion here, as Hacker observes, is that 'it is insufficient to define racism as a set of ideas that some people may hold. Racism takes its full form only when it has an impact on the real world' (1992: 29). Joseph Barndt supports this view: 'Racism is clearly more than simple prejudice or bigotry. Everyone is prejudiced, but not everyone is a racist...To be racially prejudiced means to have distorted opinions about people of other races. Racism goes beyond prejudice. *Racism is the power to enforce one's prejudices.* More simply stated, *racism is prejudice plus power*' (1991: 28 – italics added).

Viewed from this perspective, Biko's definition of racism refutes the liberals' accusatory claims that Black Consciousness is a racist philosophy. Even if Black Consciousness were to be charged with discrimination against white people, it still would not be racism in Biko's and many other people's conceptions because it does not carry the insinuation that white people are inferior to black people, nor does it have the power to universalise and prescribe the dominant norms and values which racism produces. Even Martin Luther King Jr, a committed opponent of the Black Power Movement, defends the movement against accusations of being racist: 'Black Power is an implicit and often explicit belief in black separatism. Notice that I do not call it black racism. It is inaccurate to refer to Black Power as racism in reverse...Racism is a doctrine of the congenital inferiority and worthlessness of a people...The major proponents of Black Power have never contended that the white man is inherently worthless' (1967: 48). Similarly, Black Consciousness has never been espoused as a credo for subjugation and domination of white people. In this respect, it differs tremendously from apartheid racism. Furthermore, even supposing Black Consciousness was *à la* Appiah and the liberals 'intrinsic racism', is intrinsic racism really racism? The difference between extrinsic and intrinsic racism is that the former involves regarding a racial group other than one's own as inferior. In other words, the superiority/inferiority conception is a necessary condition for racism. Intrinsic racism, according to Appiah, does not involve superiority/inferiority beliefs but simply belief in the existence of races, a notion that translates into racialism. Racialism is the belief or view that human beings are divided into different groups distinguished from one another by visible, heritable common biological descent such as physical characteristics which include skin colour, hair texture and facial structure. To be fair, Appiah does acknowledge that racialism in itself need not be morally objectionable. However, one of the salient features of racism as understood by Biko is not only power but also the belief in the given superiority of the racist group and the supposed inherent inferiority of the excluded and discriminated against racial group. Black Consciousness was black solidarity in the face of subjugation and domination, solidarity between those and by those who were subjugated and certainly did not regard themselves as inherently superior to white people. Such solidarity cannot possibly be called racist, even of the intrinsic type. Although Black Consciousness seems to fit Appiah's designation of intrinsic racism, the basis of Biko's black solidarity lies in shared or common collective historical experiences rather than in shared biological or genetic characteristics.

What does the above argument tell us? It is also a response to the now popular charge that 'Blacks are or can also be racists'. One even gets newspaper headlines such as 'BLACKS ARE THE BIGGEST RACISTS' in the *Sunday Times* (20 August 2006).[3] Earlier, I referred to Blum's assertion that not only are black people also racists, but everyone is indeed a racist. Richard Turner, one of the outspoken but sympathetic Marxist critics of Black Consciousness, also claims that black people are racists: 'It is important to notice that...there are black racists' (1972: 20). This is obviously a bizarre claim to make given that in some parts of the world, some people have not met anyone of a different colour shade. Lewis Gordon calls this kind of assertion 'equal opportunity racism', which suggests that if black people (victims of racism) are also racist like the racists themselves, each has an 'equal opportunity' to become a racist. Ultimately, if all are racists, then no one is racist! It is easy to see through this equal opportunity racism strategy. In a South African apartheid context, the assertion is often used as a strategy to ease the consciences of those who feel guilty of racism. As long as antiblack racists can be assured that black people are themselves racists, they can find reasons to justify their own antiblack racism.

For argument's sake, assuming that there are black people who are racist against white people, such racism would not even qualify for the title of racism, except from the point of view of those who define racism as racial prejudice or even defensive racial prejudice rather than pure racism. As a matter of fact, Black Consciousness cannot be compared with or even associated with white antiblack racism. Presumed 'black antiwhite racism', unlike white antiblack racism, is not a consequence of power but of powerlessness. It is what Memmi thinks of as not an 'aggressive racism' but 'defensive racism'. Memmi states that, 'while modern European racism hates and scorns more than it fears, that of the colonized fears and also continue to admire' (1965: 131). In fact, Black Consciousness has never been espoused as a credo for the subjugation and domination of white people. In this respect, it differs tremendously from apartheid. Legum argues that the problem with liberals is that they falsely equate aggressive racism with defensive separation. These are not, and cannot be, morally equivalent. To equate Black Consciousness with apartheid, even though superficially they might seem to be the same, is disingenuous because we know that they are nevertheless different 'just as we know that the killings committed by French Nazis are not morally equivalent to those committed by the Resistance' (in Husemeyer 1997: 123).

How can those who suffer from racism, argue the liberals, hope to succeed in their liberation by using the very same false instrument of 'race' used by their oppressors? Is this not another form of apartheid and was it not the outlawing of this evil system that the liberation movements were all about? Two wrongs can never make a right. Echoing these concerns of the white liberals in South Africa, Appiah states that he finds it strange that victims of racism should themselves sanction false racialist theories and themselves be racist. Is it not true, Audre Lorde insisted, that '[t]he master's tools will never dismantle the master's house' (1984)? Racism is racism no matter what it is called. But to equate the two kinds of racisms (if that is the word appropriate for both instances) as morally and fundamentally the same is flawed, because 'the hostility of one group stems not from any wrong done to it but from the wrongs it is able to *inflict* by virtue of its power...And while hostility and racial anger are unhappy facts wherever they are found, there is certainly a distinction to be made between the ideological hostility of the oppressor and the experience-based hostility of those who have been oppressed' (Fish 1994: 61). The failure to make a distinction between white and black racism, in Stanley Fish's view, is similar to equating the efforts to remedy that plight with the actions that produced it; in other words, one cannot equate the virus with the therapy applied to it. 'A virus is an invasion of the body's equilibrium, and so is an antibiotic; but we do not equate the two and decline to fight the disease because the medicine we employ is disruptive of normal functioning' (Fish 1994: 61–62).

Second, for Biko, Black Consciousness was not racist because race did not play a part in the concept of blackness as it was conceived. All people defined within the context of apartheid as races, other than white people, were negatively referred to as non-white people. Their non-whiteness was a common referent within the antiblack racism of the apartheid regime that confronted them. It was this common experience of racism, exploitation and subjugation that led to the adoption of the term 'black' as a political colour to be worn with pride against a colour-conscious apartheid regime. African, Indian and coloured medical students at the University of Natal were forced to share common university facilities different from those of their white counterparts. Because of this common experience – even though African, Indian and coloured people in South Africa were perceived and still perceive themselves as racially different – the concept 'black' was used as part of a set of constitutive ideas and principles to promote collective action. Biko and his comrades in SASO insisted that the term 'Blacks' refers to those who were by law or tradition politically, economically and socially discriminated against as a group. This political meaning can be traced back to Du Bois' assertion of his African identity:

> But one thing is sure and that is the fact that since the fifteenth century these ancestors of mine and their descendants have had a common history; have suffered a common disaster and have one long memory. The actual ties of heritage between the individuals of this group vary with the ancestors that they have in common with many others: European and Semites, perhaps Mongolians, certainly American Indians. But the physical bond is least and the badge of color relatively unimportant save as a badge; the real essence of this kinship is its social heritage of slavery; the discrimination and insult; and this heritage binds together not simply the children of Africa, but extends through yellow Asia and into the South Seas. It is this unity that draws me to Africa. (1968: 116–117)

Black Consciousness was not racist in content but was a socially, politically and ideologically constructed identity in an antiblack society that perceived colour as the central marker of inferiority and superiority. In other words, 'black' became transformed to what in William Jones' terms is 'a designation of an antagonist'. 'Black' signalled an ideological shift that repudiated whiteness and rejected assimilationism. In the same way, the words 'bad' and 'nigger' have been transformed from negatives and insults into positives and compliments or endearments respectively – as in Yancy's 'Some baaadad people we be' or 'This is my main nigger' (2002: 135). Here, 'bad' is turned on its head and made positive as a celebration of black culture, skin colour or experiences. There is a sense, therefore, that to formulate a Black Consciousness philosophy is a consequence and a tacit recognition of the fact that a philosophy that reflects or endorses a white consciousness dominates our experience. Thus, to call for Black Consciousness from this perspective is to launch an implicit attack on that very philosophy predicated on whiteness. Besides, the term 'black' as a socio-political concept – rather than a biological concept – was not necessarily all-inclusive for Biko.

To repeat, in the Black Consciousness Movement, the status of blackness was not simply based on skin colour, genetic make-up or heritage; it was also an acquired status through a process of political origination of oneself in an antiblack apartheid society. 'The fact we are all *not white*', Biko declares, 'does not necessarily mean that we are all *black*...If one's aspiration is whiteness but his pigmentation makes attainment of this impossible, then that person is a non-white' (1996: 48 – italics added). For example, all those who served, protected and maintained the oppressive system were labelled 'non-whites'. This category (differentiated from 'real' black people) included bantustan leaders, black police, black liberals, black conservatives, black soldiers and some black teachers who reproduced the apartheid mythology. Malcolm X's metaphor of the House Negro and the Field Negro mentioned earlier may here illuminate the concept of non-whites. According to Malcolm X, the House Negro was the slave living and working in the master's house, the slave doing less work and receiving better food. The House Negro was the master's ears and eyes, and was thus in a sense privileged. Such a negro identified completely with and protected the master. The House Negro embraced servitude. When the master is sick, the House Negro does not say 'the master he is sick' but 'We's sick' (Malcom X, in Karim 1971: 87). The House Negro was thus bought off and tricked, accepted oppression by the master and had benefits bestowed to him that were withheld from the Field Negro. In fact, the House Negro was positioned as a buffer between the master and the Field Negro.[4] The Field Negro, rather than being complicit in her servitude, opposed the system that oppressed her because she was the one 'catching hell' on the plantation.

The metaphor of the House Negro was applied by Biko and his comrades to refer to the apartheid grand scheme of bantustan leaders and their followers who, with some trappings of material promises and success, played the role of the House Negro and falsely convinced themselves to believe that the bantustans system could work for them. As a consequence, they became protective of and identified with the apartheid masters in an attempt to destroy the radical moves for freedom from the liberation movements and organisations of the black masses who were 'catching hell'. It is therefore only those who were 'catching hell' who constituted 'genuine Blacks', the vanguard of the liberation struggle. Against these genuine black people, the bantustan leaders and their cohorts were labelled 'Uncle Toms' or 'sell-outs'.

If Biko's Black Consciousness was not racist, how then do we explain the exclusionary practice against white people as a race in the struggle for justice? The answer still depends on how one conceives racism. If, for example, one defines racism as racial prejudice and discrimination, there is simply no moral justification for white exclusion as liberals argue. Such exclusionary practices are easily considered racist. But if one conceives racism as Biko does, as white supremacy and a white power structure according to which white people operate as a group to exclude, inferiorise, dehumanise, denigrate or kill black people, then black people's exclusion of white people is not racism but simply separation (as Martin Luther King Jr explained above). Black people were not the beneficiaries of apartheid and there was certainly no systematic, religious, cultural, social, political, economic and institutional backing or authorisation for the presumed racism of black people. To be precise, even the term 'non-collaboration' that Black Consciousness adherents used to exclude white participation in SASO has different denotative significations from 'racism'.

More importantly though is the fact that Black Consciousness used the non-collaboration with white people strategy in pursuance of its fundamental objective: the destruction of black people's psychological dependence on white people. In a similar vein as Black Consciousness, Sobukwe (outlining the Pan-Africanist non-collaborationist strategy with white and Indian people) says:

> We believed that Africans could eventually succeed if they could break their psychological dependence on whites and non-African leadership. An example of African dependence on whites was one incident at Newclare when there was a women's demonstration against passes. We went there to try to persuade the police to grant bail for the women. Because we were Africans, the police just told us to voetsek (scram). Then a certain white arrived on the scene, a man named Vincent Swart. He had started some small organization for African rights. Because he was white, the police agreed to talk to him, and naturally the friends and relatives of the women there just 'flocked' to this man, pleading with him to help with bail. We always opposed the participation of whites in any kind of action because we wanted to get the point across to our people that by their own efforts – and by these alone – change could be brought about. It was a psychological thing. (interview with Gerhart 1970)

The liberals' position actually amounts to the assumption of an ahistorical reasoning that posits both apartheid and Black Consciousness at the same moral level: separation of different races is always the same distasteful phenomenon no matter the historical circumstances and conditions of its emergence. The fight against legal and coerced apartheid separation under which black people had no choice but to be separate did not mean that those same black people had to again be coerced into integration and forsake the right to decide that their existing problems and difficulties might be alleviated by black solidarity, which they themselves freely chose. The point here is that Black Consciousness talked to black people not because their skin was black but because the blackness of their skin had generated the oppressive experiences that they suffered.

Liberalism's solution

In the face of such objections to Black Consciousness philosophy, what solutions did liberalism offer for the transcendence of apartheid racism? Put differently, what was liberalism's end (what-ought-to-be) and means for the liberation of South Africa (Azania)? Apartheid racial oppression and separatism, the liberals believed, could only be solved through its antithesis, namely racial integration, non-racialism or colour-blindness. This process could be realised through education. Compared to their critics – the Marxists (communists) and Black Consciousness adherents – the liberals' what-ought-to-be involved the maintenance, production and promotion of capitalism as the only and dominant ideology in a rights-based, non-racial egalitarian society. For how this new society should come into being, liberals proposed the civilising, legal, peaceful, gradual and non-violent method (that is, legalism, gradualism, education and non-violence). In other words, liberals proposed that the African's values be altered, her cultural deficits filled up, her apathetic soul energised, her character defects cured, and and then she should be trained and polished in a manner in which she would be ruptured from her savage ways. Maloka notes: 'South African liberals believed in gradualism as opposed to revolution, more so, they were not convinced that the oppressed could liberate themselves. They wanted a peaceful gradual process, under their leadership; as opposed to the radical or militant revolutionary struggle led and driven by the "natives"' (2014: 22).

It has been pointed out – and will be shown later – that it is precisely this liberal conception of what is to be done and how it is to be done that set it directly against Biko and his comrades' idea of emancipatory praxis. Since racism is a social construction, argued the liberals, the way to transcend it is to eliminate the word 'race' as a social signifier, adopt a colour-blind ideology and promote integration. For the liberal, racial integration (which later became known as 'non-racialism' or colour-blindness) constituted a viable solution to racism in the country and any racial identity politics was considered to be racist. Americans often make a distinction between 'desegregation' and 'integration'. The former refers to the legal (*de jure*) abolition of racial discriminatory laws and obstacles to full participation in society, while the latter speaks to the idea that black people and white people can live together in harmony, friendship and mutual respect without the necessity of legal compulsion or persuasion. What this suggests is that it is possible to have desegregation without necessarily having integration, since the latter has more to do with human attitudes and behaviour than the commands of the law. As Steinhorn and Diggs-Brown appropriately put it, '[d]esegregation may unlock doors, but integration is supposed to open minds' (2000: 5). Biko was aware of this crucial distinction between desegregation and integration, which in his opinion, was conflated by liberals and leftists.

Integrationism
Integration is not particularly contentious in itself. Indeed, after the sufferings endured for centuries under white racism, black people feel an intuitive attraction to a society free of racial oppression; a society where one's race does not have an adverse effect on one's life chance; a society where black people and white people can live together in harmony, friendship and mutual respect without the necessity of legal compulsion or persuasion. But integration as proselytised by white liberals in this country was altogether different from what Biko envisaged it to be. He thus categorically rejected the form of racial integration propagated by liberals, for numerous reasons different than those of the Afrikaner Nationalist government and its supporters. First, since integration is not about the law but about attitudes, and since liberals in their belief in the rule of law conceive of integration as a legal issue consequent to the abolition of the numerous apartheid laws, their notion of integration is in fact desegregation – which leaves untouched the question of white attitudes towards black people, namely a serious lack of white respect for black people. The latter, Biko argues, are denigrated, dehumanised and disrespected by white people, and they in turn have internalised white conceptions of themselves or (if you prefer) internalised the external. Both white people and black people consequently suffer from some form of complex (that is, a superiority and an inferiority complex respectively). In Biko's words:

> The concept of integration...is full of unquestioned assumptions that embrace white values. It is a concept long defined by whites and never examined by blacks. It is based on the assumption that all is well with the system [apartheid] apart from some degree of mismanagement by irrational conservatives at the top. Even the people who argue for integration often forget to veil it in its supposedly beautiful covering. They tell each other that were it not for job reservation, there would be a beautiful market to exploit...

> This is white man's integration – an integration based on exploitative values.
> It is an integration in which black will compete with black, using each other
> as rungs up a step ladder leading them to white values. It is an integration
> in which the black man will have to prove himself in terms of these values
> before meriting acceptance and ultimate assimilation. (1996: 91)

As long as this situation exists, Biko insists, there can never be true integration but
simply 'artificial' integration which would be a veiled form of crude assimilation
produced by white normativity.

White normativity refers to the manner in which white values, culture, norms,
beauty, language, religion and so on constitute the norm according to which
everyone else has to be measured. For example, the Miss World Beauty Pageant
determines beauty in term of white Western criteria. A white woman's beauty
is the norm in a white supremacist world; she becomes the embodiment and
personification of beauty, purity, chastity and sensuality. In short, the white woman
becomes an exemplar of femininity and beauty. White normativity expresses itself
in different forms: cultural, aesthetical, religious, sociological, institutional or
legal. At the social level, black people have to conform to white social behaviour
and norms. Institutionally, black people have to subscribe to Western institutions
such as the Westminster parliamentary system of England for the former British
colonies. In South Africa, this British parliamentary system dominates to the
exclusion of all African systems. Legally, African law has been superseded by
the Roman-Dutch law. Commenting on African invisibility as role models in
our television commercials and programmes, Sonti Maseko interrogates white
normativity: 'To my mind, to sit and watch daily programmes on television
showing one race, culture and language is a not-so-subtle form of domination. It
sends the message that there is only one "acceptable" way of life. It sends us "the
other people" in just about every area of life – the way we look, our languages, our
family structures, the way we live, the way we prepare our food and so on' (2000).[5]
What Maseko refers to as 'one "acceptable" way of life' is how white normativity
manifests itself.

In antiblack societies, therefore, whiteness has always been regarded as a
norm for what it is to be human. In the earlier chapters of this book, it was
shown that racism, among other things, is the belief that one's race is the only
one that qualifies to be regarded as human. In other words, an antiblack racist is
one who questions the humanity of black people and in so doing simultaneously
dehumanises them. If a group of people is dehumanised or reduced to the status of
subpersonhood, it means that they are abnormal when compared to those who are
supposedly human and are the norm or measurement of what it is to be human.
For example, to characterise or describe someone in negative terms such as

primitive, uncivilised, libidinous, lacking in modesty, ugly and so on is to operate on an assumed elevated position of the opposite of that description and therefore to posit oneself as the positive or normal. In reaction to this normativity myth, Biko declares Black Consciousness a philosophy that 'seeks to demonstrate the lie that black is an aberration from the "normal" which is white...[and] seeks to show the black people the value of their own standard and outlook. It urges black people to judge themselves according to these standards and not to be fooled by white society who have whitewashed themselves and made white standards the yardstick by which even black people judge each other' (1996: 49).

In a fundamental way, Black Consciousness constitutes a direct challenge to the normative status of whiteness; it does this by locating whiteness in a racial category hitherto ignored, avoided, hidden or simply rendered invisible. In the voice of Yancy, the point is that whiteness does not speak its name, an act which is a function of its power. It attempts to hide from its historicity and particularity, which is a function of how whiteness represents itself as universal and unconditioned. Whiteness functions as a universal code of beauty, intelligence, superiority, cleanliness, and spiritual and moral purity. Whiteness is the norm that is invisible, unnamed, unpronounced or unmarked; while everything outside of it must be named, pronounced and marked (Yancy 2004). When black people are seen only in terms of their race, white people are seen as simply human. Hence, in such a world, one finds professors and black professors, doctors and black doctors, engineers and black engineers, journalists and black journalists, economic empowerment and black economic empowerment, lawyers' associations and black lawyers' associations. While white political engagement is regarded simply as politics or government, black political engagement is considered racial politics or black government and so on. Although the designation 'black' accurately describes an objective biological fact, or at least a sociological construction in an antiblack world, it conceals the vital psychological fact that to an antiblack racist mind, to prefix something with '*black*' automatically relegates it to the realm of Otherness. Thus the 'black such-and-such' implies that the such-and-such is not a genuine or normal such-and-such; it is a deviation from the norm, an abnormal such-and-such. Hence Fanon speaks of the black person as an 'existential deviation' from the white norm. He writes: 'The black is not a man...The black is a black man' (1967a: 8). This statement should not be understood as a masculinist complaint about racism emasculating the black man. Rather, it is how white racism has devalued and demoted black people from the universal human being and turned them into 'a series of aberrations' from the norm (Fanon 1967a: 8).

In an African country such as South Africa, white normativity is displayed at all levels of existence. In restaurants, for example, European cuisine (food) on the menu is the unnamed and unmentioned norm; whereas other options available on the menu are labelled and described as 'African dish' or 'Zulu chicken'. Since whiteness is the norm, it acquires a position of invisibility. But, as Lewis Gordon argues, the structure of normativity is a falsification of normality. When we speak of white normativity, what we are actually saying is that '[b]lacks could become normal only by becoming white, and whites can become abnormal only by becoming black' (Gordon, in Yancy 1998: 182).

First, because of white normativity, liberal artificial integration inevitably leads to black assimilation. In a letter to all the student representative councils of black universities, Biko wrote the following about NUSAS: 'We reject their basis of integration as being based on standards predominantly set by white society. It is more of what the white man expects the black man to do than the other way round. We feel we do not have to prove ourselves to anybody' (1996: 13). Second, integration as proposed by white liberals is destined to fail to the extent that power relations between white people and black people remain skewed in favour of white people. And, since an antiblack white supremacist world is infested with white normativity, black people are in danger of being assimilated into the white value structure. Third, integration is asserted by the liberals as a superficial racial adaptation to the reality of the apartheid situation. Fourth, both black people and white people are not ready; they both, in different ways, require deracialisation in the form of conscientisation because integration is about attitudes predicated on the presence of mutual respect and human dignity. Finally, liberal integrationism is problematic because it is conceived as both a method and the goal of transcending racism. Biko argues: 'Nowhere is the arrogance of the liberal ideology demonstrated so well as in their insistence that the problems of the country can only be solved by a bilateral approach involving both black and white'. He continues that liberals, 'insist on integration not only as an end goal but also as a means' (1996: 20). This is contrary to his conviction that within an antiblack world such as South Africa, the first step towards liberation is closing ranks and forming group solidarity. In the light of all these reasons, he rejects the version of a liberal solution of integration as fundamentally artificial and designed to perpetuate and protect white interests. In response to Gail Gerhart's observation that multiracial organisations such as the Congress Alliance provided the black middle class with an escape route into white circles, thus alienating them from the ordinary black masses, Biko says:

> This is one of the things that we attacked initially about the so-called artificial integrated circles. They soothed the conscience of whites on the one hand, and they created a small comfortable microcosm of an ideal society for the blacks, which blacks knew they couldn't share with the rest of their society, but it was considered sufficient compensation by them for their efforts on behalf of those masses...

Participation in those circles was not necessarily to push an idea. Participation was regarded as something you earned by virtue of speaking out or taking a role in politics. And there is no doubt that you operate there from a position of inferiority, because the society you are now living in, this microcosm of an integrated society, is dealing with a vast number of topics now on an everyday basis, depending on where you meet. You meet in a comfortable house, and they're going to talk about art and poetry...things you are not exposed to. And the tendency is you sit and listen to these guys analyzing these things...But at that moment during your contact with these whites, it serves to dramatize your inferiority; you blame yourself for not knowing these things. You don't blame the society. Instead of sensitizing you to oppression, it tends to re-emphasize your own inferiority and emphasize their superiority.

And where these artificial circles become a farce, to me, from my own experience, is that they are so *far* from the real problem, so far from efforts toward a real solution. (interview with Gerhart 1972: 45–46 – italics in original)

Assimilationism

Given white cultural, social and political hegemony, Biko argues that white liberal integration is fundamentally a veiled form of assimilation. By assimilation generally is meant the attempt to have one racial or ethnic group absorbed, physically and/or culturally by another. The absorbed group takes on the defining characteristics of the absorbing group and renounces its own racial or ethnic uniqueness and particularity. For example, European settlers lived in the country for three-and-a-half centuries but almost all of their descendents do not speak or care to speak one African language among the many that exist. However, almost all Africans can and are expected to speak a European language, either English or Afrikaans but mostly English. As it stands, in some previously white schools in Gauteng province, Afrikaans is a necessary condition for the admission of black children – a requirement promulgated by the mainly white school governing bodies and a fact known to and allowed by the Gauteng Department of Education. Nowhere is isiZulu or Sesotho made a condition for admission to these schools. In fact, African children are often not allowed to speak or reprimanded for speaking an African language.[6] Black people have to shorten or accept shortened versions of their names simply because white people cannot or do not want to pronounce them correctly, or alternatively are given European names such as Nelson, Desmond, Jacob or Percy. If Fanon's argument is correct that to speak an alien language is to acknowledge, accept and interiorise the culture inherent in it, most black South Africans (by virtue of being speakers of foreign European languages) have taken over and interiorised Western culture and are thus alienated. Fanon describes how the Antillian native is transformed into a 'white Negro' through language: 'The Negro of the Antilles will be proportionately whiter – that is, he will come closer to being a real human being – in direct ratio to his mastery of the French language. I am not unaware that this is one of man's attitudes face to face with Being. A man who has a language consequently possesses the world expressed and implied by that language' (1967a: 18). Fanon's position resonates with Wa Thiong'o's assertion that every language carries its culture. In this case, to speak a foreign language is *ipso facto* to be alienated from one's self. To *be* Zulu, one must also *think* in *Zulu*. To *be* Zulu and then *think* in English is basically to be separated from oneself and thus alienated. Assimilation, therefore, is alienation.[7]

Even assuming that black people were willing to be assimilated into whiteness, the project would have been doomed to failure precisely because assimilation in its complete sense is impossibile for black people. Unlike the European Jew who can physically disappear within a white world, black people by their very bodily being are always already overdetermined as Other, all attempts at being white notwithstanding. European Jews are phenotypically white such that they can disappear within whiteness by the mere change of name and religion. This explains why the German Jews during the Nazi regime were required by law to wear the yellow Star of David to be distinguishable from the Germans. No matter how much they may hide their blackness through attempted modes of assimilation, black people are nonetheless phenotypically identifiable and highly visible. At an ontological level, assimilation in general (but specifically black assimilation) is, as Lewis Gordon argues, easily classifiable with hatred because '[i]t manifests a desire to eliminate the Other *as* Other – in other words, to create a world of only one *kind* of human being' (1995a: 153). Biko insists that the liberal myth of integration, which is in fact a form of progressive assimilation, must be cracked and destroyed because it ultimately turns out to be an attempt to deny black people the culture which they already possess since it involves incorporating them into white culture.

Biko anticipated the assimilationist implications of white liberal integrationism. In today's so-called non-racial New South Africa, integration as assimilation has come to mean a one-way street to whiteness. It aims to bring formerly excluded groups like black people into a white power structure mainstream. Assimilation always implies black people coming into the game after the white people have already begun, after the rules and standards have already been set, and black people have to prove themselves according to white rules and standards. Consider how black children are daily bussed from their township homes to schools in white suburbs while at the same time white parents take their children to exclusive private white schools. Consider also how, when black people move into previously assigned white neighbourhoods, white liberal people who proclaim their absolute love for Mandela move out into gated communities or golf estates. The upshot of this integration and non-racialism is that white people do not integrate – that is, they do not move into black areas or black schools even if these are far better in standards and quality than the white areas or schools. What then is presumed by many white people (liberals especially) and antirace black people as a legitimate space in which race is invisible. In fact, the demand for the invisibility of (the black) race is what the call for colour-blindness means – that is, the effective disappearance of black people.

Non-racialism (colour-blindness)

Reassuring at the sentimental level as it is, non-racialism (in many ways a euphemism for colour-blindness) is essentialist because it is predicated on some commonly held essentialist assumptions about human nature, which – as I indicated in the earlier chapter on liberalism – is rationality. By this account, human beings as humans possess certain constitutive features that operate cross-culturally and transcend racial differences. The problem with this conception is that it projects the qualities of an abstract individual onto real, concrete human beings with different physiological, racial and class determinations. Human beings have different genders and historical or racial experiences, and therefore different and specific needs and capacities. For example, the needs of a rich blind man are obviously different from those of an ordinary working-class woman, not only in terms of physical needs but also in terms of class and cultural needs. Similarly, the housing needs of a black shack dweller are radically different from those of white bourgeoisie in a white suburb. These diversities, differences and specificities resulting from particular historical trajectories, material conditions and circumstances, cultural experiences and class interests are ignored by such liberal-oriented essentialism.

White liberal conception of integration becomes even more problematic when it is touted as the now popular notion of colour-blindness in the form of 'non-racialism'. It would indeed be great to exist in a world where being black does not disadvantage one, or where being white does not privilege one. In other words, it would be wonderful to live in a non-raced truly colour-blind society, a sort of ideal society. Hence, the specific demands of colour-blindness are not in themselves controversial. Intuitively, the desire to avoid race, after centuries of racial oppression and racial hierachisation, is an *a priori* point of departure. However, in a non-ideal antiblack society, this noble vision simply remains an unfulfilled ideal. The lived experiences, the actual lived situation and conditions of black people, indicate the continuation of racist behaviour from many white people, the new Constitution of South Africa notwithstanding. After the Penny Sparrow racist saga, a number of prominent white people came out in support of her racism in the name of 'free speech' rights.

Flowing from this was the critique of any ideology-resembling racial politics. Put differently, non-racialism was and still is conceptualised as a critique of the politics of difference or particularism. While apartheid, multiracialism, ethno-politics and Black Consciousness are lumped together as accentuating difference and specificities, non-racialism is promoted as espousing a non-racial social and political order where the racial or ethnic affiliation of an individual deserves no privileged status whatsoever. Neville Alexander, a prominent South African Marxist, describes non-racialism in the following way: 'The word *non-racial* can be accepted by a racially oppressed people if it means that we reject the concept of "race", that we deny the existence of "races" and thus oppose all actions, practices, beliefs and policies based on the concept of "race"' (1985: 46). Alexander's conception highlights one interpretation of the concept 'non-racialism' in South Africa – that is, the idea that there are no races at all. To deny, as Alexander and many others such as Zack and Appiah do, the existence of races is in a significant sense to posit the unity and sameness of humanity. This is a universalism based on the humanist thought of the European Enlightenment that valorises the freedom and equality of all human beings. It claims that underneath presumed individual differences, there is one human nature and therefore a common human essence. As Barthes asserts pithily: 'Any classic humanism postulates that in scratching the history of men a little, the relativity of their institutions or the superficial diversity of the skin...one very quickly reaches the solid rock of a universal human nature' (in Donald & Rattansi 1992: 246). If human beings are by nature the same and equal, there is no valid reason why something as 'accidental' and contingent as race should count as a significant determinant of an individual's worth. Humanistic liberal philosophical anthropology therefore requires that one transcends the alleged 'accidental' differences such as race and looks 'to the *essence* thought to be the definitive constitutive aspect of the human species shared by all humans that thus makes for the *essential* unity, oneness, and identity of all persons, all other differences notwithstanding' (Outlaw 1996: 148 – italics in original).

Racial eliminativists such as Alexander and Appiah claim to transcend racism by not paying attention to race at all. One of the favourite expressions with which liberals articulate colour-blindness is: 'I don't see people as black or white. I simply see them as people.' To deny that 'races' have a reality only offers the feeble comfort that there is no problem at all. Yet there *is* a problem and it cannot be ignored, nor simply wished away by erasing the word 'race' from our vocabulary. Such denials imply that colour-blindness is incapable of confronting existing problems because it fails to recognise these for what they are. But more serious is the fact that such a negative position reaches an impasse as soon as it is confronted by what Martin Barker and Pierre-André Taguieff call 'new racism' and 'differentialist racism' respectively a racism without races – one whose presumed primary object is not biology but the unbridgeability, incommensurability, incompatibility or incommunicability of cultural differences.[8] Its articulation is in terms of culture, tradition, 'way of life', values or religions: a vocabulary of solid particularistic specificities or impenetrable group identities. In its sort of eliminativist mode, differentialist racism grants that 'races' do not exist but populations and cultures do. Racism, therefore, does not need the word 'race' in order for it to be a problem.

The problem with colour-blindness is that it becomes a metaphor for the suppression of race consciousness, a form of ignoring the reality of race or being ignorant of races. In the first place, the word 'ignorance' comes from the word 'ignore'. Ignoring is avoiding knowledge (ignorance) through forgetting or indifference. In ignoring race, non-racialists (colour-blind people) know exactly what they are ignoring precisely because ignoring is an intentional act of consciousness. In other words, to ignore is to know what it is that one is ignoring. One cannot simply ignore nothing; one ignores something which one has consciousness of. If colour-blind people do not want to see race and colour, it is perhaps because they fear that it will reveal or disclose their own racism to them. Therefore, it is specifically their hidden and undisclosed racism that they want to ignore, forget, hide or want to not know. While they know or believe that they know that their racism is possible, they do not wish to know if it is real. In other words, they want to forget the possibility of their own racism and ignore the reality of its truth. In such a case, the liberals' forgetfulness or ignorance (ignoring) is a form of bad faith, the attempt not to know what one knows. The surest and safest way to bring about a colour-blind society, Mills (2008) argues, is to ignore race, to forget it, to put it out of existence, to kill it. This strategy finds explicit expression in what he calls the 'ideal theory' of white liberals, which is an abstract and ahistorical conception of justice that refuses to deal with justice in the concrete world of the lived experience of people suffering from injustice. The ideal theory, Mills explains, though concerned with justice, confines itself in a society without a history of injustice. 'Ideal theory asks what justice demands in a perfectly just society' (2008: 1384). White liberals refuse to deal with non-ideal theory which 'asks what justice demands in a society with a history of injustice' (2008: 1384). The ideal theory of justice is therefore a conception of a raceless, race-neutral, colour-blind or non-racial society.

The absurdity of colour-blindness is made manifest by the demand not to see differences between colours and the suggestion that it really does not matter whether someone is black or white or brown or yellow. It is tantamount to asking us to ignore the colours of the traffic lights. Nikhil Singh wonders in amazement 'why a visual impairment that interferes with the perception of normal variations in the colour spectrum has become the preferred image of racial neutrality, if not racial justice, defies common-sense' (2004: 40). Those whose colour is a norm can afford to pretend that it really does not matter. However, for black people in an antiblack world, there is never a moment in their lives when colour (race) becomes a non-issue. Instead, too often race is the only relevant issue defining their very existence. No matter your educational, intellectual, social, political, economic and religious status, and no matter the fact that you may be number one in world golf rankings or tennis rankings or that you are a world boxing champion, presumptions and *a priori* assumptions about you that are solely based upon the colour of your skin are made by racist consciousness. To reiterate West's apt observation, 'race matters'. Making colour irrelevant by willing it to disappear as a fact of consciousness is impossible. Consciousness of colour is not likely to disappear unless human beings lose their eyesight or colour itself disappears. The body is that in, with and through which I am present to people and in the world. Through my body, I perceive the world and the Other, and I am perceived by the Other through my bodily presence in the world. Hence, any theory of body image is, as Merleau-Ponty correctly observes, implicitly a theory of perception. Racial classification operates on the basis of perceptual bodily differences and bodily differences belong to the realm of the visible. To this extent, racialisation has a direct connection to the realm of the visible. Because of this connection, the experience of race is predicated primordially on the perception of race manifested by bodily presence, a perception whose specific mode is a learned ability. If race is a structure of perception, it plays a dominant part in constituting the necessary background from which I know myself.

In Biko's mind, the powerful force behind integration was the struggle for the satisfaction of black people's yearning for human dignity, their desire to be regarded as mere human beings just like everyone else, free and unencumbered by the heavy burden of racism. However, Biko realised that integration under apartheid conditions and circumstances was impossible because the power relations were skewed and the credibility of white people to actually adhere to the strict requirements of 'true integration' doubtful. The same sentiment was echoed by Du Bois when he said that under American Jim Crow, human brotherhood and mutual respect were not yet a 'practical possibility' (1968: 491). I have indicated that Biko rejects a certain kind of integration, what he calls 'artificial integration'. Does he then reject integration completely? Biko is clear about what constitutes integration and what it means to him. His response is worth citing in full:

> Does this mean that I am against integration? If by integration you
> understand a breakthrough into white society by blacks, an assimilation
> and acceptance of blacks into an already established set of norms and code
> of behaviour set up by and maintained by whites, then YES I am against it.
> I am against the superior-inferior white-black stratification that makes the

white a perpetual teacher and the black a perpetual pupil (and a poor one at that). I am against the intellectual arrogance of white people that makes them believe that white leadership is a *sine qua non* in this country and that whites are the divinely appointed pace-setters in progress. I am against the fact that a settler minority should impose an entire system of values on an indigenous people. (1996: 24)

Biko here decidedly rejects artificial integrationism, assimilationism, colour-blindness, white supremacy and pure racism – all of which are predicated on the assumption that black people can only succeed if, and only if, they stand with and are led by another racial group, particularly white people, communists, workers and even capitalists.

What then does Biko understand by integration? In other words, what is Biko's synthesis? First, he offers a political interpretation of integration which involves free political participation by all irrespective of race in a society free from oppression. He states: 'If on the one hand by integration you mean there shall be free participation by all members of a society catering for the full expression of the self in a freely changing society as determined by the will of the people, then I am with you' (1996: 24). In contrast to white liberal artificial integration, Biko's conception of true integration assumes an existential and moral imperative: 'At the heart of true integration is the provision for each man, each group to rise and attain the envisioned self. Each group must be able to attain its style of existence without encroaching on or being thwarted by another. Out of this mutual respect for each other and complete freedom...there will obviously arise a genuine fusion of the life-styles of the various groups. This is true integration' (1996: 21). It is clear here that integration does not mean rendering the different racial groups within the integrated whole indistinguishable (that is, it does not mean the elimination of black people as a race). It is, in other words, a proclamation of what in Du Bois' famous essay is 'The Conservation of Races'. Hence, in Biko's view, the constituent groups remain distinct. What is important is that mutual respect among groups and respect of differences among them are the essential condition of the whole process. In this sense, Biko advocates what is known as *e pluribus unum* (the one and the many) or unity in diversity.

To use Outlaw's terms, the Bikoian synthesis is a kind of 'pluralist integration' (1996: 81) an economically, politically and socially integrated society that is also racially and culturally distinct while not threatening the integration of the social whole through cultural distinctness. In other words, for Biko, integration 'means there shall be free participation by all members of a society, catering for the full expression of the self in a freely changing society' (1996: 24). In a sense, Biko rejects Sartre's Hegelian invitation to look 'to the end of particularism in order to find the dawn of the universal'. This invitation would be tantamount to giving a negative answer to Lewis Gordon's question 'Can the achievement of black liberation avoid the elimination of the black race?' Instead, Biko insists on a synthetic moment that preserves the interplay between unity and diversity – that is, recognition of difference within sameness, of the universal and the particular, of the many in the one (*e pluribus unum*), epitomised in the post-1994 new South Africa's obsession with the concept 'Rainbow Nation' or what in Zulu is called '*Simunye*ism'. Incidentally, this synthetic view would seem to avoid the 'bad faith' which Biko sees as one of the major problems emanating from racism: the full identification with my past to the exclusion of my future possibilities, my facticity to the exclusion of my transcendence, my body to the exclusion of my consciousness, my universality to the exclusion of my particularity or vice versa.

Conclusion

The white Nationalist government did exactly what Martin Luther King Jr had predicted about the term 'Black Power'. Questioning the appropriateness of the slogan 'Black Power', he argued that denotatively the concept of Black Power is fundamentally unproblematic but that connotatively it conjures up images of violence, and this is the only meaning that the white establishment wants to hear in order to suppress legitimate black resistance. 'Why not use the slogan "black consciousness" or "black equality"?' he suggested. 'These phrases would be less vulnerable and would more accurately describe what we are about. The words "black" and "power" together give the impression that we are talking about black domination rather than black equality' (1967: 31). This critique is similar to the one offered by Appiah when he states, 'black philosophy must be rejected, for its defense depends on the essentially racist presuppositions of the white philosophy whose antithesis it is' (1992: 92). Let us look at this objection from a feminist point of view. What it would amount to is the absurd claim that 'feminist philosophy must be rejected, for its defense depends on the essentially sexist presuppositions of the male philosophy whose antithesis it is'. From this emerges the liberals' and Marxists' critique of Black Consciousness, which effectively says, 'Black Consciousness must be rejected, for its defense depends on the essentially racist presuppositions of the White Consciousness whose antithesis it is'. To these, Lewis Gordon replies: 'Why *must* "black" signify a racist presupposition? Why not a black philosophy that addresses *antiblackness*? Or a black philosophy that is antiracist?' (1997b: 128 – italics in original).

Notes

1 The media included the following newspapers: *Daily Dispatch, Daily News, Rand Daily Mail, The Star, Sunday Times, The World, Die Burger* (The Citizen).

2 See for example Zack's *Race and Mixed Race* (1993), 'Race and Philosophical Meaning' (1994) and *Thinking About Race* (2006); and Appiah's 'The Uncompleted Argument: Du Bois and the Illusion of Race' (1986), *In My Father's House: Africa in the Philosophy of Culture* (1992) and 'Race, Culture, Identity: Misunderstood Connections' (1996).

3 According to the story, this was the findings of a survey conducted by Plus 94 Research, an affiliate of the Gallup Group. The problem with such surveys is that they attempt to prove what they actually already believe to be the case. This particular survey conflates racism with ethnicity and identity. Another example (*Sunday Times*, 13 September 2009) is from a letter to the editor by one Prof. Harry Sewlall – the acting dean of the Faculty of Human Sciences of North-West University (Mafikeng Campus) – who, after suggesting that Africans are lazy and irresponsible, has this to say in response to two readers who objected to his letter: 'For Hoeane and Reddy to suggest that I traffic in stereotype and that I am driving a wedge between the Indian and African is dishonest and disingenuous. I did not invent racist minority discourse. The likes of Mbongeni Ngema and Julius Malema...have done a far better job.' The learned professor cleverly plays down his culpability in racist discourse by appeals to the supposed reality of African anti-Indian racism. The approach is to spread the blame. Africans (black people), for example Ngema and Malema, are also racists.

4 For Malcolm X's description of House and Field Negroes, see his contribution 'The Old Negro and the New Negro' in *The End of White World Supremacy: Four Speeches by Malcolm X*, edited by Imam Karim (1971).

5 Maseko S, Women's Corner, *City Press*, 16 January 2000.

6 In 2016, black students at Pretoria High School for Girls stood up against racist assimilative efforts at the former white-only institution. Black girls were forbidden to wear or style their hair into natural Afros. They were often demanded to 'relax and straighten' their hair to look like white hair. One student reported that some white teachers complained about her coming to school with a 'bird's nest' because of her dreadlocks; they told her to fix her hair 'as if it's broken'. The protest subsequently spread to schools in other big cities such as Bloemfontein and Cape Town.

7 Biko noticed this problem but insisted that English had to be used simply as a tool rather than as a mother language. Besides, most South African black people had their mother tongue as their first language and then English as a second or even third, fourth or fifth language depending on how many African languages they spoke. See pages 106 to 109 of *I Write What I Like*.

8 See Barker's *The New Racism* (1981) and Taguieff's 'The New Cultural Racism in France' (1990).

Biko, Black Consciousness and Marxism

Marxist analysis should always be slightly stretched every time we have to do with the colonial problem. Everything up to and including the very nature of pre-capitalist society, so well explained by Marx, must here be thought out again.

(Fanon 1968: 40)

AS NOTED IN THE previous chapter, negative reactions to Black Consciousness philosophy came from numerous ideological formations which can (for reasons of clarity) be broadly categorised into two main traditions: the liberal tradition and the Marxist tradition. Since the previous chapter dealt with the liberal tradition, I here focus on the Marxist tradition generally represented by the SACP, Non-European Unity Movement, Trotskyites and various socialist formations – all of which were referred to by Biko as the 'left'. These Marxist-leaning groups interpreted the problem of apartheid South Africa as fundamentally a capitalist problem founded on the economic exploitation of the working class. Accordingly, a socialist or communist classless society was the only necessary solution to the problem. Depending on their specific approaches to Marxism, Marxists differed as to the means to be employed in realising their what-ought-to-be. Some sections of the group preferred a violent revolutionary working-class approach to capitalist exploitation and others preferred what Richard Turner called a participatory democratic approach to the problem. What was Biko's response to these political solutions to the problem of racism?

Marx and race

How philosophers such as Locke, Mill, Kant, Hume and Hegel advanced racist theories and ideologies was discussed earlier. Marx, though not as explicit as Hegel, also advanced views about black and other colonised people that can easily be interpreted as racist. According to Diane Paul, Marx wrote the following in one of his several letters to Engels about Pierre Trémaux, a French traveller and scientist: 'As he [Trémaux] indicates, (he was in Africa a long time) the common Negro type is only a degenerate of a much higher one' (in Paul 1981: 115). In Poliakov's view, it was evident to both Engels and Marx that the white race, because of its civilisation, was more gifted than all the other races. Speaking of Engels' *Dialectics of Nature*, Poliakov suggests that 'a more detailed consideration, supported by references to Hegel and Lamarck, led him to conclude that the Blacks were congenitally incapable of understanding mathematics' (1974: 244). Although both Marx and Engels critiqued much of Hegel's philosophy, they were silent on his anti-African views in *The Philosophy of History*.

Like Hegel, Marx is also known for having supported the colonial subjugation of the black world. This position, Marxist apologists argue, does not stand in an essential relation to his philosophy as elaborated in, for example, *Das Kapital* or *The German Ideology* but is simply an extrinsic or accidental part of his thought. The argument constitutes what is summed up in the term *racism-separationism* – that is, the view that the racism of, for example, Kant, Locke, Hume or Rousseau can be separated from their philosophical theories. *Racism-incorporationists*, on the contrary, argue that the racism of these philosophers can be read into their texts. Tsenay Serequeberhan, for example, in a racism-incorporationist stance refutes the argument by Marxist apologists and argues that it is Marx's Eurocentric metaphysics that structures and grounds his perspective. Marx's Eurocentric metaphysics, his materialist conception of history, supports and justifies European colonialism.[1] For Marx, capitalist colonialism was a necessary historical requirement not only for the heightening of its internal contradictions but also as a civilising project for the savage natives of the colonies. Serequeberhan notes: 'Capitalist subjugation or European colonialism is the avenue through which differing non-European cultures are unified and subsumed under European civilization which, in this schema of things becomes the condition of the possibility of communism' (1990: 163). In short, the subjugation and domination of black civilisations are part of the fundamental and necessary dialectical movement of world history. Marx himself wrote the following about the British colonisation of India: 'England has to fulfil a double mission in India, one destructive, the other regenerating – the annihilation of old Asiatic society, and the laying of the material foundation of Western society in Asia' (Marx & Engels 1972: 82). This is because in Marx's view, European industrial progress signified an advanced 'civilisation' whose people (compared to the non-white peoples of the world) are the most economically, culturally and technologically advanced and civilised. The belief that white people – because of their advancement – should always be in the leadership position of control over others for human liberation to be possible is exactly the attitude Biko vehemently attacked.

Indeed, Marx's analysis and views of non-white peoples do not even constitute good grounds for his philosophical anthropology, according to which a clear understanding of human beings and the human condition requires an understanding of the socioeconomic conditions under which they exist. But Marx had hardly any firsthand knowledge of the historical development of material conditions in, for example, Africa and the structure of African societies. Most of Marx's focus involved European conditions and the historical development of European societies. His work, as a consequence, concerned itself strictly with European philosophers, historians, economists, political economists or political theorists. Yet his general philosophic concepts are regarded not only as unquestionable but also as universally applicable by his followers, despite his opinions about non-white people. Such conceptions by Marx and Marxists alike are the reasons why black philosophers such as Fanon (in the epigraph) and Nyerere warned that when applying Marx's theories to African conditions and the black world in general, one has to stretch or adjust them accordingly to suit the existing situations. In colonial conditions, Fanon argues, the economic substructure is also a superstructure. The cause and consequence are indistinguishable since you are rich because you are white and you are white because you are rich – therefore, all the reason why a Marxist analysis requires some modification and stretching every time we have to deal with the colonial problem. In fact, the 'Black Radical Tradition' articulated by Cedric Robinson in his book *Black Marxism* (1983) was an attempt to stretch Marxism to include the oppression of black people as a legitimate theoretical concern. In the same vein as Fanon, Du Bois cautions against the uncritical application of Marx to antiblack societies such as in the USA and South Africa, where blackness is a fact of inferiority and whiteness is a fact of superiority:

> It was a great loss to American Negroes that the great mind of Marx and his extraordinary insight into industrial conditions could not have been brought to bear at first hand upon the history of the American Negro between 1876 and the World War. *Whatever he said and did concerning the uplift of the working class must, therefore, be modified so far as Negroes are concerned by the fact that he had not studied at first hand their peculiar race problem here in America.* (in Walden 1972: 399 – italics added)

Marxist critique of Black Consciousness

Orthodox Marxists, following on Marx's materialist conception of history, have historically been suspicious of any philosophy that preaches subjectivism or particularism of some kind. For example, Marxists are averse to any form of race consciousness. Their critique of Black Consciousness is based on Marx and Engels' famous *Manifesto of the Communist Party* declaration that '[t]he history of all hitherto existing society is the history of class struggles' (1968: 35). Thus, within Marxist tradition, various attempts have been made to give a historical materialist explanation of race and racism, usually centring on claims about the peculiar political economy of imperial capitalism. Biko and the Black Consciousness doctrine, as I argue throughout, are locatable within the Africana philosophy of existence and therefore susceptible to charges of both subjectivism and particularism.

The responses of the Marxists (leftists) and members of the SACP toward Biko and the Black Consciousness philosophy are in many ways reminiscent of the responses of Western Marxist philosophers and the French Communist Party in particular towards Sartre's existentialism. These critiques not only lead us to consider Sartre's responses to Marxists which, I believe, are crucial to an understanding of Biko's engagement with the leftists' critique of Black Consciousness, but also provide a context within which we can situate Biko's philosophy. Fritz Heinemann, for example, reports that Marxists accused Sartrean existentialism of being 'a lost desperate attempt of a declining bourgeoisie' (1953: 166). In his 'Existentialism or Marxism?', the Hungarian Marxist philosopher Georg Lukács denounces Sartre's existentialism 'as the ideological crisis of the bourgeoisie in the epoch of imperialism, as the philosophical expression of fascism' (1966: 136). The French Communist Party's Roger Garaudy describes Sartre as a false prophet whose philosophy was simply 'metaphysical pathology', as 'all thought divorced from action'. Existentialism, he continues, 'is the middle classes' delight' (1966: 54). In his popular, though much regretted, lecture entitled *Existentialism and Humanism* (1948), Sartre contends that the communists accused him and existentialism of pure subjectivism grounded on the Cartesian '*cogito*' and also a 'quietism' that inevitably led to this philosophy being 'contemplative philosophy' and, as such, a bourgeois philosophy. Furthermore, Zack (though not from a Marxist position) accuses Sartre of being a liberal.

Interestingly, similar charges have been levelled against Biko and the Black Consciousness philosophy by Marxist and SACP members. Biko and his philosophy were derided for extreme provincialism because of his continued thinking in terms of race rather than class. He was accused of being an intellectual who loved to play with ideas but ignored reality. His views on racism were simply regarded as subjective irrational beliefs. One such vociferous Marxist critic of Black Consciousness, Toussaint (writing in the *African Communist*, the official voice of the SACP) accuses Biko of being a liberal. He claims that Biko's Black Consciousness philosophy is simply a product arising 'nebulosly in the mind, not from the substance of African life or South African society' and it was a 'sort of disembodied, rotating consciousness' (Toussaint 1979). In other words, the racism which Black Consciousness was fighting was (according to Toussaint) an illusion, a product of Biko's consciousness or imagination without concrete reality. It existed only in the minds of Biko and his comrades and was, therefore, at best a subjective idealism. In a similar vein as Roger Garaudy's description of Sartre's philosophy as simply 'metaphysical pathology...all thought divorced from action', the starting point of Biko's social change (Toussaint charges) is 'to be found in ideas'. Apparently this made Biko not only a metaphysical idealist but also a complete liberal even though a black liberal: 'For all his scorn of white liberals, liberalism penetrated deep into Biko's own thinking; for him too [just as the white liberals] the idea is the starting point of everything – the only idea must be the Black Consciousness idea, social change follows the idea' (1979: 24).

In the eyes of most left intellectuals, Biko's defence of blackness was 'reactionary' and retrogressive. The South African socialist intellectual Neville Alexander contends that the emergence of Black Consciousness philosophy 'represented a decided retrogression' (in Pityana et al. 1991: 246) because 'races' have no ontological status; they do not exist at all. In his words, 'there is no logical reason whatsoever to argue for the existence of entities called "races"' (1985: 141). However, 'races' are an invention of capitalists, a deliberate strategy for super-profits and as such a disguise for class interests. In Alexander's view, race operates as an epiphenomenon, a superstructure of the material base and thus race consciousness should be superseded by class consciousness. In effect, the argument goes, race has to be subsumed under the general rubric of working-class exploitation. This means that a class analysis of a racist social formation provides a necessary and sufficient understanding of that society. Putting up a materialist political economy view, Alexander further contends that the basic assumptions of the Black Consciousness Movement about the nature and dynamics of South African society are retrogressive mainly because racism (apartheid) is fundamentally a result of white people's desire to perpetuate 'the system of super-profit based on the exploitation of cheap black labour' (in Pityana et al. 1991: 216). While solidarity of the oppressed is necessary, he continues, the Black Consciousness Movement's conception of such solidarity or unity is problematic in so far as it 'projects the need for unity as arising from the fact of blackness' (in Pityana et al. 1991: 250). From Alexander's point of view, advocates of black solidarity such as Garvey, Du Bois, Malcolm X, Carmichael and of course Biko were all reactionaries and dangerous. For him and other Marxists, race is a superstructural phenomenon explainable in terms of and reducible to an economic material base and therefore subsumable under class conception. Accordingly, antiblack racism is merely a veiled form of class exploitation used as a divide-and-conquer strategy by the capitalist. What is, however, interesting is the convergence between liberals and Marxists' critiques of Black Consciousness through racial eliminativism. Both believe that race has no ontological reality, that it has no objective reality and therefore should be understood as an illusion. Any continued employment of racial terms and categories such as 'blackness' or 'whiteness' – as done in the Black Consciousness Movement – should be eliminated especially because they are in themselves not only subjective irrational beliefs but also dangerous and reactionary responses to South African reality.

Labelling is the standard method of critique of neo-Marxists (that is, the stigmatisation of any approach to interpreting oppressive conditions in anything other than economic and class terms). Descriptions such as 'liberal', 'bourgeoisie', 'middle-class', 'reactionary', 'counter-revolutionary', 'idealists' and so on are almost always used as standard tools for dismissing or silencing opponents. Questioning the means whereby liberation would be obtained by Black Consciousness, Toussaint compares it with the ANC–SACP alliance and concludes: 'Black liberalism [Consciousness]...compared with the forthright radicalism of the national liberation movement, developed in depth both in the realm of ideas and in the fields of action by the African National Congress and the Communist Party, it is a puny and inadequate ideology indeed – even when given a radical-sounding cloak of "Black Consciousness"' (1979: 30). In fact, what really bothers Toussaint and other Marxists such as Alexander about Black Consciousness is its exclusion of white people, its refusal to form alliances with the white working class or the left intellectuals as 'the *non-liberal* attempts, the radical attempts made for example by the African National Congress to build up an alliance with independent white organisations in what came to be called "The Congress Alliance"' (Toussaint 1979: 23). In short, the problem for neo-Marxists – just as it was for white liberals – is Biko's call for black solidarity.

Richard Turner, a devout Sartrean who wrote his PhD thesis at the Sorbonne on Sartre's *Critique of Dialectical Reason*, was (unlike Toussaint) somewhat sympathetic to Black Consciousness because of his understanding of Sartre's concept of consciousness. However, just like Toussaint, he criticised Biko for critiquing liberals so emphatically and thereby legitimising their importance. He also accused Biko of being a middle-class liberal who absolutised race over and above material conditions and class, especially the working class. Turner appeals for Black Consciousness to see different categories of white South Africans, namely: (i) racists, (ii) liberals and (iii) radicals (leftists or Marxists). He suggests that Black Consciousness's analysis of the South African white people is 'confused by a very loose grasp of the concept "liberal"' (1972: 20). Like Toussaint, he complains that Black Consciousness has given undue recognition and importance to liberalism which in actual fact is not a significant political force. He argues that since Black Consciousness is a form of radical liberalism, it needs to create alliances and solidarity with liberals rather than demonise them.

It should be noted that there is no homogeneous Marxist conception of the race problem in South Africa or in any antiblack society. West (1988), for example, identifies at least two Marxist conceptions of black oppression. First, there is the 'class reductionist' conception, according to which antiblack racism is merely a veiled form of class exploitation used as a divide-and-conquer strategy by the capitalist. In this case, race is subsumed under the general rubric of exploitation of the working class. An extreme form of this position holds that class analysis of a racist social formation provides a necessary and sufficient understanding of that society. In South Africa, this problematic position is put forward by, among others, Toussaint who argues that apartheid racism can only be understood as part of a class analysis. In his view, apartheid racism was merely a divide-and-conquer tool used to divide the working class. The second Marxist conception of black oppression holds that while black people are exploited as workers just as any other worker, they are doubly exploited because of their racial being – a racial case of 'double jeopardy', being black and being a worker. This version of Marxist class analysis is often referred to as the theory of super-exploitation, which is yet another conscious divide-and-conquer strategy of employers to encourage racial antagonisms between black workers and white workers by influencing white workers at the expense of lower wages for black workers. White workers, who fall prey to this capitalist ploy, are assumed to be suffering from 'false consciousness'.

These interpretations do not contradict one another. They differ only in terms of emphasis on oppression and possibly the method of achieving their goal, which in general is the same: socialism. However, both of these conceptions, according to West, limit and confine the struggle against racism to the workplace. They fail to explore other spheres of human existence where racism plays an integral part, for example the psychological and cultural spheres. In effect, they ignore the many forms racism assumes outside the factory. In a nutshell, black people are exploited in the Marxian sense to the degree that they are workers only. Add to this Sartre's insightful observation that because Marxists deal only with adults, 'reading them, one would believe that we are born at the age when we earn our first wages. They have forgotten their own childhoods' (1968: 61). Marxism's focus on labour and the workplace renders it incapable of understanding the effects of racism at the existential phenomenological level, on the lived experiences of children at school or SASO members at universities structured along racial lines of domination and control and so on. It renders itself incapable of comprehending the psychological damage racism causes on the psychic make-up of highly impressionable children and adolescents.

The argument that racism is used to divide the working class is based on the assumption that race solidarity is counter-revolutionary, reactionary and thus complicit in the evil capitalist system. As Lewis Gordon notes, the problem with this kind of argument is that class solidarity may in itself be equally divisive of black solidarity: 'A wealthy or even middle-class black can be deluded by the lure of class and lie to himself that money and "status" transcend racial boundaries' (Gordon 1995a: 179). Such a black person might be reminded, as West graphically describes his experience, that racism cuts across class barriers such that a black person in an antiblack society – irrespective of his class location – remains a victim of racist insults, attacks and humiliation. West (an internationally famous African-American philosopher/public intellectual who was a professor at Princeton and Harvard universities), in his popular book *Race Matters*, recounts an incident in New York where his race was more important than his class position as a middle-class university professor. After more than nine taxis passed him by, the tenth one stopped and picked up a white lady who had just emerged from nowhere. He recounts another of his experiences: 'Years ago, while I was driving from New York to teach at Williams College, I was stopped on fake charges of trafficking cocaine. When I told the police officer I was a professor of religion, he replied, "Yeh, and I'm the Flying Nun. Let's go nigger". I was stopped three times in my first ten days in Princeton' (West 1994: xv). In fact, class struggle not only creates divisions among black people by encouraging the formation of a black middle class and a black working class, but it also simultaneously irreducibly expands and intensifies the overall strength of white supremacy.

Alexander, Toussaint and Turner, among others, articulate an economistic monism which dissolves and reduces race into class and a super-exploitation position for different political terrains. Both these positions, as noted, limit the racial boundaries to the workplace. The factory is obviously not the only situation constituting the relation between black people and white people. If social relations were only confined to the workplace, it would not be possible for Biko and black existentialists to talk of *being-black-in-the-world*. The existential situation of the black person is not confined to the limited terrain of the workplace. It occurs in varied and divergent spaces where racism manifests itself, as West's experiences indicate. It is an existential manifestation of Manganyi's appropriate phrase 'being-black-in-the-world'.

Furthermore, while Marxist class reductionism and super-exploitation are in certain circumstances valid conceptions of racism, they historicise the emergence of racism to industrial and post-industrial capitalist epochs only. Although antiblack racist practices were adopted, developed and promoted in various ways during the emergence of capitalist modes of production, antiblack racism has a long history that predates capitalism and industrialism.[2] As West indicates, 'racism seems to have its roots in the early encounter between the civilizations of Europe, Africa and Asia, encounters which occurred long before the rise of modern capitalism' (1994: 262). It is true that the concept 'race', denoting primarily skin colour and physical characteristics, came into being in 1684 when Bernier classified human bodies. But this does not mean that the phenomenon and attitudes of racism emerged with the usage of the concept. Racist mythologies, legends, symbolisms and stories predate the emergence of capitalist practices and the coinage of the word 'race'. The biblical narratives of Ham and Cain, and symbolisms about blackness serve as clear examples of the genesis of Western

Christian antiblackness. Christian Delacampagne argues that racism has behind it a long and heavy history that goes back as far as the biblical curse of Ham (1990). Jordan (1968) demonstrates that unfavourable associations with black skin are considerably older than capitalism.

The traditional Marxist argument against black liberation struggles is that such efforts are bourgeois notions propagated by middle-class black people. Du Bois was described as middle class and his theory of 'race consciousness' as bourgeois when he defended black patriotism and race solidarity. Carmichael and the SNCC, which later merged with the Black Power Movement, by virtue of being a student and a student movement respectively, were described as middle class: 'the up-and-coming young man was being primed for the black middle-class. This was true of most SNCC activists in 1966' (Allen 1990: 47). The same middle-class accusations were levelled against Biko and Black Consciousness by both leftists and communists. They accused them of promoting 'middle-class' values and a bourgeois philosophy, and of having a vested interest in race analysis because it advanced and promoted their narrow bourgeois interests. In other words, the Black Consciousness Movement was regarded as a middle-class or bourgeois organisation. As a consequence, their emphasis on race rather than class was taken to be a mythical and bourgeois way of representing the class struggle. In the same manner as black nationalism, Marxists charged that Black Consciousness was separatist, racist and reactionary.

Biko's response

How did Biko and the Black Consciousness Movement respond to the Marxist criticisms? Sartre's response to communists' labelling and accusations might be instructive in appreciating Biko's response to the South African leftists' critique of Black Consciousness. Sartre's response to the 'quietism' charge is that one of the main principles of existentialism is commitment. Existentialists believe that one should commit oneself and then act on that commitment. Quietism, Sartre explains, is the attitude of people who say 'let others do what I cannot do'. However, he argues, 'there is no reality except in action...Man...is therefore nothing else but the sum of his actions' (1948: 41). For this reason, existentialism can at no point be regarded as a philosophy of quietism. What it actually does is to tell the individual that there is hope in action rather than discourage action. To the extent that Black Consciousness philosophy is existentialist in approach, at no point can it also be regarded as a philosophy of inaction. In a recent unpublished monograph, Mphutlane wa Bofelo succinctly captures the Black Consciousness Movement's philosophical praxis:

Black Consciousness does not pursue consciousness for the sake of consciousness. Black Consciousness does not subscribe to the notion of consciousness as an end in itself but to that of consciousness emanating from critical and active engagement with the prevailing conditions, experiences and realities in order to change these conditions, experiences and realities for the common good of all. Black Consciousness essentially entails moving from tangible conditions and concrete experience to consciousness, from consciousness to action and from action to the change of the conditions and transformation of experience. (2017)

For human reality, as Sartre declared, 'to be *is* to act, and to cease to act is to cease to be' (1956: 476).

The charge against subjectivity, Sartre responds, lacks substance because it is not that existentialists are bourgeois in positing the subjectivity of the individual but because the truth of the matter is that every philosophical anthropology (including that of Marx) begins with the human being, with the dignity of the individual subject since it does not reduce the human being to an object. For Sartre, all materialistic philosophies 'lead one to treat every man including oneself as an object – that is, as a set of pre-determined reactions, in no way different from the patterns of qualities and phenomena which constitute a table, or a chair or a stone' (1948: 45). Indeed, Sartre explains that the subjectivity postulated is social in the sense that it presupposes the presence of other human beings. In a statement reminiscent of Hegel's declaration that self-consciousness is only possible through the presence and mediation of the other, Sartre states: 'The man who discovers himself directly in the *Cogito* also discovers all the others, and discovers them as the condition of his own existence…I cannot obtain any truth whatsoever about myself, except through the mediation of another. The other is indispensable to my existence, and equally so to any knowledge I can have of myself' (1948: 45). This fact, Sartre contends, constitutes the world of intersubjectivity. Like Sartre, Biko sought to regenerate the subjective dimension to Black Consciousness philosophy by placing the human subject at the centre of history. Both saw human beings, rather than brute material facts, as the primary determinants of history. Both Sartre and Biko attached great significance to the power of subjective interventions in objective reality. Both subscribed to the theory of self-emancipation.

As with existentialism, Black Consciousness initially sought to restore the subjective dimension to Marxism and place the human subject at the centre of history. Later on in its development, it came to transcend dualities such as subjectivity/objectivity, idealism/materialism, finite/infinite, interior/exterior and so on – dualisms that, according to Sartre, 'have embarrassed philosophy'

(1956: xlv). It holds that existence has both objective and subjective elements, a synthesis captured by Heidegger's being-in-the-world and expressed in the title of Manganyi's book *Being-Black-in-the-World*, a hyphenated phrase that captures the interdependence between consciousness and the material world (if you prefer, between race and class, as I will indicate later). In Sartre's formulation, reality is constituted by the synthetic totality of the organisation of the object (in-itself) and the subject (for-itself). Similarly, while Biko positions the possibility of transformation within the subjective domain, he does not rule out the impact of the material forces. Ultimately, what he accomplishes is to insert self-consciousness as an objective force into the liberatory process itself. Thus, for the existentialists, both pure objectivism and pure subjectivism are to be rejected because they are outright reductionists. Referring to objectivism and subjectivism as 'the despair of necessity' and 'the despair of possibility' respectively, Kierkegaard states: 'The loss of possibility signifies...that everything has become necessary to man...The determinist or the fatalist is in despair, and in despair he has lost his self, because for him everything is necessary...The self of the determinist cannot breathe, for it is impossible to breathe necessity alone, which taken pure and simple suffocates the human self' (1951: 62). However, excessive subjectivism runs the risk of straying too far so that 'it has no necessity whereto it is bound to return...This is the despair of possibility. Possibility then appears to the self ever greater and greater, more and more things become possible, because nothing becomes actual. At last it is as if everything were possible' (Kierkegaard 1951: 54–55).

We have seen Biko's response to the liberal's charge that Black Consciousness is a racist philosophy. The leftist and Marxist make the same critique. Therefore, in both the standard liberal and standard Marxist analysis of the South African apartheid situation, there has been ongoing failure to do theoretical justice to the question of race. Liberal individualistic ontology and Marxist class ontology consider race an irrelevant and ideologically loaded explanatory category for the social and political challenges of apartheid South Africa. Captivated by their individualist and class perspectives, both the liberal and the Marxist refuse or are reluctant to acknowledge the significance of race as a determining factor in a uniquely antiblack society such as apartheid South Africa. As noted previously, the consequences of this refusal are reductionisms of all sorts including individual autonomy or class reductionisms. In short, both these positions avoid addressing racism on its own terms. What they want to do is to find a category under which to subordinate the problem of racism. For the Marxist, for example, racism is a subspecies of class exploitation.

To the question of whether a white communist and a white liberal are basically the same, Biko's answer is that although they may differ ideologically, they are the same from the point of view of the black struggle. In fact, Biko sometimes refuses to make a clear distinction between liberals and leftists, radicals, socialists and communists: 'We now come to the group that has longest enjoyed confidence from the black world – the liberal establishment, including radical and leftist groups' (1996: 63). He understood perfectly well that there is always white solidarity in the face of any presumed black threat (*swart gevaar*) – that is, the tendency among white people of different political persuasions to unite against black people, their economic, political and ideological differences notwithstanding. According to him, by virtue of their numbers and the conditions in apartheid South Africa, leftists saw themselves as threatened in the same way as liberals and conservatives. Biko argues:

> ...primarily because they want to detach us from anything relating to race, in case it has a rebound effect on them because they are white...a lot of them adopt a class analysis as a defense mechanism and are persuaded to it because they find it more comfortable. And of course a number of them are...terribly puritanic, dogmatic, and very very arrogant. They don't quite know to what extent they have to give up a part of themselves in order to be a true Marxist. (interview with Gerhart 1972: 34)

In a sense then, white people of all persuasions constitute themselves as a racial collective against Black Consciousness and this can to a large extent be understood as white solidarity. Since they are all white and are accused because of their whiteness, they use the very same category (their colour) to defend themselves even though that category is unnamed.

The Marxist charge that Biko is a liberal is indeed problematic (as indicated in Chapter 6). Recall that I made a distinction between negative and positive freedom, and argued that it is a feature of existentialist philosophy not to define freedom in the narrow sense that liberals do. I pointed out that for existentialists, freedom is distinguishable from individual liberty, which is the core concept of liberal democracy. The charge against Biko is even more curious when one understands that Black Consciousness philosophy preaches collectivism in the form of black solidarity rather than adherence to the liberal individualistic principle that gives priority to individual autonomy. While Black Consciousness philosophy's methodological approach is dialectical and synthetic, liberals are analytic in approach. As noted before, liberalism (in opposition to the Black Consciousness philosophy) is committed to an individualism which considers as basic the political, moral and legal claims of the individual over and against groups. The problems associated with the erroneous equation of Biko and the Black Consciousness thinkers with liberals, as mentioned, were addressed in previous chapters; suffice it to add here that certain concepts attributed to liberalism are actually not unique to liberalism. Many people of different races, for example, throughout history contributed concepts such as individual worth, self-respect, justice, equality or human dignity in their struggles for freedom – and these concepts have been arrogantly appropriated by liberals. More importantly, if we judge liberalism's track record on race and racism, it becomes clear that Biko cannot at any given time be likened to the liberals. In his defence of Sartre against Zack's charge that he is a liberal, Lewis Gordon helpfully reminds us that 'in fact, in practice, liberalism in itself hasn't demonstrated its antiracist calling, if the murderous history of the founding fathers of the United States and their expansion westward continue to stand as historical authority' (2000: 110).

Related to the above is the indictment that Black Consciousness promotes 'middle-class' values and a bourgeois philosophy, that its adherents have a vested interest in race analysis because it advanced and promotes their narrow bourgeois interests. In response, Biko argues that by its very nature, apartheid failed to produce a black middle class (particularly an African middle class) since it functioned as a social and economic leveller. He says:

> The Nationalists have not perfected their capitalist system. One of the
> elements of capitalism is for instance to create a...middle-class group
> among the ranks of those you are excluding from the mainstream of the
> country's economy. In other words, if you are dealing with a group of people
> who identify through one fact, for example the color of their skins, if you
> want to then exclude the bulk of those people, you have to give something
> back to a few of them in order to create a buffer-zone, so to speak, between
> you and the masses who you are exploiting. So what's happening in this
> country is that blacks don't have a very strong or large middle-class. It's
> concentrated to mainly the Indian community, that is the black middle-
> class, so to speak. In the African group, it's very little, and the same with
> the Coloured community. It's concentrated around Cape Town for the
> Coloured community.
>
> So that one effect of apartheid in a sense is that it is a great leveller. Most
> black people are about the same on an urban basis. And most black people
> are about the same on the rural basis. Out in the country, for example, each
> family is allowed a maximum say of seven cows, and five sheep, one pig,
> that type of thing. And people can only improve up to that point. And at that
> point they remain steady, there's a sort of a similarity in the community.
>
> If you look at the housing scheme of the Nationalists, it's a four-roomed
> basis for everybody in the township. The means of transport is bus and
> train for everybody. So the people participate in the same things, they share
> so many common interests. (interview with Gerhart 1972: 44)

Given these conditions under apartheid, there could thus be no middle class at all for the Africans and possibly the coloured community as well. Since the Marxists charge of black middle-classness does not make sense in apartheid South Africa, it would appear that in defence of their class position as middle class, white liberals and Marxists imagined the existence of an equally placed and privileged black middle class. Hence the constant reference to black students as middle class with bourgeois aspirations. The specificity of SASO's African students was completely ignored as they were grouped together with Indian students, the majority of whom came from wealthy families.

The category 'middle class' is often used so loosely that it loses its original Marxist meaning. If middle-class location in a colonial apartheid society consists of obtaining a loan bursary to attend university; if being middle class consists of being able to speak English; if through hard work, middle-classness consists of working for more than three years after obtaining a matriculation certificate in order to save university fees because your parents and family members do not have the means to help, as most African students at the then black universities did; if all this constitutes one being a middle class person; if living in the dusty streets of black townships without electricity – those representative instances of the colonial conditions and, in Fanon's words (1968), the embodiment of the colonial system's geographical layout – implies being middle class with bourgeois proclivities, then all Africans during the heydays of apartheid were middle class. If this is true, then a redefinition of middle-classness is required. Is middle class determined by mental ability, differential income, the relation to the means of production or all of these? Which class theory is better suited to explain the category of middle class? Is it the theory of violence, the theory of distribution, the technical organisational theory, the theory of social stratification and so on? But a charge one being a middle class person as this also fundamentally puts into question the class location of Marx and Engels themselves, let alone almost all the intellectuals who go by the name Marxist. Marx was a university graduate with a PhD, always in the library and hence not a worker.

Furthermore, if being middle class is determined by one's location in relation to the means and processes of production – and if this location automatically constitutes one as reactionary, non-progressive or conservative – then Marx, Engels, Sartre, Fanon, Nkrumah, Fidel Castro, Che Guevara, Marcuse, Angela Davis, Kenyata, bell hooks, Césaire, Winnie Mandela and a host of others too numerous to mention here should be labelled reactionaries. The irony of this charge is that the Marxists and liberals did not level the same criticism at their ally, the ANC, whose leadership has historically been constituted primarily by the educated Europeanised black 'middle class'. Furthermore, it seems the Marxists have ignored Marx and Engels' argument in *The Communist Manifesto* that '[t]he bourgeoisie, historically, has played a most revolutionary part' (1968: 37).

In the same way as Sartre's philosophy was ridiculed as 'metaphysical pathology...all thought divorced from action', Toussaint accuses Biko and Black Consciousness of being metaphysical idealists because the starting point of Biko's social change is 'to be found in ideas'. First, Toussaint seems to be caught up in the old philosophical dualism of metaphysical categories such as matter or mind (spirit or consciousness) – that is, the belief in the logic of opposites. One is either a materialist or an idealist, nothing in between; only thesis and antithesis, without a synthesis. Since, according to Toussaint, Biko was an idealist, he could not be a materialist. This kind of thinking emanates from the fundamental question that has hitherto plagued philosophy and philosophers, namely the relationship between the world (matter) and human consciousness (mind). The problem has been couched this way: Which is primary, matter or consciousness? Philosophers have thus been divided into materialist or idealist, depending on which of the two is taken to be primary and which secondary. Materialists believe that matter precedes and determines human consciousness, while idealists hold that consciousness is primary and matter is secondary. However, this debate between materialist and idealist happens within the framework of metaphysical speculation. This means that they are both metaphysical theories about the origins and intelligibility of the universe. If this is so, then '[b]y what miracle', Sartre asks, 'is the materialist, who accuses idealists of indulging in metaphysics when they reduce matter to mind [ideas], absolved from the same charge when he reduces mind to matter?' (1946/1955: 187). Since materialism is just as speculative as idealism, it is just as much a metaphysical doctrine as idealism which it condemns. Hence Sartre concludes: 'I now realize that materialism is a metaphysics hiding behind positivism; but it is a self-destructive metaphysics, for by undermining metaphysics out of principle, it deprives its own statements of any foundation' (1946/1955: 188).

To equate the 'consciousness' in Black Consciousness philosophy with a 'sort of disembodied, rotating consciousness' is simply to miss or ignore the phenomenological principle that consciousness is always consciousness of something. It is clear that Toussaint is not familiar with Africana existential phenomenology, in which I located Black Consciousness as a philosophy. The mere thought of 'disembodied consciousness' flies in the face of what Biko and his Black Consciousness comrades, especially Manganyi, refer to as embodied consciousness or what Lewis Gordon calls 'consciousness in the flesh'.[3] Indeed, to what does the descriptive 'black' attach, except to the phenomenology of the body? The concept of colour, just as the concept of consciousness, is simply not self-referential; it points to something outside itself. Colour is colour of some object. One cannot define blackness except in relation to something to which it is the colour of. To say that I am conscious makes sense only insofar as I can say or indicate what I am conscious or aware of. Human beings who regard themselves as black speak of having a black self which serves to distinguish them from those who are not black. Given this self, questions arise concerning its humanity and its Being. It is these questions about the self that constitute the concerns of Black Consciousness. Black Consciousness is a consciousness of oneself as being a black human being in an antiblack world which constantly puts one's humanity or one's Being in question. Blackness and the consciousness of it are the lived reality of millions of human beings in antiblack societies. It can hardly simply be a figment of the imagination of those whose lives are constantly threatened or terminated, whose bodies are constantly lynched, whose bodies are regarded as threatening bodies in white neighbourhoods and thus treated as criminals requiring arrest or being shot at, whose 'transcendence is condemned to fall uselessly back upon itself because it is cut off from its goals' (De Beauvoir 1994: 81). Toussaint is evidently blind to this phenomenological perspective. Even if we were to accept the Marxist principle of race as an epiphenomenon of the material conditions of existence, the bodily colour of the white worker also constitutes a material benefit because the worker's colour (a physical reality) has social, economic, political and even anthropological value over and above that of the black worker.

The reduction of consciousness to mind or ideas is equally problematic because consciousness is not merely a mental or subjective phenomenon but a physical (bodily) one, as the phrase 'consciousness in the flesh' or embodied consciousness defuses the mind/body dichotomy. Caught in the Cartesian dualism of 'mind and body', Toussaint (as a Marxist) privileges the body as a material substance in addition to the mental side. For him, ideas as mental phenomena do not change human beings and their situation; only revolutionary praxis or action brings about change. Phenomenology has long debunked the Cartesian dualism by contending that a human being is an embodied consciousness rather than the Cartesian disembodied subject. The irony of Toussaint's critique of Biko's notion of consciousness is that Marx himself employed this category in his theory. In fact, Marx contended that in order for human beings to transcend their alienated state within a capitalist mode of production, they must change from being a class in-itself (unconscious) and become a class for-itself, conscious of their own proper self-existence; they must develop 'class consciousness'. It is only through such consciousness of one's ownmost alienated existence that a revolutionary class consciousness can be developed in the long run. It is a fact that one of the problems Marxists encountered was the development of class consciousness among the workers. Substituting the word 'class' with the word 'black', the argument for revolutionary praxis stays intact. A consciousness of one's situation or conditions (one's blackness in an antiblack world or one's working-class location within a capitalist world) is a necessary condition for political action or revolution.

Effectively, Toussaint and Marxists reduce Biko's conception of Black Consciousness to what Hegel calls 'stoical consciousness'. In his master/slave paradigm, Hegel identifies three possible attitudes that the slave may take to his position in the world of servitude, namely: the stoical consciousness, the sceptical consciousness and the unhappy consciousness. The stoical consciousness in particular derives from an attitude that although one is in physical bondage, one can nevertheless feel psychologically free. 'Its principle', Hegel asserts, 'is that consciousness is a being that *thinks*' (1977: 121). This means that no one needs to view himself as a slave as long as he can turn inward for private thoughts that no one else has control over. In this case, to think means to be free and to be free implies independence from servitude. Obviously, this kind of attitude leaves out concrete reality. 'Freedom in thought has only *pure thought* as its truth, a truth lacking the fullness of life. Hence freedom in thought, too, is only the Notion of freedom, not the living reality of freedom itself' (Hegel 1977: 122). In his critique of Hegel's philosophy of law, Marx however posits that even though material force must be overthrown by material force, theory or philosophy also becomes material force as soon as it has anchored itself firmly among the masses – or, in Sartre's words, 'impregnates the masses so as to become in and through them a collective instrument of emancipation' (1968b: 6). Such has been the effect of Black Consciousness on the masses, as demonstrated particularly by the 1976 Soweto student uprising. Evidently, a philosophy can and does often become a direct motive force for praxis, and this only when it is transformed into a component of collective consciousness. Such a consciousness cannot be reduced to a form of stoical consciousness. Indeed, orthodox Marxists such as Toussaint, Turner and Alexander should have heeded Engels' warning in his *Letter to J Bloch in Konigsberg*:

> According to the materialist conception of history, the *ultimately* defining element in history is the production and reproduction of real life. More than this neither Marx nor I have ever asserted. Hence if somebody twists this into saying that the economic element is the *only* determining one, he transforms that proposition into a meaningless, abstract, senseless phrase. The economic situation is the basis, but the various elements of the superstructure – political forms of the class struggle and its results, to wit; constitutions established by the victorious class after a successful battle, etc., juridical forms, and even the reflexes of all these actual struggles in the brains of the participants, political, juristic, philosophical theories, religious views and their further development into systems of dogmas – also exercise their influence upon the course of the historical struggles and many cases preponderate in their determining their *form*. (1968: 682 – italics in original)

Biko on race and class

For most black radicals, an enduring unsettled problem has hitherto been finding the proper relationship between a fundamentally racial analysis on the one hand and a fundamentally class analysis on the other hand. This is aptly demonstrated in Cedric Robinson's analysis of Du Bois, CLR James and Wright in their various attempts to fuse class analysis with race analysis. In his magisterial *magnum opus* *Black Marxism*, Robinson mounts a critique of Western racial ontologies, a project intent on demonstrating Marxism's blind spot when it comes to race. He takes Marxism to task for its failure to understand the racial character of capitalism and its reproduction of a racial ideology. Robinson points out that this issue has been the main focus of black radical thinkers, from Toussaint L'Ouverture to Du Bois, CLR James, Wright, Lumumba, Nkrumah, Nyerere, Cabral, Césaire, Fanon to the the more recent Robert Mugabe, Agostinho Neto, Marcelino dos Santos, Angela Davis, Walter Rodney, West and others. What is common among them is a shared knowledge of the racial oppression of peoples of African descent and the failure of Marxism as a liberatory project to deal with racial capitalism. In other words, according to Robinson, black radical thinkers have often had serious problems with Marxist theory's incapacity to handle problems of racism in antiblack capitalist societies. What is more, Western Marxism parades as a universal theory of liberation yet, in actual historical fact, it is simply a particularised instance of Western (European) experience: 'Confounded it would seem by cultural zeal which accompanies ascendant civilizations, they have mistaken for universal verities the structures and social dynamics retrieved from their own distant and more immediate parts' (Robinson 1983: 2) His conclusion – one which, I may add, is shared by both Fanon and Biko – is that Western Marxism 'has proven insufficiently radical to expose and root out the racialist order which contaminates its analytic and philosophical applications...As a result, it has been mistaken for something it is not: a total theory of liberation' (1983: 451).

Biko's approach to this problem was initially strictly from a purely racial analysis, but later shifted somewhat to embrace and recognise the significance of class – a move which, in Robinson's view, locates him within the black radical tradition. This position is a familiar development in some versions of existentialism, beginning with Sartre and continuing with Fanon, Wright and Biko – that is, from an existentialist conception of individual consciousness to a socialist conception of class consciousness. The early Biko, if I may so characterise him, argued that in terms of Black Consciousness perspective, race was the only major determinant force in South Africa: The problem is White racism. It is the one force against which all others pale into insignificance. White racism '"works with unnerving totality, featuring both on the offensive and in our defence"' (1996: 50). Contrary to Marxists' view, for Biko, race in South Africa was not an epiphenomenon but the foundation of apartheid. Any analysis of the situation had to deal with the reality of racism first. White paternalistic attitudes were expressed by their desire to tell black people how to deal with white racism, the very problem which they themselves were part of: '[t]hey do so by dragging all sorts of red herrings across our paths. They tell us that the situation is a class struggle rather than a racial one'. In a clear and famous rebuttal of this position, Biko advises them to 'go to van Tonder [a reference to hardcore racist Afrikaners] in the Free State and tell him this' (1996: 89).

In South Africa, Biko argues, white people in general (including the white working class) benefit materially from their whiteness in numerous ways. First, they own the means of production. For example, they own 83 per cent of the land, major production institutions such as manufacturing industries and factories, financial institutions such as banks and insurance companies, engineering and construction conglomerates, retail business – indeed the entire economy is in their hands. Compared to white people, black people own nothing. This fact alone makes black people dependent upon the economic interest of white people. The consequences of this white ownership of the means and process of production unequally affect the employability of white and black workers. Second, the process of production (that is, relationships between white people and black people in terms of the organisation of the production process) privileges and benefits white workers and white people in general disproportionately to black people in general. For example, legal job reservation based on race protected white workers against black labour; unequal pay between white and black workers, with black workers receiving much lower wages than white workers for the same job; the Bantu Education legislation also ensured that black people remained unskilled for most jobs. Third, the alienation suffered by black workers is completely different from that suffered by white workers. For the black worker, the product created by labour belongs not only to another person (capitalist) but to a white person. It belongs to a member of a race that historically not only controlled the black worker's productive activity but also benefitted from the black person's labour. Biko insists, however, that the wages of whiteness go beyond material benefit. For him and the Black Consciousness philosophy, what was at stake was much more the humanity of black people that was questioned by white supremacy. There are different kinds of oppression, including exploitation and dehumanisation. White workers are exploited; their oppression is about how the profits are divided. Black workers, however, are not only exploited as workers but are also dehumanised as black people. For white workers, the issue is about how the profits are distributed; for black people, the issue is about how they regain their humanity and begin to be considered as a people. Given all these benefits and advantages produced by white supremacy, it is in the immediate interest of white workers to maintain their relationship with the means and processes of production which guarantee access to economic security against black workers. Indeed, the white working class makes itself white. Reminiscent of Sobukwe's statement that 'every African is a worker' (1970), Biko states:

> It should therefore be accepted that our analysis of our situation in terms of one's colour at once takes care of the greatest single determinant for political action – i.e. colour – while also validly describing the blacks as the only real workers in South Africa. It immediately kills all suggestions that there could ever be effective rapport between the real workers, i.e. blacks and the privileged white workers since we have shown that the latter are the greatest supporters of the system...Hence the greatest anti-black feeling is to be found amongst the very poor whites whom the Class Theory calls upon to be with black workers in the struggle for emancipation. This is the kind of twisted logic that the Black Consciousness approach seeks to eradicate (1996: 50)

In the face of all these facts about race, Marx and the Marxists' assertion that the working class represent human emancipation rings hollow and unconvincing: '...in their [the workers'] emancipation is contained universal human emancipation. The reason for this universality is that the whole of human servitude is involved in the relation of the worker to production, and all relations of servitude are nothing but modifications and consequences of this relation' (Marx 1975: 333). Unfortunately, in Marx's Eurocentrism, the workers he referred to as the vehicle for universal human emancipation excluded black workers; they were white workers in Germany: '*The emancipation of the German is the emancipation of man...its heart is the proletariat*' (1975: 257 – italics in original).

Marxists in South Africa conceived of liberation from apartheid capitalism in terms of a two-stage liberatory programme: a national democratic revolution followed by a socialist revolution. While the ANC (as an ally of the SACP) was to realise the first stage of the national democratic revolution, the SACP was assigned the task of realising the second stage, the socialist phase. The two-stage programme, however, faced a huge obstacle when viewed against the interests of the white workers in the oppression of black workers. The success of the programme would be guaranteed if the interests of the white workers coincided with those of the black workers, namely the transcendence of white racism and exploitation. This, however, is often not the case in historical situations of white supremacy. In South Africa, for example, although white workers are oppressed under capitalism, they nonetheless benefitted from the exploitation of black people and have greater access to the means of production than black workers. This means that the more white workers have access to or work with the means of production, the greater the white working class' interest in the exploitation of black workers. In other words, much like the bourgeoisie, the white worker has an immediate interest in the preservation of the capitalist system. In the super-exploitation of black workers in South Africa, the surplus value extracted was partially redistributed among white workers. There was, therefore, a transfer of black workers' value to white workers through higher wages for the same job and better provision of shelter, food and clothing. The white workers sold their labour and so were, by the very fact, proletariats while at the same time they had control over the labour of black workers. The control over black labour made them into part owners of the means of production and therefore capitalist in relation to black workers. Hence, the white workers did not find it necessary to form a single trade union with the black working class. We still find racially segregated trade unions within the mineworkers' unions, teachers' unions, civil servants' unions and so on. For example, the National Union of Mineworkers is a black trade union in opposition to Solidarity, which is a white mineworkers' union. The white workers' relation to the means of production, therefore, in effect encouraged a perverse interest in preserving antiblack racist oppression, which overrides what Marx refers to as the working-class interest in universal human emancipation.

What critics such as Toussaint conveniently ignore is that just like the two-stage liberatory programme of the ANC and SACP, Black Consciousness envisaged a two-phase revolutionary strategy, namely consciousness awakening and political praxis. However, unlike the ANC and SACP's strategy, the two stages of the Black Consciousness Movement's strategy overlapped. This move was predicated on the assumption that before black people can gain complete political, social, cultural, economic and even religious liberation, they ought to first free themselves from mental or psychological slavery and domination. Put differently, Biko believed that transformation of consciousness precedes political praxis. Psychological freedom and political freedom are interconnected, even though they are not the same. This is because an individual cannot fight for political freedom unless he is psychologically or existentially free and is conscious of that. Another reason is because any oppressive society, such as apartheid South Africa, which seeks to justify its oppression appeals to the false premise that human beings are by nature bound by some accident of birth (such as race or gender) and not free.

The problem of race for Biko always cuts across white class lines. As noted above, when it comes to racial oppression, Biko declared that white people are all the same (that is, the problem in South Africa is nothing else but white racism). In this early phase, Biko's position resonates with that of Césaire, whose letter of resignation from the French Communist Party Biko cites on several occasions. In the letter, Césaire argues that racism can be transcended neither by liberal notions of the mere equality of humanity nor by reduction to class consciousness. In his view, what is a precondition for any surpassing of racism is black people coming to concrete consciousness of their situation. In the letter of resignation addressed to Maurice Thorez, Césaire makes it clear that the black problem cannot be reduced to a working-class problem. He contends that these problems are completely different: 'It is clear that our struggle – the struggle of colonial peoples against colonialism, the struggle of peoples of color against racism – is more complex, or better yet, of a completely different nature than the fight of the French worker against French capitalism, and it cannot in any way be considered a part, a fragment, of that struggle' (1956/2010: 3). African-American thinkers such as DuBois, LeRoi Jones (aka Amiri Baraka), Maulana Ron Karenga and the early Malcolm X also privileged race over class. For example, Karenga states: 'The international issue is racism, not economics. White people are racists not just capitalists. Race rules out economics and even if it doesn't wipe it out completely, it minimizes it. Therefore we conceive of the problem today not as a class struggle but a global struggle against racism' (in Allen 1990: 166). Indeed, Biko also moves beyond the boundaries of South African racism (just like Du Bois, Karenga, Baraka, Malcolm X and Carmichael) to a global conception of the racial problematic. He recognises that racism has become a problem affecting the entire 'Third World' and that as a consequence, '[t]he surge towards Black Consciousness is a phenomenon that has manifested itself throughout the so-called Third World' (1996: 49). There was therefore no doubt in Biko's mind that racism against black people is rampant the world over.

A closely related critique of Marxist socialist utopia on racism is De Beauvoir's response to the Marxist explanation of woman's absolute Otherness. If one were to replace 'woman' with 'black person', there would be very little to modify in De Beauvoir's critique. According to her, the specificity of sex and race resist conflation or reduction into class. She questions historical materialism's assumption that women can be emancipated only when they can take part in production on a large social scale. This view, according to her, intimately binds together the fate of women and socialism. Marxists, she states, hold that '[w]oman and the proletariat are both downtrodden' (1989: 55). Both are to be set free through the economic development consequent upon the social upheaval brought about by machinery. The problem of woman is thus reduced to the problem of her capacity for labour. For De Beauvoir, this kind of solution to women's oppression is not only disappointing but also inadequate. Focusing specifically on Engels' *The Origin of the Family*, De Beauvoir points out that his theory does not account for the oppression that is a result of human consciousness's constitution of the Other and its original aspiration to dominate that Other. One of the major problems with Engels, she argues, is his attempt 'to reduce the antagonism of the sexes to class conflict'

(1989: 58). This reductionism ignores the specificity of women oppression and is for that very reason untenable: 'It is true that division of labor according to sex and the consequent oppression bring to mind in some ways the division of society by classes, but it is impossible to confuse the two. For one thing, there is no biological basis for the separation of classes' (De Beauvoir 1989: 58).

De Beauvoir argues that Engel's economic analysis of women's oppression, first, ignores the deep confrontation between individuals and not merely groups. Second, the Otherness of women is prior to property relations and is needed to understand why these property relations take the form that they do. Hence, to see the situation of women only at the level of property or to reduce it to economics is not exactly the right way to change the self/other dialectic endemic to it but merely to force it into other institutional expressions. Finally, the fundamental project of the proletariat is its own disappearance as a class. This, however, is not true of women. Unlike the proletariat, women have absolutely no desire to disappear as women; there is not 'any thought of her own disappearance as a sex' (De Beauvoir 1989: 58). Besides, contemporary socialist states have not rendered the liberation of women possible at all. Patriarchy still reigns in hitherto existing socialist and communist societies.

Biko held the same sentiment as De Beauvoir about existing socialist societies. If class was the determinant force of black or even women oppression, why are racism and sexism still social realities in most socialist countries? Antiblack racism, for example, is still a phenomenon of even the most advanced socialist states. For Marxists to assume that socialism will be the solution to the problem of racism is to ignore the realities of the life-world and lived experiences of black people. African students in communist China, for example, have been subjected to racial slurs such as being called monkeys. In Cuba, Afro-Cubans do experience racial discrimination. As Lewis Gordon aptly states: 'Racism, particularly antiblack racism, has existed and continues to exist in socialist environments, or at least settings that claim to be socialist, too' (1995a: 178). So socialist countries are no less racist or sexist than capitalist societies. But, Marxists may object, [t]he hitherto existing socialist states have merely approximated but not achieved the ideal socialist society and hence cannot be made the measure of what a true socialist society can be'. In their present state, the objection may continue, such societies still contain vestiges of the old capitalist order in the form of attitudes such as sexism and racism which will only be transcended with the realisation of *true* socialism or communism. In response, Biko might have pointed out that such genuine socialist states have historically not come into being. They exist only as unrealisable utopia – at least, as present historical events seem to indicate.

Biko understood that in terms of Marx's sense of class formation, the white working class is a class 'in-itself' (that is, a class that is merely potentially itself or a class unconscious of itself as a working class). It is not a class 'for-itself', meaning a class in actuality, a class conscious of itself as a working class and aware of its historic mission. People or a group of individuals sharing interests based on a common situation cannot constitute a class unless they share the same political and ideological consciousness that promotes their shared interests. Because of the differential access to the mode and processes of production engendered by race, white workers and black workers cannot become a class since, as noted, their situation does not promote a political movement and a class ideology promoting their shared interests. Pityana explains this issue thus: 'A class is formed when persons who perform the same function in the production process become aware of their common interests and unite to promote them against the opposing class. Thus, in order that a group of people can bring about change, there must be an identity of interests which they seek to protect and promote. I submit that any identity of interest between Black and White is effectively stifled by the colour conflict' (in Van der Merwe & Welsh 1972: 185). The fact that in South Africa racism was pervasive, involving almost all white people (including the white working class), is ironically even acknowledged by hardcore South African black Marxists. Writing in the *The African Communist*, Mncane Mkhize grudgingly admits:

> By and large, the white trade union movement has played a sorry and disreputable role in South Africa. Drenched in race and colour prejudice, selfishly monopolising all skilled and well-paid employment, it has made itself an adjunct of monopoly capitalism and the capitalist farmers in upholding white domination.
>
> After more than a century in which they have turned their backs on the sufferings of their black fellow-workers, have not raised a finger to help them organise and have deliberately thwarted their aspirations to acquire and use industrial skills, today, we suddenly find the leaders of the white unions affiliated to TUCSA deciding to organise 'parallel' African unions in *their* industries, for which purpose they solicit financial aid from the British TUC and the US CIO-AFL.
>
> No change of heart, no conversion or good motives lie behind this manoeuver. These 'trade unionists', like their employers, have been struck with terror at the great strikes of African workers in 1973; and at the dramatic advance of 'black consciousness' and political consciousness among them. (1974: 76 – italics in original)

Mkhize's lamentations support some of the issues Biko raised about white South Africans: First, that in the face of black resistance, white solidarity emerges; second, that white people often use black people for their own interests, such as fundraising for themselves in the name of black people; and, lastly and more importantly, this supports Biko's constantly stated view that race in South Africa supersedes class.

Later in their ideological development, however, Biko and some of the members of the Black Consciousness Movement such as Mafika Gwala began to recognise the significance of class analysis as well.[4] Since South Africa is a colonial racist capitalist society, it became clear to Biko and his comrades that to ignore a class analysis completely would be folly. Gwala, a staunch member of the Black Consciousness Movement, insists: 'We cannot talk of Black Solidarity outside of class identity' (1974: 29). As Biko became more radical, he began to recognise the difficulty of abolishing apartheid without at the same time transforming the 'system' from capitalism to some form of socialism. He did not reject the significance of class, but held that racial solidarity was a necessary precondition. This means that there can be no workers' solidarity (even non-racial humanism) without black solidarity first, as shall be seen in the next chapter. Using the colonial model according to which black people are seen as exploited by capitalists, Biko argues that the issue is not simply about the *haves* and the *have-nots* (as both white liberals and communists declare) but about who constitutes the *haves* and who constitutes the *have-nots*. In colonial capitalist South Africa, Biko argues, race and class often converge such that those who *have* are white and those who do not *have* are essentially black – an argument reminiscent of Fanon's claim that in the colonial situation 'you are rich because you are white, you are white because you are rich. This is why Marxist analysis should always be slightly stretched every time we have to do with the colonial problem' (1968: 40). For Biko, in South Africa, there is a perfect correlation of race and class so that all black people are workers and all white people are the ruling class. Therefore, it is possible to talk of the 'black class' and the 'white class'.

> There is for instance no worker in the classical sense among whites in South Africa, for even the most down-trodden white worker still has a lot to lose if the system is changed. He is protected by several laws against competition at work from the majority. He has a vote and he uses it to return the Nationalist Government to power because he sees them as the only people who, through job reservation laws, are bent on looking after his interest against competition with the 'Natives'. It should therefore be accepted that an analysis of our situation in terms of one's colour at once takes care of the greatest single determinant for political action – i.e. colour – while also validly describing the blacks as the only real workers in South Africa. (Biko 1996: 50)

Even though Biko still accuses the so-called white workers of racism, he concedes that the system has used them for its benefit. 'True enough, the system has allowed so dangerous an anti-black attitude to build up amongst whites that it is taken as almost a sin to be black and hence the poor whites, who are economically nearest to blacks, demonstrate the distance between themselves and the blacks by an exaggerated reactionary attitude towards blacks' (1996: 50). His introduction of what Halisi refers to as 'racial proletarianisation', meaning 'a process that provided a social foundation for multiclass race consciousness among blacks and whites' (1999: 14), is an attempt at reconciling race and class in South Africa.

As noted earlier, Biko followed in the footsteps of existentialists such as Sartre and Fanon by moving from a purely existentialist category of lived experience to a materialist conception, even though not completely. Moving from the categories of *Being and Nothingness* to the *Critique of Dialectical Reason*, Sartre fuses existentialism with Marxism and attempts to show that they are dialectically connected. Fanon does the same from the phenomenological-existentialist *Black Skin, White Masks* to *The Wretched of the Earth*, by demonstrating that race and class, phenomenology and politics, are dialectically and actively intertwined such that in antiblack worlds, one cannot properly understand classes without considering race as a determinant of social relations. In such worlds, Fanon argues, the base (substructure) can dialectically be viewed as the superstructure and the superstructure can in turn be viewed as the base. I am here, however, not subscribing to the problematic standard division between the young presumably immature Sartre of *Being and Nothingness* or the Fanon of *Black Skin, White Masks* as opposed to the mature Sartre of the *Critique of Dialectical Reason* or the Fanon of *The Wretched of the Earth*, which from a Marxist point of view represent the immature early Sartre or Fanon concerned with the bourgeois philosophy of subjective freedom against the mature Sartre or Fanon concerned with the revolutionary praxis of Marxism. Instead of viewing Sartre or Fanon as two distinct manifestations, I consider this division a mistake. There is no radical rupture in the works of both Sartre and Fanon; there is simply a development from the early categories to the later ones – that is, a continuity of thought.

The shift towards a synthesis of race and class was inevitable considering that both Marxist and Black Consciousness philosophies have more in common than differences. They both aim at the same object (the human being), even though Marxism seeks him in the workplace and Black Consciousness seeks him everywhere – at work, at home and in the streets. Both remain committed to the disalienation of the human being. For Marx, alienation (because it is dehumanisation) is the negation of the worker's essential being. For Biko, racism (because it is dehumanisation) is the negation of the black subject's essential being. Both Black Consciousness and Marxism have as one of their main foci the critical analysis of ordinary existence and offer means of transcending the alienation experienced towards the goal of radical change. In addition, both philosophies call for a significant transformation of consciousness, which is assumed to bring about an end to alienation and false consciousness. And yet, in both philosophies, alienation or suffering cannot be overcome simply by thought alone – *practice* is necessary (albeit the traditions differ on the forms of practice required). Just like what may be called the early Marx, Biko was a humanist – though in the Africanist and ontological sense of the term. His mind was concerned with the quest for the humanity of black people just as Marx was concerned with the humanity of the working class. Black Consciousness belongs to a philosophical tradition that is deeply rooted in the project of liberation and that liberation is understood as, among other things, liberation from racial oppression with its attendant acute alienations from the self and humanity in a racist capitalist society. This concern is in many ways similar to both the early and later Marx's concern with human alienation and dehumanisation as the fundamental problems of human existence in a capitalist society, the fact that most Marxists emphasise liberation in strictly materialistic terms notwithstanding.

There has been a significant movement by many twentieth-century Marxists away from orthodox Marxism to a position that takes into serious account the interconnections between race and class – or better still, the base and the superstructure. Philosophers such as Antonio Gramsci and Sartre have taken seriously Engels' warning that 'if somebody twists this into saying that the economic element is the *only* determining one, he transforms that proposition into a meaningless, abstract, senseless phrase'. Sartre rejects Marxism's deterministic materialism, yet he accepts the historical aspect of it. Determinism of whatever kind, for Sartre, negates human subjectivity and freedom and constitutes human beings purely as objects.[5] Gramsci reformulates the base and superstructure relation away from the one-way cause and effect notion of orthodox Marxism. For him, the relationship between the base and the superstructure is not and has never been static, rigid or one-way cause and effect. A constant and dialectical interaction between the base and the superstructure takes place, such that often the superstructure (rather than the base) becomes the decisive determinant of development.

Black radicals such as Du Bois, Césaire, CLR James, West, Mills and Outlaw – some even before Sartre and Gramsci – long held the position that although class analysis is a sufficient condition for understanding an antiblack society, it is not a necessary condition. They realised that it is impossible to understand capitalism in an antiblack world without linking it to racism. As Biko admits, '[c]apitalistic exploitative tendencies, coupled with the overt arrogance of white racism, have conspired against us' (1996: 96). Furthermore: 'There is no doubt that the colour question in South African politics was originally introduced for economic reasons...[however] after generations of exploitation, white people on the whole have come to believe in the inferiority of the black man, so much so that while the race problem started as an offshoot of the economic greed exhibited by white people, it has now become a serious problem on its own' (1996: 87–88). Mills also moved away from orthodox Marxist class reductionism by attempting to combine the materialist dynamic that is important to Marxism with accounts of issues that take personhood and white supremacy seriously.[6] He argues that white supremacy is a system of domination in its own right, whose power has attained autonomy of its own albeit initially generated by capitalist expansionism. He states: 'When...the working class excludes blacks from unions and joins lynch mobs, they are not just (as a top-down, bourgeois manipulation model would have it) serving capitalist interests but affirming and developing an identity that would, in certain respects, pay off for them.' David Roediger, inspired by Edward Thompson, argues in *The Wages of Whiteness* that the white American working class '*makes itself* as white' (in Mills 2012). Even Outlaw, a defender of the conservation of races, articulates the same position:

> A class analysis...is necessary if we are to understand the nature and foundations of the constraints upon human freedom in terms of economic exploitation and other forms of oppression. Still, such an analysis is not sufficient. It must be complemented by analyses grounded in an appreciation of the value of racial/ethnic nationality. And praxes, in themselves and in terms of their goals and objectives, must be acts that are structured by an understanding that is the appropriate achievement of both modes of analysis. (1983: 126)

In a similar fashion, Biko moved from a purely race analysis position to one that took into account the relevance of class though not a fundamental determinant of existence. In acknowledgment of class analysis, He states: 'Being part of an objective society in which we are often the direct objects of exploitation, we need to evolve a strategy towards our economic situation. We are aware that blacks are still colonized within the borders of South Africa. Their cheap labour has helped to make South Africa what it is today...Capitalist exploitative tendencies, coupled with the overt arrogance of white racism, have conspired against us' (1996: 96). Such statements and the 'coming into consciousness', as he put it, signalled a development in his thinking about *what-is* to *what-ought-to-be* (that is, from an apartheid racist world to a future liberated and free Azania).

Conclusion

In their criticism of the Black Consciousness philosophy as articulated by Biko, both the liberals and the Marxists specified their conceptions of what-ought-to-be in a future transformed or liberated South Africa. Liberalism, Marxism and Black Consciousness agree on the necessity of social, economic and political transformation. At the ideological level, however, they all disagree significantly. Added to this is the disagreement between Black Consciousness and the other two philosophies over cultural issues. The disagreement points directly to the differences in the movements about *what-is* and *what-ought-to-be*, that is the 'how' of achieving this. In the next chapter, the focus is on Lenin's longstanding question 'What is to be done?'

Notes

1   For the distinction between 'racism-separationism' and 'racism-incorporationism', see Matthew Bruenig's 'Atomistic Individualism and the Hermeneutics of Racist Philosophy' (2011). For defenders of 'racism separation', see for example Bernard Boxill's 'Rousseau, Natural Man, and Race' (2005). For defenders of 'racism incorporation', see, for example, Shlomo Avineri's (Ed.) *Karl Marx on Colonialism and Modernization* (1968), Eze's 'The Color of Reason: The Idea of "Race" in Kant's Anthropology' (1997) and Mills' *The Racial Contract* (1997).

2   For discussions on this historical evidence, see David Davis' *The Problem of Slavery in Western Culture* (1966), Jordan's 'Modern Tensions and the Origins of American Slavery' (1970) and Philip Mason's *Patterns of Dominance* (1970).

3   For the notion 'consciousness in the flesh', see Gordon's *Bad Faith and Antiblack Racism* (1995a, from page 34).

4   See Halisi's *Black Political Thought in the Making of South African Democracy* (1999), and Gwala's 'Towards the Practical Manifestation of Black Consciousness' (1974) and 'Steve Bantu Biko' (1981).

5   For a sustained critique of orthodox Marxism's deterministic metaphysics, especially directed at Engels and French Marxists, see Sartre's 'Materialism and Revolution' (1946/1955), *Search For a Method* (1968) and *Critique of Dialectical Reason: Theory of Practical Ensembles* (1982).

6   See Mills' *Radical Theory, Caribbean Reality: Race, Class and Social Domination* (2010), especially Chapter 3 'Race and Class: Conflicting or Reconcilable Paradigms?', and *From Class to Race: Essays in White Marxism and Black Radicalism* (2003).

9

Biko and liberation

Those who profess freedom, and yet depreciate agitation, are men who want crops
without plowing up the ground. They want rain without thunder and lightning.
They want the ocean without the awful roar of its waters. This struggle may be a
moral one; or it may be a physical one; or it may be both moral and physical; but
it must be a struggle. Power concedes nothing without a demand. It never did, and
it never will...The limits of tyrants are prescribed by the endurance of those whom
they oppress.
(Douglass 1857: 437)

The system concedes nothing without demand, for it formulates its very method
of operation on the basis that the ignorant will learn to know, the child will grow
into an adult and therefore demands will begin to be made. It gears itself to resist
demands in whatever way it sees fit. When you refuse to make these demands and
choose to come to a round table to beg for your deliverance, you are asking for the
contempt of those who have power over you.
(Biko 1996: 91)

We must learn to accept that no group, however benevolent, can ever hand
power to the vanquished on a plate. We must accept that the limits of tyrants are
prescribed by the endurance of those whom they oppress.
(Biko 1996: 90)

IN THE PREVIOUS CHAPTERS of this book, I located Black Consciousness philosophy
and Biko within Africana existential philosophy, which is also a particular kind of
philosophical anthropology asserting that a human being is best understood as
a free being (that is, a being who, because her existence precedes her essence, is
capable of making decisions which will determine what she is to become). Among
the primary concerns of the Africana philosophy of existence are the ontological
and teleological issues involving questions of identity and liberation respectively.
Teleological questions are questions of purpose dealing with what-ought-to-be and
therefore what-ought-to-be-done. These teleological questions speak to concerns
about liberation from what-is. To repeat, every philosophy originates from the
conflict between *what-is* and *what-ought-to-be*. While some philosophies affirm

what-is, others like Black Consciousness negate the what-is by positing what-ought-to-be. The last century, for example, was marked by a proliferation of liberation struggles based on the vision of what-ought-to be, seeking emancipation from oppressions of different kinds (such as colonialism, anti-Semitism, antiblack racism, slavery, sexism and homophobia). But the last and present centuries are still plagued by the emergence of new forms of oppression and racism, and the persistence of the old ones.

One of the most popular burning questions to be asked about a movement and its philosophy is Lenin's 'What is to be done?' This question relates to the means-ends issue of political, social and economic transformation of the existing what-is to what-ought-to-be. What is to be done about apartheid? We saw the attempts made by liberals and Marxists to transcend apartheid racism. However, the distressing persistence of racism worldwide not only gives credence to Du Bois' prophetic haunting prognosis, 'Herein lie buried many things which if read with patience may show the strange meaning of being black here at the dawning of the Twentieth Century. This meaning is not without interest to you, Gentle Reader; for the problem of the Twentieth Century is the problem of the color line' (1968: xi). However, it has also raised doubts about its transcendability in the eyes of thinkers such as the leading originator of critical race theory Derrick Bell, who pronounced the permanence of racism.

Indeed, although all three oppositional philosophical doctrines of apartheid have been in agreement about the necessity of abolishing the system, Biko's foremost concern was, in the words of Sartre, to 'oblige those who have vainly tried throughout the centuries to reduce him to the status of a beast, to recognize that he is a man' (1988: 296). Since antiblack racism in particular is fundamentally the denial of black people's humanity by reducing them either to subhuman beings or animals, black people have constantly been engaged in – to use Biko's apt words – the 'quest for true humanity'. This suggests that the black subject's struggle against antiblack racism is fundamentally an ontological struggle for Being which has to include psychological and political awakening dimensions (that is, the recognition that there is a necessity for a liberated consciousness in the ultimate creation of a new human being and a transformed society). My aim in the present chapter is to articulate Biko's thoughts on how the quest for true humanity would be fulfilled (that is, how the transcendence of racism would come about) and his vision of what-ought-to-be.

The dialectical approach

The fundamental problem in South Africa, Biko emphatically declares, is white racism. At the bottom of this white racism is the questioning of the humanity of black people and the demand for black people to justify their existence. In an attempt to find a solution to this fundamental problem, Biko formulates the problem through the Hegelian dialectical method. By dialectic, Hegel refers to a logical process of thought or the pattern of development through inner conflict. This pattern proceeds by triads consisting of thesis (affirmation), antithesis (negation) and synthesis (integration). Hegel believes that reason always follows this pattern. It begins by laying down a positive thesis which is at once negated by its antithesis, and then further thought produces a synthesis in the form of a new idea. What Hegel is driving at is that opposites are mutually interdependent in the form of what he calls 'the identity of opposites'. The same process gets repeated until reason reaches a synthetic moment of the Absolute Idea which is identical with its starting point, except that all that was implicit in the beginning is rendered explicit in a higher most developed form. The driving force behind the dialectic, Hegel argues, is the power of the negative. It is the pressure to overcome negativity, which gives the dialectical process its potency. The transcendence of the negative moment is accomplished through the act of negating negation. This act constitutes the moment of synthesis which is not only destructive of the negative but is also an absolute affirmation, the consequence of which is the unity of opposites. Even though there are numerous theories of dialectics and their applications, what is common to almost all of them is the idea that opposition, contradiction, antagonism or conflict are a necessary condition for change. For example, conflict among nations, classes, races or even individuals may constitute a necessary condition for political, social or economic transformation. Marx employed the dialectic in his class analysis of hitherto existing societies.

According to Biko, the unquestioned maxim for dealing effectively with racism has automatically been presumed to be integration. In his view, this integration ideology became so powerful that in a sense, it assumed a religious faith. 'In fact, it became a *sine qua non* that before you even started entering the arena of politics and fighting for social change, you must be a non-racialist [integrationist]' (interview with Gerhart 1972: 13). For Biko, this kind of solution is shortsighted because it posits as antithesis (negation) what is the synthesis (negation of the negation) in a dialectical progression. He then launches a scathing attack on liberals for deliberately conflating the antithetical moment of the dialectical progression with the synthetic moment, which they interpret as an expression of integration or non-racialism:

> For the *liberals*, the *thesis* is apartheid, the *antithesis* is non-racialism, but the *synthesis* is very feebly defined. They want to tell the blacks that they see integration as the ideal solution...The failure of the liberals is in the fact that their *antithesis* is already a watered-down version of the truth whose close

proximity to the thesis will nullify the purported balance. (1996: 90 –
italics added)

Liberal integration, Biko insists, is a trick to foist white norms and values upon
black people and thus achieve black assimilation into white culture, norms and
values. The logical point is that integration as non-racialism cannot both be the
antithesis and the synthesis of the dialectical process. The synthetic moment is
a product of and therefore must be a higher expression of both the thetical and
antithetical moments. To equate the antithetical with the synthetical moments is to
arrest the process of change at a particular stage and thus to reproduce the status
quo in a veiled and masked form. For in this kind of integration envisaged by
liberals, the 'in-built complexes of superiority and inferiority...continue to manifest
themselves even in the "nonracial" set-up of the integrated complex. As a result,
the integration so achieved is a one-way course' (Biko 1996: 20).

It should be noted, however, that Biko is here guilty of conflating Hegel's
'dialectical idealism' with Marx's 'dialectical materialism'. This conflation renders
his understanding of Hegel suspect and calls into question his conception of
racism. First, it was not Hegel who posited dialectical materialism, as Biko
contends. Dialectical materialism is Marx and Engels' theory whereby the world
is understood not as a complex of ready-made things, but a network of processes
in which all material things go through an undisrupted change of coming into
being and passing out of being. It considers that matter is always in motion and in
flux. It is the process of change, flux and movement in the material world (nature)
that gives rise to development and history. In this sense, dialectical materialism
claims that concrete material reality and history follow the dictates of dialectical
development. Second, if Biko indeed believed in Hegel's dialectical idealism
rather than Marx's dialectical materialism, he threw racism into the realm of the
ahistoricity of dialectic as a method. In this method, the antithetical moment is
given as the immediate consequence of the thesis and therefore privileges the
immediacy of racism at the expense of its historicity. Issuing a warning against the
understanding of racism in such ahistorical terms, Lewis Gordon asserts: 'We have
to recognize that we are historically structured as the essential negation of whites.
But we're not in our being the essential negation of anybody' (in Yancy 1998: 109).
Furthermore, racism is abandoned to Hegel's ahistorical idealism as opposed
to the historicity of Marx's materialism. Hegel believed that ideas constitute the
essence of all reality and that it is the development of ideas that encourages the
rest of reality towards the Absolute Idea. Thus Hegel's conception of history is the
history of the realisation of the Absolute Idea – that is, God. The result of Hegel's
idealistic dialectic is the removal of history from the concrete realm to the spiritual.
A Hegelian idealistic dialectic also occludes class exploitation – an issue which

Biko emphasised quite often as a feature of the South African apartheid system, a system in which class and race converged.

Biko's appeal to the dialectic is in many ways similar to Sartre's application of it in 'Black Orpheus', where he describes Negritude as the negative moment of a dialectical process:

> In fact, negritude appears like the upbeat [unaccented beat] of a dialectical progression: the theoretical and practical affirmation of white supremacy is the thesis; the position of negritude as the antithetical value is the moment of negativity. But this negative moment is not sufficient in itself, and these black men who use it know this perfectly well; they know that it aims at preparing the synthesis or realization of the human being in a raceless society. Thus Negritude is *for* destroying itself; it is a 'crossing to' and not an 'arrival at', a means and not an end. (1988: 327 – italics in original)

Sartre unfortunately goes on to describe this negative moment as 'antiracist racism' (Sartre 1988: 296). Both Biko and Sartre conceived of the negative moment (antithesis) as a means, a 'crossing to', and not an end, an 'arrival at'. White liberals (especially the doyen of liberalism in South Africa, Alan Paton) objected strongly to Biko's formulation of the South African apartheid problem: 'I am also strongly critical of Mr. Biko's use of the *thesis, antithesis,* and *synthesis*' (1972: 10). Responding to Biko's Hegelian approach, Paton accused him of the same objection Biko himself levelled against liberals' notion of synthesis: feebly defined. When Biko declares that the synthesis will be 'true humanity', Paton retorts: 'The *synthesis* is just as likely to be war.' Either Paton had not read Hegel or Marx, or he completely misunderstood their theory of dialectics and Biko's application of it. In terms of the dialectical progression, war or conflict is inevitable at the antithetical rather than at the synthetic moment. This is one point which all theories of dialectics agree upon: the idea that opposition, contradiction, antagonism or conflict is a necessary condition for change. As mentioned, conflict or war among nations, classes, races or even individuals may constitute a necessary condition for political, social or economic transformation which would be the synthetic moment (that is, an absolute affirmation, the consequence of which is the unity of opposites). To then confuse the antithetical moment and the synthetical moment, as Paton does, is to arrest the process of change at a particular stage and thus reproduce the status quo in a veiled and masked form. Paton's position is a familiar characteristic of formal Aristotelian logic which, in many ways, is the opposite of the dialectical thought process. For example, while the law of contradiction in formal logic asserts, to use George Novak's example, that 'a democracy cannot be undemocratic' (1971: 21), the same law in dialectical thinking states that a democracy can both be democratic and undemocratic. In formal thinking, things are what they are and remain that way forever. In other words, this kind of thought does not allow much change; whereas dialectics posits that change is the driving force of development. The basic laws of formal Aristotelian logic (the laws of identity, contradiction and excluded middle) are resistant to change or movement because in different forms, they all assert that a thing is always equal to or identical with itself.

I have mentioned Fanon's serious objection to Sartre's location of Negritude at the antithetical moment of the dialectic. What, however, seems to agitate Fanon more than anything was the fact that in the phrase 'antiracist racism', the concentrated focus is on the term 'racism' – which implicitly is intended to point an accusatory finger at the victims of racism as the ironic perpetrators of that which they are victims of: racism. Instead of creating an affinity between Negritude and humanism, Sartre establishes an affinity with racism. Negritude's negative moment, the moment of separation, Sartre describes as 'antiracist racism'. It is this appearance of blaming the victim that seems to enrage Fanon.[1]

Fanon's critique of Sartre's dialectic may *mutatis mutandis* apply to Biko. The latter's representation of Black Consciousness in Hegelian terms notably and deliberately recalls Sartre's characterisation of Negritude not only as an antithesis, a negative moment responding to white racism, but also as antiracist racism (Sartre 1988: 296). Unlike Fanon who objects to Sartre's description of Negritude, Biko endorses the latter's conclusion because he probably realised the significance of the expression 'the moment of separation or negativity' for emancipatory solidarity praxis. Unfortunately, as Fanon suspected, a lot of the critics of Black Consciousness embraced the 'antiracist racism' expression. Taking their cue from this unfortunate characterisation of antiracist racism and placing a heavy emphasis on the last word, many of those opposed to Black Consciousness or any form of race loyalty or solidarity labelled them racist. In the book *African Philosophy*, which he co-authored with Kane Anyanwu, Ernest Ruch conveniently interprets the antithetical moment (Black Consciousness) as racist. Referring to the advocates of Black Consciousness, he states: 'In order therefore to find their identity as a race, they become racialist in their turn, belittling their former superiors, burning what they used to adore, and showing by all means at their disposal that they themselves and not their oppressors are in fact the superior beings' (Ruch 1981: 201).

Besides the contestable claim that Biko and his Black Consciousness comrades were 'showing by all means at their disposal that they themselves and not their oppressors are in fact the *superior* beings', Ruch fails to make the important distinction between racism and racialism.[2] These are often conflated to mean one thing, namely the belief that one's race is superior to others and therefore has the right to dominate others. Even supposing these concepts were synonymous, Biko repeatedly emphasises that the goal of Black Consciousness is not the domination or exploitation of white people. Indeed, Sartre also says this much of Negritude: 'The Negro himself...wishes in no way to dominate the world, he desires the abolition of *all* kinds of ethnic privilege' (1988: 326 – italics in original). The aim, Biko argues, is not the subjugation or domination of white people but the liberation of black people. The two are, however, distinct and do not necessarily entail each other. A racialist believes in the existence of races and that these races are different, both physiologically and phenotypically. Racialism by its very nature does not posit racial hierarchical value judgements about one race or another. It limits itself merely to distinguishing between races without attribution of negative or positive valuations. In this sense, racialism is not necessarily – certainly not always practically – pernicious and to be opposed automatically. Even Appiah acknowledges that racialism is not in itself necessarily a dangerous doctrine. What distinguishes racialism from racism is that in the latter, there is an assertion of the superiority of one race over another. A racist, in other words, would not only say that there are different races but also that certain races (especially her own) are superior to other races and because of that they have to dominate the inferior ones. In other words, racism adds to racialism a hierarchically discriminating value judgement predicated on power relations.

Sartre is responsible for generating this erroneous interpretation by describing the 'moment of separation' as a kind of racism instead of racialism. For it is evident from the context of 'Black Orpheus' that his intention was not to label the Negritude thinkers 'racist' in the usual pejorative sense. If he had meant to suggest that they were racist, it would imply that they not only had the power to dominate Europeans but also that they considered themselves superior to them and furthermore that black people questioned the humanity of white people – a claim neither Sartre nor the Negritudinists would defend. He makes this point clear when he asserts that through Negritude, 'the Negro himself, we have said, creates a kind of antiracist racism. *He wishes in no way to dominate the world: he desires the abolition of all kinds of ethnic privileges; he asserts his solidarity with the oppressed of every color* (Sartre 1988: 326 – italics added). It is clear that to describe Negritude as racism is misleading. Not all separatisms are necessarily racist. In the context of the situation of black people in an antiblack white world, black solidarity may not necessarily amount to racism. At best, it may be correctly described as 'racialism' – which in and by itself is not dangerous, pernicious or racist. Indeed, Sartre's idea would make more sense if it were to be rephrased from 'antiracist racism' to 'antiracist racialism'.

However, certain invidious separations are racist to the core. One such example of separation as racism is apartheid. Fundamental to the problem of alienation is the notion of separation of someone from herself, others and (for Marx) her products. For Biko, the black subject's alienation manifests itself in a black self-hatred and inferiority complex produced by invidious white racism which can only be transcended by ontological, psychological, political and cultural processes of the antiracism articulated by Black Consciousness philosophy.

> This is the first truth, bitter as it may seem, that we have to acknowledge before we can start on any programme designed to change the status quo. It becomes more necessary to see the truth as it is if you realise that the only vehicle for change are these people who have lost their personality. The first step therefore is to make the black man come to himself; to pump back life into his empty shell; to infuse him with pride and dignity, to remind him of his complicity in the crime of allowing himself to be misused and therefore letting evil reign supreme in the country of his birth. This is what we mean by an inward-locking process. (Biko 1996: 29)

In an almost similar context, Du Bois states that the negro, '[a]fter the Egyptian and Indian, the Greek and Roman, the Teuton and Mongolian', is the seventh son, 'born with a veil, gifted with second-sight in this American world – a world which yields him no true self-consciousness, but only lets him see himself through the revelation of the other world. It is a peculiar sensation, this double consciousness, this sense of always looking at one's self through the eyes of others, of measuring one's soul by the tape of a world that looks on in amused contempt and pity, one feels the twoness...' (1969: 45).

Alienation

Fundamental to Black Consciousness is the problem of alienation and its corollary, bad faith. In the antiblack apartheid world, alienation was not only the separation or attempted separation of one racial group from another, or of the individual from herself, it was also an 'effort to evade one's humanity' by asserting this 'humanity as what it is not' (Gordon 1997b: 124) – that is, as either black or white consciousness. This view is a consequence of the principle in dialectical thought whereby a being realises itself in direct proportion to the degree of its opposite, such that interiority, for example, is realised in direct proportion to exteriority, transcendence to facticity, whiteness to blackness, and so on. So black consciousness is posited as the antithesis of white consciousness, purging from black people a consciousness that alienates them from who they are not essentially but situationally. This alienation has its origin in the antiblack racism that affects the black subject from the cradle to the grave. Because of the injustices, differential treatment, inequality, 'you begin to feel that there is something incomplete in your humanity, and that completeness goes with whiteness' (Biko 1996: 101).

The problem with antiblack racism is that black people not only acquiesce in it but are psychologically, economically and physically coerced to participate in their own oppression. The black subject, Biko insists, must be reminded of 'his complicity in the crime of allowing himself to be misused and therefore letting evil reign supreme in the country of his birth' (1996: 29). The natural consequence of this acquiescence and complicity is that black subjects end up deceiving themselves into believing in the naturalness and givenness of their situation. 'What makes the black man fail to tick?', Biko asks in earnest. Because 'reduced to an obliging shell, he looks with awe at the white power structure and accepts what he regards as the "inevitable position"' (1996: 28). However, deep inside, the black person knows that he is lying to himself for, '[i]n the privacy of his toilet his face twists in the silent condemnation of white society but brightens up in sheepish obedience as he comes out hurrying in response to his master's impatient call' (1996: 28). In the presence of a white person, the black person assumes an attitude of pure facticity. She plays the role assigned to her by the master. She lives her situation by fleeing it; she chooses either to deny it or to deny her responsibility.

One of the tragedies arising from racism, Biko argues, is the effect of self-negation which characterises the black subject's situation: '[T]he black man in himself has developed a certain state of alienation, he rejects himself, precisely because he attaches the meaning white to all that is good, in other words he associates good and he equates good with white' (1996: 100). This point is articulated with disturbing precision by Tocqueville in *Democracy in America*:

> The Negro makes a thousand fruitless efforts to insinuate himself among men who repulse him; he conforms to the taste of his oppressors, adopts their opinions, and hopes by imitating them to form a part of their community. Having been told from infancy that his race is naturally inferior to that of whites, he assents to the proposition and is ashamed of his own nature...if it were in his power, he would willingly rid himself of everything that makes him what he is. (1981: 203)

Lamenting the impact of white normativity on the consciousness of black people, Fanon declares, 'For the Black man, there is only one destiny. And it is white' (1968: 10). In an echo of Fanon, Elijah Muhammad (Malcolm X's mentor) complained about this black self-hatred: 'The Negro wants to be everything but himself. He wants to be a white man. He processes his hair. Acts like a white man. He wants to integrate with the white man, but he cannot integrate with himself or his own kind. The Negro wants to lose his identity because he does not know his own identity' (in Silberman 1964: 71). Having learned from his mentor, Malcolm X acknowledged with sadness that racism had indeed taught him and black people to despise and hate themselves: 'The worst crime the white man has committed has been to teach us to hate ourselves' (1965: 53). It is this selfsame black self-loathing that produces black-on-black violence, crime and disrespect. It is this self-hatred that is responsible for the idealisation and valorisation of everything white that leads black people to despise and disrespect their own kind and makes them unable to work together in business, the medical profession, law – in anything except for funerals, parties and fun. Even in these rather mundane activities, it is almost impossible to get full-blown collaboration.

In his autobiography, Malcolm X describes the false consciousness expressive of his self-hatred, self-degradation, shame of self, and his consequent desire to 'look white' or 'to go white'. In order 'to go white', Malcolm X bought lye, eggs and potatoes as ingredients for the concoction he applied to his hair and head:

> A jelly-like, starchy-looking glop resulted from the lye and potatoes, and Shorty [Malcolm X's friend] broke in two eggs, stirring real fast. The congolene turned pale-yellowish. 'Feel the jar' Shorty said. I cupped my hand against the outside, and snatched it away. 'Damn right, *its hot*, that's the lye', he said. 'So you know its going to burn when I comb it in – it burns *bad*. But the longer you can stand it, the straighter the hair. The congolene just felt warm when Shorty started combing it in. But then my head caught fire. (1965: 54 – italics in original)

After enduring the excruciating pain of the process of straightening his hair, Malcolm X says: 'This was my first step toward self-degradation: when I endured all that pain...to have my hair look like a white man's hair. I had joined that multitude of Negro men and women...who are brainwashed into believing that the black people are 'inferior' – and white people 'superior' – that they will even violate and mutilate their God-created bodies to try to look 'pretty' by white standards' (1965: 55). The upshot of Malcolm's narrative is that the reason why he went through such an excruciating and masochistic experience was the intense sense of shame he had about who and what he was. Indeed, he was not alone in being gripped by this sense of shame about self. Most jazz musicians, boxers, singers and ordinary black people of his time suffered from this terrible malaise of racial shame: Billy Eckstein, Dizzy Gillespie, Clark Terry, Nat King Cole, Duke Ellington, Ray Brown, Herbie Hancock, Jack McDuff, Brooke Benton, Sugar Ray Robinson, *ad infinitum*. Even the great Miles Davis (the quintessential rebel against racism) and James Brown (who ironically popularised the slogan and the hit song *Say it Loud! I'm Black and I'm proud!!*) fried their heads and conked their hair. The jazz musician and composer Charles Mingus, in his autobiography, narrates how as a child he styled his hair to be accepted, how he burned his hair with his mother's hot-comb hair straightener (More 2007). Sadly, still in this age and time, a number of African soccer players in the European league continue to conk their hair. Didier Drogba, the former Chelsea striker and a host of African players in France and Spain are examples of those still trapped in the morass of shame.[3]

Shame is shame of something and that something is in most cases me. Shame is therefore, primordially, shame of self. I am ashamed of what I am, which means that I am essentially ashamed of myself as I appear to the Other (in this case, the white Other). Elsewhere I wrote: 'Because of the negative stigma attached to kinky, nappy hair by Whites, I am thus put in a position of passing negative aesthetic judgment on myself. Thus, shame is shame of oneself before the Other. It is a product of Du Bois' double consciousness, the attitude of seeing oneself through the eyes of the White Other' (2007). Most people would definitely be ashamed to appear naked before others. And that is precisely why clothes were invented. To put on clothes, Sartre would say, is to hide one's nakedness, object-hood and vulnerability to the look and thus consciousness of the Other; it is to claim the right of seeing without being seen. It is indeed the desire to be God, to be the unlooked-look. Shame is of course not always the result of self-exposure, of nudity. Shame is also a constant problem of stigmatised identity, whether the stigma is physical (having a black body or being crippled) or social (being African in a white world or being a Jew in Nazi Germany). Such stigma presents the stigmatised person with a choice of attempting either to hide or to reveal the stigmatising feature (for example hair), to be ashamed of it or to accept it with pride. As a stigmatised person, I choose the way in which I constitute the stigma (for example my hair texture) as 'humiliating', 'to be hidden', 'to be revealed to all', 'an object of pride', 'as justification for my failure or success' and so on. In short, it is always possible – through my choice – to reject or accept the authority of those who stigmatise my hair (indeed my whole black body) as ugly, undesirable or repugnant.

In her book *Black Looks: Race and Representation*, bell hooks (Gloria Watkins) recounts a tragic incident during a visit to friends whose pre-teen daughter showed serious racial concern over her hair and skin colour. She explains:

> Their little girl is just reaching that stage of pre-adolescent life where we become obsessed with our image, with how we look and how others see us. Her skin is dark. Her hair chemically straightened. Not only is she fundamentally convinced that straightened hair is more beautiful than curly, kinky, natural hair, she believes that lighter skin makes one more worthy, more valuable in the eyes of others. Despite her parents' effort to raise their children in an affirming black context, she has internalized

white supremacist values and aesthetics, a way of looking and seeing the world that negates her value. (1992: 3)

This negation of the black self is not new. It is pervasive and can be said of most black people and expressed not only in terms of negativity towards one's hair but also, and more fundamentally, to the very Being of Blackness (including language, religion, culture, body and politics). Maya Angelou, the famous black writer and poet, recounts her anguish and pain as a little girl when she realised that the only way she could become truly beautiful was to become white:

> Wouldn't they be surprised when one day I woke out of my black ugly dream, and my real hair, which was long and blond, would take the place of the kinky mass that Momma wouldn't let me straighten?...Then they would understand why I had never picked up a Southern accent, or spoke the common slang, and why I had to be forced to eat pigs' tails and snouts. Because I was really white and because a cruel fairy stepmother...had turned me into a too-big Negro girl, with nappy black hair. (1969: 2)

Oppression often makes black people turn against their own in an attempt to flee and evade their blackness. They assert a white consciousness by adopting an antiblack standpoint on human reality. This they attempt to achieve in several ways. For example, seduced by the seeming non-racialism and equal treatment in liberal organisations, mixing with white people at wine, beer and tea parties in white suburbs, '[t]his serves to boost up their own ego to the extent of making them feel slightly superior to those blacks who do not get similar treatment from whites' (Biko 1996: 23). What these black people try to forget is that even in those 'mixed' circles, it is as black people that they are received. In doing so, they lie to themselves because they know perfectly well that they cannot cease being black. They conceal from themselves the truth which, despite their futile attempts to deny, they nevertheless carry in the depths of their being. By assuming an antiblack consciousness, by trying to flee from the black reality, by attempting to cut themselves off from the mistakes of their race, by making themselves judges of other black people, they exhibit an alienated consciousness in bad faith.

The other way in which antiblack consciousness manifests itself in black people through apartheid oppression is when a black person, 'because of the accumulation of White insults in his being, vents his anger on his fellow man in the township instead on the White person who is the direct source of his anger' (Biko 1996: 28). This is normally called black-on-black violence. Several reasons may be advanced for this phenomenon. One of them is certainly the fact that such a black person in a displacement of his anger towards white people, may either be hiding from his own desire for white recognition, which is a clear expression of bad faith. Since violence often breeds more violence, the victims of this violence (lacking the will or the resources to engage in counter-violence with the white power structure), instead of directing their anger at the oppressor, invariably turn the violence inward upon themselves. As Fanon correctly insists, when deprived of a channel to express itself against its real target, the violent environment turns inwards (that is, the victim turns the aggression against his own people): 'The colonized man will first manifest this aggression which has been deposited in his bones against his own people...you will see the native reaching for his knife at the slightest hostile or aggressive glance cast on him by another native' (Fanon 1968: 52, 54). This condition of absolute auto-violence is the theme of many black South African novelists such as Mphahlele, Modisane and Sepamla. In *Down Second Avenue*, Mphahlele graphically describes not only the violent and dehumanising conditions under which black people in South Africa's black townships live but also the violence on oneself and the violence on other black people.

In the text referred to above, Modisane recounts the violence that was part and parcel of the African existential condition in the heart of the apartheid world. Violence, he avers, 'exists in our day-to-day group relationships, the expression of the public conscience. It is the instrument maintaining law and order.' This state and police violence invariably turns into auto-violence, black-on-black violence, '[t]he African directs his aggression, perhaps more viciously, against his own group' (Modisane 1986: 59). Complaining about the pervasiveness and debilitating effects of violence in these apartheid townships, Modisane states: 'I am saturated with violence, it was a piece of the noise that was Sophiatown [a black township], of the feverish intensity of Sophiatown life, it was, and is, the expression and the clarification of our society...Violence is often the term of reference in our relationships.' He adds, 'violence and death walk broad...striking out in revenge or for thrill or caprice' (1986: 59).

Drawing from Fanon, Biko argues that as a consequence of apartheid's violent and brutal state repression, life in the zone where the natives live (township life) 'alone makes it a miracle for anyone to live up to adulthood. There we see a situation of absolute want in which black will kill black to be able to survive' (1996: 75). This self-destruction happens while the real source of black anger – white people – are sun-tanning or relaxing in a completely diametrically opposed zone of peaceful exclusive beaches and beautiful bourgeois homes with 'brightly lit town' streets 'covered with asphalt', where the 'garbage cans swallow all the leavings, unseen, unknown, and hardly thought about' (Fanon 1968: 39). This world, as Biko shows, is constituted by two zones whose logic is simply 'reciprocal exclusivity'. While there was peace and tranquility in Lower Houghton, Bishopscourt, Waterkloof and Westville (the zones where white people live), high cases of violence and murder occurred in the neighbouring black townships of Alexandria, Gugulethu, Mamelodi, Umlazi and Soweto. Evidence of this claim was obtained from the 1979 crime statistics. During that year, Bulhan reports, 'the average rate of homicide in Soweto only was 27.7 per 100,000 compared to 9.7 per 100,000 in the United States. In 1980, there were 1,221 victims of homicide among a population of about one and one-half million in Soweto compared to 1,733 persons out of 7.4 million residents in New York City' (1985: 174). As Biko indicates above, if by any chance a Sowetan (that is, a black South African) escapes being murdered by the police, he still runs a high risk of being murdered by another Sowetan – a typical example of JanMohamed's 'Death-Bound-Subject'.

At the bottom of all this violence and auto-violence is, as a consequence of the anguish experienced in the face of freedom, the anguish that comes with making difficult choices and taking responsibility for those choices. In apartheid conditions, a large section of the black population saw themselves through the eyes of the white people and thus constituted themselves purely in their factical mode. In bad faith, they refused to face the fact that it was in their power to choose not to consent to those despicable and violent conditions imposed upon them; they refused to face up to their freedom and attempted to frame themselves as objects and not as subjects. From an existentialist point of view, 'freedom is impossible to distinguish from the *being* of human reality'.

Part of the source of this alienation, Biko believed, was the education system as a whole – a system in whose content a black child did not recognise herself. This system taught the black child about Europe and Europeans to a point where '[t]he African child learns to hate his heritage in his days at school. So negative is the image presented to him that he tends to find solace only in close identification with the white society' (Biko 1996: 29). Bantu education constituted what is called the calculated miseducation of the black child, an education system that taught black people to accept with humility their inferior status in their country of birth. Evidently, whenever education is either denied or intentionally falsified, self-knowledge becomes impossible.

Racism and alienation

But how does this black antiblackness, this alienated consciousness immersed in bad faith, occur? From an ontological perspective, human reality is such that as consciousness, it lacks Being. This means that no one is full, complete and necessary precisely because existence – including ours – is contingent. Contingency is here understood to refer to an antideterminism according to which existence, and human existence in particular, lacks necessity. What is contingent is that which is not necessary; even though it *is*, it need not *be* or be as it is. Put differently, what is contingent happens to be the case but could have been otherwise. In a somewhat different sense, contingency includes the chance happening or the accidental. What happens by chance or is accidental is that which *is* but could have been otherwise. The contingent, therefore, lacks necessity, justification, or rational or logical explanation because whatever we are is not always what we have to be. However, in the face of such contingency – in the face of our incompleteness, our unjustifiability – we seek fulfilment, completeness, necessity or justification. We thus desire to be as complete as God is omnipresent, omnipotent, omniscient and self-justifying. This desire constitutes human reality as the desire to be God, which Sartre calls the 'original project'.

The peculiarity of antiblack racism is that because it questions the humanity of black people, it does – by that very fact – constitute the questioner (white people) as the norm of what it is to be human. In an antiblack world where white is superior to black, whiteness regards itself and is regarded as self-justified, as its own foundation, necessary and existing by (divine) right. The implication is that blackness as inferior to whiteness is or must be unjustified and superfluous. Since black existence is unjustified, black people are required to justify their existence. This demand for justification adopted by one who regards herself as an 'existent-that-exists-because-it-has-the-right-to-exist' (Sartre 1963) is at the core of antiblack racism. The demand for justification may be a demand that one explains why one exists or why, if one already exists, one should be regarded as a human being. Lewis Gordon captures the consequences of such a situation when he notes that in an antiblack world, '[f]or the black, to be white…is to be a human being and hence one step closer to God. But since such a goal is out of his reach, he might as well regard whiteness as divine. If the black *is* human, and whiteness is above blackness, then to be white is tantamount to being a god' (1995a: 147). If the original project of human reality is the desire to be God, and if white people are human and black people are non-human or subhuman, then the original project of black people is to be human – which means to be white. To repeat what Fanon posits: 'For the Black man, there is only one destiny. And it is white' (1968: 10).

Freire argues that the oppressed invariably recognise themselves in the images established by the oppressing group. But, rather than accept those images, they do everything they can to distance themselves from them. This generally manifests in the desire to become like or be accepted by members of the dominant group. He states: 'At a certain point in their existential experience, the oppressed feel an irresistible attraction toward the oppressor and his way of life. Sharing this way of life becomes an overpowering aspiration. In their alienation, the oppressed want at any cost to resemble the oppressor, to imitate him, to follow him' (Freire 1985: 49). Freire's words unveil an important dimension of internalised racism. The desire to be white (to be like the oppressor) implies a degree of dissatisfaction with the self among the oppressed, or what in Kierkegaard's terms is a failure to be a relation which relates itself to its own self and in relating itself to its own self, relates to another. This failure or dissatisfaction with the self may extend to how the oppressed feel about other members of their group.

In the face of such self-hatred, inauthenticity, bad faith and alienation, what should black people do to liberate themselves from the racism that generates such an identity crisis, such a 'double consciousness'? Is there a way of deliverance and salvation from the clutches of bad faith? If racism is a form of bad faith, if there is 'No Exit' from bad faith (as Sartre seems to suggest), is there then equally 'No Ontological Exit' or salvation from the terror of racism? Salvation and deliverance cannot be realised, according to Biko, until there is a radical move by black people from a state of inauthenticity (the desire to be white) to an authentic mode of existence which is the acceptance of our contingent, superfluous and unjustifiable existence. This conversion from an inauthentic mode of existence or bad faith to an authentic state in which freedom is the absolute value requires a process of conscientisation that would ultimately lead to what Sartre calls a 'radical conversion'. Indeed, for Biko and his Black Consciousness comrades, conscientisation is the first step towards liberation.

Conscientisation

The term 'conscientisation' is derived from Paulo Freire's notion *conscientização*, which refers to 'learning to perceive social, political, and economic contradictions, and to take action against the oppressive elements of reality' (Freire 1985: 19) – that is, the awakening of critical consciousness. According to Freire, '*conscientização* is the deepening of the attitude of awareness' (1985: 101); it is the subjective perception of a situation which, through action, prepares human beings for the struggle against the obstacles to their humanisation. Conscientisation was also the major aim of the Black Power Movement, as articulated by Carmichael and Hamilton: 'We aim to define and encourage a new consciousness among black people...This consciousness...might be called a sense of peoplehood: pride, rather than shame, in blackness, and an attitude of brotherly communal responsibility among all black people for one another' (1967: viii). One of the primary aims of SASO was to heighten black students' sense of consciousness and encourage them to become involved in the political, economic and social development of the black people. The 'envisaged self', according to Biko, has to be attained through the process of conscientisation.

There is a close correlation between the concepts 'conscientisation' and 'consciousness'. The one ('consciousness') is a noun referring to a state of mind; while the other is a derivative of the first, a verb derived from 'consciousness' which means the process of making aware, of bringing or making something appear to consciousness – it is a 'coming to consciousness', what Heidegger might term 'a call of conscience', not with its moral connotations but in its existential presence to self. The call of conscience is a call to authentic ownmost potentiality to Being, to the authentic one's own self-defining self. Put differently, the call of conscience is a call that summons one to choose to become oneself, authentic, and to resolutely take responsibility for one's choices.

Just like the Negritude thinkers and Fanon, it is to the black people that Biko addressed his exhortations, encouragements, criticisms and well-thought-out arguments. In its Black Consciousness dimension, conscientisation is that process which brings to the consciousness of black people the task of taking charge of their destiny, of resolutely taking responsibility for who they are and the choices they make, of committing themselves to authentic possibilities, thus taking over their freedom and uniqueness, and resolutely engaging in the projects through which they create themselves. Conscientisation is thus a moment in which a critical demystification of the edifices and arrangements of domination are exposed to the consciousness of the oppressed. In other words, conscientisation may be regarded as akin to the removal or disappearance of false consciousness and the emergence of a true consciousness which involves the necessity of political engagement. At the trial of his comrades (the SASO Nine Trial) in 1976, Biko confirmed the following definition of conscientisation:

> Conscientization is a process whereby individuals or groups living within a given social and political setting are made aware of their situation. The operative attitude here is not so much awareness of the physical sense of their situation, but much more their ability to assess and improve their own influence over themselves and their environment. Thus in the South African setting for instance, it is not enough to be aware that one is living in a situation of oppression or residing in a segregated and probably inferior educational institution. One must be committed to the idea of getting oneself out of the morass, one must be aware of the factors involved and dangers imminent in such an undertaking, but must always operate from the basic belief that one is in a struggle that must be seen through in spite of the dangers and difficulties. Thus then conscientization implies a desire to engage people in an emancipatory process, in an attempt to free them from a situation of bondage. (Woods 1987: 188–189)

Thus conscientisation for Biko is the process of consciousness raising by uncovering, unmasking and laying bare the sources of oppression and seeing the world in a new way. In other words, it is politicisation of the mind, what he calls 'coming into consciousness' of oppression and the commitment to end that oppression. Perhaps a similar articulation of conscientisation is that provided by Fanon in terms of his practice as a psychoanalyst: 'As a psychoanalyst, I should help my patient to become conscious...to act in the direction of a change in the social structure...my objective, once his motivations have been brought into consciousness, will be to put him in a position to choose action (or passivity) with respect to the real source of conflict...that is, toward the social structure' (1967a: 100). It is a process whereby black people are made to enter history as subjects, humanising themselves and becoming more fully human. The aim, for the Black Consciousness Movement, was therefore to rebuild and recondition the consciousness of the oppressed black masses in such a way that they would be willing and unafraid to demand what was rightfully theirs: human dignity, freedom and self-worth.

Interviewed by Gerhart, Biko explained the process of conscientisation as 'basically a raising of the level of critical awareness of what is going on around town. And it promotes self-reliance in the area of making decisions for yourself, looking at things and analysing them. It's a much slower process' (interview with Gerhart 1972: 30). Biko here emphasises the idea of self-liberation, proposing a conscientisation process to unlock the intrinsic humanity of black people – what Freire terms 'the ontological vocation to become human'. For Biko, concientisation ultimately meant the unveiling of reality in such a way that it engendered in the consciousness of black people the fact that society and history can be made and remade by human actors and organised groups, the consciousness of whom in reality exercises domination and power in society.

In an effort to discredit conscientisation as a potent liberatory process and method, critics such as Toussaint reduce it to a mere liberal form of education. In his view, Biko was no more than a black liberal in method and inclination; hence, his solution to the problem in South Africa is characteristically liberalistic. Biko's means or method for liberation, Toussaint charges, is '*not* by violence; *not* by law-breaking; *not* by mass struggle...[but to] change their [black people's] idea' (1979: 27–28). From this, Toussaint equates Biko's means towards the liberation of black people from apartheid with the liberal method of educational reform. In his Marxist view, Toussaint believes that education as a means to liberation is idealism at its best with no materialist foundation at all. Contrary to Du Bois' suggestion that all knowing is knowing for the sake of doing, Toussaint whines, '[w]hereas white liberals believe in universal education as the great leveler, Biko believes in black re-education' (1979: 24). Just as the starting point for the liberals is 'the idea', so too is 'the idea' the first step toward liberation for Biko. In other words, Toussaint – just as the leftists' standard criticism of Black Consciousness – accuses Biko of being a philosophical idealist, a pacifist, without any political programme.

This is clearly ridiculous reasoning, but it did not stop him because he goes on to claim that for Biko, 'consciousness is what is important, the material basis of society secondary, almost unimportant' (1979: 24) – a claim which, of course, is far from the truth.

It is surprising that in their critique of Black Consciousness as a philosophy, Toussaint and other Marxists conveniently forget not only that Marxism itself is a philosophical theory but also what Marx said about philosophy: 'Just as philosophy finds its *material* weapons in the proletariat, so the proletariat finds its *intellectual* weapons in philosophy; and once the lightning of thought has struck deeply into the virgin soil of the people, emancipation will transform the *Germans* into *men...The emancipation of the German is the emancipation of man*. The *head* of this emancipation is *philosophy*, its heart the *proletariat*' (1975: 257 – italics in original).

Even though Toussaint's description of Biko's liberation project is to a certain extent correct (that is, it is intended to educate black people), he falls prey to the common erroneous and conservative belief that education is the same for every situation and time. For him, education is the practice of domination (teacher = subject, learner = object) rather than 'the practice of freedom' (dialogical interaction of two subjects) (Hooks 1994: 4). Education for domination involves knowledge as information without any relation to how one lives one's life-world and life struggles, and navigates one's lived experiences. It is knowledge about obedience, authority, submissiveness, manipulation, self-restraint, brainwashing and reinforcement of control. This is what education represents to Toussaint: education for domination, which basically amounts to brainwashing. Referring to this kind of conception of education, Biko warns: 'A long look should also be taken at the educational system for blacks...Who can resist losing respect for his tradition when in school his whole cultural background is summed up in one word – barbarism?'(1996: 94). In a colonial setting such as South Africa, the missionaries 'were in the vanguard of the colonisation movement to "civilise and educate" the savages and introduce the Christian message to them' (Biko 1996: 93). And it is precisely this education in the form of Bantu Education that Biko and his comrades wanted to destroy and replace with education for liberation. Mafika Gwala emphatically captures this mood: 'We who uphold and want to promote Black Consciousness principles have a firm opinion of what things we appreciate; and also what we reject. We appreciate, as students – education that is geared for liberation. We appreciate social progress in the Black community...We definitely reject education that makes us sophisticated slaves' (1974: 17). It is therefore evident that Toussaint misunderstood Biko's concept of conscientisation as education for liberation rather than education for domination.

Biko's philosophy, as written in his book, is fundamentally a basic revolutionary lesson in what Freire called the 'Pedagogy of the Oppressed' – knowing for the sake of doing and acting, which at any point in time is completely different, distinguishable and antagonistic to Eurocentric liberal education, the oppressive and dehumanising Bantu Education and the colonial civilising missionary education. As the pedagogy of the oppressed and even practised in SASO Formation Schools. Black Consciousness philosophy was designed to awaken the long-dormant consciousness of black people from its political and revolutionary slumber. With deliberate care, this pedagogy located and identified the foundation and origins of their oppression. In doing this, it demonstrated to black people that their oppression was not natural, God-given or of their own making, that there is nothing like 'the Black problem', but that there is everything wrong with white racism which questions their humanity at every level of existence. Ultimately, it is a pedagogy whereby human beings are encouraged to deal critically and creatively with the reality that confronts them, and learn or understand how to participate in the transformation of that reality and their world of existence. This is not the kind of education that Fanon says we are just all too eager to call 'political education': 'we often believe with criminal superficiality that to educate the masses politically is to deliver a long political harangue from time to time'. Education for freedom means 'to teach the masses that everything depends on them; that if we stagnate it is their responsibility, and that if we go forward it is due to them too, that there is no such thing as a demiurge, that there is no famous man who will take the responsibility for everything, but that the demiurge is the people themselves and the magic hands are finally only the hands of the people' (Fanon 1968: 197).

The necessity for conscientisation

Why then is conscientisation so crucial to the Black Consciousness Movement? De Beauvoir asserts that there are times when the slave is not conscious of his servitude and when it becomes necessary to bring the seed of his liberation to him from the outside. Marx makes the same claim about what he calls the 'false consciousness' of the worker. The fact that the slave is submissive is because the slavemaster 'has succeeded in mystifying him in such a way that his situation does not seem to him to be imposed by men, but to be immediately given by nature, by the gods, by the powers against whom revolt has no meaning; thus he does not accept his condition through a resignation of his freedom since he cannot even dream of any other, (De Beauvoir 1994: 85). What must be done in such a situation is to provide the ignorant slave with the means of transcending her situation, to put an end to her ignorance by means of conscientisation. The same phenomenon applies to black people in an antiblack society. Indeed, in such a world, black people are vulnerable to all sorts of mystifications and myths propagated by white people, to the extent that they can give themselves up to an inhuman myth by fleeing from their freedom. They are given ample evidence that the situation in which they find themselves is natural. 'In order to prevent...revolt, one of the ruses of oppression is to camouflage itself behind a natural situation since, after all, one cannot revolt against nature. When a conservative wishes to show that the proletariat is not oppressed, he declares that the present distribution of wealth is a natural fact and that there is thus no means of rejecting it' (De Beauvoir 1994: 83). Given this condition, Biko and his comrades found it necessary to expose, through the process of conscientisation, the mystifications and to restore black humanity in the presence of its freedom. lf the black subject – as Biko declares – has become a shell, a shadow of a man, completely defeated, drowning in his own tears of misery, a slave, an ox bearing the yoke of oppression with sheepish timidity, then the only vehicle for change is the very same black people who lost their identity and dignity. Hence, the first thing to do is to make black subjectivity re-apprehend itself, relate its own self to itself and in doing so, relate itself to another, and in Biko's phrase, 'pump back life into his empty shell...infuse him with pride and dignity, to remind him of his complicity in the crime of allowing himself to be misused' (Biko 1996: 29).

Part of the reason why conscientisation was necessary lies in the fact that the most popular liberation movement, the ANC, moved from the assumption that the 'black problem' in South Africa was predominantly a white man's problem. This assumption led to the belief that the problem would be resolved through black people being granted full political rights and power by white people. What this approach really did was that it made little attempt to solve what Silberman might call the black people's 'black problem' (1964). For the Black Consciousness proponents, the 'black problem' was first and fundamentally a black person's problem before being a white person's problem. This means that the emphasis on political and civil rights did not even begin to deal with the black people's 'black problem' at all. Their 'black problem' manifests in the ever-so-important-question of identity: Who am I? This question bothers every black person in a way no white or any other colour person can ever know. This is because a black person always comes up against the knowledge of the white world's distaste for her. This experience leads to low self-esteem that ultimately ends up transforming into self-hatred. Self-hatred manifests itself in a number of ways. The most obvious is what Fanon refers to as the 'denegrification' practice – the practice of black people to straighten their hair and apply skin lightening creams in a desperate but futile attempt to achieve whiteness, which is presumably the measure not only of beauty but also of one's humanity. Wa Bofelo captures this messages from what he calls 'White high society to the primitive Black body' thus: 'Here are skin-enlightening creams and hair-dyes, we have generously produced them in large quantities for you to bleach your skins and perm your hair to at least look as possible as it can be like human beings' (2017). Given this developed externally induced sense of self-hatred, black alienation involves an attempt to flee one's black body, 'the way they make up and so on, which tends to be a negation of their true state and in a sense a running away from their colour; they use lightening creams, they use straightening devices for their hair and so on' (Biko 1996: 104). It is reported that in Jamaica, black women inject themselves with chicken hormones in an attempt to lighten their skin. In a sense, the recent hair extensions that are often blond and the bleaching of the skin throughout Africa is a reproduction of the Fanonian 'White Mask'.[4]

The quest for the white ideal in this manner is not only a sign of self-hate, but also a road that inevitably leads to further self-hatred and continuous frustration. Like Garvey, Césaire, Fanon, Carmichael and Malcolm X, the Black Consciousness activists strove to conscientise black people that their blackness should not be a source of self-hatred and shame but a badge of honour. The real enemy or problem is not the white person but the black person herself; the one who because of prolonged racist oppression has learned to despise herself and is therefore unable to liberate herself. Echoing Malcolm X's statement that the worst crime white people have committed against black people was to teach them to hate themselves, Biko states: 'The Black man in himself has developed a certain state of alienation, he rejects himself, precisely because he attaches the meaning white to all that is good' (1996: 102). It is at the conquest of this debilitating self-hatred that conscientisation is aimed. The success of conscientisation as a pedagogical politics of conversion ultimately rests upon and requires a radical conversion.

Radical conversion

If we are ontologically contingent beings, if our existence (including our racial make-up) is contingent, then no one can justifiably demand or has a right to require that I recognise her claim to necessity. Therefore, racism or oppression – precisely because it is based on contingency – requires a lucid consciousness of our contingency to generate resistance of a revolutionary nature to a consciousness previously corrupted. 'The revolutionary's conscience demands that the privileges of the oppressor class be *unjustifiable,* that the primordial *contingency* he finds in himself also be a constituent part of his very existence, that the system of values set up by his masters, the purpose of which is to confer *de jure* existence upon *de facto* advantages, may be transcended towards an organization of the world which does not yet exist and which will exclude, both in law and in fact, all privileges' (Sartre 1946/1955: 218–219 – italics added).

To complete the movement, the revolutionary requires a revolutionary philosophy which ought to show: (i) that human beings are unjustifiable, that their existence is contingent, in that neither they nor any providence has produced it; and (ii) that, as a result of this, any collective order established by human beings can be transcended towards other orders (Sartre 1946/1955: 219). Here, Sartre makes a clear break from ontology to the ontic level of revolutionary politics. Thus, in the realm of action, contingency generates some measure of optimism. If contingency is a source of anguish, then that very contingency should provide relief from it: None of the oppressed groups or individuals has to be what she is; each could be something other than what she is or do otherwise. All are free and responsible for their situations in the ontological sense, which urges them on to freedom in the ontic sense where anything *is* possible and nothing *has* to be the case because it is contingent. This realisation should bring hope to the oppressed, hope of changing the oppressive situation.

The realisation of the contingency of our Being is what Sartre refers to as a conversion of a radical type. 'Radical conversion' or 'existential conversion' is a subjective project of radically transcending bad faith, alienation and the contingency of our Being. In other words, within the context of an antiblack world, radical conversion is the resolve of a black subject which involves renouncing the original project of desiring to be white. But this renunciation of the original project cannot just be given; it must be *willed*. As *willed*, it becomes an attitude of mind. Hence Biko's characterisation of Black Consciousness as an attitude of mind, which involves an existential conversion from a corrupted consciousness or 'the self-recovery of being, which was previously corrupted' (Sartre 1956: 70). Thus when the vibrant truth that Black is Beautiful emerged, and that this blackness is immutable because it is one's facticity, '"Ahaa!" the blacks said, at that moment the radical transformation came into being. Those with adequate inner resources could now snap out of the trance of the false consciousness and become, through much pain and anguish, the rebels who understood history and have a deep-seated conviction that it is on their side' (Manganyi 1981: 170). Manganyi's 'Ahaa!' is the moment of the emergence of a lucid consciousness, the moment of the self-recovery of being which was previously corrupted. In this new attitude of my 'radical conversion', I not only recognise that I am condemned to be free and thus without excuse, but I also cease to value the impossible or vain attempt to be white. I come to realise that my existence or Being is unjustified, unnecessary, superfluous and without foundation. Ephraim insightfully captures this process when he states: 'Unless an individual *understands* that he is being oppressed, he will remain politically and spiritually inert. Once he becomes conscious of his oppression, he itches to understand the *source*, the causal agency, of his oppression – of his existential discomfiture. Then, and only then, will he be in a position to do whatever he must to liberate himself (he becomes actional). And self-liberation is an existential imperative for any awakened consciousness' (2003: 414 – italics in original).

Among the objectives of radical conversion is self-motivation. The self-motivating consciousness may seek self-recovery by proposing authenticity and thus freedom as a value. This self-recovery requires that one *assumes* that which one seeks to find. To assume involves the resoluteness to adopt as one's own, to claim responsibility for one's freedom. By assuming responsibility for one's freedom, one recognises that one is the 'incontestable author' of one's choices (Sartre 1956: 553) and that there is absolutely no excuse. This responsibility, this act of radical conversion, speaks to and is an expression of the Black Consciousness Movement's injunction 'Black man, you are on your own!' In this form, the radical conversion calls for the immergence of a lucid self-consciousness that would bring about a radical break with the history of dehumanised existence. The acute clarity of this awakened consciousness brought with it the stark realisation that their freedom, their redemption, laid exclusively in their own hands. Pityana understands the importance of the radical conversion as 'self-recovery' when he argues that since black people cannot depend on anyone else except themselves for their liberation, '[t]his therefore necessitates a self-examination and a rediscovery of ourselves' (in Mngxitama et al. 2008: 173).

The Black Consciousness philosophy, in its conscientisational moment, was for Biko and his comrades a pedagogical politics of conversion. From the subjective moment of conversion came the realisation of the political need for collective action, for the politics of solidarity. This conscientisation process, this pedagogy of the oppressed, is not simply passive contemplation or speculation about the world and reality. This philosophy, in its engagement with the issues of the existential world of everydayness, moves away from what *is* and points to the *oughtness* of the world with respect to the possibility of humanistic relations among human beings. Construed in this way, the Black Consciousness philosophy becomes a very dangerous activity to the oppressor. The catalyst for the disalienation processes is the antithetical moment represented by the Black Consciousness in the dialectical movement which will produce a liberated consciousness among black people that will eventually develop into a collective quest for black freedom and a new true humanity. The antithetical moment which constitutes the moment of disalienation ironically has to take the form of separation from separation (negation of the negation) in the form of black solidarity.

Black solidarity

Questions of liberation from oppression involve questions about the means to overcome that oppression. George Kateb, for example, poses these questions: How should human beings react when others constitute them into a collectivity based on certain features deemed to warrant hostile and negative treatment of those so characterised? What kind of response would be appropriate when such classification 'supported by superior force is meant to invade the psyches of those categorized, generation after generation, and make them accept the categorization and cooperate with it to their own injury'? (Kateb 1998: 48). Put in a specific context, how should black people respond when they are grouped together and oppressed on the basis of the contingency of their physical characteristics? Throughout the ages of struggle against racial oppression, competing paradigms of liberation have existed. Apart from the liberal solutions of assimilation (universal humanity) and integration, black identity and solidarity have been one of the favourite responses and rallying calls for social justice and liberation for most black people. Black leaders repeatedly exhorted their followers to become a more unified collective agent for emancipation. Thus, many prominent theorists in the history of black political and social thought defended a collective black identity theory tied up with liberatory black solidarity.[5]

Black solidarity as the primary objective of Black Consciousness was articulated early in the Manifesto (1971), which described Black Consciousness as black people's awareness of the power they wield as a cohesive group and black solidarity as a significant element of the philosophy. This policy document, borrowing from Carmichael and Hamilton, put forward the view that '[b]efore the Black people should join the open society, they should first close their ranks, to form themselves into a solid group to oppose the definite racism that is meted out by the White society' (Langa 1973: 10). This was consistent with the view of some of the foremost African and African-American and some European thinkers. Du Bois advocated 'self-segregation' as a necessary condition for the development of black consciousness and self-assertion. Likewise, Carmichael and Hamilton called for black people to close ranks before integration. And Samir Amin advocated what he called 'delinking' as the only strategy to free colonised people from oppression. Finally, Sartre called for the moment of separation or negativity, 'antiracist racism', as the only way to abolish racial differences.

Du Bois persistently calls for black solidarity as a liberatory praxis. He states: 'As a race, we must strive by race organization, by race solidarity, by race unity to the realization of that broader humanity which freely recognizes difference in men... For the accomplishment of these ends, we need race organizations' (1998: 272). Like many black radicals before him, Biko moved from the premise that group solidarity or collective action, rather than individual action, is the only appropriate and necessary agent for liberation from white racism. If effective resistance to racism needs to be a group or collective project of solidarity, the critical question which arises is: What should be the organising principle or criterion on which this solidarity is grounded? Biko argues that a reasonable response from the point of view of the victims of racism would be: If the problem is racism, and racism is predicated on race, race becomes the legitimate ground and point of departure for emancipatory solidarity. Indeed, what else can solidarity be based upon except the criterion or category which is used as a foundation for that very oppression? 'We are in the position in which we are because of our skin. We are collectively segregated against – What can be more logical than for us to respond as a group?' (1996: 25). In his Hegelian dialectical formulation, Biko insists that since '[t]he *thesis* is in fact a strong white racism and therefore, the *antithesis* to this must *ipso facto* be a strong solidarity among the blacks on whom this white racism seeks to prey' (1996: 90). Elaborating on this point of view, Biko is led to define Black Consciousness in solidaristic terms as 'the realisation by the black man of the need to rally together with brothers around the cause of their operation – the blackness of their skin – and to operate as a group in order to rid themselves of the shackles that bind them to perpetual servitude' (1996: 49).

To claim, as Biko and others do, that racial solidarity is a rational way to deal with racism is *ceterus peribus* to utter a banality since, as Biko himself comments, '[w]hen workers come together under the auspices of a trade union to strive for the betterment of their conditions, nobody expresses surprise in the Western world. It is the done thing. Nobody accuses them of separatist tendencies. Teachers fight their battles, garbagemen do the same, nobody acts as a trustee for another' (1996: 25). However, the banality of such a claim assumes a different dimension when it becomes a source of national controversy and its legitimacy is called into question by competing paradigms of racial liberation posited by prominent thinkers. A famous contesting paradigm that rejects race as a foundation for racial solidarity was largely spearheaded by Appiah, among others, and subsequently used in its South African variant by liberals of all kinds.

As noted earlier, in Appiah, we have what is perhaps the most powerful and well-known critic of race-based solidarity. I shall therefore pay more attention to his position – as critique of black solidarity as a type of racism and nativism – not only for its philosophical sophistication but also (as mentioned earlier) because of its characteristic liberalistic position. Appiah's argument is that black solidarity, especially the kind advocated by Du Bois, constitutes racism of a special kind but racism all the same, namely *intrinsic racism*. Intrinsic racism consists in giving preference to one's own 'racial' group to the exclusion of other groups, not because the other groups are inferior to one's own but simply on the basis of racial solidarity with members of one's race. He claims that 'the discourse of [racial] solidarity is usually expressed through the language of *intrinsic* racism... the bare fact of being of the same race...provides the basis for solidarity...[and] makes the idea of fraternity one that is naturally applied in nationalist discourse' (Appiah 1992: 17). Accordingly, Du Bois' Pan-Africanism – and by extension Negritude, the Black Consciousness Movement, Afrocentricity and so on – serves as an emblematic doctrine of intrinsic racism. He concludes that the Pan-Africanists must abandon the idea of race as a regulative principle in order to escape from racism fully, and from the racialism it presupposes. The reason for this judgement emanates from Appiah's denial that races exist. For him, any belief or claim that there are human races is *ipso facto* racist even in the absence of any value judgement being made about the superiority or inferiority of the races or hierarchising them according to physical, moral or intellectual traits. He finds support for this claim in scientific findings of biology and genetics.[6]

Having thus argued that races do not have a biological or scientific legitimacy, Appiah insists that racial solidarity should be rejected not only on the grounds that it is predicated on a falsehood but, equally important, because it involves treating an irrelevant factor (morphological characteristics) as a basis for being concerned about one's group rather than about another. In short, because races do not exist, he concludes that race is an unworthy basis for identity and political solidarity. Indeed, anyone who preaches solidarity on the basis of race is a racist. In Appiah's view, colour-blind interracial solidarity – to be sure, cosmopolitanism – is the only morally defensible strategy to fight racism.

Part of Appiah's problem is his disregard of the racist consciousness that always operates at the level of collectives. It is this indifference to racism's collectivist nature that makes him blind to its viciousness and the danger or threat it poses to the millions of black people whose circumstances differ from his. The word 'race' itself signifies not a single individual person but a collection or group of people distinguishable by certain morphological and phenotypical characteristics. If, as it is commonly agreed, racism is predicated on the assumption of the existence of races (real or imagined), if race refers to a collectivity or a group of human beings with certain identifiable physical traits, then racism cannot be a phenomenon directed against a single individual; its reference is to a group. To the racist consciousness, human beings always exist as collective wholes and their identities inhere in those collectives. To such a consciousness, human beings will always appear as black people, white people, Jews or Indians. A person, according to this logic, is not an isolated being within a collective whole but a part of a homogenised crowd. An individual person with a self-identity is unheard of to the racist consciousness because the foundation of being is the racial group or collective – nothing else.

Since racism is fundamentally not a phenomenon about the uniqueness of an autonomous individual but about collectives (groups, the superiority or inferiority of a presumed racial group) each individual person belonging to that particular collective is replaceable and changeable in the manner of each individual within Sartre's seriality. For this reason, it is impossible to fight racism as an autonomous individual. This point is given explicit expression by the African proverb that the individual cannot fight the king's troops alone even though she is designated as a target of their bullets. While an individual can refuse to be broken and demoralised or downtrodden by racism, even though she can act to diminish the extent to which she suffers from racism and can make a significant contribution to the emancipatory effort against racism, she cannot abolish or destroy racism all by herself. Racial solidarity is a necessary condition for emancipation from racism. Hence Du Bois, in the 'Conservation of Races', emphatically declares: 'The history of the world is the history, not of individuals, but of groups, not of nations, but of races' (1898/1998: 270). It is thus groups, not individuals acting on their own, that bring about liberation and make history. Following on Du Bois, Biko emphatically states: 'We are oppressed not as individuals...we are oppressed because we are black. We must use that very concept to unite ourselves and to respond as a cohesive group. We must cling to each other with the tenacity that will shock the perpetrators of evil' (1996: 97).

In fact, it is not only black radical thinkers who take George Kateb's question seriously; some non-black thinkers have responded in a similar manner as, for example, Biko and Du Bois. Hanna Arendt articulates the sentiment from her experience with National Socialism: 'If one is attacked as a Jew, one must defend oneself as a Jew. Not as a German, not as a world citizen, not as an upholder of the Rights of Man' (in Bernasconi 2001: 290). And Sartre insists that, since the black person 'is oppressed within the confines of his race and because of it, he must first of all become conscious of his race' (1988: 296). For Sartre, a necessary moment towards a socialist universal humanism requires that black people in particular must realise that they are oppressed primarily because of their blackness – a position articulated well in the SASO Policy Manifesto.

I stated above that Biko rejected the liberal dialectic which constitutes the antithetical moment as the resolution of apartheid antiblack racism. However, Biko argues that this solution leaves the contradictions unresolved. For him, since the *thesis* is strong white racism and the *antithesis* necessarily strong black solidarity, this contradiction requires a transcendence of the contradiction at the synthetical moment. It is only through such transcendence, Biko argues, that 'we can therefore hope to reach a kind of balance – a true humanity' (1996: 90).

Humanism

What does Biko mean by a 'true humanity'? In the chapter 'The Quest for a True Humanity' of his book, Biko declares that Black Consciousness proponents have 'set out on a quest for true humanity...In time, we shall be in a position to bestow upon South Africa the greatest gift possible – a more human face' (1996: 98). Why would human beings be in a *quest* for something that they already really are? The answer is simple: antiblack white racism. When Biko declares '[w]e have set out on a quest for true humanity', the 'true humanity' is not only a critique of liberal humanism but fundamentally also a denunciation and rejection of the dehumanisation of black people by the constant and systematic calling into question of their humanity by the antiblack racist white supremacist system that is apartheid. This declaration locates Biko in the category of the humanist. But Biko was not simply a humanist; he was also, paradoxically, an antihumanist. Just as Fanon and Sartre do, Biko criticises Enlightenment liberal conceptions of humanism which proclaim the essential equality of human beings while excluding black people from the realm of the human.

Recall that for Kant, Hume, Mill, Hegel and indeed also liberals, rationality constitutes human essence. To be human is to be rational. Given the views of some of these liberal philosophers about black people and rationality, it becomes evident that the humanity of black people is seriously and systematically questioned while the equality and dignity of all human beings as rational beings is preached. Thus statements such as 'It is impossible for us to suppose that these beings [black people] should be men' (Montesquieu) and 'The Negro race is a species of men as different from ours as the breed of spaniels is from that of the greyhounds' (Voltaire) exclude black people from the category of the human even though their authors hold humanistic philosophies. It is precisely this kind of hypocritical liberal or bourgeois humanism that Biko questions and criticises vehemently even among white South African liberals. To this extent, he is antihumanism. So, when Biko talks of 'true humanity', he is referring to and distinguishing it from liberal humanism that surreptitiously tolerated, encouraged and embraced racism. This kind of liberal humanism is a humanism of bad faith, since the racism upon which it is predicated is partly misanthropic by nature.

Sartre makes the same antihumanist critique of what he considers to be a perverted Western liberal humanism whose principle of universality provides moral, political and economic justification for racism. In the preface to Fanon's book, Sartre rhetorically denounces Western humanism in these strong words: 'Let us look at ourselves, if we can bear to, and see what is becoming of us. First, we must face that unexpected revelation, the striptease of our humanism. There you can see it, quite naked, and it's not a pretty sight. It was nothing but an ideology of lies, a perfect justification for pillage; its honeyed words, its affectation of sensibility were only alibis for our aggression' (1968b: 24–25). His critique of liberal humanism is predicated on the belief that the category of the human, however noble in its conception, deliberately excludes gender and race. It does not only openly put male before female, but also relegates black people to the subhuman. While proclaiming the equality of all human beings, this abstract humanism in fact simultaneously promotes the interests of one race against the interests of the rest of humanity. Hence humanistic principles such as equality, justice, freedom and individuality are to be seriously questioned because of the 'inappropriate restrictions of the range of various groups covered by the principles, as in the cases involving the flagrant contradiction of the universalism of the principles when their application is restricted to privileged groups on the basis of racial or ethnic distinction' (Outlaw 1996: 149). It is this weakness that probably led Sartre to lament '[h]umanism is the counterpart of racism; it is a practice of exclusion' (1982: 752). While racism begins by positing the Other as subhuman or non-human, liberal humanism begins by positing the Other as human but then blames the Other for not being human enough, for being subhuman and alien, and hence morally deserving to be treated as such.

It is the individualism of liberal humanism which Biko attacks and contrasts with African humanism. He writes: '[I]n all we do, we place Man first and hence all our action is usually joint community oriented action rather than the individualism which is hallmark of the capitalist approach' (1996: 42). Pushing this point to almost absurd limits, he claims that even African music is collective rather than the individualistic approach of the Western art form. Elsewhere he emphatically declares: 'We must reject, as we have been doing, the individualistic cold approach to life that is the cornerstone of Anglo-Boer culture' (1996: 95). The cultural dimension of African humanism is articulated in an essentialist manner in the chapter entitled Some African Cultural Concepts, in which he offers a list of some fundamental elements constitutive of African culture. The list smacks much more of Senghor's essentialist notions of African culture than Fanon's, and includes human centeredness, the belief in the inherent goodness of human beings, collective ownership of property, caring, communicativeness, sharing and closeness to nature. Problematic as this list might be, it encapsulates much of what has been called African humanism or, from a South African perspective, ubuntu.[7] This cultural essence of Africans is translatable into an ideological conception of communalism (African socialism) as articulated especially by Nyerere, Nkrumah and others.

Biko's antihumanism does not entail total rejection of humanism as such. His problem, as I have indicated, was simply with the hypocrisy of liberal humanism. For him, 'true humanity' is a product of what Gibson and Pithouse refer to as 'revolutionary humanism', a humanism that is universal in its conception because of its inclusion in the category of the human those who have been systematically implicitly or explicitly excluded by Western humanism. It is the humanism that believes in the commonality and unity of all human beings irrespective of race, gender and creed. However, unlike the liberal or even Marxist forms of humanism, Biko's version does not harbour essentialist notions of human nature assumed by the other two forms. The differences notwithstanding, most humanisms are essentially emancipatory because of their belief in human agency as a fountain of liberation. Biko's true humanism was a humanism stripped of any racist vestiges; his 'true humanity' symbolised the synthetical moment of the dialectical progression, an antiracist humanistic moment.

But how would this synthetic moment manifest itself into a true humanity? Would it be through the liberal's ruse of assimilation or integration? Put differently, when Biko speaks of a 'synthesis' in the white/black dialectic, is he articulating a position that would presumably lead to the elimination of both the white and black races (colour-blindness) or a solution whereby one is completely absorbed into the other in the manner of miscegenation resulting in the emergence of a completely mixed-race society (assimilation)? Like Sartre in *Anti-Semite and Jew*, Biko understood that the white liberals' putative humanism rescues black people as universal (read Western) human beings but annihilates them as black people; that it denies them their black particularity. The reason is because the white liberal by disposition is someone afraid of group or collective consciousness, someone who wishes to destroy the black person as a black person 'and leave nothing in him but the man, the abstract and universal subject of the rights of man and the rights of the citizen' (Sartre 1965: 57). The liberal is, in fact, an assimilationist – one who wants black people to be full members of an abstract humanity only if they renounce their concrete blackness. Understood this way, liberal humanism is intent on erasing black Otherness, black identity, in favour of an assimilative universal humanity which is nothing more than simply a veiled particularised Europeanism. This, as shown earlier, is the kind of solution Biko emphatically rejected.

Whereas the white apartheid bigot believes in a dehumanised black particularity (that is, the black racial side of the black person and attaches a negative value to it), the liberal's humanistic universalism focuses on the human side and attaches a positive value to it. Whereas the white racist refuses to recognise the human being in the black person by reducing her to a subhuman or animal, the liberal refuses to recognise the black in the human being. The black person is reproached by the white racist for *being* black while the liberal reproaches the black person for believing herself black (Sartre 1965). By blaming the black person for *being* a black person, the white racist is in fact attributing an essence (a nature) to the being of the black subject. Accordingly, one *is* a black person, like a rock *is* a rock and nothing else. The liberal, however, rejects such particularised essence in favour of a universal human essence in which the black person is by virtue of her blackness excluded from the human. Therefore, both the white racist and the liberal are guilty of essentialism. For black people (as both Sartre and Biko would say), there is virtually no difference between the enemy, the white racist and the friend of the black people, the 'do-gooders', the liberal, because (as Biko noted) white power presents itself as a totality. In the liberal, Biko detects a hint of antiblack racism precisely because the liberal is hostile to the black person insofar as the latter thinks of herself as a black person. Consequently, Biko arrives at the conclusion that neither the white racist's particularism nor the liberal's universalism can resolve the racial problem confronting black people.

Freedom for black people, Biko insists, is only possible through the elimination of fear and the demand for a true humanity. Among the conditions of the quest for humanity, Biko argues, is that true humanity requires the acceptance of death as a possibility for the attainment of freedom. That Biko accepted the possibility of death in the struggle for liberation reveals his revolutionary radicalism. The struggle for liberation begins with the individual's ontological and political consciousness; the understanding that as human beings, they must break the chains of psychological oppression before transforming the social order. Psychological freedom and political freedom are inextricable even though they are distinguishable. First, the human being cannot fight for her political freedom unless she is free mentally and can recognise that she is so. Second, any society which seeks to justify oppression must base itself upon the false premise that human beings are not free beings who can make themselves what they are, but that they are born with an absolute nature bound up with some accidents of birth.

This means that a society free of antiblack racism would require the depoliticisation of black identity. But this depoliticisation of black identity would ironically require the very politicisation of identity which it aims to transcend. A radical politicisation of black identity (Black Consciousness), however contradictory it may seem, is necessary for black liberation from antiblack racism. Such an identity would constitute the moment of particularism, of separation which precedes the concrete reality of universal humanity – socialism. This process takes place in a Hegelian dialectical manner, with white racism as the thesis, Black Consciousness as the antithesis and a raceless socialist society (universal humanity) as the synthesis.

Traditional and critical ontologies

Ontology is the study not only of what *is* the case, of existence, but also a study of '*what is treated as being the case* and *what is realized as the contradiction of being the case*' (Gordon 1995a: 133 – italics in original). From this perspective, a distinction can be made between traditional or distorted ontology on the one hand and critical or undistorted mediated ontology on the other hand. The former commits itself strictly to the first moment by focusing on 'what is the case', thereby becoming a 'Metaphysics of Presence'. This kind of ontology often ascribes necessity instead of contingency to being by simply positing the primacy of essence over existence, a notion that in fact introduces the deterministic conception of human nature.

Dehumanisation predicated on conceptions of human nature, as indicated in the preceding chapters, has its roots right here. But more importantly, this ontology risks rendering the question of Being ever more remote from concrete political and moral concerns.

Critical, existential, undistorted or radical ontology, however, acknowledges the three moments in the conception of ontology. Its radical character emanates from its recognition of the importance of contingency in existence. The danger of committing ourselves to an ontology that focuses exclusively on *what must be the case* resides in our forgetfulness of the contingency of Being and thus the failure to appreciate that what *is* the case need not always *be* the case. Liberation from distorted ontology, then, requires the rejection of the kind of ontology that is predicated on the idea of necessity but instead requires the admission of the fact that fundamentally the situation does not have to be as it is. As indicated, when existentialists ask 'What is the meaning of Being?', Black Consciousness raises the question 'What is the meaning of the Being of a black person in an antiblack political, social, cultural, religious and moral world?' Such ontology has liberatory potential because human beings do indeed judge that the way things are in their lived political, social and moral world is certainly not the way they ought to be; that what *is* need not *be* as it is. From this judgement, human beings do set about to change the way things *are* to what they must and *ought* to be. The realisation that their situation need not be as it is, meant the acceptance by the Black Consciousness activists that the power to define people and their identity need not rest on the shoulders of external agents but purely on their subjective selves. This self-definition, according to Gwala, 'will take the form of a negation...negating all that has been imposed' (1972: 13) on the black subject. In fact, because apartheid was a systematic negation of the black Other, a resolute decision to refuse the black Other all the attributes of humanity, Black Consciousness positioned itself as the negation of the negation, a summoning of black people (in Heidegger's phrase) to their 'ownmost potentiality-for-Being'. This requires resoluteness toward a self that will make it possible 'to let the others who are with [them] "be" in their ownmost potentiality-for-Being" (Heidegger 1962: 344).

In her review of Merleau-Ponty's *Phenomenology of Perception,* De Beauvoir asserts that the ontological question about the meaning of human existence cannot be separated from political or moral questions about the meaning of *lived human experience.* In short, what De Beauvoir suggests is that our moral or political point of view (whatever it may turn out to be) must in the long run depend upon an ontological account or description of human beings. If, for example, we understand the question of human rights as distinctively a political question, then we have to understand that any justification of human rights must be understood in terms of a more fundamental ontological account of what it means to be a human being. This approach would therefore inevitably provide a defence of political and moral action against any violation of human rights. Addressing the same issue of the ontological and its relation to the political within the Black Consciousness Movement, Gibson argues that even though this philosophy as expressed by Pityana's insistence on the ontological category of TO BE may contain an individualist existential moment of self-examination, the emphasis is still 'connected to becoming actional social beings' (2011: 50). Thus, in constituting black solidarity as an essential condition for political liberation, the Black Consciousness Movement enabled individual members to confront the anguish of apartheid non-Being by submerging the identity of the individual in the collective. It was this possibility of self-affirmation within the collective that made Black Consciousness attractive to many black people.

This consciousness of being-black-in-the-world is an ideal that has to be pursued relentlessly by black people. Black consciousness must assume a positive image and identity; it should not be a *lack* of whiteness. The achievement of this consciousness of black self-identity, and the purging of sedative Western values from the consciousness of black people, is a necessary first step to black liberation. In other words, subjective liberation has to be succeeded by objective liberation. Therefore, psychological or mental liberation is the essential condition for liberation from racism. Indeed, freedom is more than the mere absence of external restraint; it requires the presence of a liberated consciousness, a consciousness that has undergone a *radical conversion*. This consciousness is not another's to give; it is a state of mind or attitude to be won. For without a change from within, the changes without are superficial.

Liberation from a traditional or distorted ontology which posits human essence as given requires a critical mediated ontology that calls for a radical or existential conversion of a corrupted consciousness. Such a consciousness, in the context of Black Consciousness, is the consciousness of any black person who has been forced (through a variety of historical, social, political or even religious practices) to internalise black being as non-being. Such a consciousness is one that is immersed in the mud of bad faith that renders human reality an 'unhappy consciousness'. This state of unhappiness constitutes the reason why consciousness has to recover itself from its corrupted and buffeted condition. A radical conversion is thus an ontological transformation of the individual from the clutches of inauthenticity (bad faith) to authentic existence. Inauthenticity is a flight from self and therefore from one's freedom. Salvation and deliverance from inauthenticity to an authentic existence requires making freedom an absolute value. In this sense, therefore, the radical conversion becomes a project aimed at a radically different type of being, a being who has freedom as her foundation and goal.

Biko and his comrades understood the necessity of a radical and existential conversion. They understood that they themselves have the responsibility of transforming themselves from an imposed state of non-being, of subhumanity, to full humanity. Their project, as Biko forcefully articulates, was '[t]he quest for a true humanity'. Black people, Gwala also emphasises, 'are their own redeemers' (interview with Gerhart 1972: 7). Redemption, it was understood, means that the radical conversion should involve recognising themselves as human beings and human reality as a source of value. Indeed, it is this very recognition that led one author in the *SASO Newsletter*, who (because of style and diction) sounds more like Gwala than Biko, to declare: 'We must know that we don't have to prove our humanity in spite of our blackness. Rather the reverse should be the case. We should prove our blackness by our own humanity...the quintessence of our *being* is our humanity. Our blackness is inseparable from our humanity. This is the truism of Black Consciousness' (interview with Gerhart 1972: 7). In this sense, then, radical conversion becomes the self-recovery of the black being which was previously corrupted by the fundamental project of apartheid racism.

As Pityana states, the conversion means the desire and courage '*to be*'. 'The first method of our liberation', Biko explains, 'is self-conception, i.e., the definition of self in terms of the motivating factor that makes man what he essentially is... the desire to be' (interview with Gerhart 1972: 12). This Tillichian desire and the 'courage to be' became a determination to affirm one's ownmost potentiality-for-being. Compelled to experience the conversion, the Black Consciousness activists – just like the Negritudinists – in a moment of 'new self-discovery', authentically acknowledged their blackness and began to define themselves accordingly. To repeat Sartre's incisive words cited earlier, having 'his back against the wall of authenticity: having been insulted and formerly enslaved, he picks up the word "nigger" which is thrown at him like a stone, he draws himself erect and proudly proclaims himself a black man, face to face with white men'. So, in line with SASO's principle not to allow the white establishment to define them with all sorts of degrading labels such as 'non-whites', 'non-beings', 'nobodies', 'plurals', 'Bantus', 'natives' and 'kaffirs', the black students passed a resolution at the beginning of the General Students' Council of 1972 urging all newspapers to refrain from using these degrading labels but to call them 'Blacks'.

Let us be clear about what was at stake here. At the heart of the matter was an issue of authority, the authority of black people to describe reality as they perceived it and to define themselves as they saw fit within that reality. At stake here was the power and authority to define. Is the white person to be the sole definer of reality, including black reality? By attaching a positive meaning to the term 'black' for their identity, the proponents of the Black Consciousness Movement seized the power of defining and naming difference itself and invalidated the stigmatising meaning of blackness and the implicit and explicit definition of it as deviance to the norm of whiteness. In the very act of reclaiming the identity and definition which the white world taught them to hate, and affirming it as an identity to celebrate and valorise, the Black Consciousness Movement activists eradicated from their consciousnesses the 'double consciousness' that Du Bois saw afflicting black existence. Hence, from a Black Consciousness perspective, Biko concludes that this philosophy 'makes the black man see himself as a *being* complete in himself. It makes him less dependent and more free to express his manhood [personhood]. At the end of it all, he cannot tolerate attempts by anybody to dwarf the significance of his manhood [personhood]' (1996: 92).

Conclusion

In the concluding paragraph of the chapter entitled 'Black Consciousness and the Quest for a True Humanity', Biko states: 'We have set out on a quest for true humanity, and somewhere on the distant horizon we can see the glittering prize. Let us march forth with courage and determination, drawing strength from our common plight and our brotherhood. In time, we shall be in a position to bestow upon South African the greatest gift possible – a more human face' (1996: 98). This quest for humanity within the context of apartheid dehumanisation assumed a consciousness which was a negating activity structured and saturated by the desire *to be*. In this sense, Black Consciousness became the black people's fundamental project: a humanist project demanding a new humanism reminiscent of Fanonian revolutionary humanism. For fundamental to this radical and critical humanism is the requirement of what it is to be human in the realm of Being and therefore in the realm of ontology. Salvation and deliverance from non-Being to Being require making freedom in its multifarious manifestation an absolute value. For a human being wills herself free so that there be Being: 'To will that there be being is also to will that there be men by and for whom the world is endowed with human signification...to make being "be" is to communicate with others by means of being' (De Beauvoir 1994: 70–71). To communicate with others by means of Being implies that a radical transformation from *being to doing* occurs and this transformation is one from the ontological sphere to the everydayness of the political. Black Consciousness can thus be seen both as a philosophy of problematic ontology and a philosophy of existential (political, social, religious and cultural) freedom from that very problematic ontology.

Notes

1   For an intensive discussion on 'Blaming the Victim', see Marilyn Nassim-Sabat's 'Victim No More' (1998) and William Ryan's *Blaming the Victim* (1976).

2   For a similar distinction between racism and racialism, see Albert Mosley's *African Philosophy: Selected Readings* (1995), Alain de Benoist's 'What is Racism?' (1999) and Outlaw's *On Race and Philosophy* (1996).

3   For a detailed engagement with the question of black hair, see my unpublished paper 'The Politics of Race and Hairdo' (2007); Ingrid Banks' *Hair Matters: Beauty, Power, and Black Women's Consciousness* (2000), Patricia Hill Collins' *Black Feminist Thought: Knowledge, Consciousness, and the Politics of Empowerment* (1990) and *Black Sexual Politics* (2004), Michael Adams' *The Multicultural Imagination* (1996), Angelou's *I know Why the Caged Bird Sings* (1969), hooks' *Black Looks: Race and Representation* (1992), Jonathan Jansen's 'King James, Princess Alice, and the Ironed Hair: A Tribute to Stephen Bantu Biko' (2007), *The Autobiography of Malcolm X* (2000) and the *Sunday Times* (26 November 2016).

4   For a more extensive discussion on this phenomenon, see my unpublished paper 'The Politics of Race and Hairdo' (2007).

5   For a thorough discussion on the differences among theories of black solidarity (for example common oppression theory, collective self-determination theory and collective identity theory), see Tommie Shelby's 'Foundations of Black Solidarity: Collective Identity or Common Oppression' (2002); for a much more expanded version of discussion on this issue, see Shelby's *We who are Dark: The Philosophical Foundations of Black Solidarity* (2005).

6   For a critique on this view, see Mosley's *African Philosophy: Selected Readings* (1995) and 'Are Racial Categories Racist?' (1997), as well as Alain de Benoist's 'What is Racism?' (1999).

7   For a critique and defence of Biko's cultural concepts and his humanism, see Frank Wilderson III's 'Biko and the Problematic of Presence' (2008) and Oliphant's 'A Human Face: Biko's Conception of African Culture and Humanism' (2008). A detailed philosophical exposition of the ubuntu philosophy may be found in Ramose's *African Philosophy Through Ubuntu* (1999).

References

Adams H (1985) Variation of ethnicity: Afrikaner and black nationalism in South Africa. *Journal of Asian and African Studies* July, 20: 169–180

Adams M (1996) *The multicultural imagination.* London: Routledge

Adam H & Moodley K (1993) *The negotiated revolution: Society and politics in post-apartheid South Africa.* Johannesburg: Jonathan Ball

Ahluwalia P & Zegeye A (2001) Frantz Fanon and Steve Biko: Towards liberation. *Social Identities* 7(3): 455–469

Alcoff LM (1991) The problem of speaking for others. *Cultural Critique* 20: 5–32

Alcoff LM (2000) Habits of hostility: On seeing race. *Philosophy Today* 44: 30–40

Alexander N (1985) *Sow the wind: Contemporary speeches.* Johannesburg: Skotaville

Allen RL (1990) *Black awakening in capitalist America.* Trenton, NJ: Africa World Press

Allport G (1954) *The nature of prejudice.* Boston, MA: Beacon

Andersen ML & Collins PH (1992) *Race, class, and gender: An anthology.* Belmont, CA: Wadsworth

Angelou M (1969) *I know why the caged bird sings.* New York: Bantam

Appiah AK (1986) The uncompleted argument: Du Bois and the illusion of race. In HL Gates Jr (Ed.) *'Race' writing, and difference.* Chicago, IL: University of Chicago Press

Appiah AK (1986/1987) Racism and moral pollution. *The Philosophical Forum* XVII(2–3): 185–202

Appiah AK (1992) *In my father's house: Africa in the philosophy of culture.* New York: Oxford University Press

Appiah AK (1996) Race, culture, identity: Misunderstood connections. *The Tanner Lectures on Human Values* 17: 51–136

Appiah AK (1997) Liberalism and the plurality of identity. In N Cloete, J Muller, MW Makgoba and D Ekong (Eds) *Knowledge, identity and curriculum transformation in Africa.* London: Maskew Miller

Arnold M (Ed.) (1987) *Steve Biko: No fears expressed.* [Place of publication]: [Publisher]

Asante MK (1990) *Kemet: Afrocentricity and knowledge.* Trenton, NJ: Africa World Press

Avineri S (1968) *Karl Marx on colonialism and modernisation.* New York: Doubleday

Ayer AJ (1945) Novelist-Philosopher V, Jean-Paul Sartre. *Horizon* 12(67): 12–26

Baartman E (1973) Black Consciousness. *Pro Veritate* 11(11): 4–6

Badat S (2009) *Black man, you are on your own.* Braamfontein: STE Publishers

Baier K (1978) Merit and race. *Philosophia* 8(2–3): 121–151

Baker M (1983) Racism and empiricism. *Radical Philosophy* 33: 6–15

Baldwin J (1993 [1961]) *Nobody knows my name: More notes of a native son.* New York: Vintage International

Banks I (2000) *Hair matters: Beauty, power, and black women's consciousness.* New York: New York University Press

Baraka A (1992) Malcolm and ideology. In J Wood (Ed.) *Malcolm X in our own image.* New York: St Martin's Press

Barker M (1981) *The new racism.* London: Junction Books

Barndt J (1991) *Dismantling racism: The continuing challenge to white America.* Augsburg: Fortress

Barzun J (1937) *Race: A study in modern superstition.* London: Methuen

Berlin I (1969) *Four essays on liberty.* Oxford: Oxford University Press

Bernal M (1991) *Black Athena: The Afroasiatic Roots of Classical Civilization.* Volume 1. London: Vintage

Bernasconi R (Ed.) (2001) *Race.* Malden, MA: Blackwell

Biko S (1972) I write what I like. *SASO Newsletter* 2(1) Jan/Feb: 9–10

Biko S (1996) *I write what I like: A selection of his writings.* Randburg: Ravan Press

Blum L (2002) *'I'm not a racist, but...': The moral quandary of race.* Ithaca, NY: Cornell University Press

Bodunrin P (1981) The question of African philosophy. *Philosophy* 56: 161–179

Boesak AA (1983) Apartheid is a heresy. In JW de Grouchy and C Villa-Vicenco (Eds) *Apartheid is a heresy*. Cape Town: David Philip

Bogues A (2012) And what about the human? Freedom, human emancipation, and the radical imagination. *Boundary* 2, Fall: 29–46

Boxill B (2005) Rousseau, natural man, and race. In A Valls (Ed.) *Race and racism in modern philosophy*. Ithaca, NY: Cornell University Press

Bracken H (1978) Philosophy and racism. *Philosophia* 8(2–3): 241–259

Breitman G (Ed.) (1965) *Malcolm X speaks*. New York: Grove

Brookfield S (2005) On malefic generosity, repressive tolerance and post-colonial condescension: Considerations on white adult educators racializing adult education discourse. Proceedings of the 44th Adult Education Research Conference, Athens, University of Georgia

Bruenig M (2011) Atomistic individualism and the hermeneutics of racist philosophy. *American Philosophical Association Newsletter on Philosophy and the Black Experience* 11(1): 28–33

Buber M (1967) *Between man and man* (trans. RG Smith with an introduction by M Friedman). New York: Macmillan

Bulhan HA (1985) *Frantz Fanon and the psychology of oppression*. New York: Plenum

Buthelezi S (1987) The Black Consciousness Movement in South Africa in the late 1960s. *CEAPA Journal* 1(2): 23–33

Camus A (1974) *The rebel* (trans. A Bower). Harmondsworth: Penguin

Carmichael S (Kwame Ture) (2007) *Stokely speaks: From Black Power to Pan-Africanism*. Chicago, IL: Lawrence Hill Books

Carmichael S & Hamilton CV (1967) *Black power and the politics of liberation in America*. New York: Vintage

Carroll L (1992 [1930]) *Alice in Wonderland*. New York: WW Norton

Césaire A (1972) *Discourse on colonialism* (trans. J Pinkham). New York: Monthly Review Press

Césaire A (1956/2010) *Letter to Maurice Thorez* (trans. C Jeffers). *Social Text* 28(103): 145–152

Chomsky N (1975) *Reflections on language*. New York: Pantheon

Cilliers C (2008) *For whites only: What whites think about the new SA*. Johannesburg: X-Concepts

Cleaver E (1968) *Soul on ice*. Palo Alto, CA: Ramparts Press

Cohen-Solal A (1987). *Sartre: A life*. London: Heinemann

Collins PH (1990) *Black feminist thought: Knowledge, consciousness, and the politics of empowerment*. New York: Routledge

Collins PH (2004) *Black sexual politics*. New York: Routledge

Cone JH (1969) *Black theology and Black Power*. New York: The Seabury Press

Cone JH (2000) Whose Earth is it anyway? Accessed 8 March 2001, www.crosscurrents.org/cone.htm

Davis D (1966) *The problem of slavery in Western culture*. Ithaca, NY: Cornell University Press

Davis AY (1971) *If they come in the morning: Voices of resistance*. New Rochelle, NY: Third Press

De Beauvoir S (1945) La phenomenology de la perception de Maurice Merleau-Ponty. *Le Temps Modernes* 1(2): 363–367

De Beauvoir S (1989) *The second sex* (trans. HM Parshley). New York: Vintage

De Beauvoir S (1994) *The ethics of ambiguity* (trans. B Frechtman). New York: Carol

De Benoist A (1999) What is racism? *Telos* 114: 11–48

Delacampagne C (1990) Racism and the West: From praxis to logos. In DT Goldberg (Ed.) *Anatomy of racism*. Minneapolis, MN: University of Minnesota Press

Derrida J (1985) Racism's last word. *Critical Inquiry* 12: 290–299

Derrida J & Tlili M (1987) *For Nelson Mandela*. New York: Seaver Books

Diop CA (1974) *The African origin of civilization: Myth or reality*. Chicago, IL: Third World Press

Donald J & Rattansi A (Eds) (1992) *'Race', culture and difference*. London: Sage

Douglass F (1857/1950) West [Indian] emancipation. In PS Foner (Ed.) *The life and writings of Frederick Douglass* (Vol. 2). New York: International Publishers

Douglass F (1983) *Narrative of the life of Frederick Douglass*. New York: Penguin

Du Bois WEB (1968) *Dusk of dawn: An essay toward an autobiography of a race*. New York: Schocken

Du Bois WEB (1969) *The souls of black folk* (introduction by N Hare and A Poussaint). New York: Signet

Du Bois WEB (1898/1998) On the conservation of the races. In EC Eze (Ed.) *African philosophy: An anthology*. Oxford: Blackwell

Dyson ME (1993) *Reflecting black: African-American cultural criticism*. Minneapolis, MA: University of Minnesota Press

Ellison R (1995) *The invisible man*. New York: Vintage

Encyclopaedia *Britannica* (1798) (American edition). New York: Encyclopaedia Britannica Inc

Engels F (1968) Letter to J Bloch in Königsberg. September 21, 1890. In *Marx Engels: Selected works*. Moscow: Progress Publishers

English P & Kalumba KM (1996) *African philosophy: A classical approach*. Englewood Cliffs, NJ: Prentice Hall

Ephraim WC (2003) *The pathology of Eurocentrism: The burden and responsibility of being black*. Trenton, NJ: Africa World Press

Eze, EC (Ed.) (1997) *Race and the Enlightenment: A reader*. Cambridge, MA: Blackwell

Eze EC (1997/2001) *Achieving our humanity: The idea of the postracial future*. New York: Routledge

Fanon F (1965) *A dying colonialism* (trans. H Chevalier with an introduction by Adolfo Gilly). New York: Grove Weidenfield

Fanon F (1967a) *Black skin, white masks* (trans. CL Markmann). New York: Grove

Fanon F (1967b) *Toward the African revolution* (trans. H Chevalier). New York: Grove

Fanon F (1968) *The wretched of the Earth* (trans. C Farrington). New York: Grove

Fatton R (1986) *Black Consciousness in South Africa*. New York: SUNY Press

Fish S (1994) *There is no such thing as free speech*. New York: Oxford University Press

Frederickson GM (1997) *The comparative imagination: On the history of racism, nationalism, and social movements*. Berkeley, CA: University of California Press

Freire P (1985) *Pedagogy of the oppressed* (trans. MB Ramos). New York: Continuum

Friedman S (2014) The ambiguous legacy of liberalism: Less a theory of the society, more a state of mind? In P Vale, L Hamilton and E Prinsloo (Eds) *Intellectual traditions in South Africa: Ideas, individuals and Institutions*. Pietermaritzburg: University of KwaZulu-Natal Press

Garaudy R (1966) False prophet: Jean-Paul Sartre. In G Novack (Ed.) *Existentialism versus Marxism: Conflicting views on humanism*. New York: Delta

Garcia JLA (1997) Current conceptions of racism: A critical examination of some recent social philosophy. *Journal of Social Philosophy* 28(2): 5–42.

Gates HL Jr & West C (1996) *The future of the race*. New York: Alfred A Knopf

Gibson N (1988) Black Consciousness 1977–1987: The dialectics of liberation in South Africa. *Africa Today* 35(1): 5–20

Gibson N (2003) *Fanon: The postcolonial imagination*. Cambridge: Blackwell

Gibson NC (2011) *Fanonian practices in South Africa: From Steve Biko to Abahlali baseMjondolo*. Scottsville: University of Kwazulu-Natal Press

Gilmore RW (2006) *Golden Gulag*. Berkeley, CA: University of California Press

Glass M (1978) Anti-racism and unlimited freedom of speech: An untenable dualism. *Canadian Journal of Philosophy* 8(3): 559–575

Glausser W (1990) Three approaches to Locke and the slave trade. *Journal of the History of Ideas* 51(2): 199–216

Glendinning S (Ed.) (1999) *The Edinburgh encyclopedia of continental philosophy*. Edinburgh: Edinburgh University Press

Goldberg DT (1993) *Racist culture: Philosophy and the politics of meaning*. Oxford: Blackwell

Goldberg DT (1995) 'Hate, or power?' *American Philosophical Association Newsletter* 94(2) :12–14

Goldberg DT (2009) *The threat of race: Reflections on racial neoliberalism*. Malden, MA: Wiley-Blackwell

Gordon JA (2014) *Creolizing political theory*. New York: Fordham University Press

Gordon LR (1995a) *Bad faith and antiblack racism*. Atlantic Highlands, NJ: Humanities

Gordon LR (1995b). *Fanon and the crisis of European man: An essay on philosophy and the human sciences*. New York: Routledge

Gordon LR (1995c) Critical 'mixed race'? *Social Identities* 1(2): 381–395

Gordon LR (Ed.) (1997a) *Existence in black: An anthology of black existential philosophy*. New York: Routledge

Gordon LR (1997b) *Her majesty's other children: Sketches of racism from a neocolonial age*. Lanham: Rowan & Littlefield

Gordon LR (2000) *Existentia Africana: Understanding Africana existential thought*. New York: Routledge

Gordon LR (2001) Sartre in Africana philosophy. Paper presented at Lewis University, Romeoville, Illinois

Gordon LR (2002) Foreword. In SB Biko *I Write What I Like*. Chicago, IL: University of Chicago Press

Gordon LR (2006) *Disciplinary decadence: Living thought in trying times*. Boulder, CO: Paradigm

Gordon LR (2008) *An introduction to Africana philosophy*. Cambridge: Cambridge University Press

Gordon LR & Gordon JA (Eds) (2006) *Not only the master's tools: African-American studies in theory and practice*. Boulder, CO: Paradigm

Gordon LR, Sharpley-Whiting TD & White RT (Eds) (1996) *Fanon: A critical reader*. Cambridge: Blackwell

Gwala MP (1972) 'The black thing...is honest...is human'. *SASO Newsletter* 2(1) Jan–Feb: 13–15

Gwala MP (1974) Towards the practical manifestation of Black Consciousness. In T Thoahlane (Ed.) *Black renaissance. Papers from the Black Renaissance Convention*. Johannesburg: Ravan Press

Gwala MP (1981) Steve Bantu Biko. In M Mutloase (Ed.) *Reconstruction: 90 years of black historical literature*. Johannesburg: Ravan Press

Hacker A (1992) *Two nations: Black and white, separate, hostile, unequal*. New York: Charles Scribner's Sons

Hadfield L (2016) *Liberation and Development: Black Consciousness Community Programs in South Africa*. East Lansing, MI: Michigan State University Press

Hadot P (1995) *Philosophy as way of life*. Malden, MA: Blackwell

Halisi CRD (1999) *Black political thought in the making of South African democracy*. Bloomington, IN: Indiana University Press

Harris L (1983) *Philosophy born of struggle*. Dubuque, IA: Kendall/Hunt

Hayman R (1987) *Sartre: A biography*. New York: Carroll & Graf

Hegel GWF (1952a) *The philosophy of history* (trans. J Sibree). In *The great books of the Western world* (Vol. 46). Chicago, IL: Encyclopaedia Britannica Inc

Hegel GWF (1952b) *The philosophy of right* (trans. TM Knox). In *The great books of the Western world* (Vol. 46). Chicago, IL: Encyclopaedia Britannica Inc

Hegel GWF (1977) *Phenomenology of spirit* (trans. AV Miller). Oxford: Oxford University Press

Heidegger M (1962) *Being and time* (trans. J Macquarrie & E Robinson). Oxford: Basil Blackwell

Heinemann FH (1953) *Existentialism and the modern predicament*. New York: Harper

Heinz G & Donnay H (1969) *Lumumba: The last fifty days* (trans. JC Seitz).. New York: Grove

Heller A (1984) *A radical philosophy* (trans. J Wickham). Oxford: Basil Blackwell

Hemson D (1995) The antinomies of black rage: A review of *I write what I like* by Steve Biko. *Alternation* 2(2): 184–206

Hoernle RFA (1939) South African native policy and the liberal spirit. Lecture delivered at the University of Cape Town

Hook D (Ed.) (2014) *Steve Biko: Voices of liberation*. Cape Town: HSRC Press

Hooks B (1992) *Black looks: Race and representation*. Boston, MA: South End

Hooks B (1994) *Teaching to Transgress: Education as the Practice of Freedom*. London: Routledge

Hountondji P (1983) *African philosophy: Myth or reality?* (trans. H Evans with the collaboration of J Ree). London: Hutchinson

Husemeyer L (Ed.) (1997) *Watchdogs or hypocrites? The amazing debate of South African liberalism*. Johannesburg: Friedrich-Naumann-Stiftung

Imbo OS (1998) *An introduction to African philosophy*. Lanham, MD: Rowman & Littlefield

Jackson, G (1970) *Soledad brother: The prison letters of George Jackson*. New York: Bantam Books

Jackson G (1971) *Blood in my eye*. New York: Random House

Jackson JL (2008) *Racial paranoia*. New York: Basic Civitas Books

JanMohamed A (2005) *The death-bound-subject: Richard Wright's archaeology of death*. Durham, NC: Duke University Press

Jansen J (2007) King James, Princess Alice, and the ironed hair: A tribute to Stephen Bantu Biko. In C Van Wyk (Ed.) *We write what we like*. Johannesburg: University of the Witwatersrand Press

Jaspers K (1995) The question of German guilt. In NJ Kritz (Ed.) *Transitional justice* (Vol. 1). Washington, DC: United States Institute of Peace Press

Johnson CS (2005) (Re)Conceptualizing blackness and making race obsolescent. In G Yancy (Ed.) *White on white/black on black*. Lanham, MD: Rowman & Littlefield

Jordan WD (1970) Modern tensions and the origins of American slavery. *Journal of Southern History* 28: 18–30

Jordan WD (1974) *The white man's burden: Historical origins of racism in the United States*. London: Oxford University Press

Kalumba KM (1995) The political philosophy of Nelson Mandela: A primer. *Journal of Social Philosophy* 26(3): 161–171

Karim IB (Ed.) (1971) *The end of white world supremacy: Four speeches by Malcolm X*. New York: Arcade.

Kateb G (1998) Response to Robert Gooding-Williams. *Constellation* 5(1): 48–50

Kendall FE (2006) *White privilege: Creating pathways to authentic relationships across race*. New York: Routledge

Kennedy R (1997) 'My race problem – And ours'. *The Atlantic Monthly* 279(5): 55–66

Kierkegaard S (1941) *Concluding unscientific postscripts* (trans. W Lowrie). Princeton, NJ: Princeton University Press

Kierkegaard S (1951) *The sickness unto death* (trans. W Lowrie). Princeton, NJ: Princeton University Press

Kimmerle H & Wimmer FM (1997) *Philosophy and democracy in intercultural perspective*. Amsterdam/Atlanta, GA: Radopi

King ML Jr (1967) *Where do we go from here: Chaos or community?* New York: Harper & Row

Kiros T (Ed.) (2001) *Explorations in African political thought*. New York: Routledge

Kuper H (1979) Commitment: The liberal as scholar in South Africa. In P van den Berghe *The liberal dilemma in South Africa*. London: Croom Helm

La Guma A (Ed.) (1971) *Apartheid*. New York: International Publishers

Laing RD (1965) *The divided self*. Baltimore, MD. Penguin

Langa B (Ed.) (1973) *SASO on the attack: An introduction to the South African student organisation*. Durban: SASO

Larrain J (1994) *Ideology and cultural identity*. Cambridge: Polity Press

Leach G (1989) *The Afrikaners: Their last Great Trek*. London: Macmillan

Leatt J, Kneifel T & Nurnberger K (Eds) (1986) *Contending ideologies in South Africa*. Cape Town: David Philip

Legum M (1997) I was a white liberal and survived. In L Husemeyer *Watchdogs or hypocrites? The amazing debate on South African liberals and liberalism*. Johannesburg: Friedrich-Naumann-Stiftung

Locke J (1980) *Second treatise of government*. Indianapolis, IN: Hackett Publishing Company

Lorde A (1984) *Sister outsider*. Trumansburg, NY: Crossing Press

Losurdo D (2011) *Liberalism: A counter-history* (trans. G Elliot). London: Verso

Lötter H (1992) The intellectual legacy of Stephen Bantu Biko (1946–1977). *Acta Academica* 24(3): 22–36

Lötter H (1993) On interpreting Biko and the 'new' South Africa: A reply to Teffo and Ramose. *Acta Academica* 25(2 & 3): 14–26

Lukács G (1966) Existentialism or Marxism? In G Novack (Ed.) *Existentialism versus Marxism: Conflicting views on humanism*. New York: Delta

MacDonald M (2006) *Why race matters in South Africa*. Scottsville: University of KwaZulu-Natal Press.

Macey D (2000) *Frantz Fanon: A biography*. New York: Picador

Magaziner DR (2010) *The law and the prophets: Black Consciousness in South Africa, 1968–1977.* Athens, OH: Ohio University Press

Maloka E (2014) *'Friends of the natives': The inconvenient past of South African liberalism.* Durban: 3MS Publishing

Mandela N (1995) *Long walk to freedom: The autobiography of Nelson Mandela.* London: Abacus

Manganyi NC (1973) *Being-black-in-the-world.* Johannesburg: Sprocas/Ravan Press

Manganyi NC (1977) *Alienation and the body in a racist society.* New York: Nok

Manganyi NC (1981) *Looking through the keyhole.* Johannesburg: Ravan Press

Mangcu X (1999)

Mangcu X (2012) *Biko: A biography.* Cape Town: Tafelberg

Mangena M (1989) *On your own: Evolution of Black Consciousness in South Africa/Azania.* Braamfontein: Skotaville

Marable M & Felber G (2013) *The portable Malcolm X reader.* New York: Penguin

Marcano D-D L (2009) White racial obligation and the false neutrality of political and moral liberalism. *The Southern Journal of Philosophy* 47: 16–24

Marcuse H (1955) *Eros and civilization: A philosophical inquiry into Freud.* New York: Beacon Press

Marx K (1975) *Early writings* (trans. R Livingstone and G Benton). Harmondsworth: Penguin

Marx K & Engels F (1968) Manifesto of the Communist Party. In *Selected works.* Moscow: Progress Publishers

Marx K & Engels F (1972) *On colonialism.* Moscow: Foreign Language Publishing House

Mason P (1970) *Patterns of dominance.* London: Oxford

Mbembe A (2017) *Critique of black reason* (trans. L Dubois). Johannesburg: University of the Witwatersrand Press

McGary H (1992) Paternalism and slavery. In H McGary and B Lawson (Eds) *Between slavery and freedom.* Bloomington, IN: Indiana University Press

Mead M & Baldwin J (1971) *A rap on race.* London: Michael Joseph

Memmi A (1965) *The colonizer and the colonized.* New York: Orion

Merleau-Ponty M (1962) *Phenomenology of perception* (trans. C Smith). London: Routledge & Kegan Paul

Mészáros I (1979) *The work of Sartre (Vol. 1). Search for Freedom.* Atlantic Highlands NJ: Humanities Press

Mills CW (1997) *The racial contract.* Ithaca, NY: Cornell University Press

Mills CW (1998) *Blackness invisible: Essays on the philosophy and race.* Ithaca, NY: Cornell University Press

Mills CW (2003) *From class to race: Essays in white Marxism and black radicalism.* Lanham: Rowan & Littlefield

Mills CW (2006) Modernity, persons, and subpersons. In J Young and JE Braziel (Eds) *Race and the foundations of knowledge.* Urbana Champaign, IL: University of Illinois

Mills CW (2008) Racial liberalism. *PMLA (Publication of the Modern Language Association of America)* 123: 1380–1397

Mills CW (2010) *Radical theory, Caribbean reality: Race, class and social domination.* Jamaica: UWI Press

Mills CW (2013) *An illuminating blackness.The Black Scholar* 43(4): 32–37

Mkhize M (1974) Thoughts on race and consciousness. *The African Communist* 58: 71–83

Mngxitama A, Alexander A & Gibson NC (Eds) 2008. *Biko lives! Contesting the legacies of Steve Biko.* New York: Palgrave Macmillan

Modisane B (1986) *Blame me on history.* Parklands: AD Donker

Montagu A (1965) *Man's most dangerous myth: The fallacy of race.* New York: Oxford University Press

Montesquieu Baron de (1952) *The spirit of laws* (trans. T Nugent). In J Adler, C Fadiman and PW Goetz (Eds) *The great books of the Western World.* Chicago, IL: Encyclopaedia Britannica Inc

Moodley S (1972) Black Consciousness: The black artist and the emerging culture. *SASO Newsletter* May/June

More MP (1998) The philosophical bases of Steve Biko's thought in *Contributions of the African and German Philosophies to the Formation and Creation of Communities in Transition* Johannesburg: The Goethe Institute

More MP (1996a) African philosophy revisited. *Alternation* 3(1): 109–129

More MP (1996b) Complicity, neutrality or advocacy? Philosophy in South Africa: Ronald Aronson's *Stay out of politics*. A review essay. *Theoria: A Journal of Social and Political Theory* (87): 124–135

More MP (2004a) Biko: Africana existentialist philosopher. *Alternation* 11(1): 79–108

More MP (2004b) Albert Luthuli, Nelson Mandela and Steve Biko: The philosophical bases of their thought and practice. In K Wiredu (Ed.) Philosophy and an African culture. Cambridge: Cambridge University Press

More MP (2006) Fanon and the Azanian existentialist tradition. In C Headley and M Banchetti (Eds) *Shifting the geography of reason: Science, gender, and religion*. Selected proceedings from the First Annual Meeting of the Caribbean Philosophical Association. Newcastle Upon Tyne: Cambridge Scholars Publishing

More MP (2008) Sartre and South African apartheid. In J Judaken (Ed.) *Race after Sartre*. Albany, NY: SUNY Press

More MP (2009) Black solidarity: A philosophical defense. *Theoria: A Journal of Social and Political Theory* (120): 20–43

More MP (2010/2011) Gordon and Biko: *Africana existential conversation*. *Philosophia Africana* 13(2): 71–88

More MP (2007) The politics of race and black hairdo. Unpublished paper

More MP (2012) Black Consciousness Movement's ontology: The politics of being. *Philosophia Africana* 14(1): 23–39

More MP (2014) The intellectual foundations of the Black Consciousness Movement. In P Vale, L Hamilton and E Prinsloo (Eds) *Intellectual traditions in South Africa: Ideas, individuals and institutions*. Pietermaritzburg: University of KwaZulu-Natal Press

More MP (2016) Biko and Douglass: Existentialist conception of death and freedom. *Philosophia Africana* 17(2): 99–116

More MP (2017) Locating Frantz Fanon in (post)apartheid South Africa. *Journal of Asian and African Studies* 52(2): 127–141

Mosley A (1995) *African philosophy: Selected readings*. Englewood Cliffs, NJ: Prentice Hall

Mosley A (1997) Are Racial Categories Racist? *Research in African Literature* 28(4): 101–115

Mphahlele E (1959) *Down Second Avenue*. London: Faber & Faber

Mphahlele E (1962) *The African image*. New York: Praeger

Mudimbe VY (1988) *The invention of Africa: Gnosis, philosophy, and the order of knowledge*. Bloomington, IN: Indiana University Press

Nassim-Sabat M M (1998) Victim no more. *Radical Philosophy Review* 1(1): 17–34

Nengwekhulu HR (1976) The meaning of Black Consciousness in the struggle for liberation in South Africa. United Nations Centre Against Apartheid No. 16/76, July

Neugebauer C (1991) Hegel and Kant: A refutation of their racism. *Quest* V(1): 51–69

Newfield J (1964) Mugging the white liberal. *The Village Voice* June 25, 9(36): 5

Nolutshungu SC (1983) *Changing South Africa*. Cape Town: David Philip

Novack G (1971) *An introduction to the logic of Marxism*. New York: Pathfinder

Nteta CJ (1987) Revolutionary self-consciousness as an objective force within the process of liberation: Biko and Gramsci. *Radical America* 21(5): 54–61

Nyerere J (1968) *Ujamaa: Essays on socialism*. Dar es Salaam: Oxford University Press

Obenga T (1989) *Ancient Egypt and black Africa: A student's handbook for the study of Ancient Egypt in philosophy, linguistics and gender relations*. London: Karnak House

Oguejiofor JO (Ed.) 2003. *Pilosophy, democracy and responsible governance in Africa*. Munster: Lit Verlag

Okolo CB (1974) *Racism – A philosophic probe*. New York: Exposition Press

Oliphant A (2008) A human face: Biko's conception of African culture and humanism. In A Mngxitama, A Alexander and NC Gibson (Eds) *Biko lives! Contesting the legacies of Steve Biko*. New York: Palgrave Macmillan

Oruka OH (1990) *Trends in contemporary African philosophy*. Nairobi: Shirikon

Outlaw LT (1983) Race and class in the theory and practice of emancipatory social transformation. In L Harris (Ed.) *Philosophy born of struggle*. Dubuque: Kendall/Hunt

Outlaw L (1991) The Future of Philosophy in America. *Journal of Social Philosophy* 22(1): 162–182

Outlaw LT (1992/1993) African, African American, Africana philosophy. *The Philosophical Forum* 25(1–3): 63–93

Outlaw LT (1996) *On race and philosophy*. New York: Routledge

Parry B (1996) Reconciliation and remembrance. *Die Suid Afrikaan* 55: 10–12

Paton A (1972) Black Consciousness. *Reality: A Journal of Liberal and Radical Opinion* March: 9–10

Patterson O (1973) *The sociology of slavery*. London: Granada

Paul D (1981) 'In the interest of civilization': Marxist views of race and culture in the nineteenth century. *Journal of the History of Ideas* 42(1): 115–138

Philips M (1984) Racist acts and racist humor. *Canadian Journal of Philosophy* 15(1): 75–96

Pityana NB (1970) The politics of powerlessness. *SASO Newsletter* September: 8–10

Pityana NB (1971) From the president's desk. *SASO Newsletter* June, 1(2): 8–9

Pityana NB (1972) Power and social change in South Africa. In H van der Merwe and D Welsh (Eds) *Student perspective on South Africa*. Cape Town: David Philip

Pityana NB (1979) Afro-American influence on the Black Consciousness Movement. Paper presented at the Conference on Afro-American Interrelationships with Southern Africa, 27–29 May, Howard University, Washington DC

Pityana NB (2002) *Steve Biko: An enduring legacy*. Accessed June 20 2012, www.unisa.ac.za/contents/about/principle/docs/Biko.doc

Pityana BN (2012) Black Consciousness, black theology, student activism, and the shaping of the new South Africa. Inaugural Steve Biko Memorial Lecture. Europe, London School of Economics and Political Science

Pityana NB, Ramphela M, Mpumlwana M & Wilson L (Eds) (1991) *Bounds of possibility: The legacy of Steve Biko and Black Consciousness*. Cape Town: David Philip

Poliakov L (1974) *The Aryan myth: A history of racist and nationalist ideas in Europe* (trans. E Howard). New York: Meridian

Presbey G (1996) Fanon on the role of violence in liberation: A comparison to Gandhi and Mandela. In LR Gordon, TD Sharpely-Whiting and RT White (Eds) *Fanon: A critical reader*. Oxford: Blackwell

Price L (2005) *Steve Biko*. Cape Town: Maskew Miller Longman

Ramose MB (1991) Hegel and universalism: An African perspective. *Dialogue and Humanism* 1(1): 75–87

Ramose MB (1999) *African philosophy through Ubuntu*. Harare: Mond

Ramphela M (1995) *A life*. Cape Town: David Philip

Rand A (1967) *Capitalism: The unknown ideal*. New York: Signet

Ranuga TK (1986) Frantz Fanon and Black Consciousness in Azania. *Phylon* 47(3): 182–191

Robertson J (1971) *Liberalism in South Africa, 1948–1963*. Oxford: Clarendon

Robinson CJ (1983) *Black Marxism: The making of the black radical tradition*. London: Zed Books

Ruch EA & Anyanwu KC (1981) *African philosophy*. Rome: Catholic Book Agency

Ryan W (1976) *Blaming the victim* (revised and updated edition). New York: Vintage

Sartre J-P (1946/1955) Materialism and revolution. In *Literary and philosophical essays* (trans. A Michelson). New York: Macmillan

Sartre J-P (1948) *Existentialism and humanism* (trans. P Mairet). London: Methuen

Sartre J-P (1955) Materialism and revolution. In J-P Sartre (Ed.) *Literary and philosophical essays*. London: Collier Books

Sartre J-P (1956) *Being and nothingness* (trans. HE Barnes). New York: Philosophical Library

Sartre J-P (1965) *Anti-Semite and Jew* (trans. GJ Becker). New York: Schrocken

Sartre J-P (1966) Those who are confronting apartheid should know they are not alone. Statement at a Press Conference of the French Liaison Committee against Apartheid, Paris

Sartre J-P (1968a) *Search for a method* (trans. HE Barnes). New York: Vintage

Sartre J-P (1968b) Preface. In Frantz Fanon *The wretched of the earth* (trans. C Farrington). New York: Grove Press

Sartre J-P (1970) Intentionality: A fundamental idea of Husserl's phenomenology (trans. J Fell). *Journal of the British Society for Phenomenology* 1(2): 4–5

Sartre J-P (1974a) A more precise characterization of existentialism. In M Contat and M Rybalka (Eds) *The writings of Jean-Paul Sartre* (trans. R McCleary). Evanston: Northwestern University Press

Sartre J-P (1974b) The purpose of writing. In *Between existentialism and Marxism* (trans. J Mathews). New York: Patheon Books

Sartre J-P (1974c) Black presence. In M Contat and M Rybalka (Eds) *The writings of Jean-Paul Sartre* (Vol. II). Evanston, IL: Northwestern University Press

Sartre J-P (1982) *Critique of dialectical reason (Vol. 1): Theory of practical ensembles* (trans. A Sheridan-Smith). London: Verso

Sartre J-P (1984) *War diaries: Notebooks from a phony war* (trans. Q Hoare). London: Verso

Sartre J-P (1988) Black Orpheus (trans. J MacCombie). In *What is literature? and other essays*. Cambridge, MA: Harvard University Press

Sartre J-P (1989) *The respectful prostitute* (trans. L Abel). In *No exit and three other plays*. New York: Vintage

Sartre J-P (1992) *Notebooks for an ethics* (trans. D Pellauer). Chicago: Chicago University Press

Sartre J-P (2001) Colonialism is a system. In *Colonialism and neocolonialism* (trans. A Haddour, S Brewer and T McWilliams). London: Routledge

Sartre J-P (2013) The republic of silence. IR Aronson and A van den Hoven (Eds) *We have only this life to live: The selected essays of Jean-Paul Sartre 1939–1975*. New York: New York Review Books

SASO Manifesto (1971)

SASO Policy Manifesto (1973)

SASO Newsletter (1970, 1971, 1972) Durban: SASO

Scott D (2000) The re-enchantment of humanism: An interview with Sylvia Wynter. *Small Axe: A Caribbean Journal of Criticism* 8: 119–207

Sekyi-Otu A (1996) *Fanon's dialectic of experience*. Cambridge, MA: Harvard University Press

Senghor LS (1964) *On African socialism*. New York: Praeger

Senghor LS (1974) Negritude. *Optima* 16: 1–8

Senghor LS (1977) *Anthologie de la Nouvelle Poésie Nègre et Malgache de Langue Française* Paris: Presses Universitaire de France

Serequeberhan T (1989) The idea of colonialism in Hegel's *Philosophy of right*. *International Philosophical Quarterly* 29(3): 301–312

Serequeberhan T (1990) Karl Marx and African emancipatory thought: A critique of Marx's Euro-centric metaphysics. *Praxis International* 10(1/2): 161–181

Serequeberhan T (1991) *African philosophy: The essential readings*. New York: Paragon

Serequeberhan T (1994) *The hermeneutics of African philosophy: Horizon and discourse*. New York: Routledge

Shelby T (2002) Foundations of black solidarity: Collective identity or common oppression? *Ethics* 112 (Jan): 231–267

Shelby T (2005) *We who are dark: The philosophical foundations of black solidarity*. Cambridge: Harvard University Press

Shutte A (1993) *Philosophy for Africa*. Rondebosch: University of Cape Town

Silberman CE (1964) *Crisis in black and white*. New York: Vintage

Siloane M (2008) The development of Black Consciousness as a cultural and political movement (1967–2007). In CW du Toit (Ed.) *The legacy of Stephen Bantu Biko: Theological challenges*. Pretoria: University of South Africa, Research Institute for Theology and Religion

Singer MG (1978) Some thoughts on race and racism. *Philosophia* 8(2–3): 153–183

Singh NP (2004) *Black is a country: Race and the unfinished struggle for democracy*. Cambridge: Harvard University Press

Sithole T (2016) *Steve Biko: Decolonial meditations of Black Consciousness*. Lanham, MD: Lexington

Sivanandan A (1983) Challenging racism: Strategies for the 80s. *Race and Class* 26(2): 1–12

Smith G (2002). Death by memory. *Chimurenga* 3: 6–8

Sono T (1971) Some concepts of negritude and black identity. *SASO Newsletter* 1(2): 18

Sono T (1972) From the President's Desk *SASO Newsletter* 3(1)

Sono T (1993) *Reflections on the origin of Black Consciousness in South Africa*. Pretoria: HSRC Press

Squadrito K (1979) Racism and empiricism. *Behaviorism* 7: 105–115

Steinhorn L & Diggs-Brown B (2000) *By the color of our skin: The illusion of integration and the reality of race*. New York: Plume

Steve Biko Foundation (2009) *The Steve Biko memorial lectures: 2000–2008*. Johannesburg: Pan Macmillan

Taguieff P-A (1990) The new cultural racism in France. *Telos* 83: 109–122

Taiwo O (2003) The prison called my skin: On being black in America. In PC Hintzen and JM Rahier (Eds) *Problematizing blackness*. New York: Routledge

Teffo LJ & Ramose MB (1993) Steve Biko and the interpreters of Black Consciousness: A response to Lötter. *Acta Academica* 25(2&3): 1–13

Tempels P (1959) *Bantu philosophy*. Paris: Présence Africaine

Thomas A & Sullen S (1972) *Racism and psychiatry*. New York: Citadel Press

Thompson L (1985) *The political mythology of apartheid*. New Haven, CT: Yale University Press

Tocqueville A de (1981) *Democracy in America* (trans. G Lawrence). New York: Anchor Books

Toussaint (1979) 'Fallen among liberals': An ideology of Black Consciousness examined. *African Communist* 78: 23–39

Turner L & Alan J (1986) *Frantz Fanon, Soweto and American black thought*. Chicago: News and Letters

Turner R (1972) Black Consciousness and white liberals. *Reality: A Journal of Liberal and Radical Opinion* July: 20–22

Vale P, Hamilton L & Prinsloo E (Eds) (2014) *Intellectual traditions in South Africa: Ideas, individuals and institutions*. Pietermaritzburg: University of KwaZulu-Natal Press.

Vasey C (2000) *Being and race*. Accessed 13 September 2015, http/www.bu.edu/wcp/Papers/Soci/SociVase.htm

Van den Berghe PL (1978) *Race and racism: A comparative perspective*. New York: John Wiley & Sons

Van Wyk C (Ed.) *We write what we like*. Johannesburg: University of the Witwatersrand Press

Verwoerd W (2000) The TRC and apartheid beneficiaries in a new dispensation. Paper presented at Politics and Promises: Evaluating the Implementation of the TRC's Recommendations Conference, Centre for the Study of Violence and Reconciliation, Johannesburg, 27 October

Von Wolferen K (1990) *The enigma of Japanese power*. New York: Vintage

Wa Bofelo M (2017) Black body, intellect and soul are sites of struggle: Treatise on black consciousness. Unpublished monograph

Walden D (Ed.) (1972) *W.E.B. Du Bois: The crisis writings*. Greenwich, CT: Fawcett

Wa Thiong'o N (2003) Consciousness and African Renaissance: South Africa in the black imagination. Steve Biko Memorial Lecture, Cape Town, University of Cape Town

Watts J (1989) *Black writers from South Africa: Towards a discourse of liberation*. London: Macmillan

Webster N (1952) *Webster's New Twentieth Century Dictionary*. New York: Hibiscus Press

West C (1982) *Prophesy and deliverance! An Afro-American revolutionary Christianity*. Philadelphia, PA: Westminster

West C (1988) Marxist theory and the specificity of Afro-American oppression. In C Nelson and L Grossberg (Eds) *Marxism and the interpretation of culture*. Hampshire: Macmillan Education

West C (1994) *Race matters*. New York: Vintage Books

Wilderson FB III (2008) *Biko and the problematic of presence*. New York: Palgrave Macmillan

Wilson L (2011) *Steve Biko*. Auckland Park: Jacana Media

Wiredu K (1980) *Philosophy and an African culture*. Cambridge: Cambridge University Press

Wise T (2004) *White like me: Reflections on race from a privileged son*. Berkeley, CA: Soft Skull Press

Wittgenstein L (1953) *Philosophical investigations* (trans. GEM Anscombe). New York: Macmillan

Woods D (1987) *Biko* (revised and updated edition). New York: Penguin

Wynter S (1994) No humans involved: An open letter to my colleagues. *Knowledge on Trial* 1(1): 42–73

Yancy G (Ed.) (1998) *African-American philosophers: 17 conversations*. New York: Routledge

Yancy G (Ed.) (2002) *The philosophical I: Personal reflections on life in philosophy.* Lanham, MD: Rowman & Littlefield

Yancy G (Ed.) (2004) *What white looks like.* New York: Routledge

Yancy G (Ed.) (2005) *White on white, black on black.* Lanham, MD: Rowman & Littlefield

Young R (1990) *White mythologies: Writing history and the West.* New York: Routledge

Zack N (1993) *Race and mixed race.* Philadelphia, PA: Temple University Press

Zack N (1994) Race and philosophical meaning. *American Philosophical Association Newsletter on Philosophy and the Black Experience* 91(1): 14–20

Zack N (2006) *Thinking about race.* Belmont, CA: Wordsworth

Zylstra B (1993) Steve Biko on Black Consciousness in South Africa. *Acta Academica* 25(2 & 3): 27–41

Interviews

Biko S, interview with GM Gerhart, Durban, 24 October 1972

Biko S, interview with BBC, 1977 (transcript in *Umtapo Focus*, November 1987: 7–8)

Mills CW, interviewed with Tom Mills (in *New Left Project*), 12 April 2012

Sobukwe MR, interview with GM Gerhart, 1970
(http://www.aluka.org/action/showMetadata?doi=10.5555/AL.SFF.DOCUMENT.gerharto_005)

About the author

Mabogo Percy More is a former professor of philosophy at the University of the North, University of Durban-Westville and University of KwaZulu-Natal. He is the 2015 winner of the Frantz Fanon Lifetime Achievement Award and has published widely on Fanon, Sartre, Biko and Black Consciousness. He is currently professor of philosophy at the University of Limpopo.

Index

rejection of racial solidarity 197–198,
   274–275
Aristotle 61–62, 89, 118, 253–254
assimilation 26–27, 213, 216n9
   Fanon on 211–212
   Gordon on 212
   integration as form of 207–208,
   210–213, 216–217
   see also colour-blindness, principle of;
   multiracialism
authenticity 9, 28, 54, 88, 93, 95–96, 101,
   103, 106, 110
   and consciousness of death 13–15, 18
   radical/existential conversion to
   282–283
   see also inauthenticity
Azania 20, 24, 26, 30, 32–33, 56n3,
   104–105, 109, 206, 247

B
bad faith 106–107, 142–143, 154, 156, 215,
   218, 260–262, 264, 271, 282
   and argument of ignorance 188–189
   Lewis Gordon on 149–151, 153, 256
   Sartre on 15, 90–91, 93, 115, 149–150,
   171, 188–189, 277
   see also under Biko/black consciousness
   existential philosophy
Baldwin, James 54, 104, 136–137, 153,
   159–160, 164
Banda, Hastings Kamuzu 22–23, 103, 175
Baraka, Amiri (LeRoi Jones) 1, 160, 241
being-black-in-the-world 15, 106–107
   black consciousness as mode of 107,
   117, 139–141, 149, 227, 230, 235, 281–282
   Negritude as mode of 11, 26, 29, 42,
   48, 76, 99–100, 103–104
Berlin, Isaiah 111, 183, 183
Bernier, Francois 124, 227
Biko, Bantu Stephen 4
   and authentic being 13–15, 18, 84, 87,
   116, 139–140, 149, 181, 265, 272
   banning orders/censorship 10–11
   commodification of 7
   conception of racism 199–200, 252
   consciousness of imminent death 13,
   18, 149
   criticism of black liberals 180–184
   detention/torture of 11–12
   intellectual legacy of 2–4, 82–83
   leadership style 2–3
Biko/black consciousness existential
   philosophy 1–5, 9, 35, 51, 112

antiracist 2, 86–87, 95–96, 111, 129,
   199, 256, 279
conception of freedom/liberation
   108–111, 114, 139, 184, 194–195, 210,
   240, 246
and conscientisation towards radical
   conversion 24–25, 47, 51, 54, 87, 114,
   116, 149, 264–272, 272, 282–283
and emergence of black selfhood 28,
   40–42, 54–56, 75–76, 80, 108, 117,
   147–148, 181, 264
influence of Hegelian ideas on 40,
   84–87, 138, 217, 251–253
influence of Sartre on 84–88, 93,
   95–96, 98, 104–105, 138, 140–141,
   186–187
non-collaboration strategy 195–196,
   198, 205
and notion of bad faith 14–15, 84, 87,
   115–116, 149, 151–153, 155–156, 218
as quest for humanity 86–87, 109, 140,
   147, 156, 179, 246, 250, 276–277, 280,
   284
synthesis of race and class in 245–247,
   253
as 'way of life' 72–76, 108
and *what-ought-to-be* teleology 16, 58,
   78, 115–116, 152, 247–248, 250
see also Black Consciousness
   Movement; being-black-in-the-world;
   Negritude Movement; white racism:
   Biko's lived experience of
Biko's criticism of white liberals 5, 10–11,
   24, 29, 103, 116, 159, 164–167, 169–170,
   173, 175–176, 184, 192, 199, 277,
   279–280
   regarding individualism versus
   collectivism 178–180
   regarding integration/assimilation
   210–212, 216–218, 251–252
Biko's writing 84
   Frank Talk 11, 114
   I write what I like 4, 7, 10, 12, 26, 103,
   114, –147, 249
Black Consciousness Movement 3, 5, 7,
   9, 140
   African indigenous influences 22–24
   Biko as voice of 19, 21–25, 58, 79–80,
   82
   blackness/Negritude as sociopolitical
   concept 11–12, 19, 27–29, 45–54, 79,
   90, 139–141, 145, 195, 203–204, 224,
   253, 283
   and concept of African heroes 7–8

ontology of freedom/liberation 78,
183–184
two-stage liberation project 240, 267
see also under Black Power Movement,
USA; Negritude
Black First Land First movement 5
black identity in an antiblack world 25–29,
33, 35, 49, 52, 102, 105–107, 149, 203,
209, 235
see also black consciousness philosophy; blackness; Negritude; racial
solidarity; slavery: impact on black
identity
Black Power Movement, USA 47, 200–201,
218, 228, 264
Black Panthers 20, 25
influence on Black Consciousness
Movement 20–25, 34, 56n4, 183, 273
see also under SASO
blackness 19, 28, 47, 49
negative connotations of 11, 35–40, 42,
45–46, 171, 218, 227–228
political sense of 49–51, 117–118, 140,
203–205
as racial identity 40, 50, 74, 93, 101,
120, 122, 203
Blum, Lawrence 136, 201
Bofelo, Mphutlane wa 228–229, 269
Buber, Martin 71–72, 142
Buthelezi, S 28, 194, 196

C
Cabral, Amilcar 103–104, 237
Camus, Albert 13, 15, 17, 77, 104, 107–108,
186
see also under rebellion, existential
Carmichael, Stokely (Kwame Ture) 104,
129, 165, 167, 170, 200, 224, 228, 241,
264, 270, 273
influence on Biko 21
views on white liberalism 160
Césaire, Aimé 20, 79, 104
influence on Biko 25–26, 84, 147
philosophy of Negritude 22, 25, 27–29,
69, 197, 141
class analysis 103, 194, 224, 226, 231, 237,
246–247, 251
Biko's views on 244
class consciousness 178, 224, 235, 237,
241, 243
class exploitation 162, 194, 224–225, 230,
252
class struggle 222, 228, 236, 238, 241
and intensification of white supremacy 227

colonial consciousness 43–44
colour-blindness, principle of 183–184,
197–198, 206, 213–215, 275, 279
communism 221, 242
Cone, James 13, 21, 84, 86, 104, 111, 157n7
influence on Biko and black consciousness movement 21, 47, 169
on saying NO to the oppressor 9
conscientisation 24–25, 29, 79, 210,
264–266, 268–270 *see also under*
Biko/black consciousness existential
philosophy

D
Damas, Léon-Gontras 25–26, 104
Davis, Angela 21, 104, 148, 233, 237
De Beauvoir, Simone 15, 83, 88, 97, 104,
153, 235, 268–269, 281, 284
notion of women as absolute other 143
on oppression of women 241–242
de Tocqueville, Alexis 44, 257
dehumanisation 245–246, 281
dehumanisation of black people 26, 54, 71,
119, 143–144, 250, 272, 277, 279, 284
and concept of subpersonhood 43, 72,
142, 145, 208, 250, 263, 278
Fanon's zone of nonbeing 30, 43, 98,
143
racism as 45, 135, 142, 147, 157n7, 205,
208, 245
through the Sartrean Other's look/
gaze 53, 90, 92–95, 97, 99–100, 117,
120, 138, 142–144
see also negation of black humanity
dehumanisation of black people under
apartheid 10, 12, 29, 109, 114–116, 132,
146, 207, 238, 261, 268
being-towards-death/enforced
nonbeing 14, 25, 30, 141–142, 144–145,
148–149, 154, 156
black-on-black violence as symptom of
260–262
non-white label 25, 203–204, 221–222,
283
Saartjie Baartman case 146
denegrification
Fanon's concept of 269–270
and desire to be white 45, 98–99, 106,
204, 212, 260, 263–64
and shame/negation of self 28, 38,
257–259, 270
see also Fanon, Frantz: zone of
nonbeing

denial/negation of black humanity *see
under* rationality
Derrida, Jacques 82, 130
Descartes, Rene 61, 65, 83, 89
    Cartesian 'cogito' 10, 18, 42, 55, 62–63,
    76, 89, 92, 172, 195, 223, 235
Diop
    Cheik Anta 25–26, 60
    David 25–26
Douglass, Frederick 44, 50–51, 144, 148,
    184, 249
du Bois, William 10, 20, 23–24, 83–84,
    104, 107, 120, 148, 151
    notion of double consciousness 27, 45,
    151, 153–154, 228, 256, 259, 264, 284

E
Elkins, Stanley 154, 172
Engels, Fredrick 118, 220–222, 233, 236,
    246, 252
    de Beauvoir's criticism of 241–242
ethnicity/ethnic identity 70, 101, 121, 168,
    176, 197, 211, 214, 255, 278
    conflation of racism with 219n3
Eurocentrism 61, 268 *see also under*
    Marxist
European Enlightenment 36, 62, 66–67,
    70, 122, 144, 147, 214, 277
existential phenomenology 10, 64–65,
    87–90, 93, 96–97
    liberal denouncement of 66
    see also Africana existential
    philosophy; Biko/black consciousness
    existential philosophy; philosophy as
    way of life
existentialism, definition of 60, 63–64
Eze, Emmanuel 58, 121–122, 145

F
false consciousness 14–15, 246, 258, 265,
    271
    Marxist concept of 15, 226, 246, 268
    see also bad faith
Fanon, Frantz
    on apartheid/colonial world 30–34, 44,
    77, 129, 133–134, 152, 169, 173, 220, 233,
    261
    critique of Hegel's ontology 99–100
    critique of liberalism 192, 194, 277
    critique of Western Marxism 32, 103,
    220, 222, 237, 244
    on freedom and liberation 111
    influence of Sartre on 32, 87–88, 93,
    96–97, 99–102, 141–142, 186, 254

    influence on Biko/Black
    Consciousness Movement 15, 24–27,
    29–30, 33, 85, 96, 103, 149, 152, 178,
    237, 244–245, 261, 270
    phenomenology of blackness 15–16, 20,
    40, 42, 54, 82–83, 96, 106–107, 144,
    148–149, 277–278, 284
    philosophical influences 97–98,
    102–103
    on political education/conscientisation
    265–266, 268
    on racism 30, 98, 101–102, 121, 169,
    209
    synthesis of race and class 245
    on violence 261
    on white normativity 98, 169, 257
    see also under dehumanisation of
    black people; denegrification; Sartre,
    Jean-Paul
Fanon's writings 104
    Black Skin, White Masks 12, 30, 44, 93,
    96, 98, 100, 103, 107, 121, 245
    The Wretched of the Earth 30–31, 34, 88,
    96–97, 103, 130, 186, 220, 245
    Toward the African Revolution 30–31,
    103
Fatton, Robert 3, 22, 186
Fish, Stanley 202–203
Fisher, Bram 3, 185
France 26, 133
    French Communist Party 147, 223,
    240
Frederickson, George 22–23
Freire, Paulo 84, 184, 263–264, 266–267
    influence on Biko 24–25, 267–268

G
Gandhi, Mahatma 57n12, 129, 180
Garvey, Marcus 20, 23, 84, 104, 148, 224,
    270
    Universal Negro Improvement associa-
    tion 160
genocide 32, 35, 72, 142, 146, 157n11, 189
Gerhart, Gail 10, 24, 26, 166, 175–176,
    181–183, 205, 210–211, 231–232, 251,
    266, 283
Goldberg, David 135, 170
Gordon, Jane 133
Gordon, Lewis 1, 10, 19, 35, 72, 87, 114–115,
    145, 199, 280
    on black consciousness/racial
    solidarity 55, 96, 134, 218, 226

complicity in racism 69, 159, 161–167, 169–170, 187–188, 215

myth/fiction of race 5, 184, 197–198, 224

see also Appiah, Anthony; colour-blindness, principle of; multiracialism; non-racialism

Locke, John 83, 89–90, 118, 147, 220–221

as father of liberalism 161–164

see also under antiblack racist theories and ideology

L-Ouverture, Toussaint 20, 223, 225–227, 234–237, 240, 266–267

Lumumba, Patrice 12, 23, 88, 148, 237

M

Macey, David 27, 96–97

Madondo, Bongani 3

Magaziner, Daniel 3–4, 20–21

Malcolm X 21, 26, 44, 52, 104, 137, 148, 160, 170, 180, 193, 224, 241, 257–258, 270

'House Negro' metaphor 182, 204

iconisation of 7

rebellious attitude of 10, 12, 17–18

Maloka, E 165–167, 173–174, 206

Mandela, Nelson 82, 146, 148, 180, 185, 213

iconisation of 1–3, 7–8

Manganyi, Chabani 7–8, 12, 34–35, 42, 48, 140, 227, 230, 234, 271

criticism of white liberals 195

philosophical influences 33, 93, 107–108

see also being-black-in-the-world

Manifesto of the Communist Party 222, 233

Marcuse, Herbert 10, 233

Marx, Karl 103, 129, 233, 236, 239

concept of dialectical materialism 79, 246, 252–253

Marxism 68, 106 *see also under* Fanon, Frantz

Marxist

class reductionism 194, 225–227, 230, 242, 247

criticism of Sartre's existentialism 223, 228–230, 234

Eurocentrism 221, 239

ideology/what-ought-to-be 59, 103, 120

views on race/antiblack racism 194, 224–227, 230, 237, 239, 242

Marxist critiques of black consciousness 2, 193, 201, 218, 220, 222–224, 228, 234–236, 240, 248, 267

accusations of liberalism 231–233

Biko's responses to 223, 228–233, 237, 239, 242, 267

convergence with liberals 224–225, 230

master/slave consciousness 43–45, 69–70, 102, 138, 182, 204, 268

Hegelian paradigm 33, 40, 85–86, 103, 142, 152–153, 172, 191, 236

masking 153–155, 158n14

Mbembe, Achille 67, 131, 172

Memmi, Albert 44, 88, 137, 142, 166, 202

Merleau-Ponty, Maurice 4, 64, 96–97, 216, 281

Mill, John Stuart 69, 147, 161–162, 172, 220, 277

Mills, Charles W 72, 76, 118, 134, 143, 161, 163, 168, 172, 215, 246–247

conception of black philosophy 36

Mngxitama, Andile 3–5, 87, 272

modernity 29, 36, 69, 112, 144, 161

Modisane, Bloke 34, 57n12, 104, 155, 174, 182, 261

Mokoape, Nchaupe Aubrey 24, 33, 57

Montagu, Ashley 124, 126

Moodley, Strinivasa 50–51

moral responsibility, Biko's concept of 185–192

Mphahlele, Ezekial (Es'kia) 12, 34, 57n12, 104, 261

Mtshali, Oswald 25, 141

Muhammad, Elijah 105–106, 257

multiracialism 165, 180, 210, 214

N

National Association for the Advancement of Colored People (NAACP) 18, 160

National Union of South African Students (NUSAS) 5, 27, 169, 210

criticism of black consciousness 193–195

white liberal stance 166

see also under SASO

Nationalist Party *see under* apartheid

Nazi Germany *see* Nazism

Nazism 31–32, 43, 110, 157, 189, 202, 212, 259

Negritude 20

importance to Black Consciousness Movement/SASO 25–27, 29, 61

origins/definition of 22, 26–29, 47–48, 61

and Sartre's concept of antiracist racism 87, 95–96, 101–102, 253–255

see also being-black-in-the-world; denegrification

Negritude Movement 29, 60–61, 84, 87,
94–95, 102–103, 107, 138, 141, 265, 274
founding of 25–27
see also Césaire, Aimé: philosophy of
Negritude
Nietzsche, Friedrich 13, 16, 48, 83, 105
Nkrumah, Kwame 23–24, 61, 79, 103–104,
118, 129, 175, 233, 237, 278
Nolutshungu, Sam 87, 108, 140
non-racialism 5 12, 49, 120, 166, 182, 194,
196, 198, 206, 212–215, 244, 251–252,
260 *see also* colour-blindness, principle
of
non-white consciousness 44, 51–52, 54, 141,
156, 169, 190, 198, 221
and collusion with apartheid regime
190–191, 204–205
Nyerere, Julius 23–24, 61, 82–84, 103–104,
175, 222, 237, 278

O
Okolo, Chukwudum B 124–125, 128
Oruka, Odera 48, 61
Outlaw, Lucius 49, 61, 70–71, 123, 214, 217,
246–247, 278

P
Pan-Africanism 3, 20, 84, 196, 205,
274–275
Pan-Africanist Congress (PAC) 24, 159
banning of 19
Parry, Benita 2, 82
Paton, Alan 180, 253
phenomenology 38, 59, 64, 77, 85, 87, 97,
107 *see also* existential phenomenology
philosophy
critique of western tradition 61, 63–66,
72
definition of 58–60, 80
institutionalisation/professionalisation
of 73–74, 89
is/ought-to-be gap 77–79, 105–106
as pursuit of truth 114
rejection of race and racism 117, 119
philosophical anthropology 35, 56, 61–62,
71–72, 79, 89, 108, 116, 140–142, 214,
221, 229, 249
philosophy as way of life 73–75
and Sartre's drama of existence/
human reality 75–76, 88–90, 96–98,
184
see also under Biko/black consciousness
existential philosophy

Pityana, Barney N 3, 20, 33, 40, 56n4, 85,
87, 145, 168, 243, 272, 282–283
as SASO president 140–141, 282
Plato 61–62, 75, 77, 89, 114
post-apartheid apartheid 2, 5, 191–192
pre-reflective consciousness 33, 139, 141

R
race, conceptions of 48–49, 123–124
interconnections with class 32, 117,
190, 226–227, 230, 237, 244–247, 253
see also liberalism and notions of race;
Marxist: views on race/anti-black
racism
racial discrimination 128–129, 131, 135, 138,
199–200, 242
racial domination 128–129, 199, 201, 221,
226, 243
Biko on 138, 202, 254–255
see also white supremacy
racial prejudice 126–128, 131, 200, 202,
205, 243
racial segregation
South Africa 31, 131, 134, 138, 166–167,
240, 265
Jim Crow laws (US) 21, 164, 216
see also apartheid
racial (black) solidarity 179, 195, 197–198,
228, 255, 272, 274–276
Biko on 180, 224, 244, 272–274, 276
see also under Appiah
racism 2, 17, 112, 119–120, 240–241, 275
anti-Semitism as 93, 101, 115, 143, 151,
171, 189–190, 250
colonialism as product of 122, 166
definition/theories of 124–129, 138,
199–200
power relations as foundation of 129,
135–139, 167, 199–200, 202, 216
see also antiblack racism; Fanon,
Frantz: on racism; white racism; white
supremacy
racist consciousness 38, 43–45, 47, 138, 179,
216, 275
Ramphela, Mamphela 3, 25, 165
rationality 60, 68–70, 75, 89, 125, 145, 160,
170, 180, 200, 213, 277
as defining feature of human beings
61–62, 66, 70, 89–90
existentialism as reaction to 66
and denial/negation of black/African
humanity 43, 54, 66, 68–69, 86,
95, 109, 119–120, 144–145, 148, 252,
162–163, 281